KAZUKI TAKAHASHI

ITO-KUN WAS ONE OF MY ASSISTANTS WHO WORKED ON *YU-GI-OH!*, AND NOW HE'S GOING TO WRITE A BRAND NEW *YU-GI-OH!* SERIES. I'LL BE LOOKING FORWARD TO EVERY EPISODE. ENJOY, EVERYONE!

Artist/author Kazuki Takahashi first tried to break into the manga business in 1982, but success eluded him until *Yu-Gi-Oh!* debuted in the Japanese *Weekly Shonen Jump* magazine in 1996. *Yu-Gi-Oh!*'s themes of friendship and fighting, together with Takahashi's weird and imaginative monsters, soon became enormously successful, spawning a real-world card game, video games, and three anime series (two Japanese *Yu-Gi-Oh!* series and *Yu-Gi-Oh! GX*). A lifelong gamer, Takahashi enjoys shogi (Japanese chess), mahjong, card games, and tabletop RPGs, among other games.

AKIRA ITO

KAZUKI TAKAHASHI SENSEI'S *YU-GI-OH!* HAS COME TO AN END, AND NOW THERE'RE NO MORE NEW CHAPTERS FOR US TO READ. *YU-GI-OH! R* FOCUSES ON THINGS THAT WE COULDN'T INCLUDE IN THE ORIGINAL SERIES. I HOPE YOU LIKE IT!

Akira Ito worked on the original *Yu-Gi-Oh!* manga as an assistant to Kazuki Takahashi. He also assisted in the creation of *Yu-Gi-Oh! GX*. *Yu-Gi-Oh! R* is his first work as lead creator.

Volume 1
SHONEN JUMP Manga Edition

Original Concept by **KAZUKI TAKAHASHI**
Story and Art by **AKIRA ITO**

Translation & English Adaptation **KINAMI WATABE & IAN REID, HC LANGUAGE SOLUTIONS**
Touch-up Art & Lettering **ERIC ERBES**
Cover Design **CAROLINA UGALDE**
Interior Design **COURTNEY UTT**
Editors **MICHAEL MONTESA & JASON THOMPSON**

VP, Production **ALVIN LU**
VP, Publishing Licensing **RIKA INOUYE**
VP, Sales & Product Marketing **GONZALO FERREYRA**
VP, Creative **LINDA ESPINOSA**
Publisher **HYOE NARITA**

Printed in the U.S.A.

Published by VIZ Media, LLC
P.O. Box 77010
San Francisco, CA 94107

10 9 8 7 6 5 4 3 2 1
First printing, October 2009

www.viz.com

PARENTAL ADVISORY
YU-GI-OH! R is rated T and is
recommended for ages 13 and
up. Contains fantasy violence.
ratings.viz.com

THE WORLD'S
MOST POPULAR MANGA
SHONEN JUMP
www.shonenjump.com

Yu-Gi-Oh! 遊戯王 R

VOLUME 1
A WICKED SHADOW!

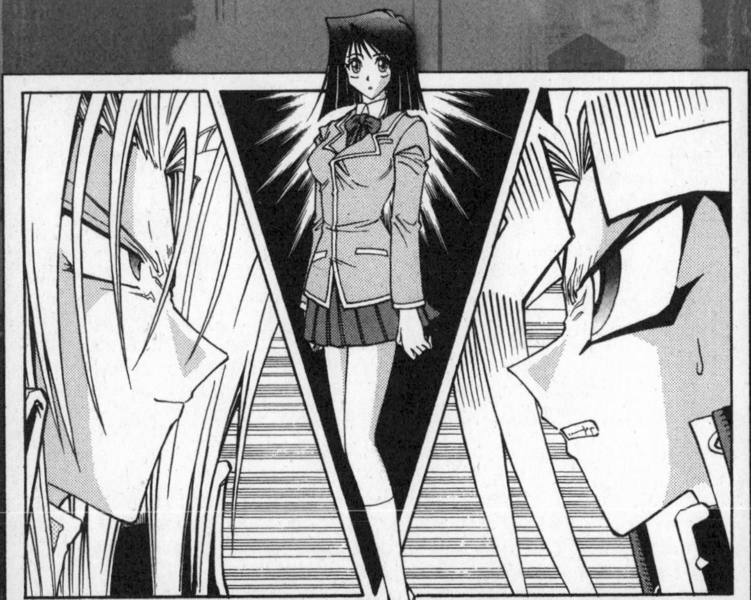

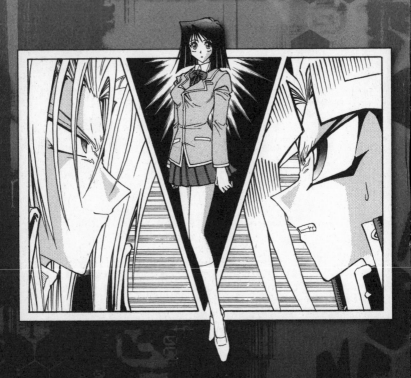

Original Concept/Supervised by **KAZUKI TAKAHASHI**
Story & Art by **AKIRA ITO**

CAST & STORY

YUGI MUTOU

But Yugi's other great rival Seto Kaiba, the teenage CEO of Kaiba Corporation, was not so easily defeated. Discovering that Pegasus had created three incredibly rare cards known as the "Egyptian God Cards," Kaiba announced a new tournament, "Battle City," to draw out the owners so he could get the cards for himself. But Yugi won the tournament and acquired the three most powerful cards in the world: "Slifer the Sky Dragon," "The God of the Obelisk" and "The Sun Dragon Ra." Within the cards dwells a mystic power which is linked to Yu-Gi-Oh's Egyptian past. But now, a new enemy has appeared...

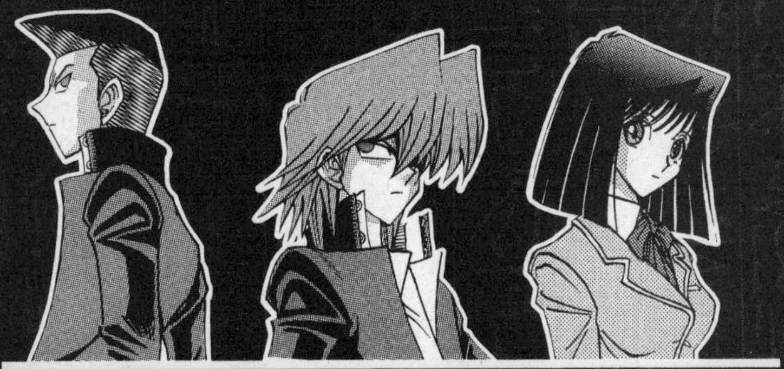

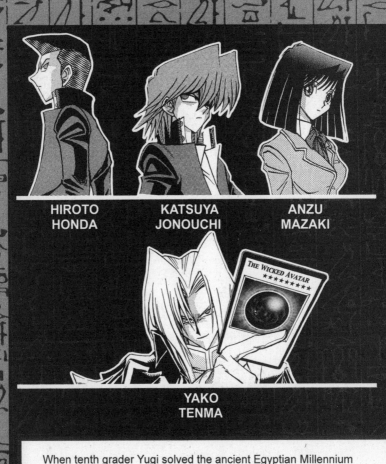

HIROTO
HONDA

KATSUYA
JONOUCHI

ANZU
MAZAKI

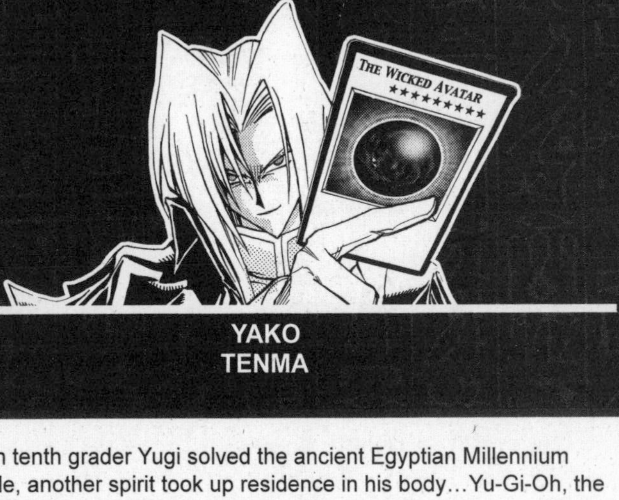
THE WICKED AVATAR

YAKO
TENMA

When tenth grader Yugi solved the ancient Egyptian Millennium Puzzle, another spirit took up residence in his body…Yu-Gi-Oh, the King of Games! Using his gaming skills, Yugi fought many ruthless enemies at "Duel Monsters," the most popular collectible card game in the world. Eventually, Yugi's skills got the attention of Maximillion Pegasus, the game's multimillionaire creator…and the bearer of another ancient Egyptian artifact, the Millennium Eye. Using his strange powers, Pegasus stole the soul of Yugi's grandfather and forced Yugi to participate in "Duelist Kingdom," a tournament held on a remote island. After many tough battles, Yugi beat Pegasus and rescued his grandfather's soul. After the battle, Pegasus suffered a terrible fate.

Yu-Gi-Oh! 遊☆戯☆王 R

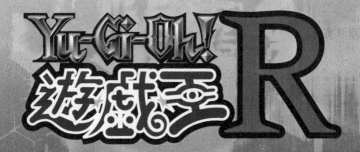

VOLUME 1

A WICKED SHADOW!

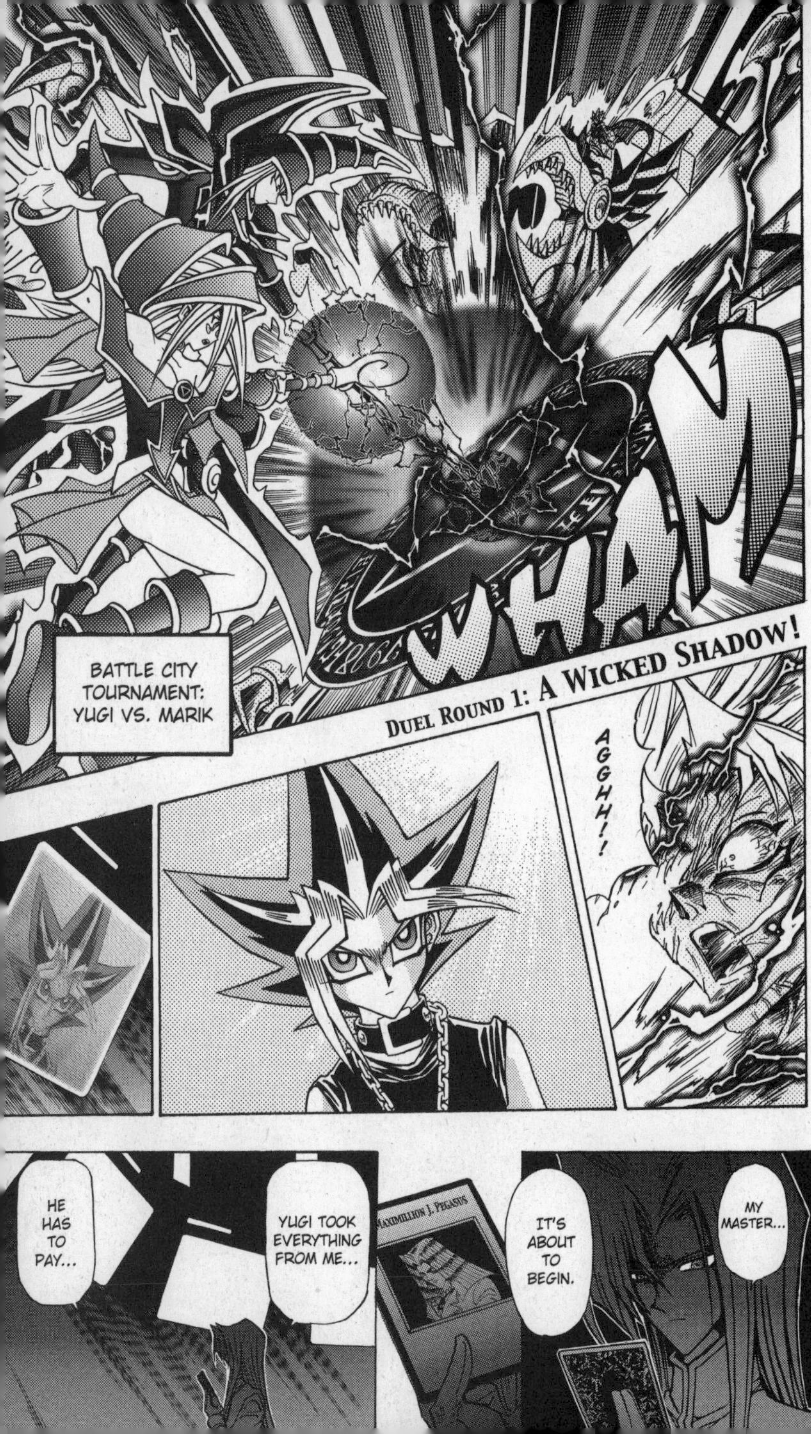
WHAM
BATTLE CITY TOURNAMENT: YUGI VS. MARIK
DUEL ROUND 1: A WICKED SHADOW!
AGGHH!!
MY MASTER...
IT'S ABOUT TO BEGIN.
MAXIMILLION J. PEGASUS
YUGI TOOK EVERYTHING FROM ME...
HE HAS TO PAY...

Duel Round 1: A Wicked Shadow!

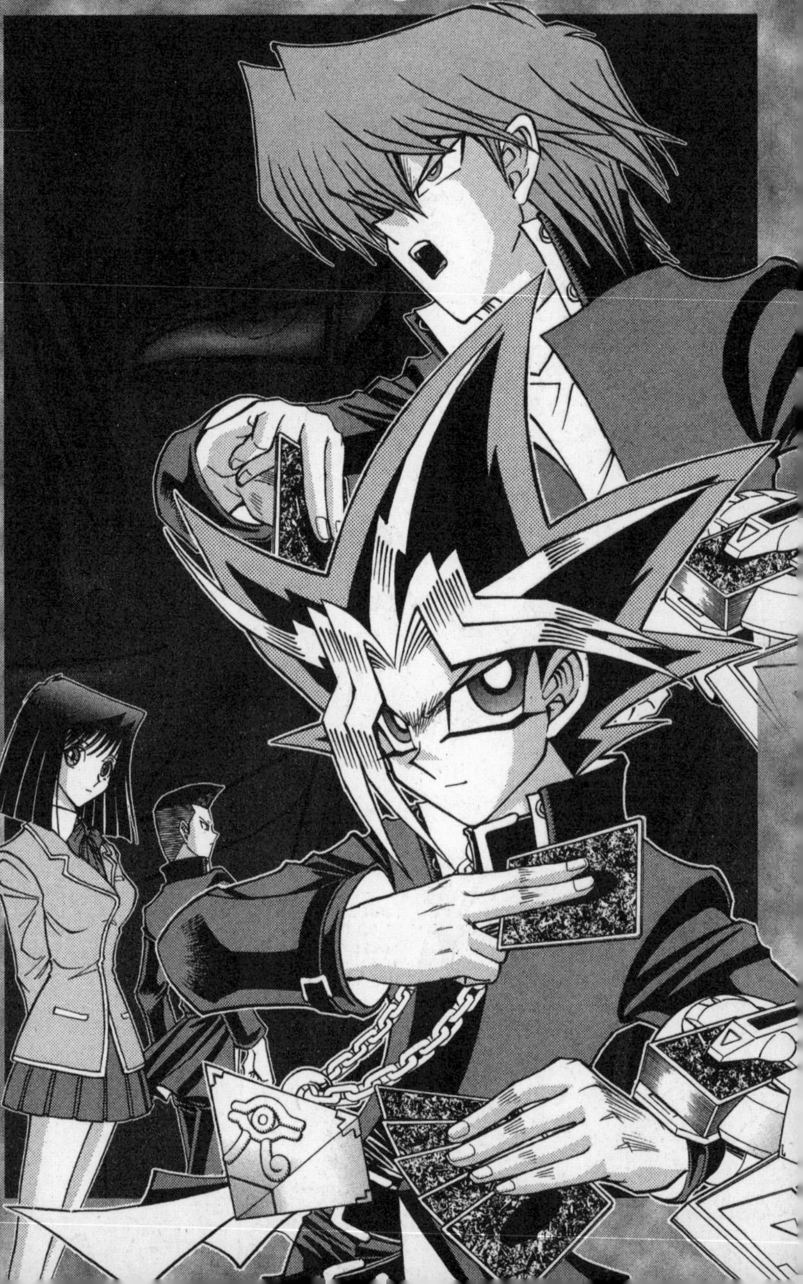

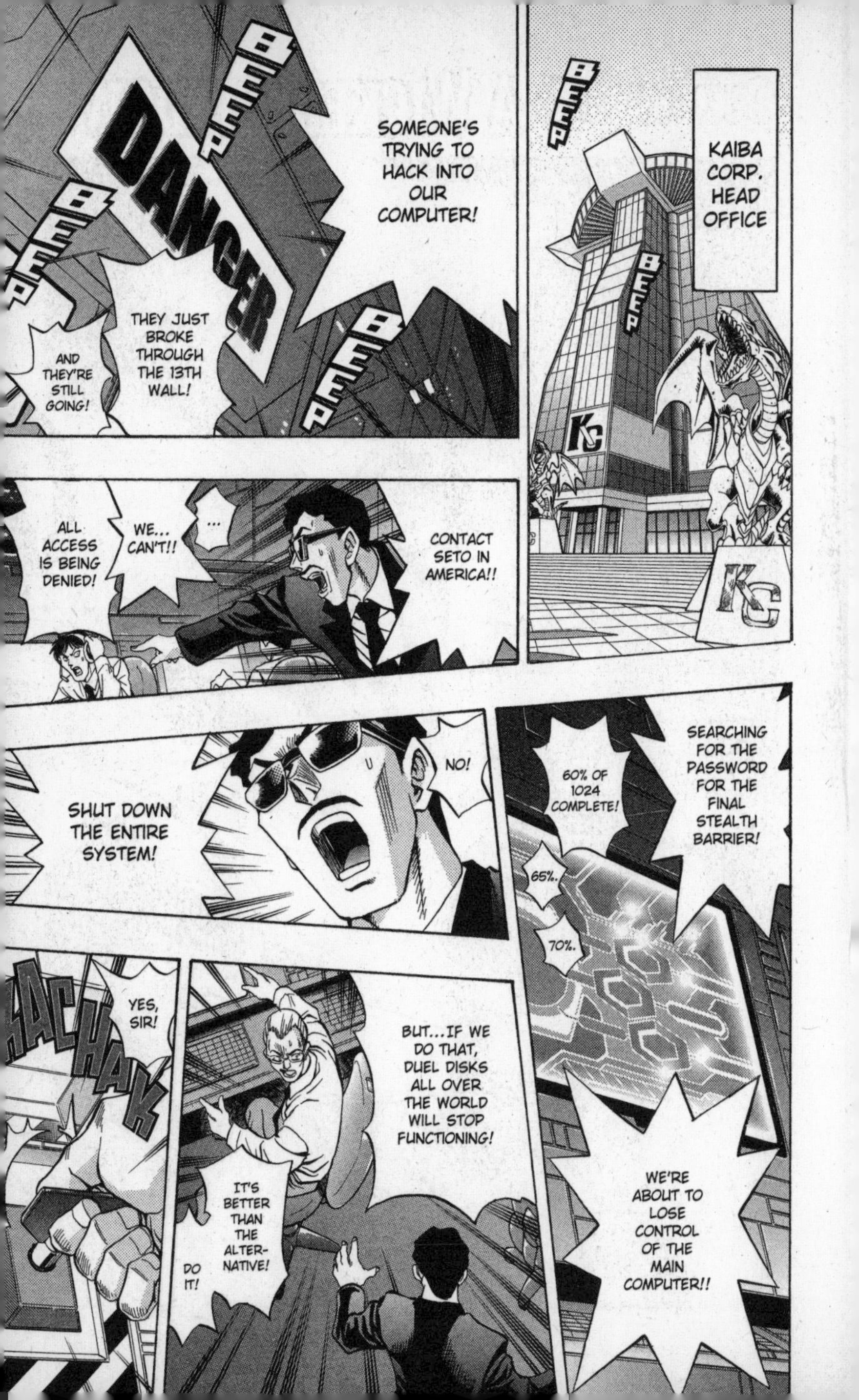
BEEP
KAIBA CORP. HEAD OFFICE
BEEP
SOMEONE'S TRYING TO HACK INTO OUR COMPUTER!
BEEP
DANGER
BEEP
THEY JUST BROKE THROUGH THE 13TH WALL!
AND THEY'RE STILL GOING!
BEEP
CONTACT SETO IN AMERICA!!
...
WE... CAN'T!!
ALL ACCESS IS BEING DENIED!
SEARCHING FOR THE PASSWORD FOR THE FINAL STEALTH BARRIER!
60% OF 1024 COMPLETE!
65%.
70%.
WE'RE ABOUT TO LOSE CONTROL OF THE MAIN COMPUTER!!
NO!
SHUT DOWN THE ENTIRE SYSTEM!
BUT...IF WE DO THAT, DUEL DISKS ALL OVER THE WORLD WILL STOP FUNCTIONING!
IT'S BETTER THAN THE ALTER-NATIVE!
DO IT!
YES, SIR!
HACHAK

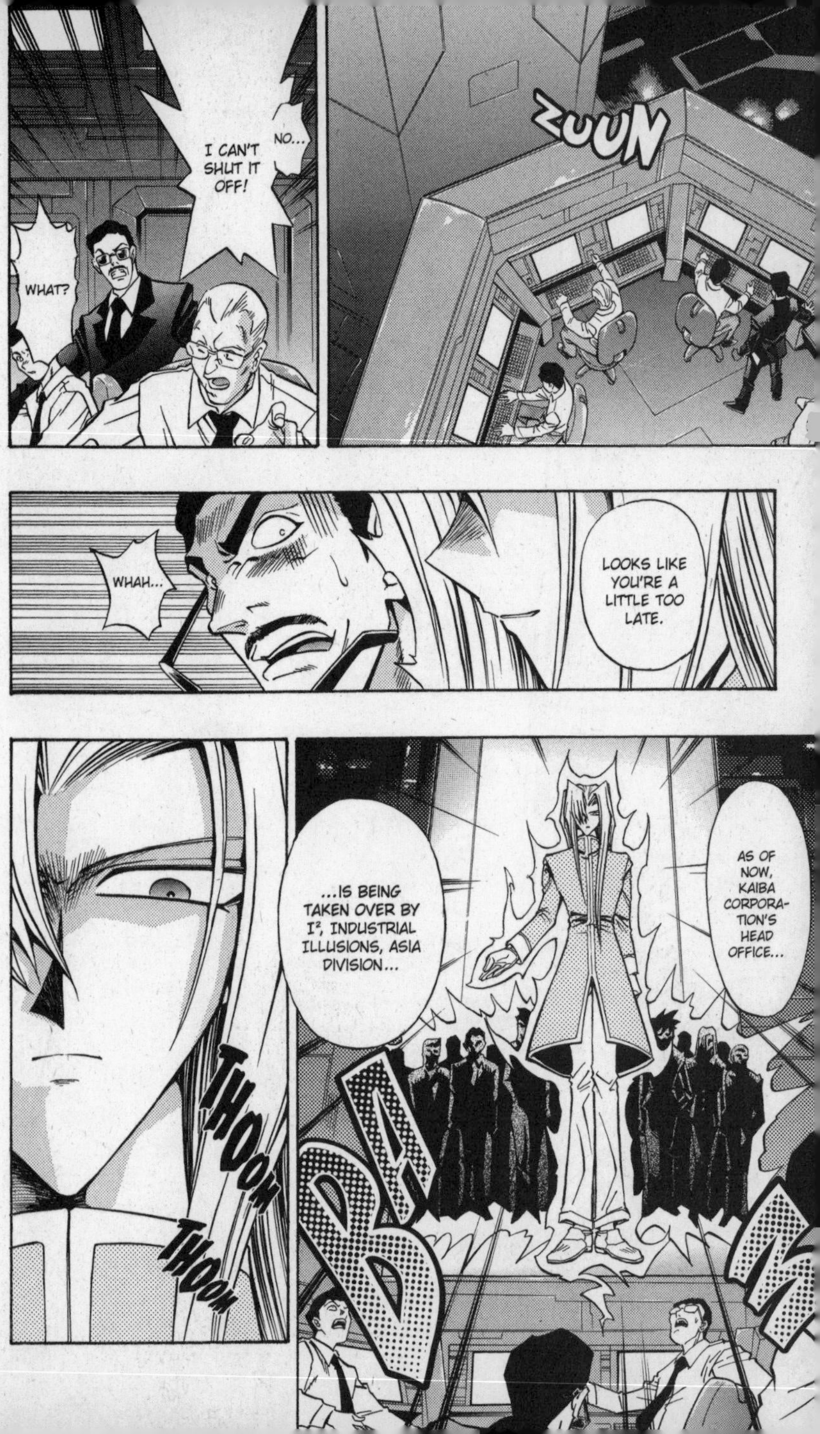
ZUUN
NO...
I CAN'T SHUT IT OFF!
WHAT?
LOOKS LIKE YOU'RE A LITTLE TOO LATE.
WHAH...
AS OF NOW, KAIBA CORPORATION'S HEAD OFFICE...
...IS BEING TAKEN OVER BY I^2, INDUSTRIAL ILLUSIONS, ASIA DIVISION...
BAM
THOOM THOOM

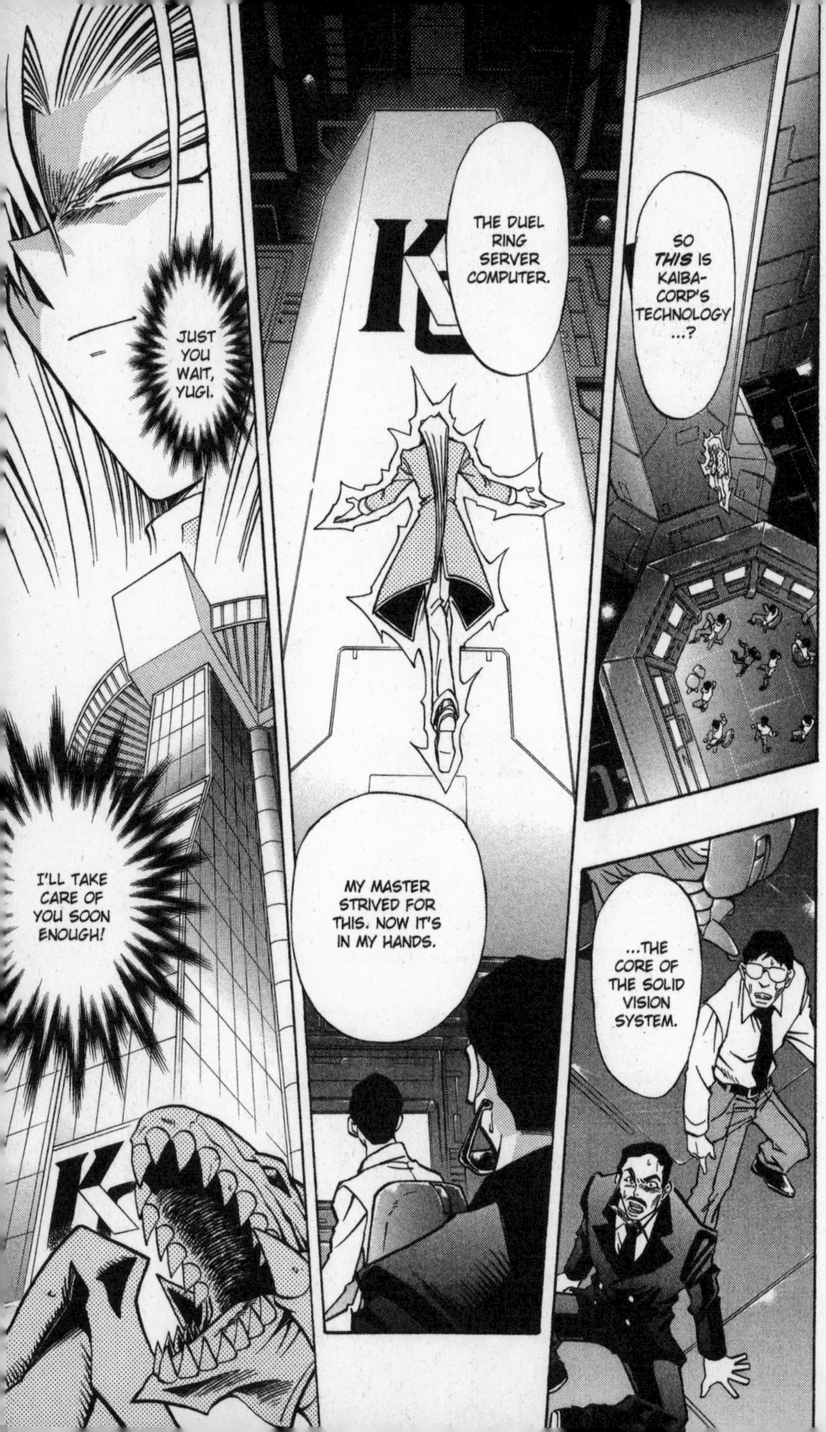
SO THIS IS KAIBA-CORP'S TECHNOLOGY ...?
...THE CORE OF THE SOLID VISION SYSTEM.
THE DUEL RING SERVER COMPUTER.
MY MASTER STRIVED FOR THIS. NOW IT'S IN MY HANDS.
JUST YOU WAIT, YUGI.
I'LL TAKE CARE OF YOU SOON ENOUGH!

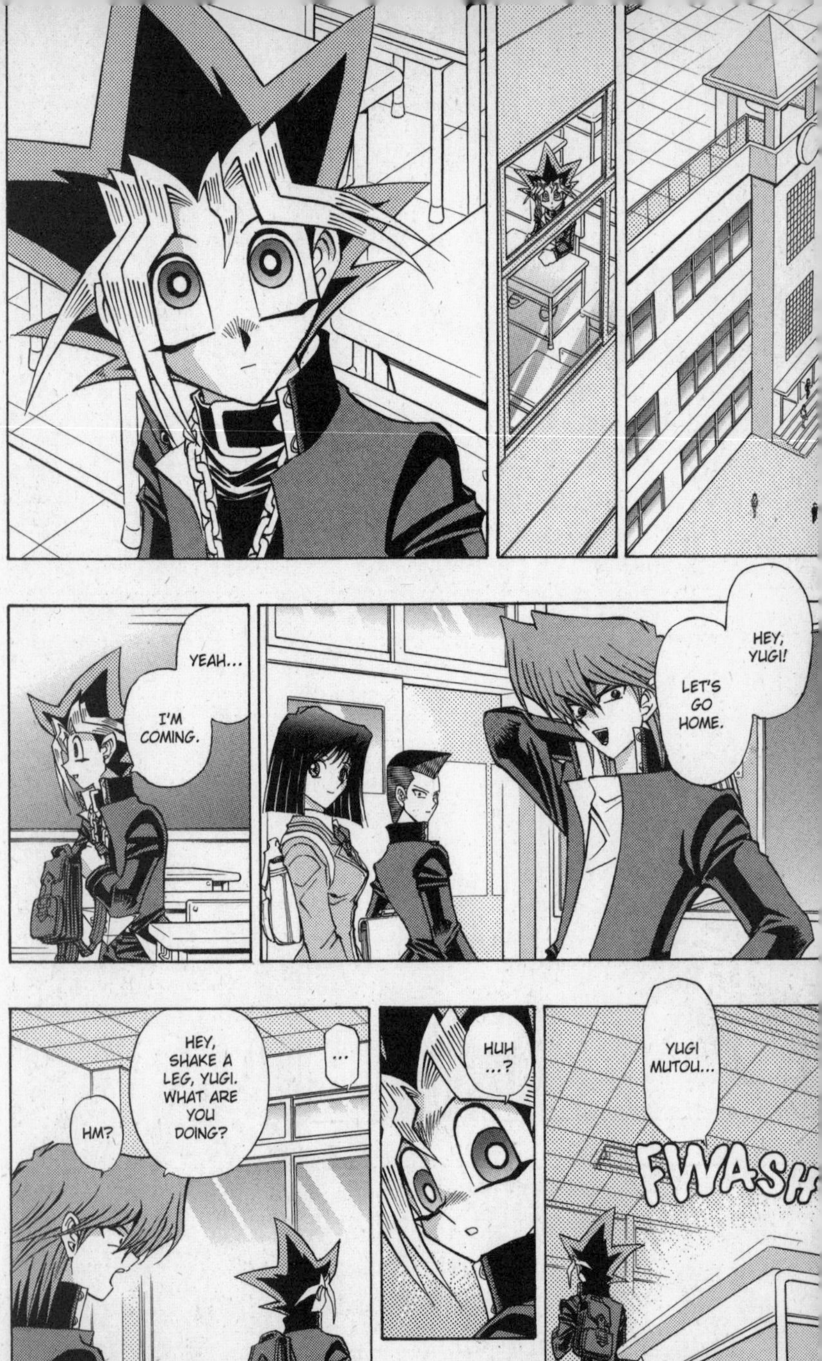
HEY, YUGI!
LET'S GO HOME.
YEAH...
I'M COMING.
YUGI MUTOU...
FWASH
HUH ...?
...
HEY, SHAKE A LEG, YUGI. WHAT ARE YOU DOING?
HM?

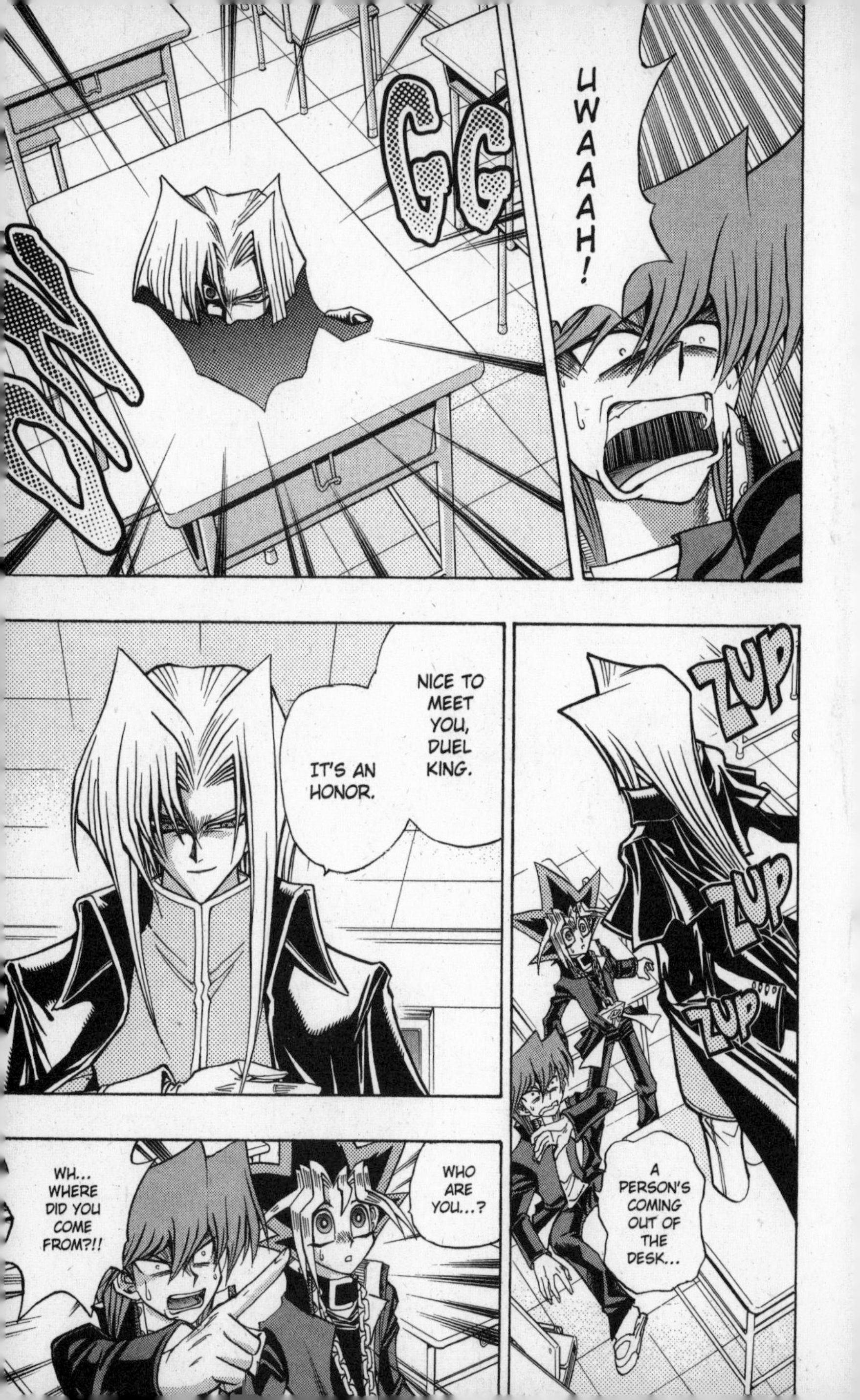
UWAAAAH!
GG
ZUP
ZUP
ZUP
A PERSON'S COMING OUT OF THE DESK...
NICE TO MEET YOU, DUEL KING.
IT'S AN HONOR.
WHO ARE YOU...?
WH... WHERE DID YOU COME FROM?!!

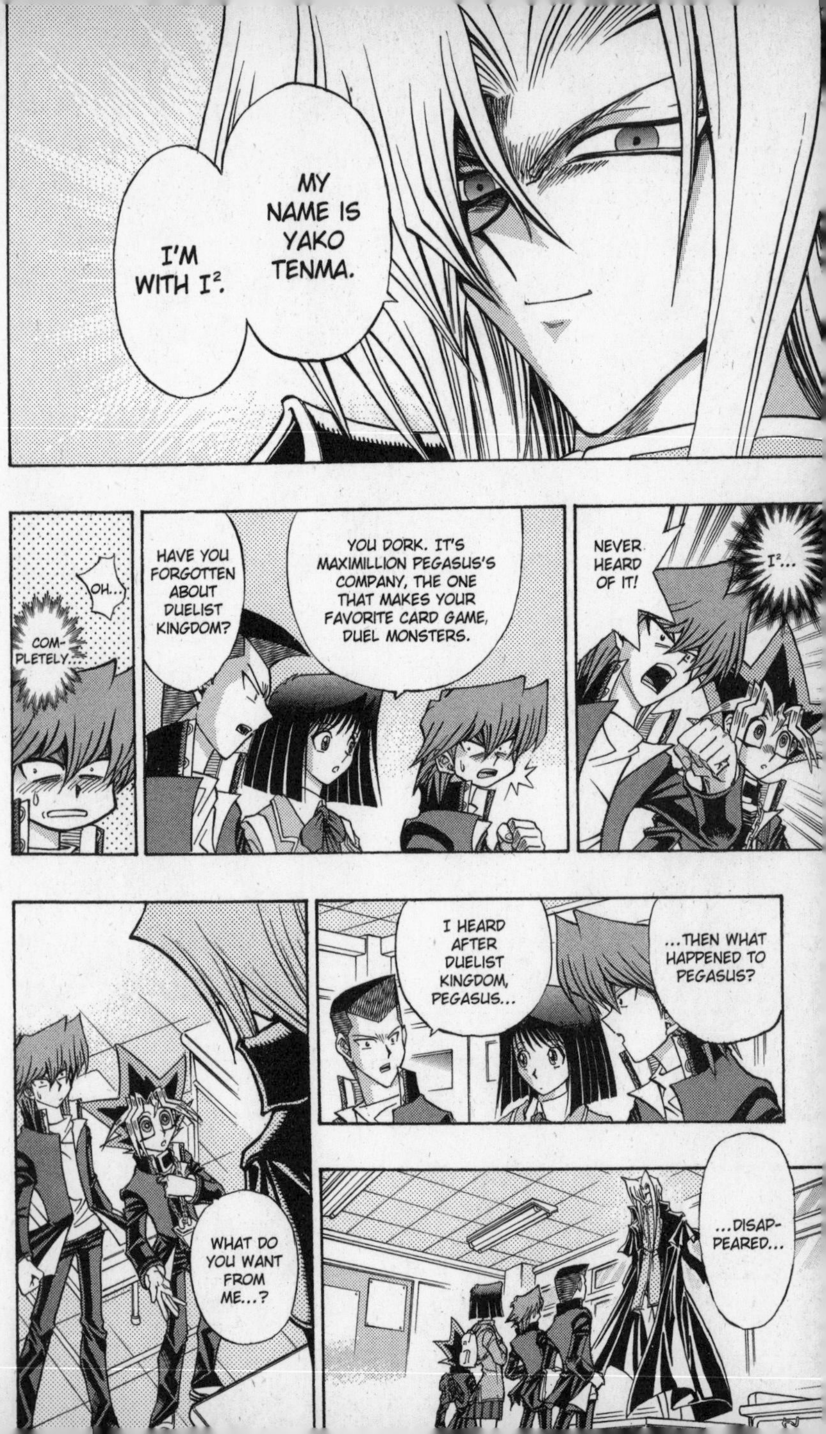
MY NAME IS YAKO TENMA.
I'M WITH I^2.
I^2...
NEVER HEARD OF IT!
YOU DORK. IT'S MAXIMILLION PEGASUS'S COMPANY, THE ONE THAT MAKES YOUR FAVORITE CARD GAME, DUEL MONSTERS.
HAVE YOU FORGOTTEN ABOUT DUELIST KINGDOM?
OH...
COM-PLETELY...
...THEN WHAT HAPPENED TO PEGASUS?
I HEARD AFTER DUELIST KINGDOM, PEGASUS...
...DISAP-PEARED...
WHAT DO YOU WANT FROM ME...?

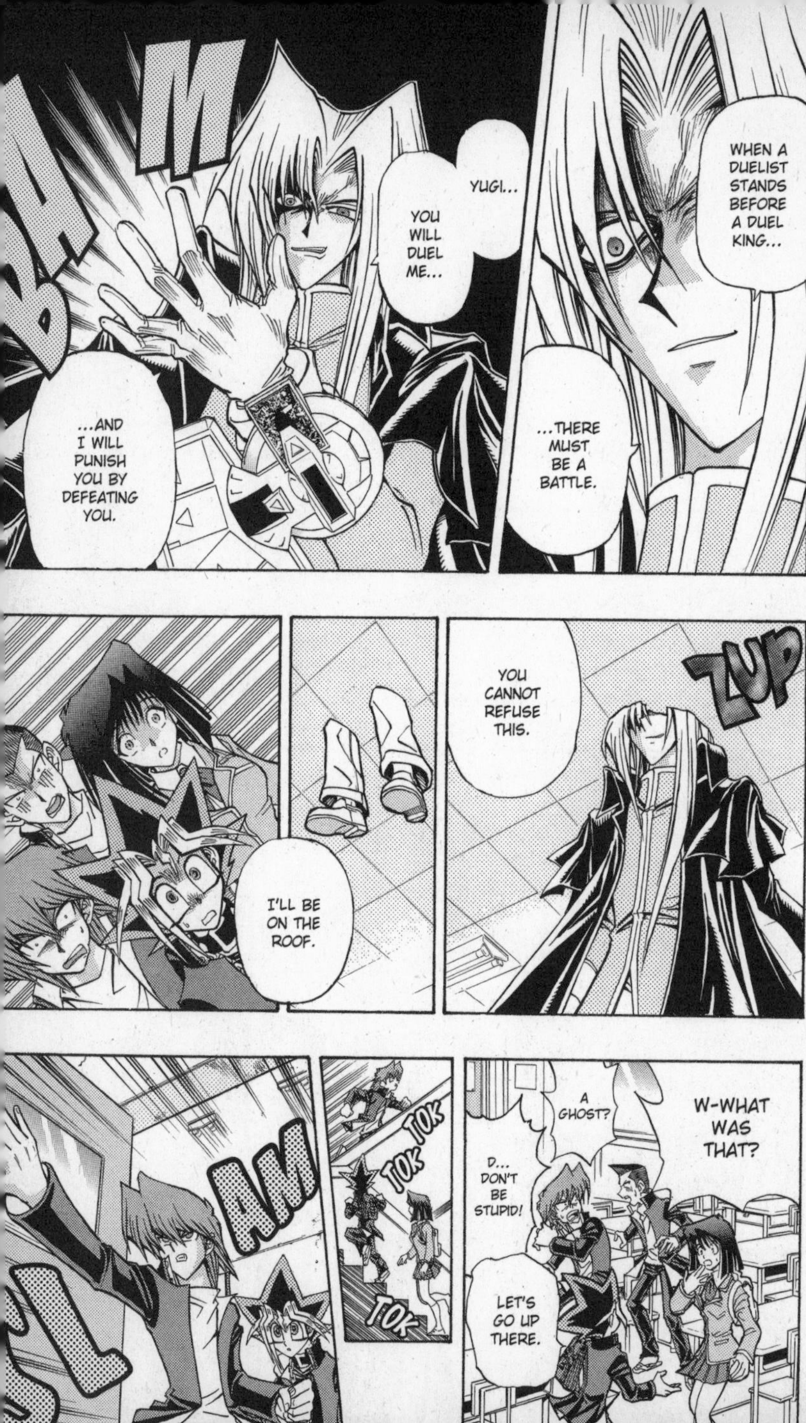
WHEN A DUELIST STANDS BEFORE A DUEL KING...
...THERE MUST BE A BATTLE.
YUGI...
YOU WILL DUEL ME...
BAM
...AND I WILL PUNISH YOU BY DEFEATING YOU.
ZUP
YOU CANNOT REFUSE THIS.
I'LL BE ON THE ROOF.
W-WHAT WAS THAT?
A GHOST?
D... DON'T BE STUPID!
LET'S GO UP THERE.
TOK
TOK
TOK
SLAM

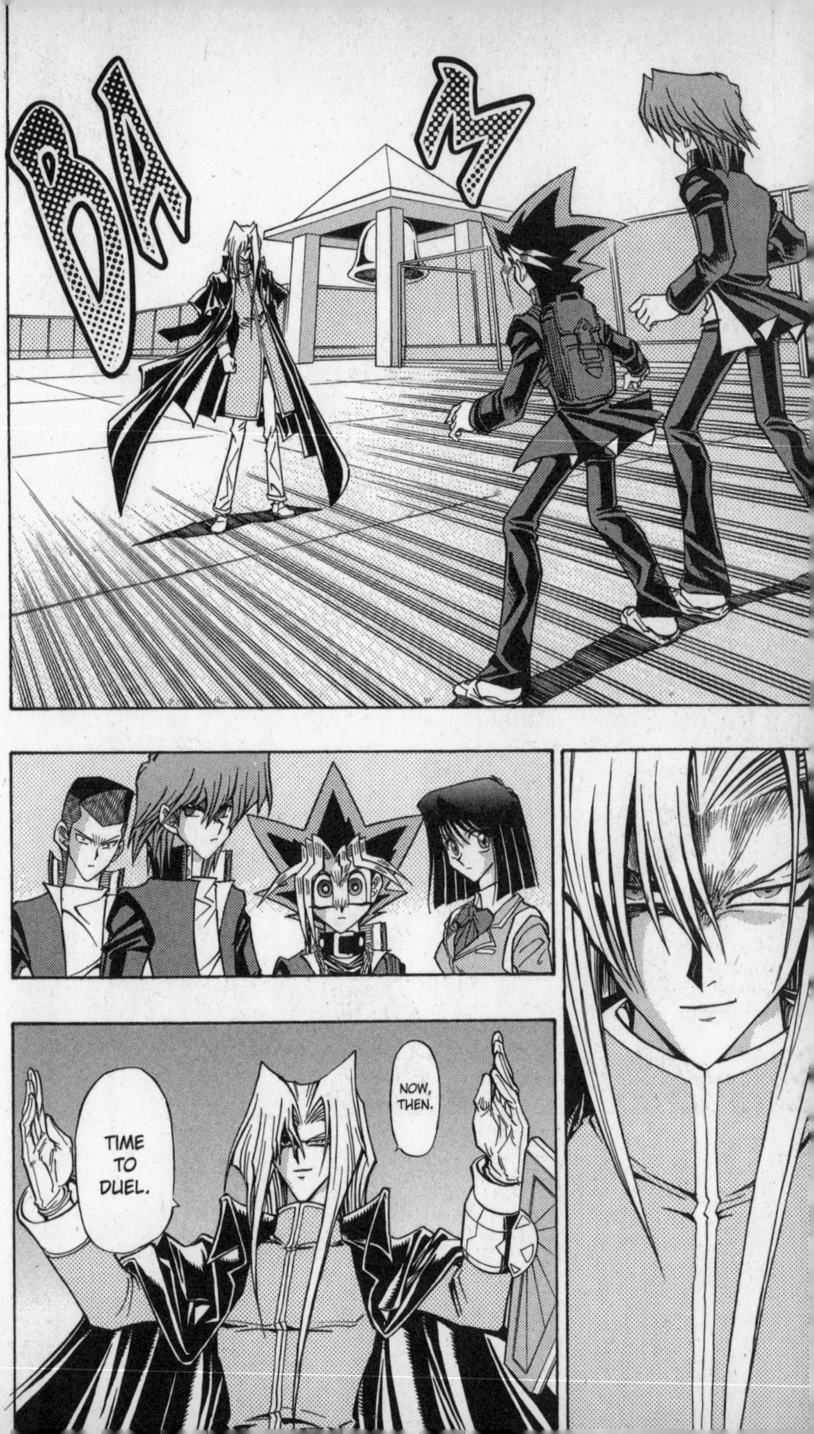
BAM
NOW, THEN.
TIME TO DUEL.

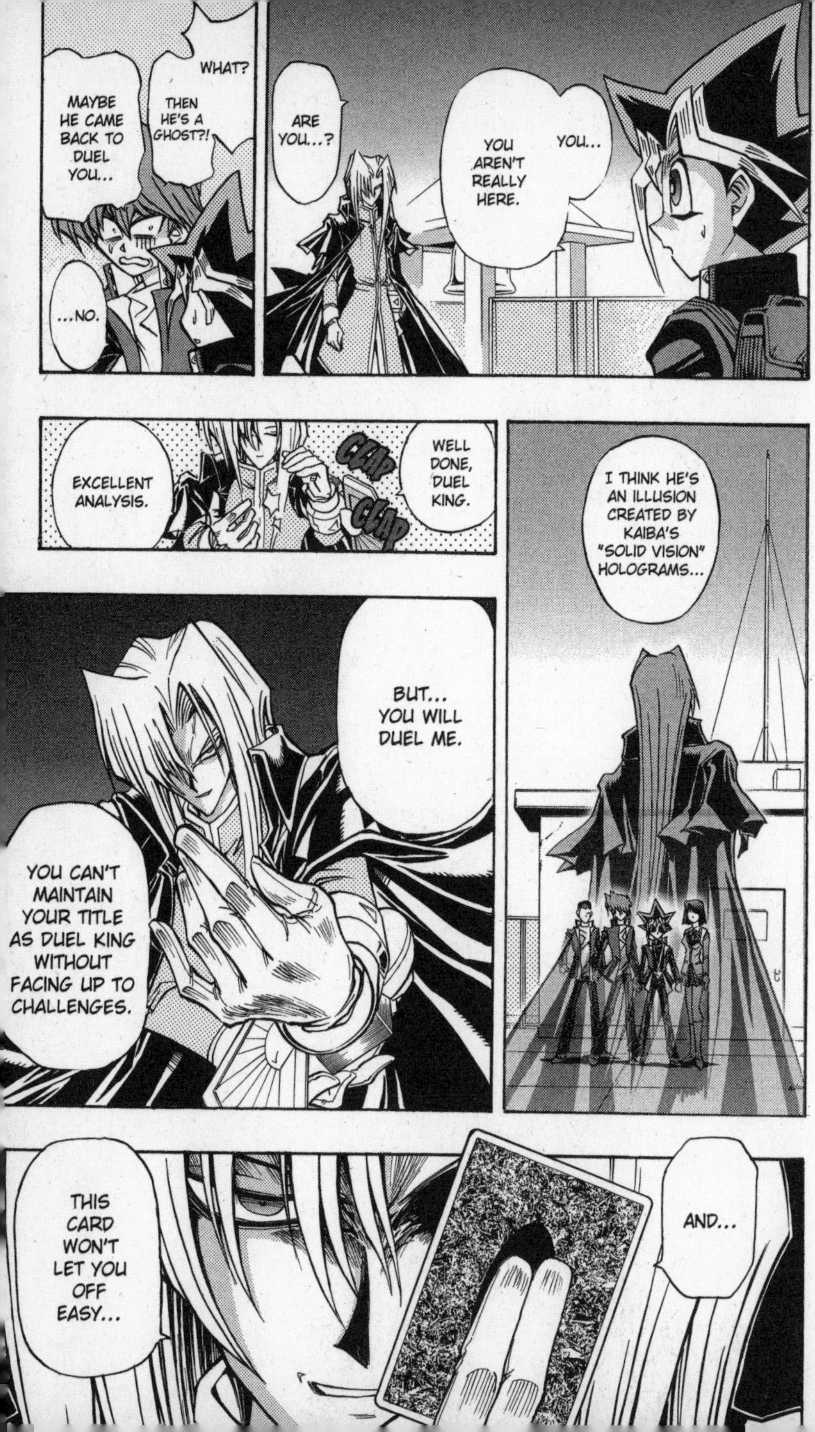
YOU...
YOU AREN'T REALLY HERE.
ARE YOU...?
WHAT?
THEN HE'S A GHOST?!
MAYBE HE CAME BACK TO DUEL YOU...
...NO.
I THINK HE'S AN ILLUSION CREATED BY KAIBA'S "SOLID VISION" HOLOGRAMS...
WELL DONE, DUEL KING.
CLAP
CLAP
EXCELLENT ANALYSIS.
BUT... YOU WILL DUEL ME.
YOU CAN'T MAINTAIN YOUR TITLE AS DUEL KING WITHOUT FACING UP TO CHALLENGES.
AND...
THIS CARD WON'T LET YOU OFF EASY...

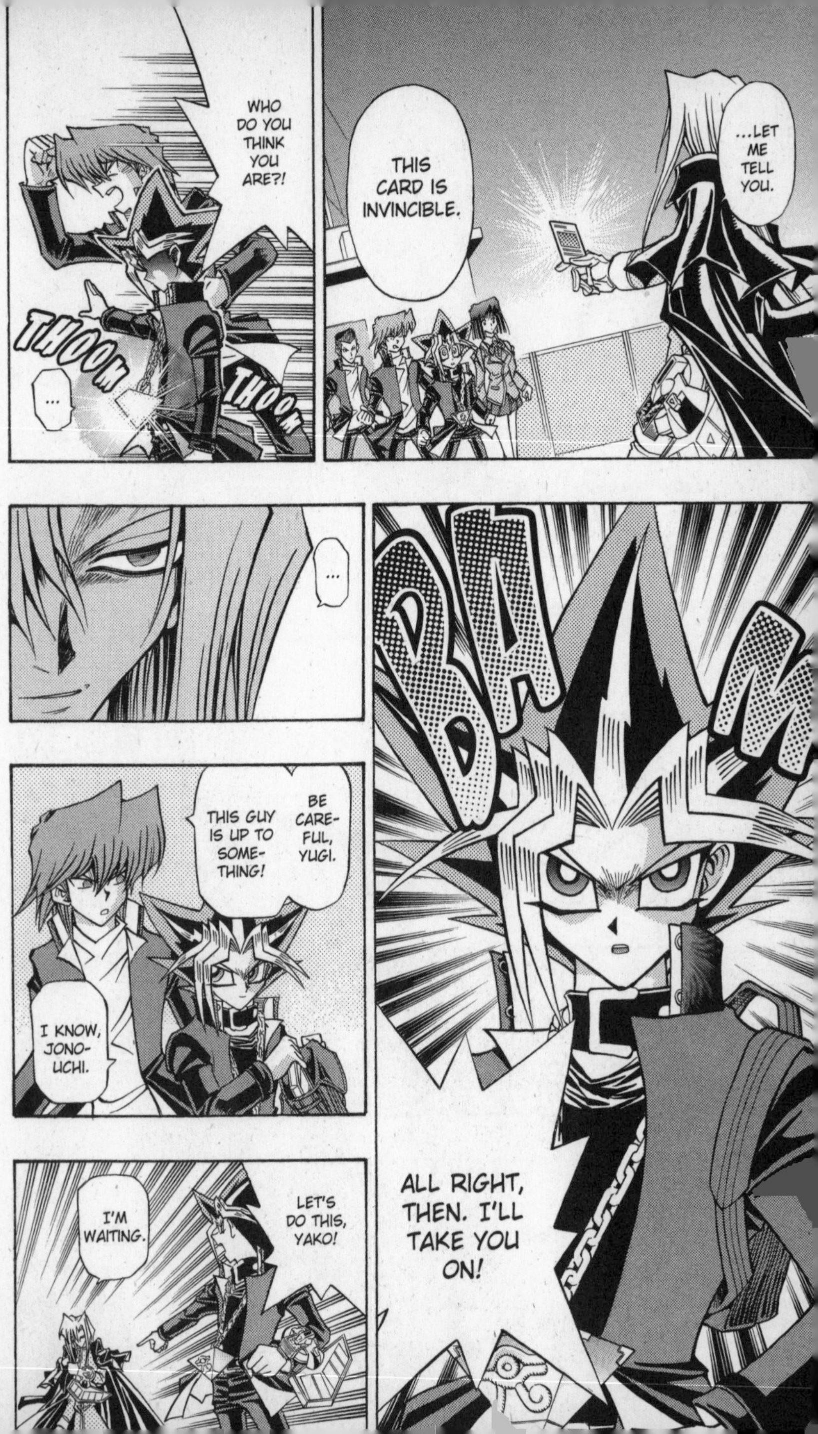
...LET ME TELL YOU.
THIS CARD IS INVINCIBLE.
WHO DO YOU THINK YOU ARE?!
THOOM
THOOM
...
BAM
ALL RIGHT, THEN. I'LL TAKE YOU ON!
...
BE CARE-FUL, YUGI.
THIS GUY IS UP TO SOME-THING!
I KNOW, JONO-UCHI.
LET'S DO THIS, YAKO!
I'M WAITING.

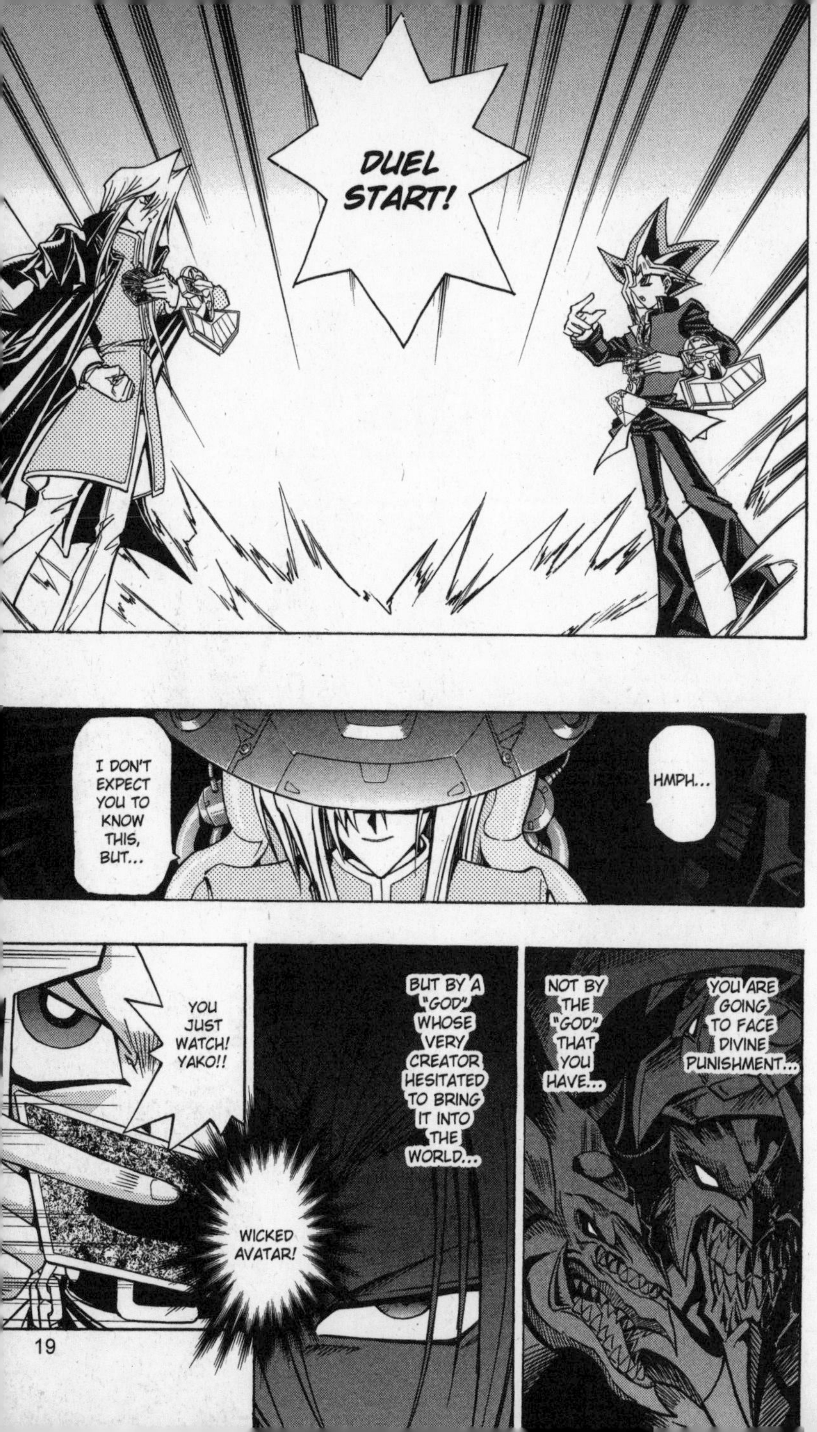
DUEL START!
HMPH...
I DON'T EXPECT YOU TO KNOW THIS, BUT...
YOU ARE GOING TO FACE DIVINE PUNISHMENT...
NOT BY THE "GOD" THAT YOU HAVE...
BUT BY A "GOD" WHOSE VERY CREATOR HESITATED TO BRING IT INTO THE WORLD...
YOU JUST WATCH! YAKO!!
WICKED AVATAR!

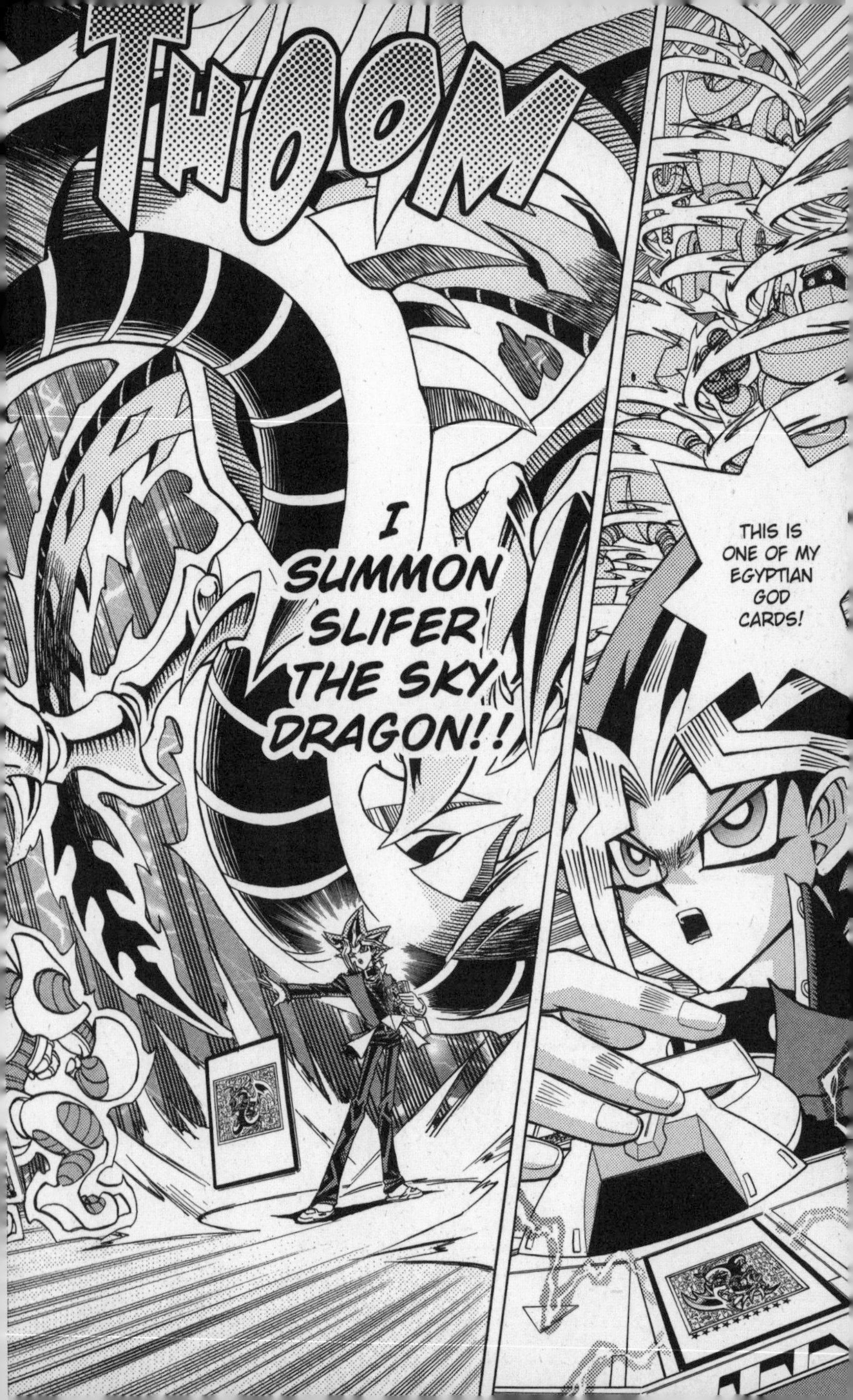
THIS IS ONE OF MY EGYPTIAN GOD CARDS!
THOOM
I SUMMON SLIFER THE SKY DRAGON!!

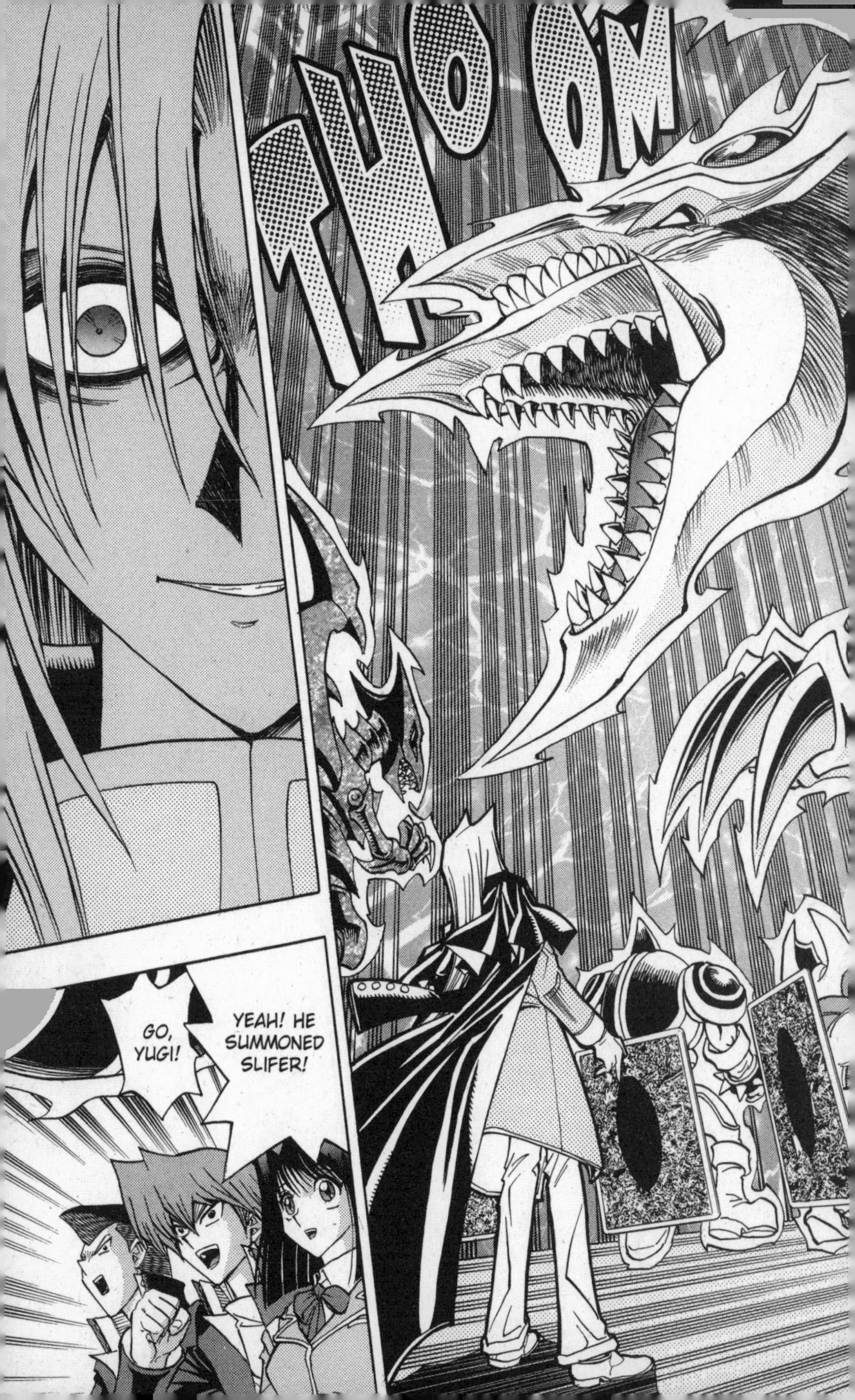
THOOM
YEAH! HE SUMMONED SLIFER!
GO, YUGI!

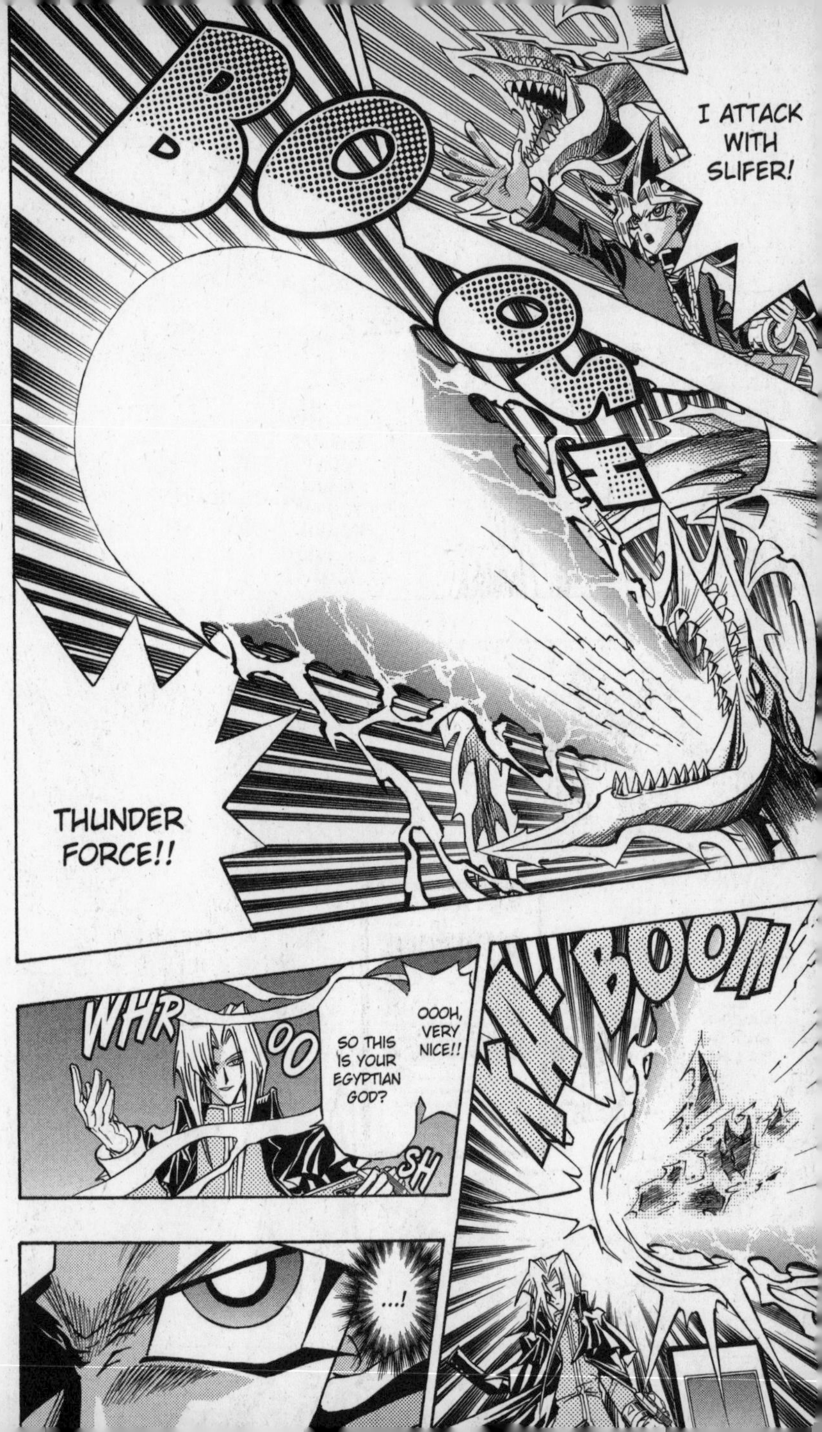
I ATTACK WITH SLIFER!
BOOOOOOOM
THUNDER FORCE!!
WHHHBOOM
OOOH, VERY NICE!!
SO THIS IS YOUR EGYPTIAN GOD?
WHROOSH
...!

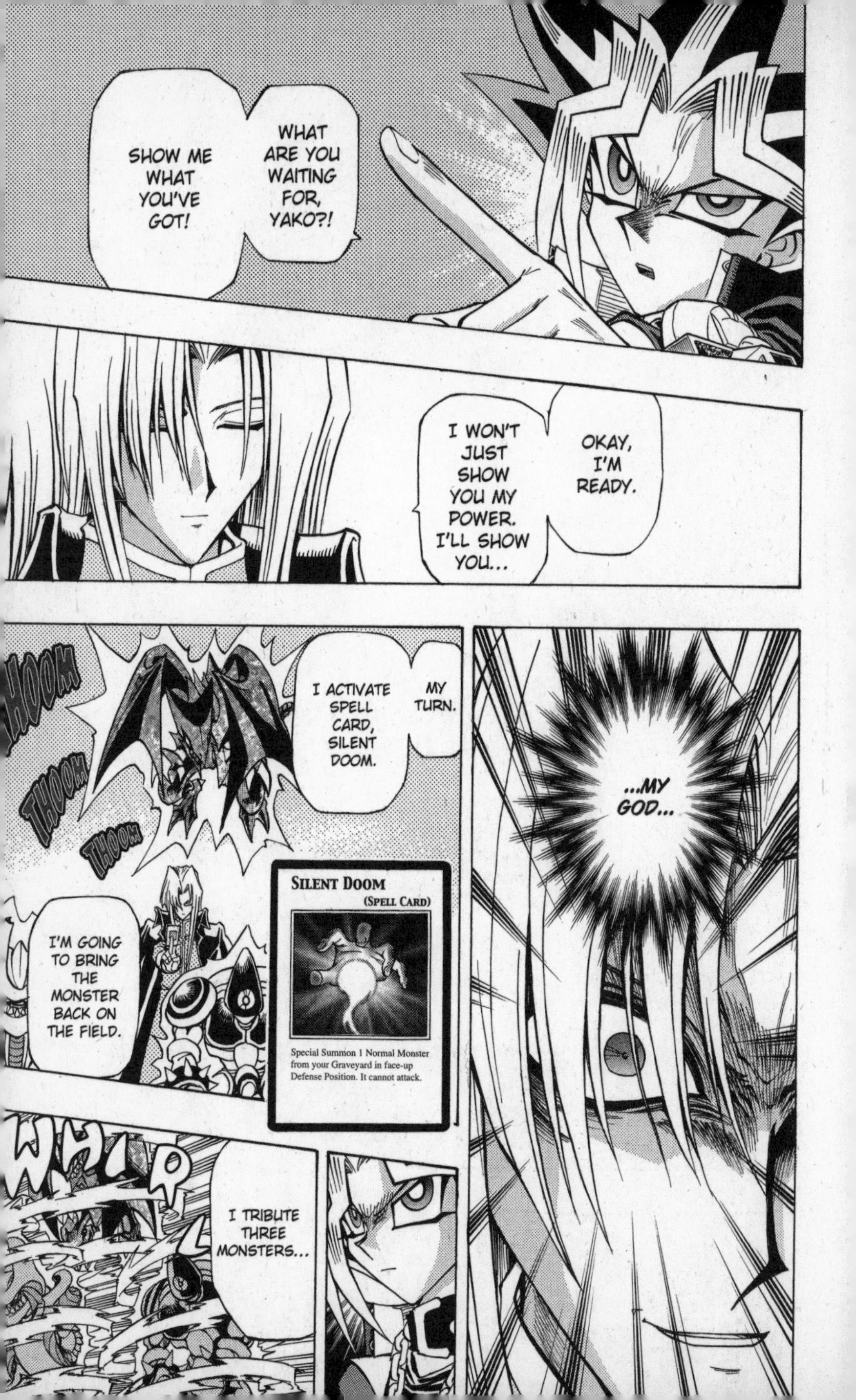
WHAT ARE YOU WAITING FOR, YAKO?!
SHOW ME WHAT YOU'VE GOT!
OKAY, I'M READY.
I WON'T JUST SHOW YOU MY POWER. I'LL SHOW YOU...
...MY GOD...
MY TURN.
I ACTIVATE SPELL CARD, SILENT DOOM.
HOOM
THOOM
THOOM
SILENT DOOM
(SPELL CARD)
Special Summon 1 Normal Monster from your Graveyard in face-up Defense Position. It cannot attack.
I'M GOING TO BRING THE MONSTER BACK ON THE FIELD.
I TRIBUTE THREE MONSTERS...
WHIP

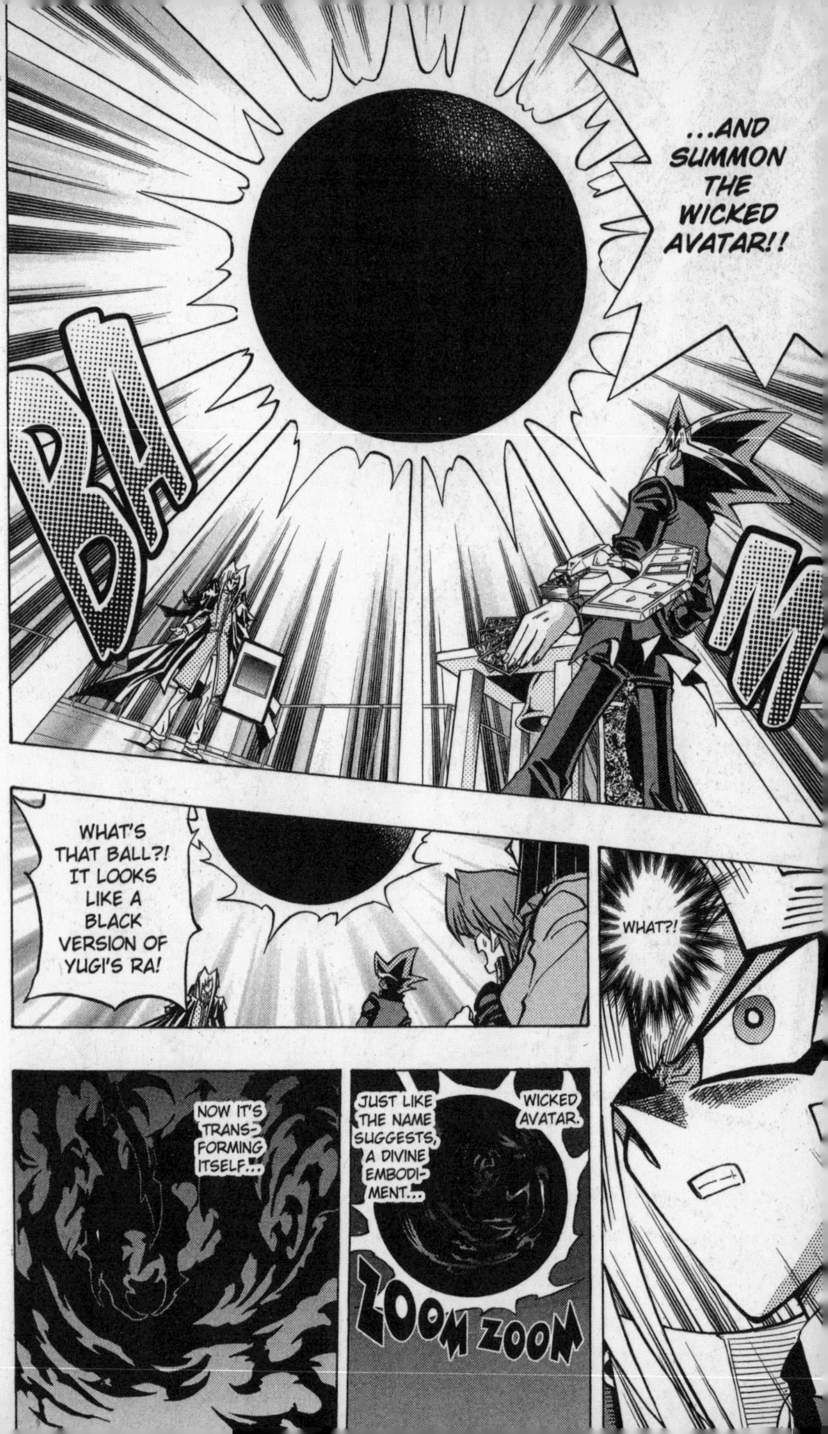
...AND SUMMON THE WICKED AVATAR!!
BA
M
WHAT?!
WHAT'S THAT BALL?! IT LOOKS LIKE A BLACK VERSION OF YUGI'S RA!
WICKED AVATAR.
JUST LIKE THE NAME SUGGESTS, A DIVINE EMBODI-MENT...
ZOOM ZOOM
NOW IT'S TRANS-FORMING ITSELF...

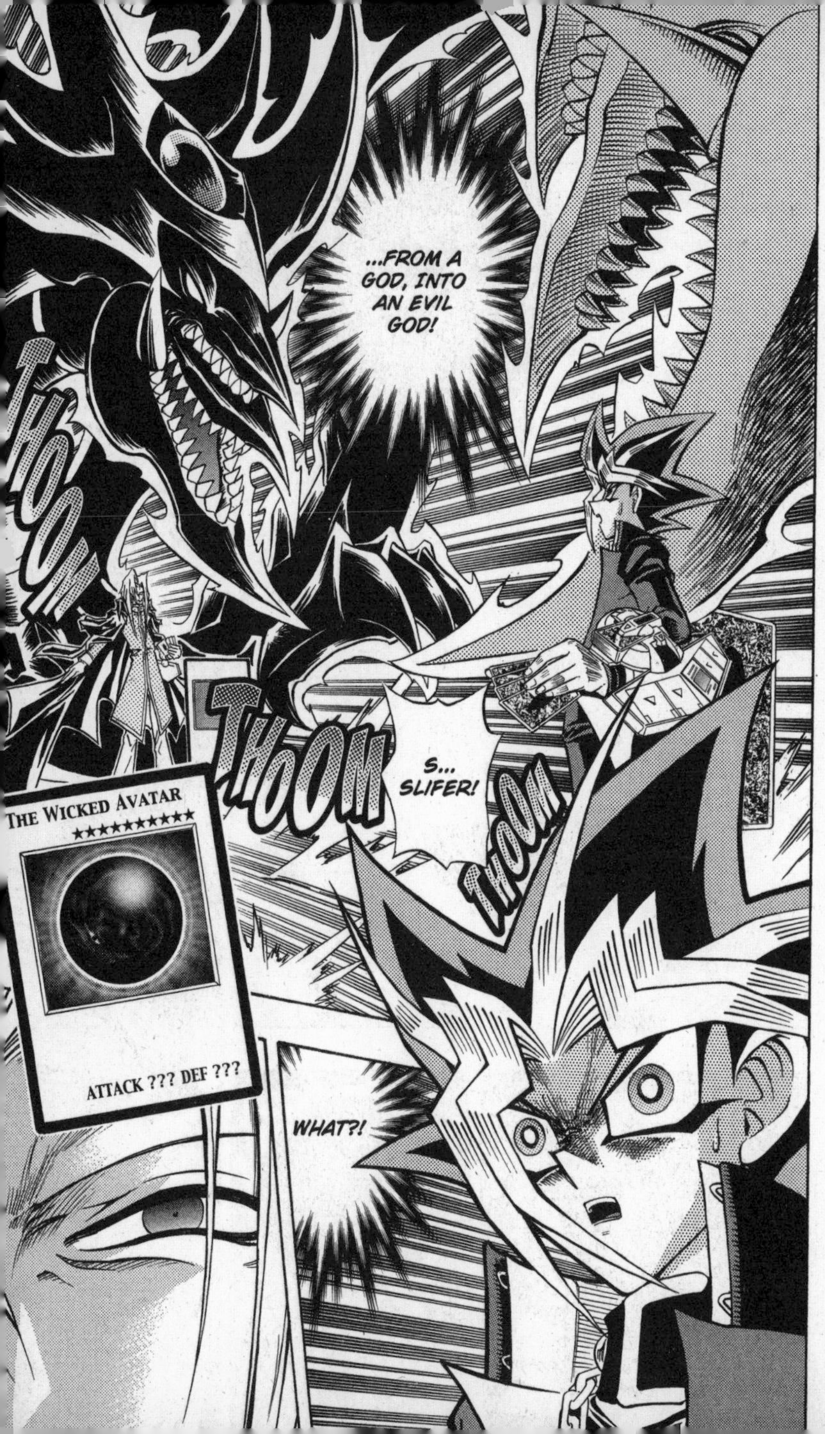
...FROM A GOD, INTO AN EVIL GOD!
THOOM
THOOM
THOOM
S... SLIFER!
WHAT?!
THE WICKED AVATAR
★★★★★★★★★★
ATTACK ??? DEF ???

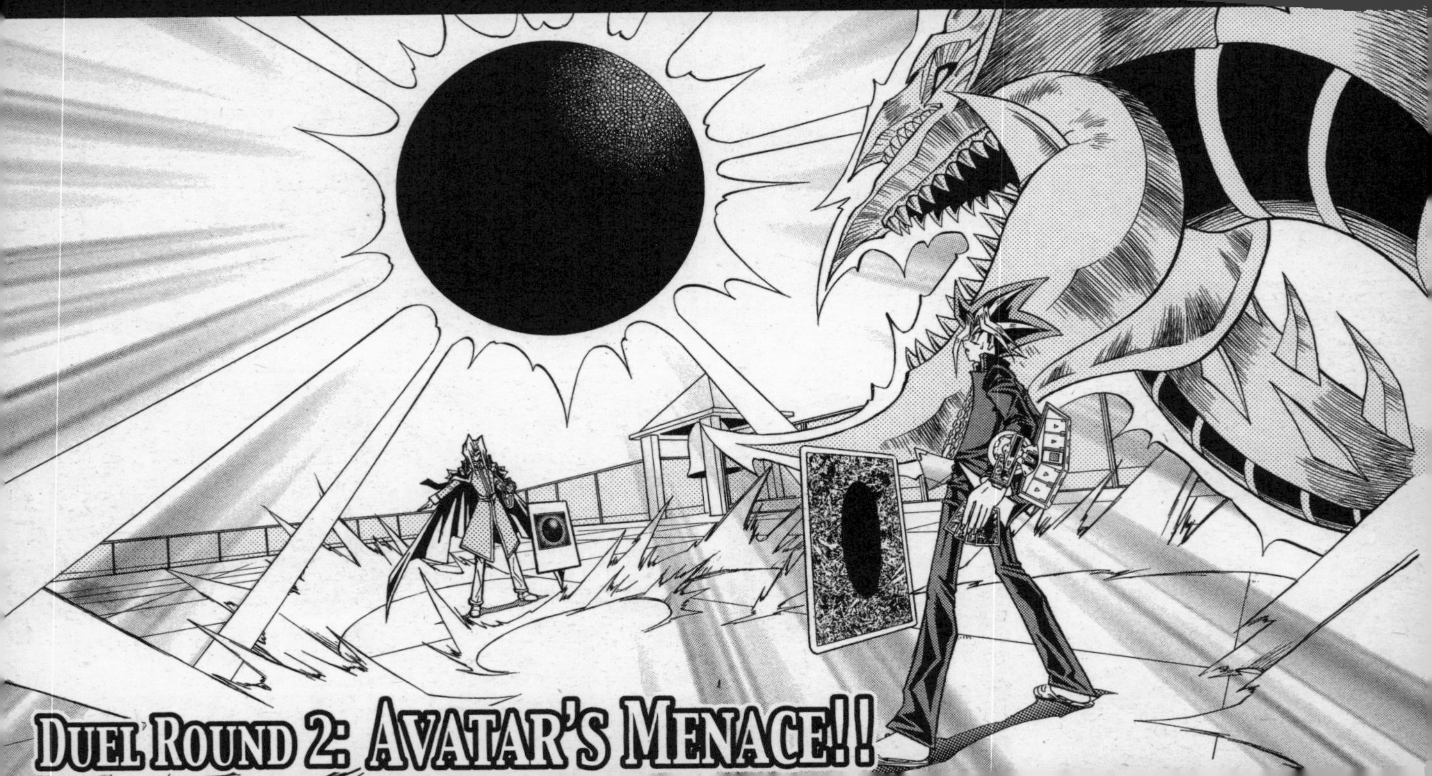

Duel Round 2: Avatar's Menace!!

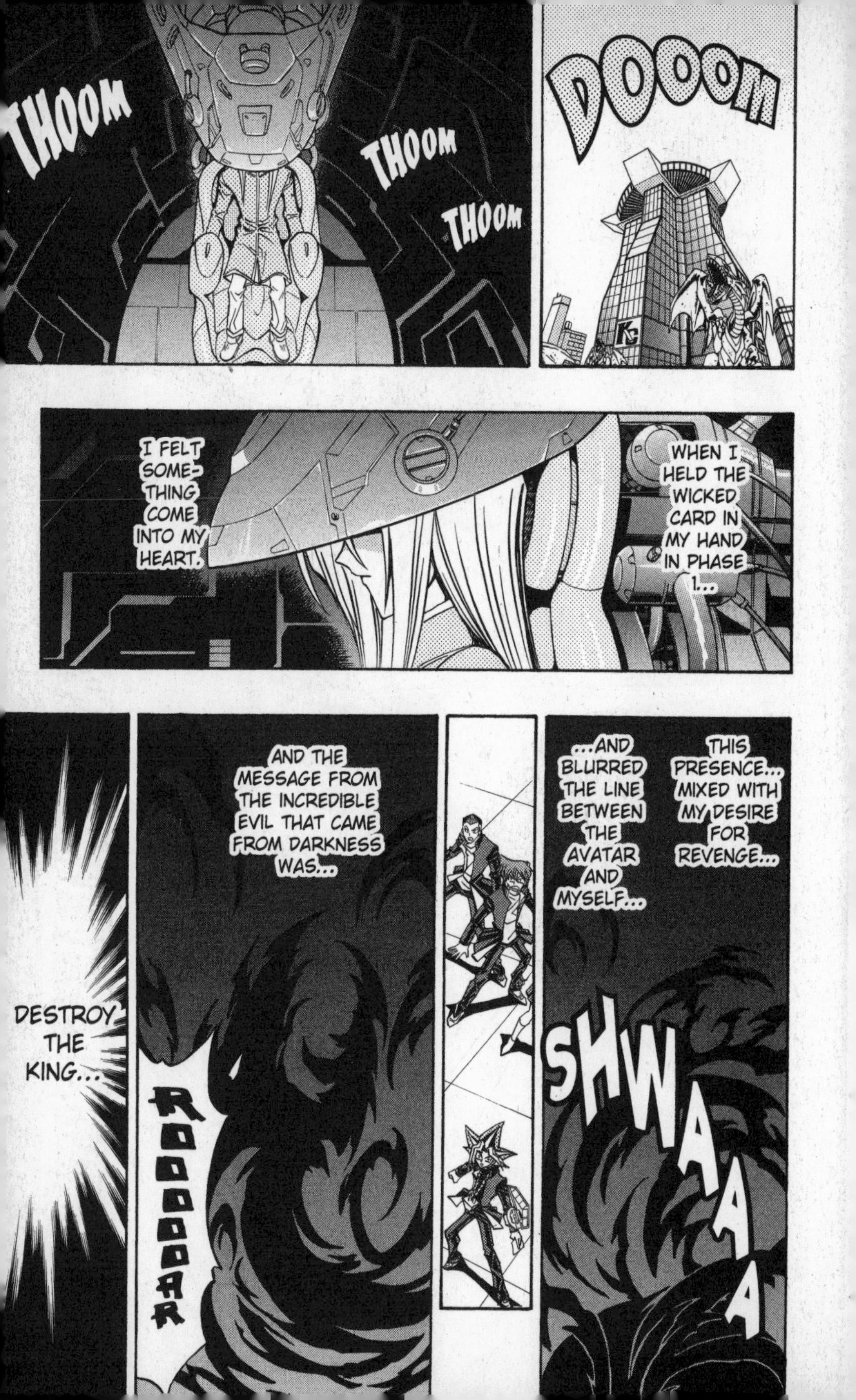
DOOOOM
THOOM
THOOM
THOOM
WHEN I HELD THE WICKED CARD IN MY HAND IN PHASE 1...
I FELT SOME-THING COME INTO MY HEART.
THIS PRESENCE... MIXED WITH MY DESIRE FOR REVENGE...
...AND BLURRED THE LINE BETWEEN THE AVATAR AND MYSELF...
SHWAAAA
AND THE MESSAGE FROM THE INCREDIBLE EVIL THAT CAME FROM DARKNESS WAS...
ROOOOOAR
DESTROY THE KING...

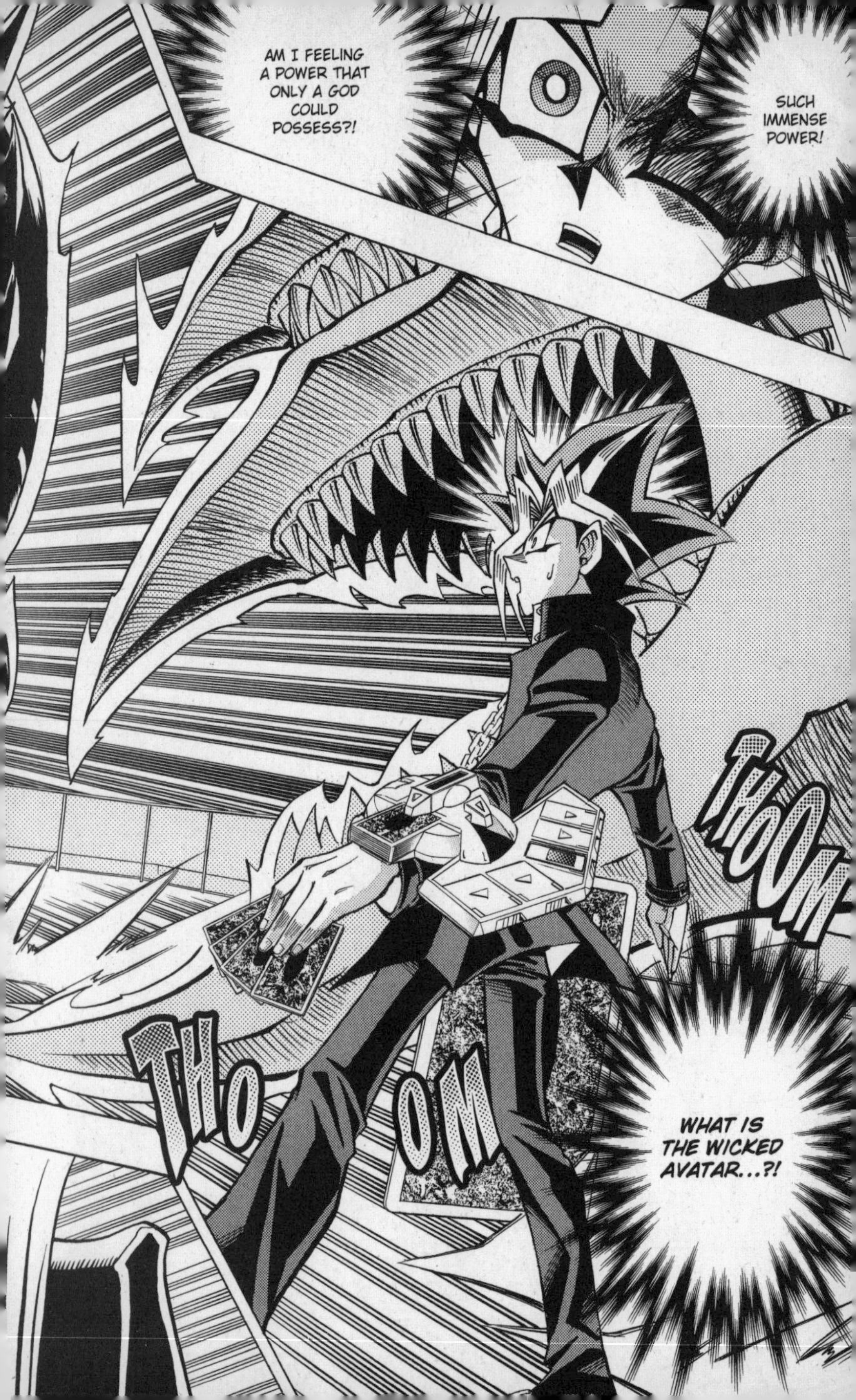
SUCH IMMENSE POWER!
AM I FEELING A POWER THAT ONLY A GOD COULD POSSESS?!
THOOM
WHAT IS THE WICKED AVATAR...?!
THO OM

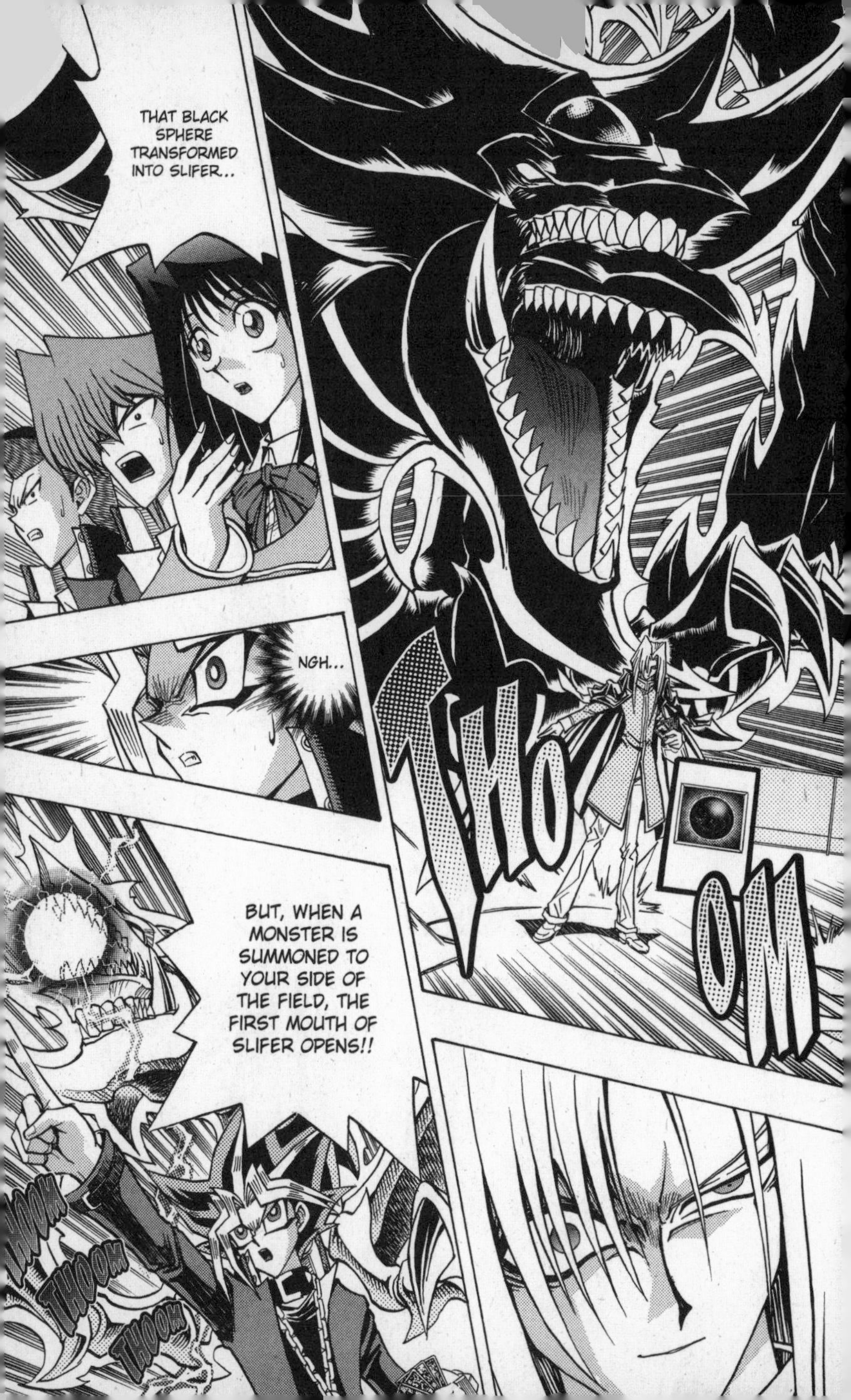
THO OM
THAT BLACK SPHERE TRANSFORMED INTO SLIFER...
NGH...
BUT, WHEN A MONSTER IS SUMMONED TO YOUR SIDE OF THE FIELD, THE FIRST MOUTH OF SLIFER OPENS!!
THOOM
THOOM

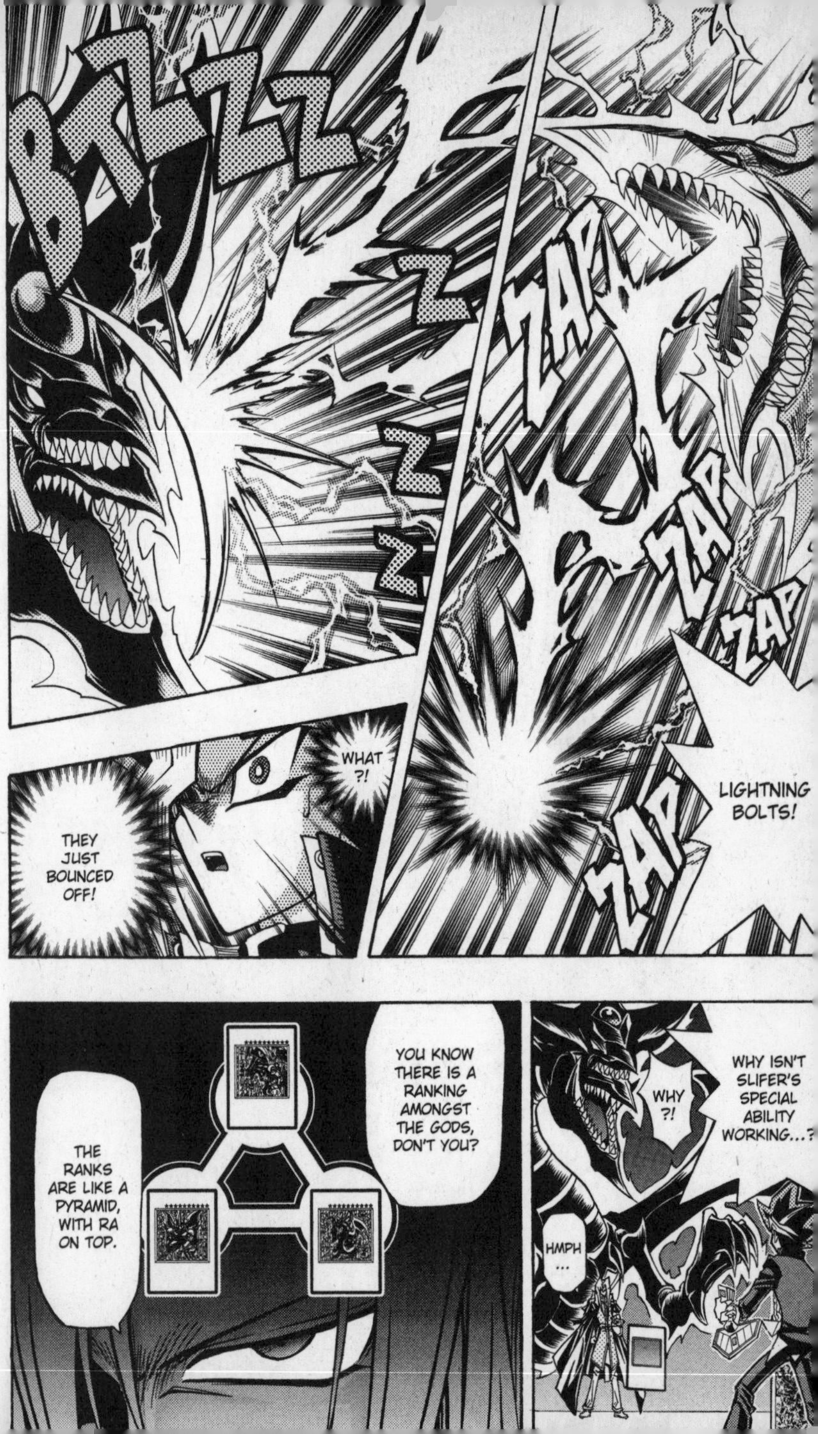
ZAP!
ZAP
ZAP
ZAP
LIGHTNING BOLTS!
BZZZ.
Z
Z
Z
WHAT ?!
THEY JUST BOUNCED OFF!
WHY ISN'T SLIFER'S SPECIAL ABILITY WORKING...?
WHY ?!
HMPH ...
YOU KNOW THERE IS A RANKING AMONGST THE GODS, DON'T YOU?
THE RANKS ARE LIKE A PYRAMID, WITH RA ON TOP.

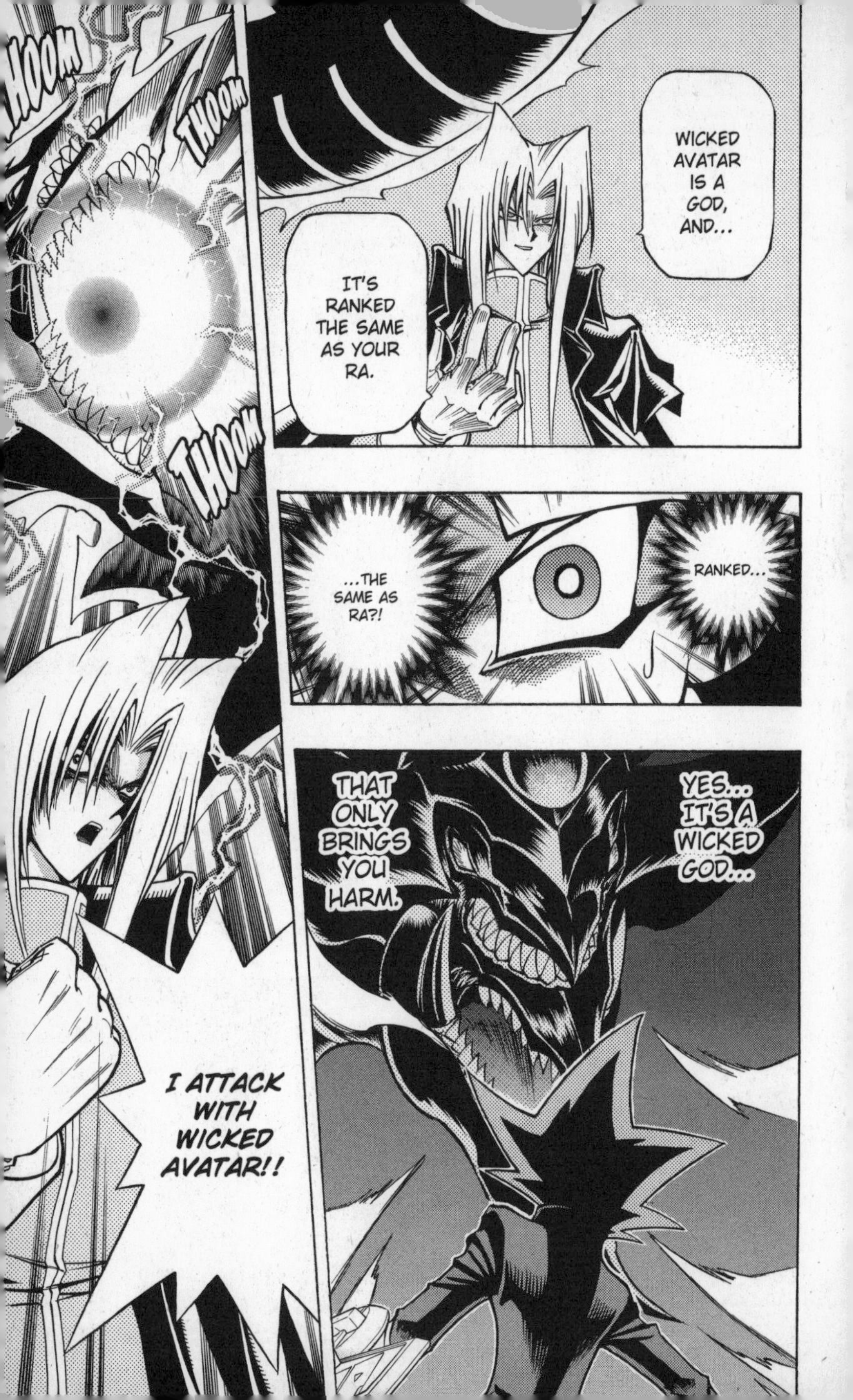
WICKED AVATAR IS A GOD, AND...
IT'S RANKED THE SAME AS YOUR RA.
RANKED...
...THE SAME AS RA?!
YES... IT'S A WICKED GOD...
THAT ONLY BRINGS YOU HARM.
THOOM
THOOM
THOOM
I ATTACK WITH WICKED AVATAR!!

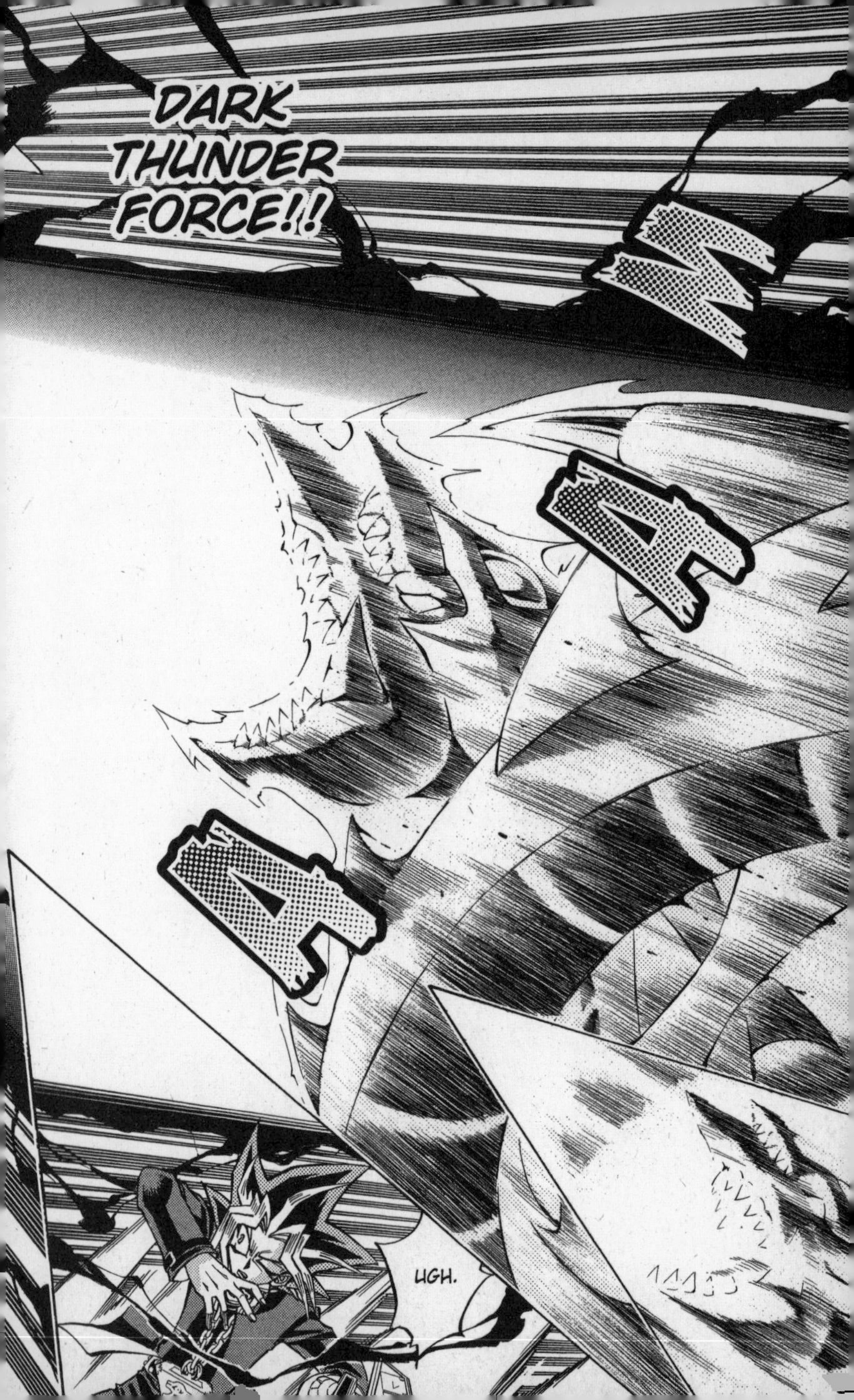
DARK THUNDER FORCE!!
UGH.

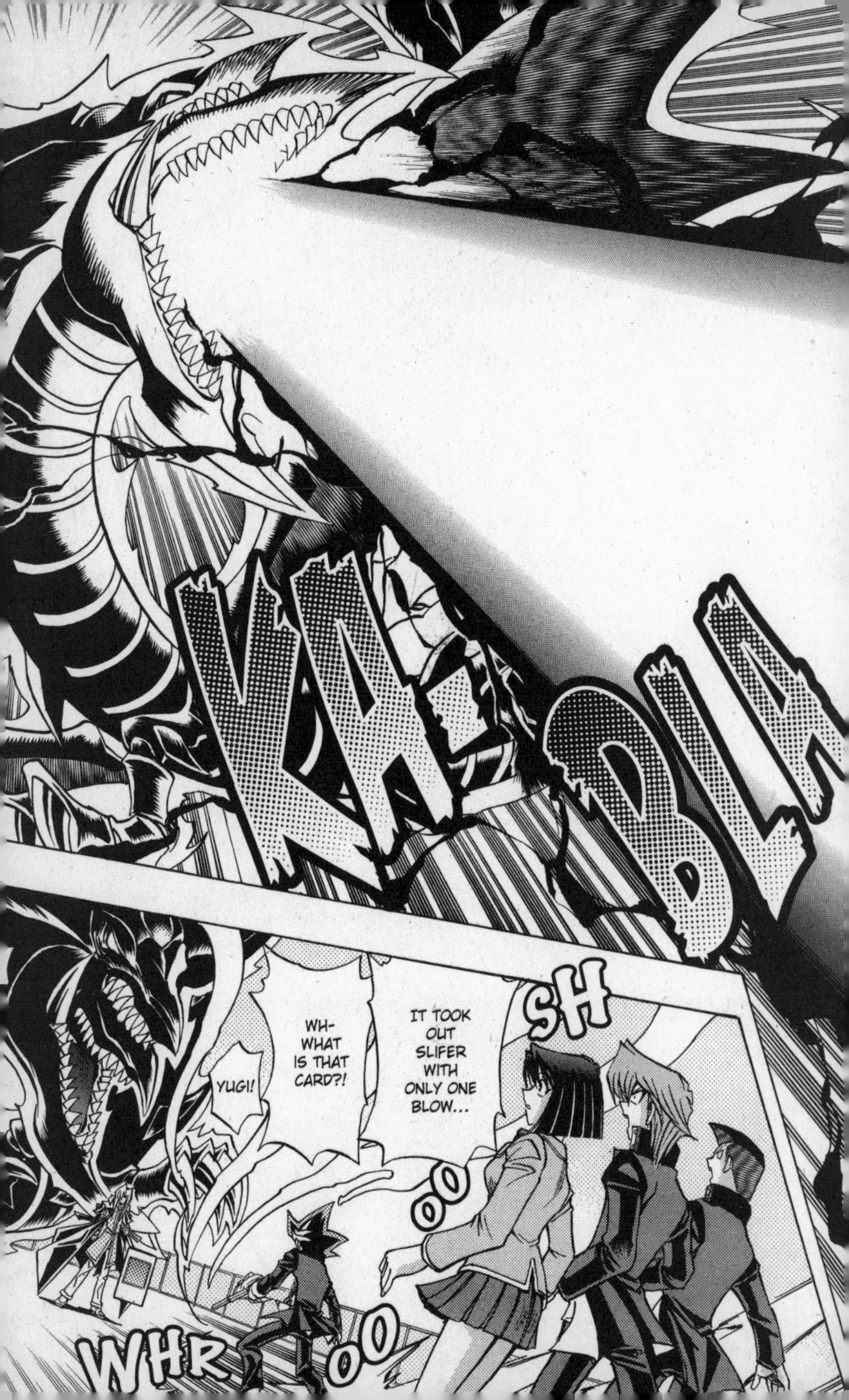
KA-BLA
IT TOOK OUT SLIFER WITH ONLY ONE BLOW...
WH-WHAT IS THAT CARD?!
YUGI!
SH
OO
OO
WHR

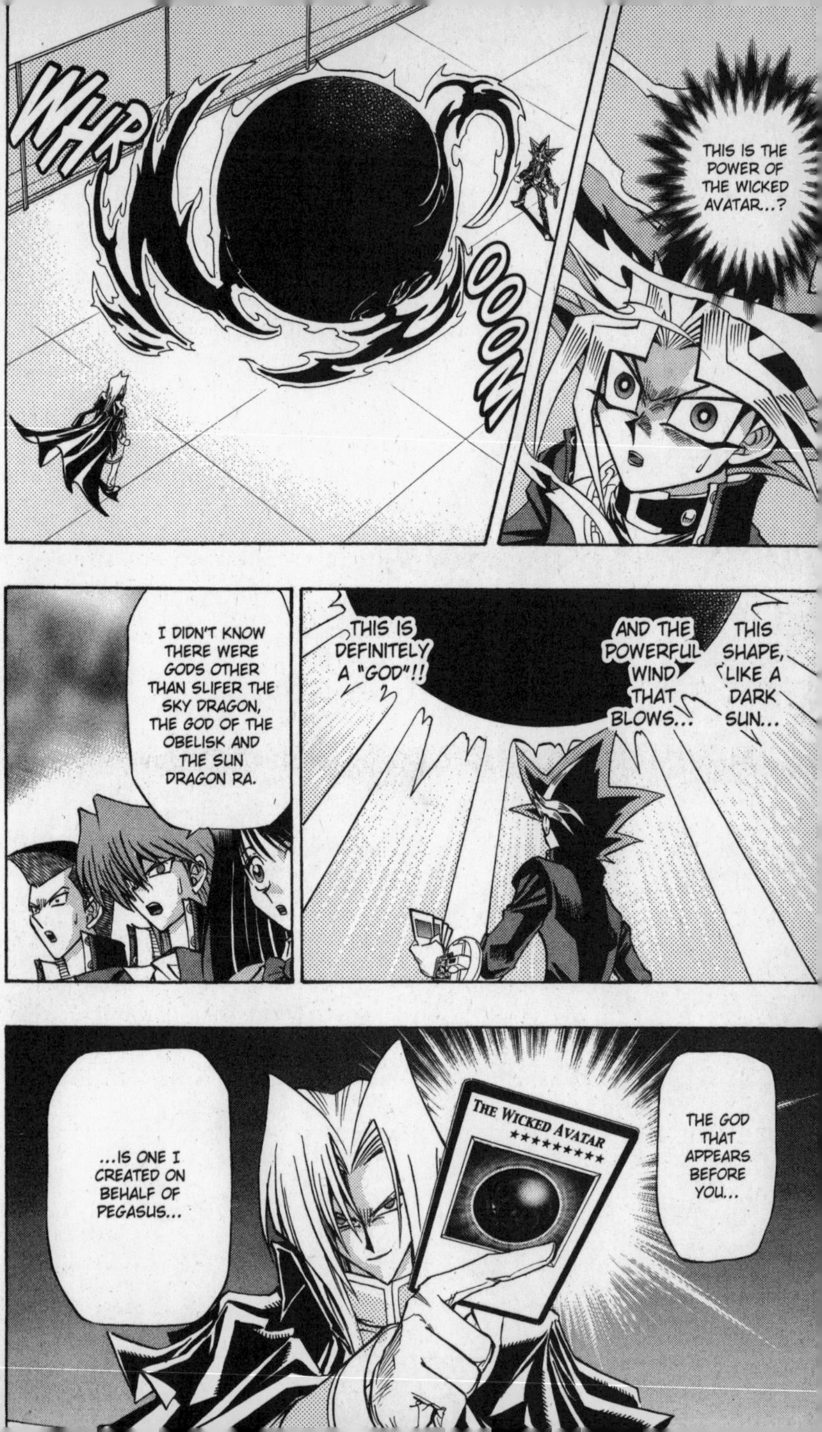
THIS IS THE POWER OF THE WICKED AVATAR...?
WHROOOOM!
THIS SHAPE, LIKE A DARK SUN...
AND THE POWERFUL WIND THAT BLOWS...
THIS IS DEFINITELY A "GOD"!!
I DIDN'T KNOW THERE WERE GODS OTHER THAN SLIFER THE SKY DRAGON, THE GOD OF THE OBELISK AND THE SUN DRAGON RA.
THE GOD THAT APPEARS BEFORE YOU...
THE WICKED AVATAR
...IS ONE I CREATED ON BEHALF OF PEGASUS...

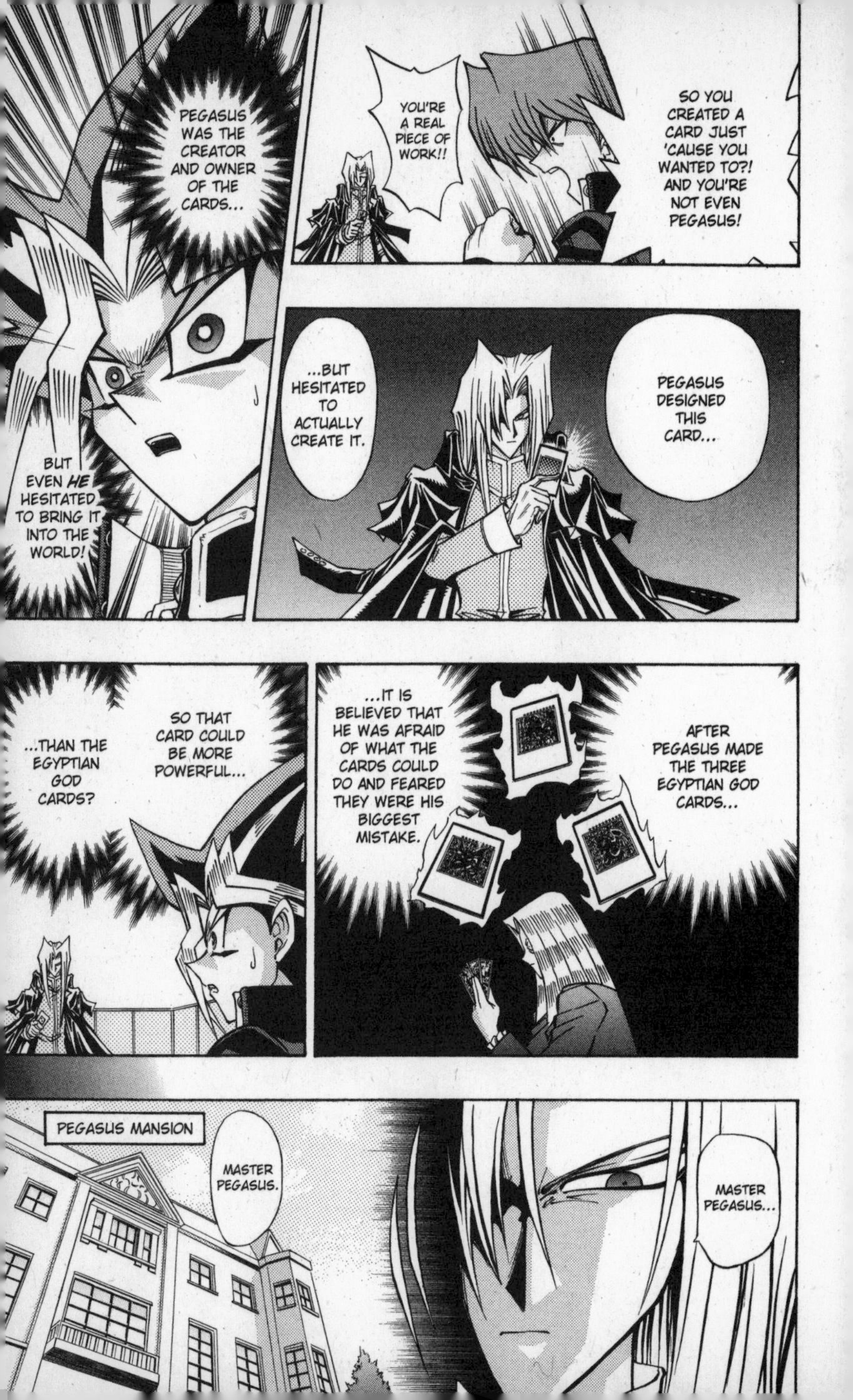

SO YOU CREATED A CARD JUST 'CAUSE YOU WANTED TO?! AND YOU'RE NOT EVEN PEGASUS!
YOU'RE A REAL PIECE OF WORK!!
PEGASUS DESIGNED THIS CARD...
...BUT HESITATED TO ACTUALLY CREATE IT.
PEGASUS WAS THE CREATOR AND OWNER OF THE CARDS...
BUT EVEN *HE* HESITATED TO BRING IT INTO THE WORLD!
AFTER PEGASUS MADE THE THREE EGYPTIAN GOD CARDS...
...IT IS BELIEVED THAT HE WAS AFRAID OF WHAT THE CARDS COULD DO AND FEARED THEY WERE HIS BIGGEST MISTAKE.
SO THAT CARD COULD BE MORE POWERFUL...
...THAN THE EGYPTIAN GOD CARDS?
MASTER PEGASUS...
PEGASUS MANSION
MASTER PEGASUS.

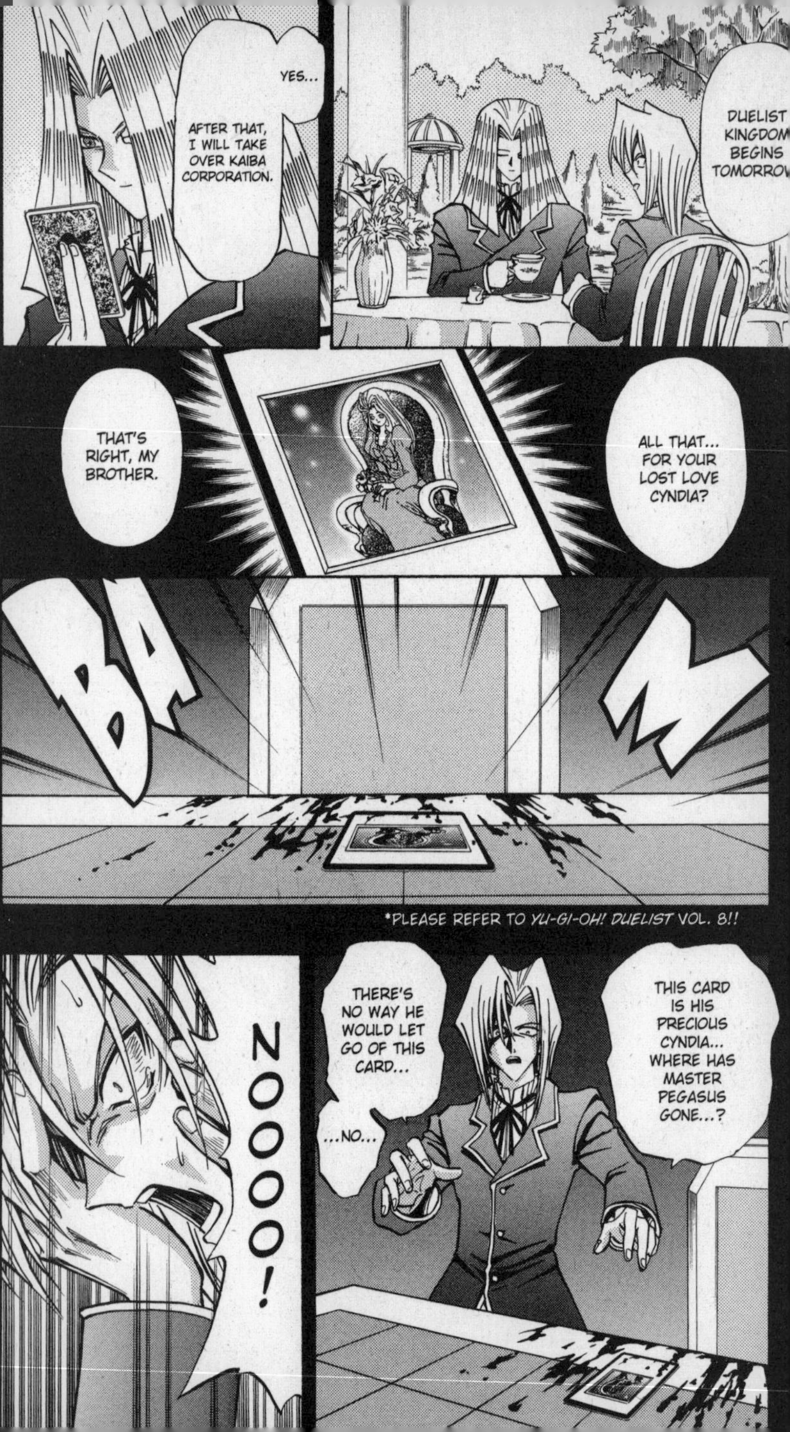
DUELIST KINGDOM BEGINS TOMORROW
YES...
AFTER THAT, I WILL TAKE OVER KAIBA CORPORATION.
ALL THAT... FOR YOUR LOST LOVE CYNDIA?
THAT'S RIGHT, MY BROTHER.
BAM
*PLEASE REFER TO *YU-GI-OH! DUELIST* VOL. 8!!
THIS CARD IS HIS PRECIOUS CYNDIA... WHERE HAS MASTER PEGASUS GONE...?
THERE'S NO WAY HE WOULD LET GO OF THIS CARD...
...NO...
NOOOOO!

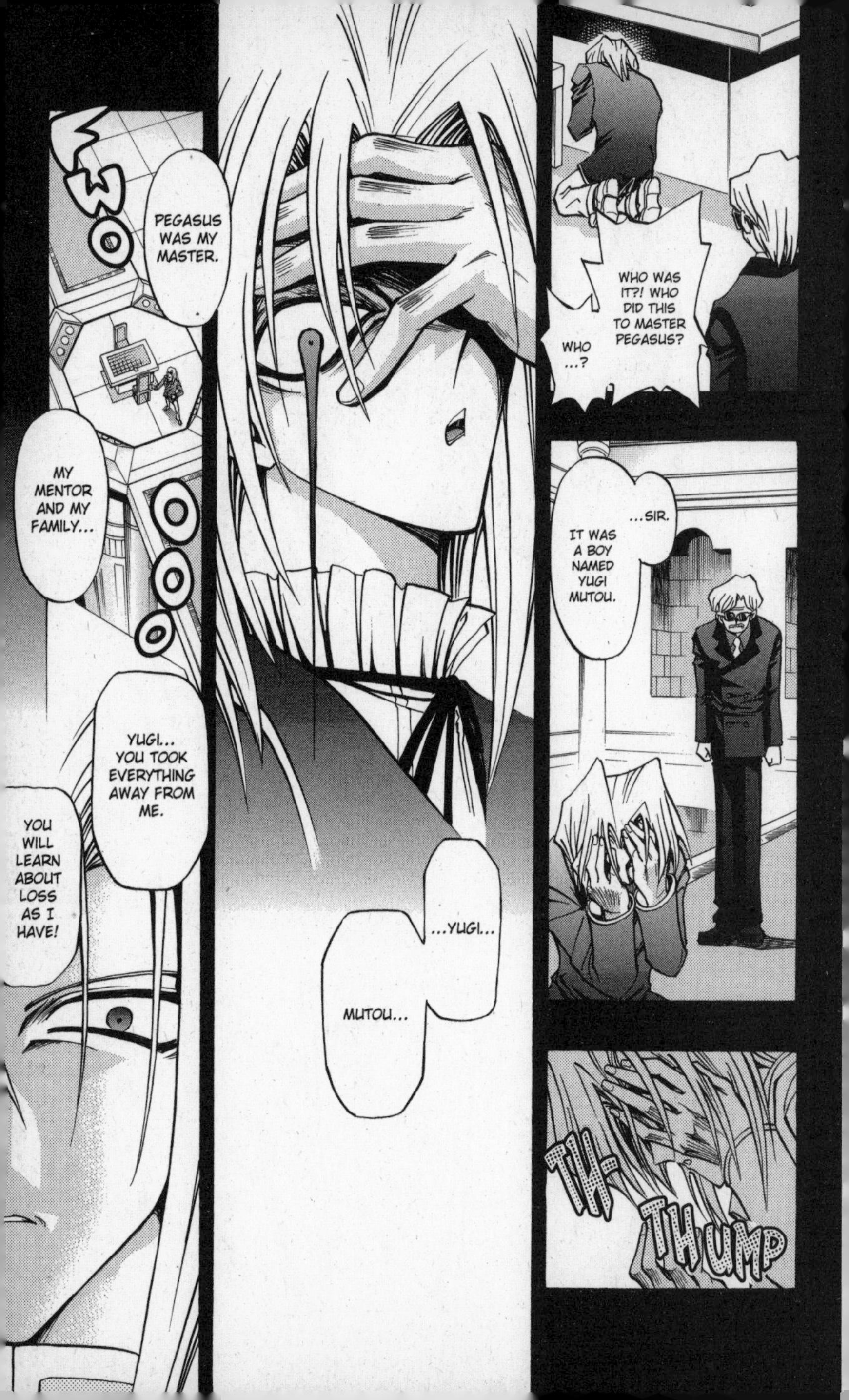
WHO WAS IT?! WHO DID THIS TO MASTER PEGASUS?
WHO ...?
...SIR.
IT WAS A BOY NAMED YUGI MUTOU.
TH-THUMP
...YUGI...
MUTOU...
PEGASUS WAS MY MASTER.
WOOOO
MY MENTOR AND MY FAMILY...
YUGI... YOU TOOK EVERYTHING AWAY FROM ME.
YOU WILL LEARN ABOUT LOSS AS I HAVE!

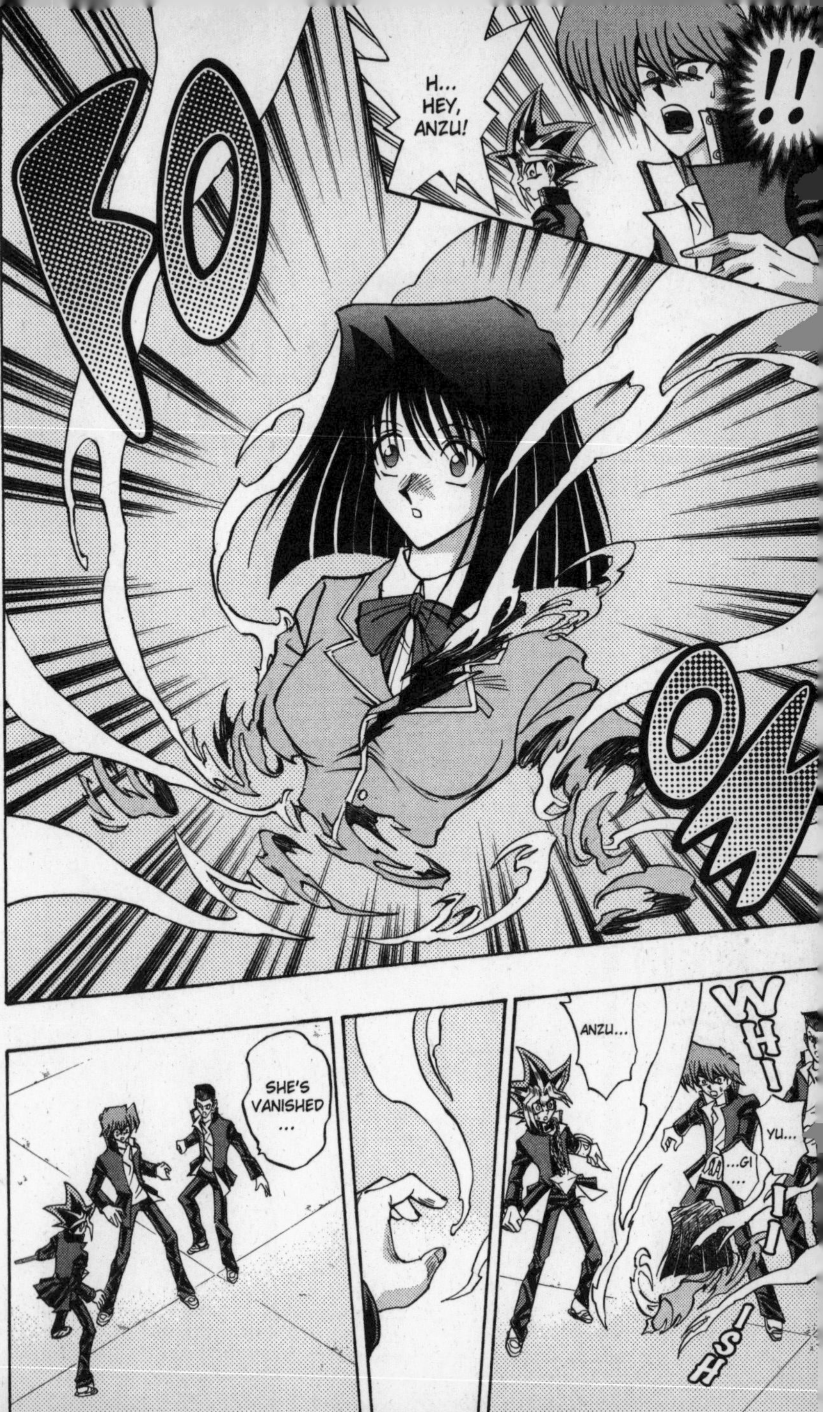
!!
H... HEY, ANZU!
ANZU...
YU...
...GI ...
SHE'S VANISHED ...

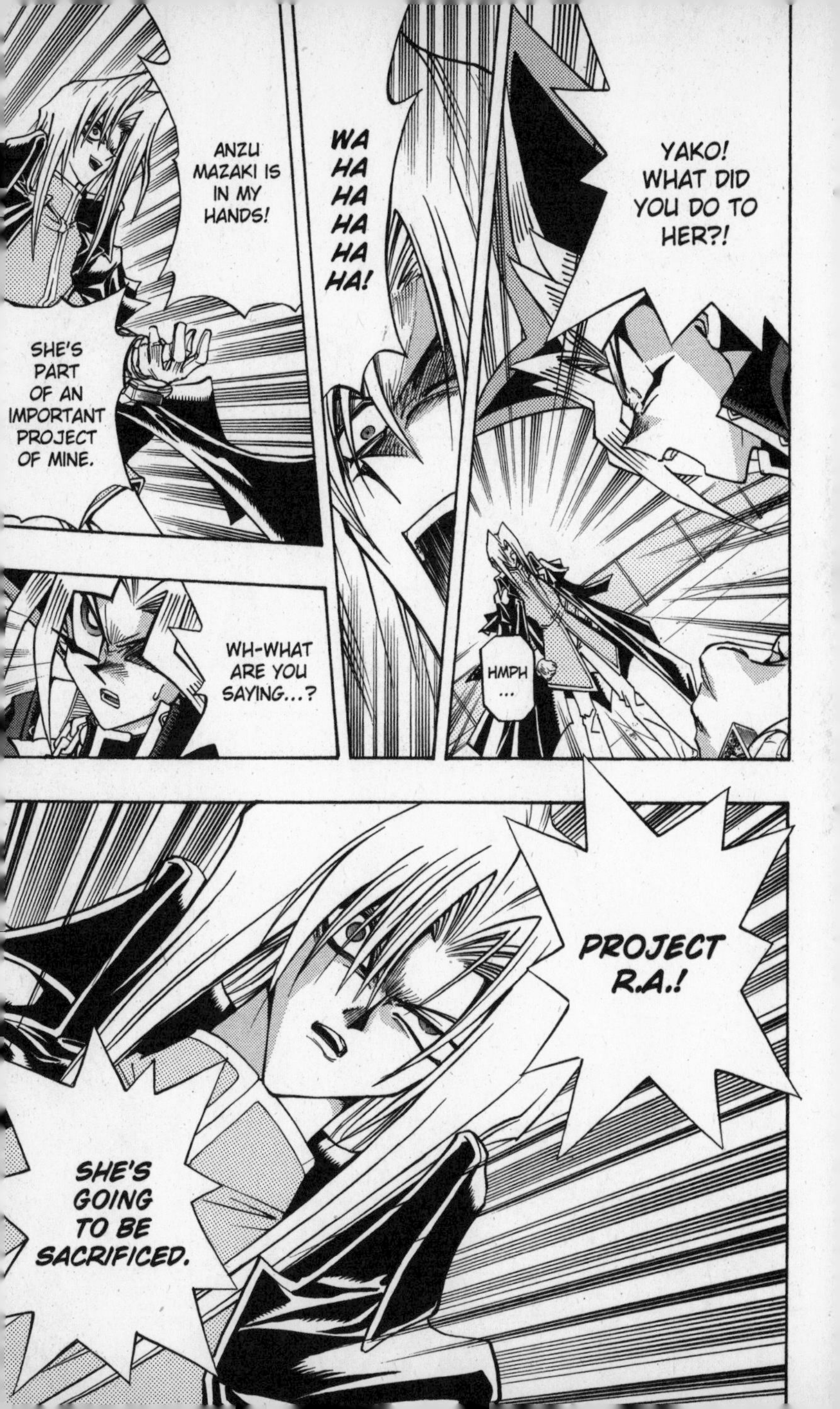
YAKO! WHAT DID YOU DO TO HER?!
HMPH ...
WA HA HA HA HA HA!
ANZU MAZAKI IS IN MY HANDS!
SHE'S PART OF AN IMPORTANT PROJECT OF MINE.
WH-WHAT ARE YOU SAYING...?
PROJECT R.A.!
SHE'S GOING TO BE SACRIFICED.

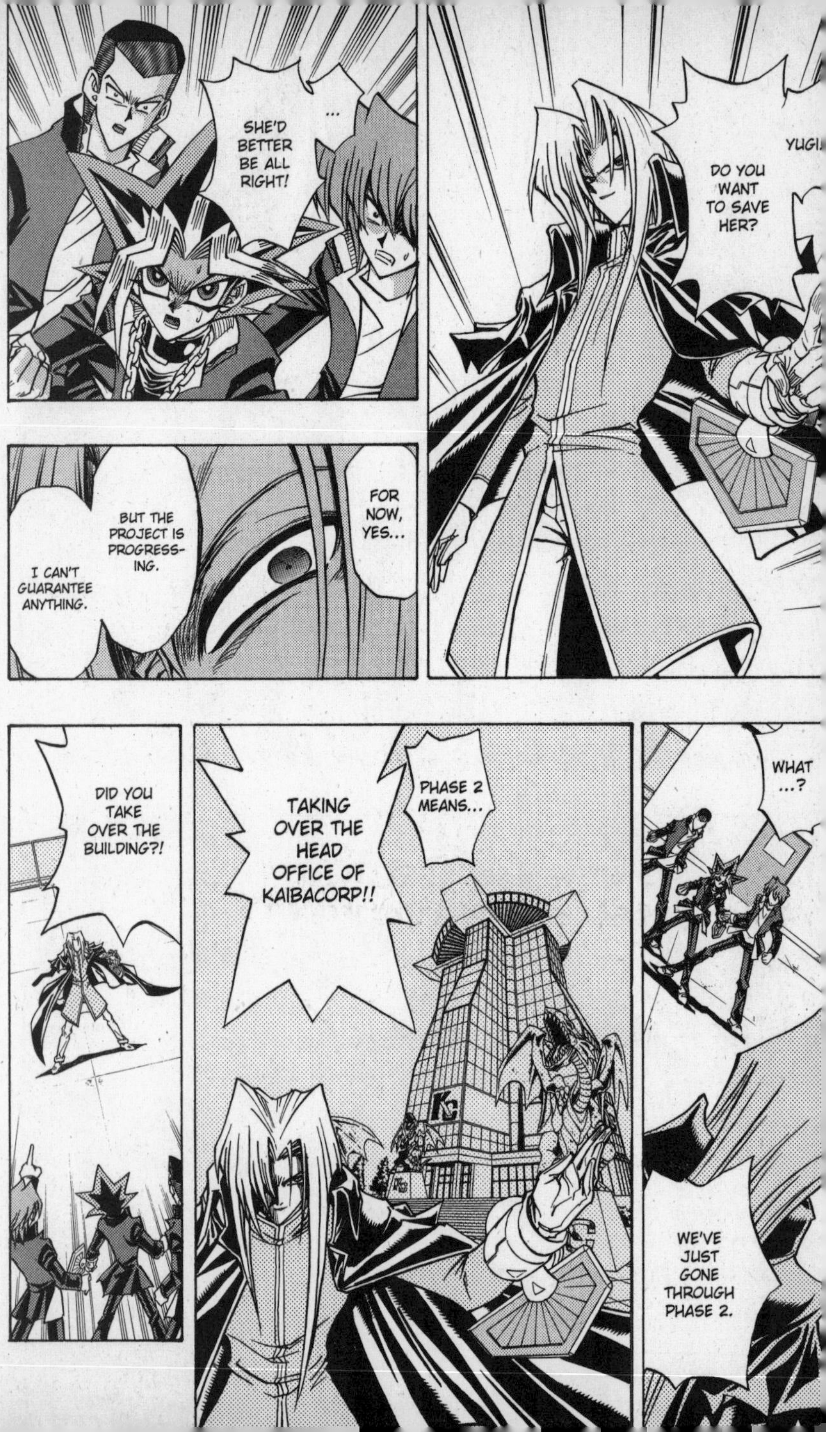
YUGI.
DO YOU WANT TO SAVE HER?
...
SHE'D BETTER BE ALL RIGHT!
FOR NOW, YES...
BUT THE PROJECT IS PROGRESS-ING.
I CAN'T GUARANTEE ANYTHING.
WHAT ...?
WE'VE JUST GONE THROUGH PHASE 2.
PHASE 2 MEANS...
TAKING OVER THE HEAD OFFICE OF KAIBACORP!!
DID YOU TAKE OVER THE BUILDING?!

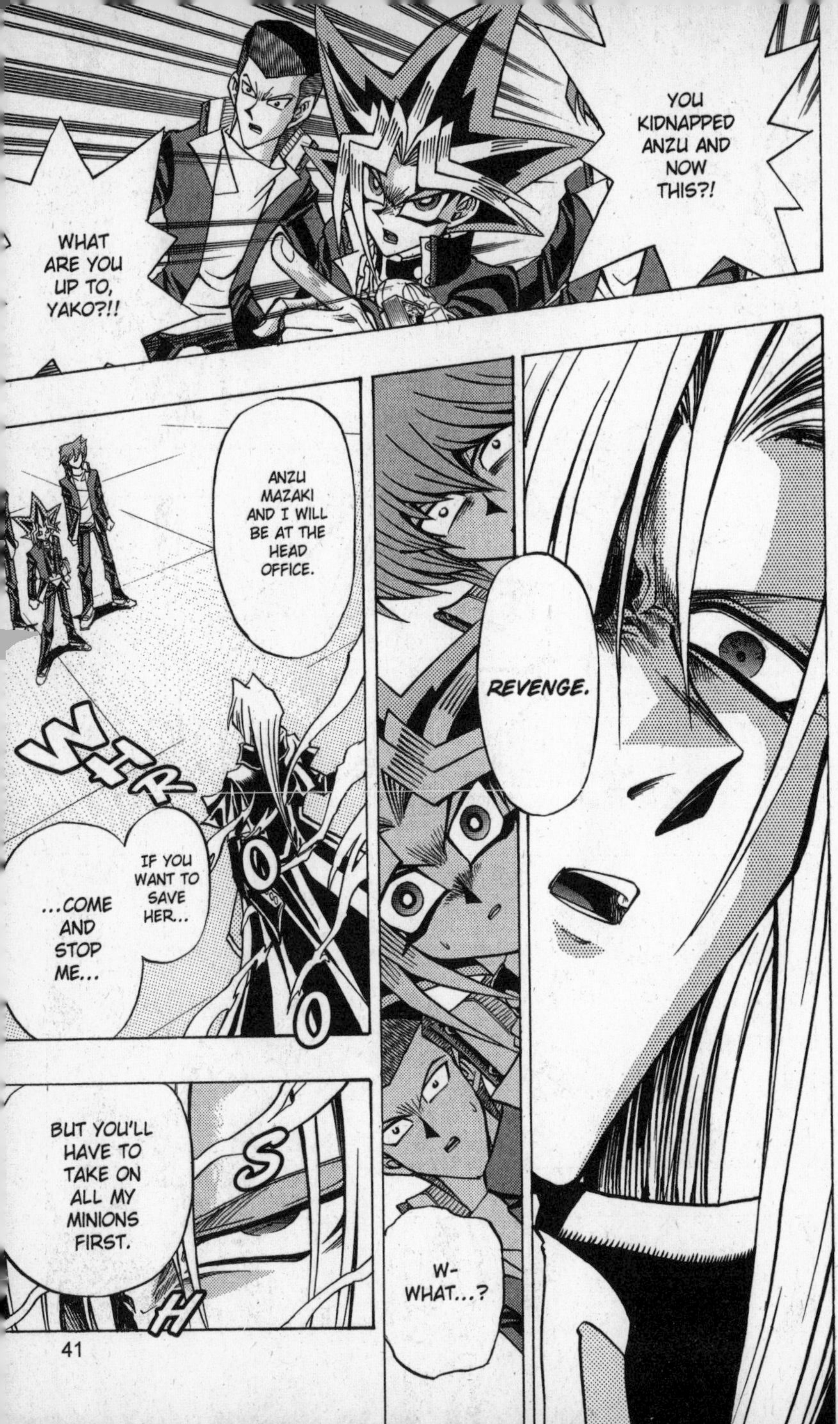

YOU KIDNAPPED ANZU AND NOW THIS?!
WHAT ARE YOU UP TO, YAKO?!!
REVENGE.
W- WHAT...?
ANZU MAZAKI AND I WILL BE AT THE HEAD OFFICE.
WHROOOSH
IF YOU WANT TO SAVE HER...
...COME AND STOP ME...
BUT YOU'LL HAVE TO TAKE ON ALL MY MINIONS FIRST.

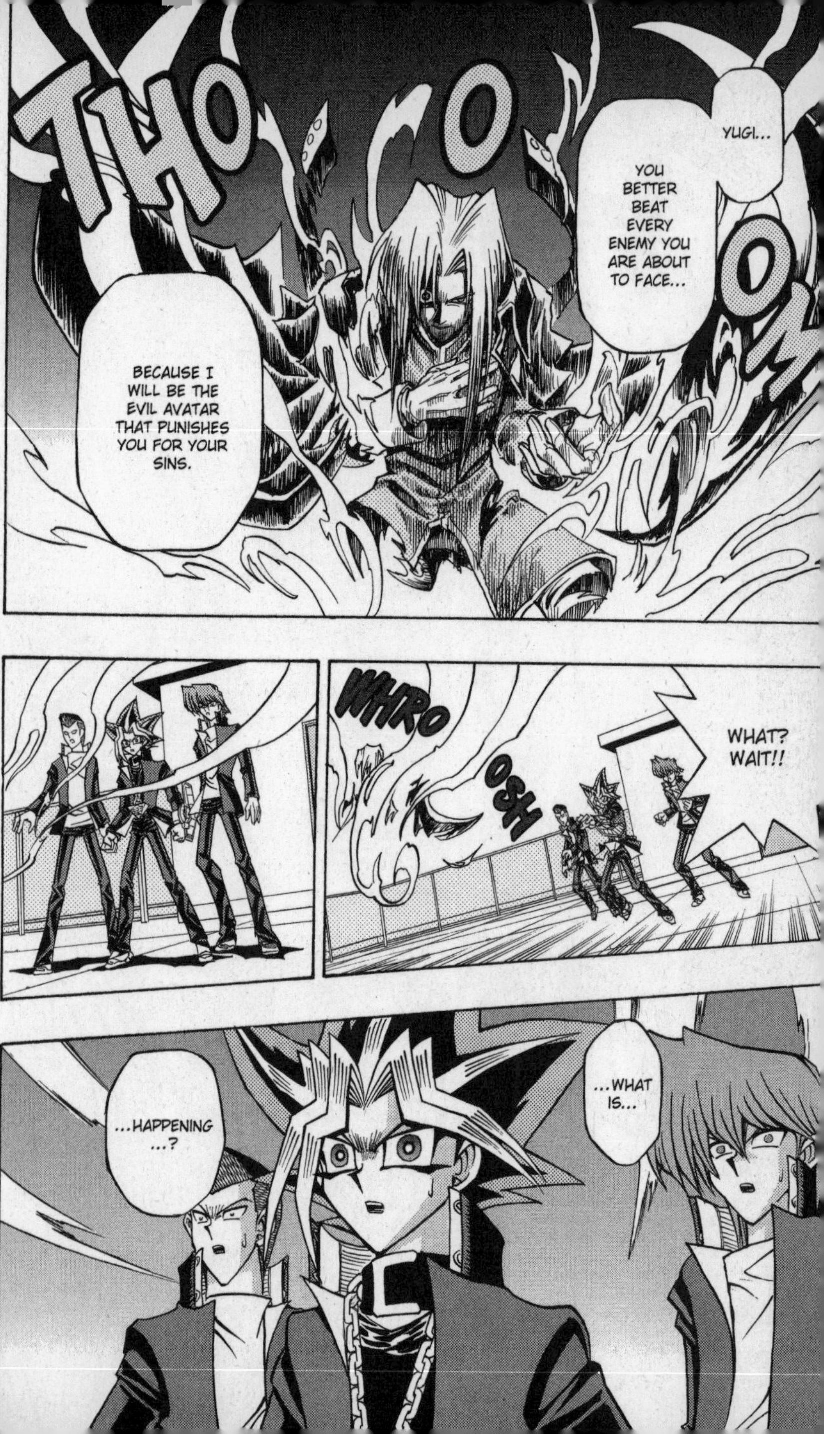
THO-O-OM
YUGI...
YOU BETTER BEAT EVERY ENEMY YOU ARE ABOUT TO FACE...
BECAUSE I WILL BE THE EVIL AVATAR THAT PUNISHES YOU FOR YOUR SINS.
WHAT? WAIT!!
WHROOSH
...WHAT IS...
...HAPPENING ...?

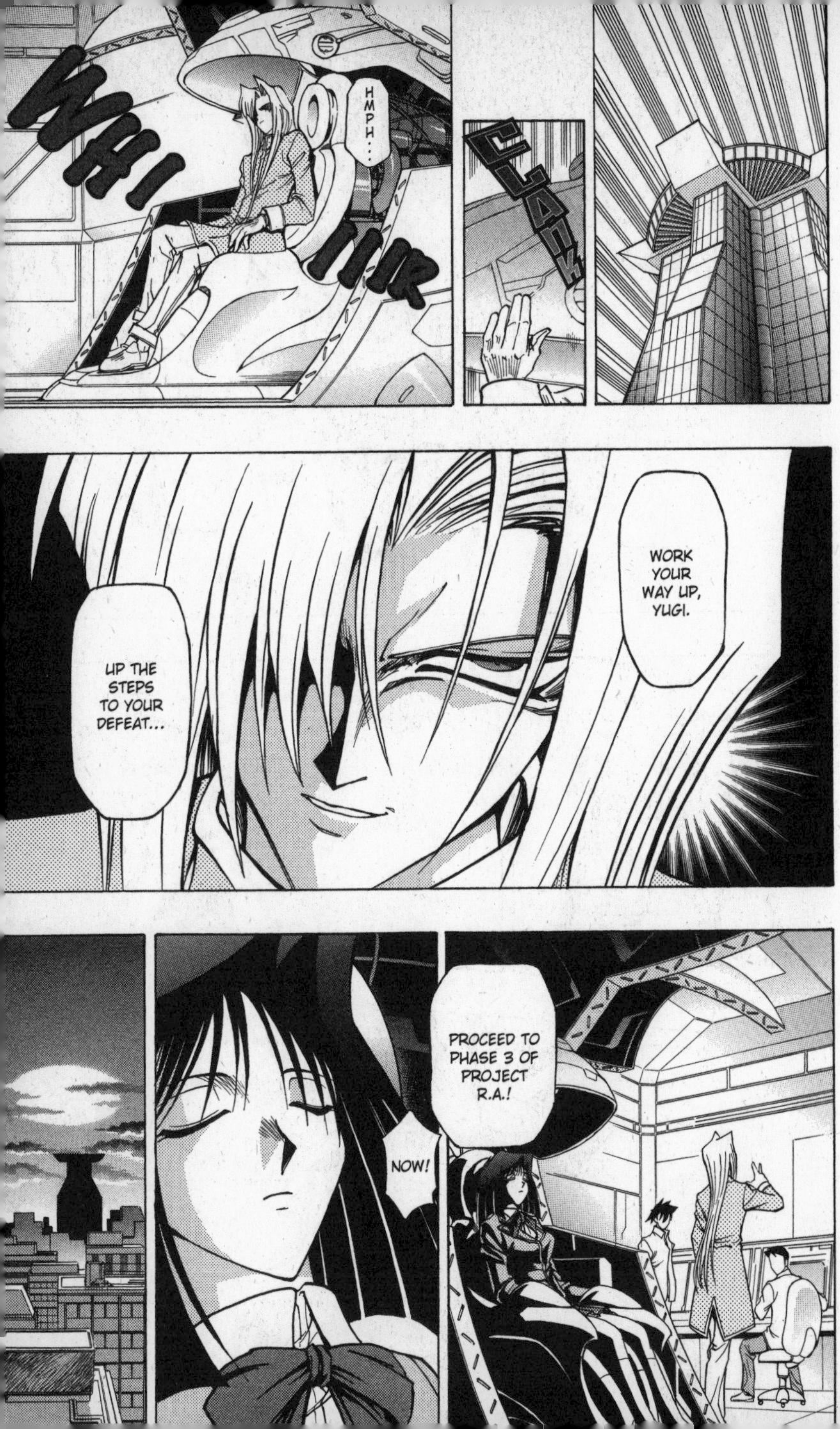
CLANK
HMPH...
WHIIIIR
WORK YOUR WAY UP, YUGI.
UP THE STEPS TO YOUR DEFEAT...
PROCEED TO PHASE 3 OF PROJECT R.A.!
NOW!

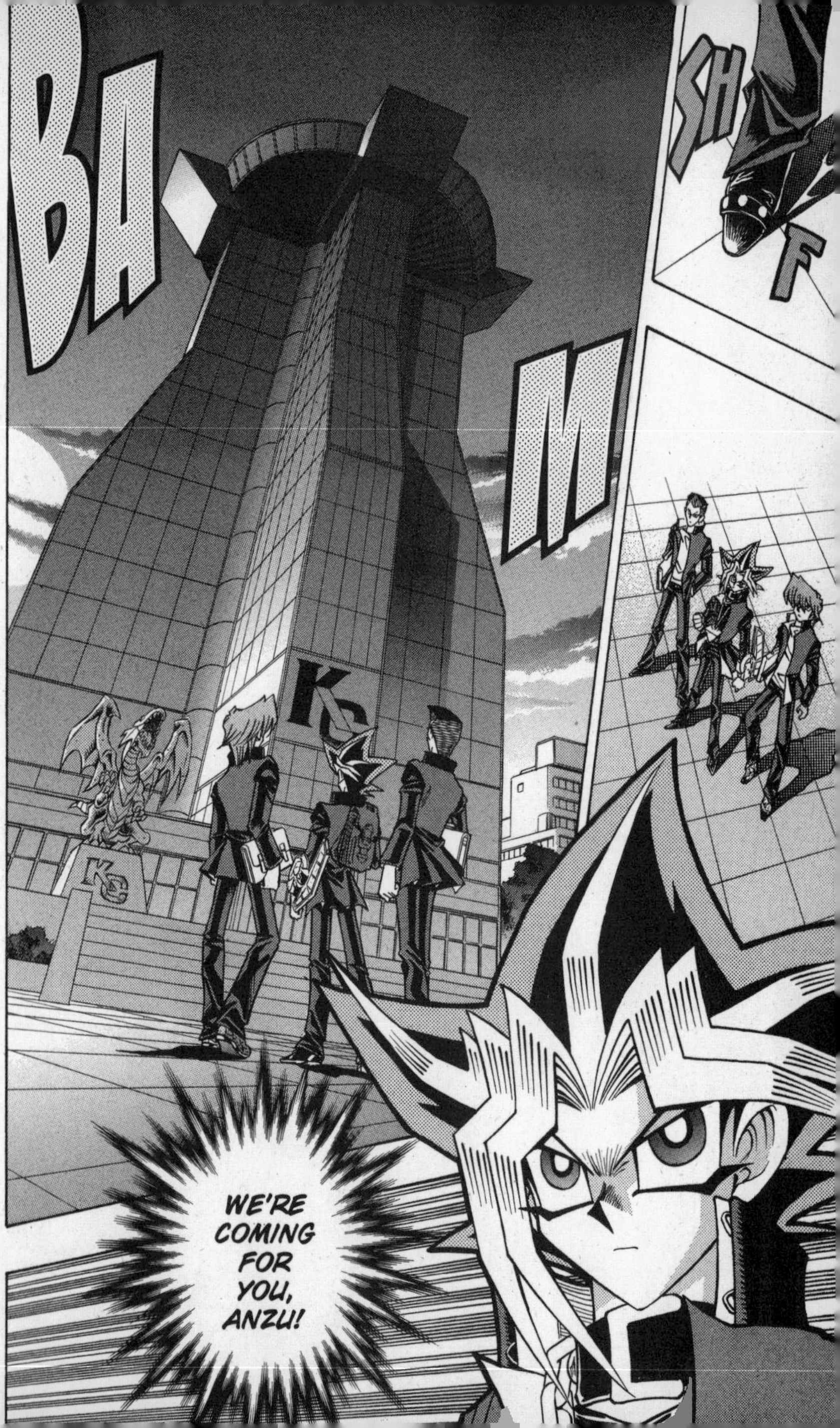
SH
F
BA
M
WE'RE COMING FOR YOU, ANZU!

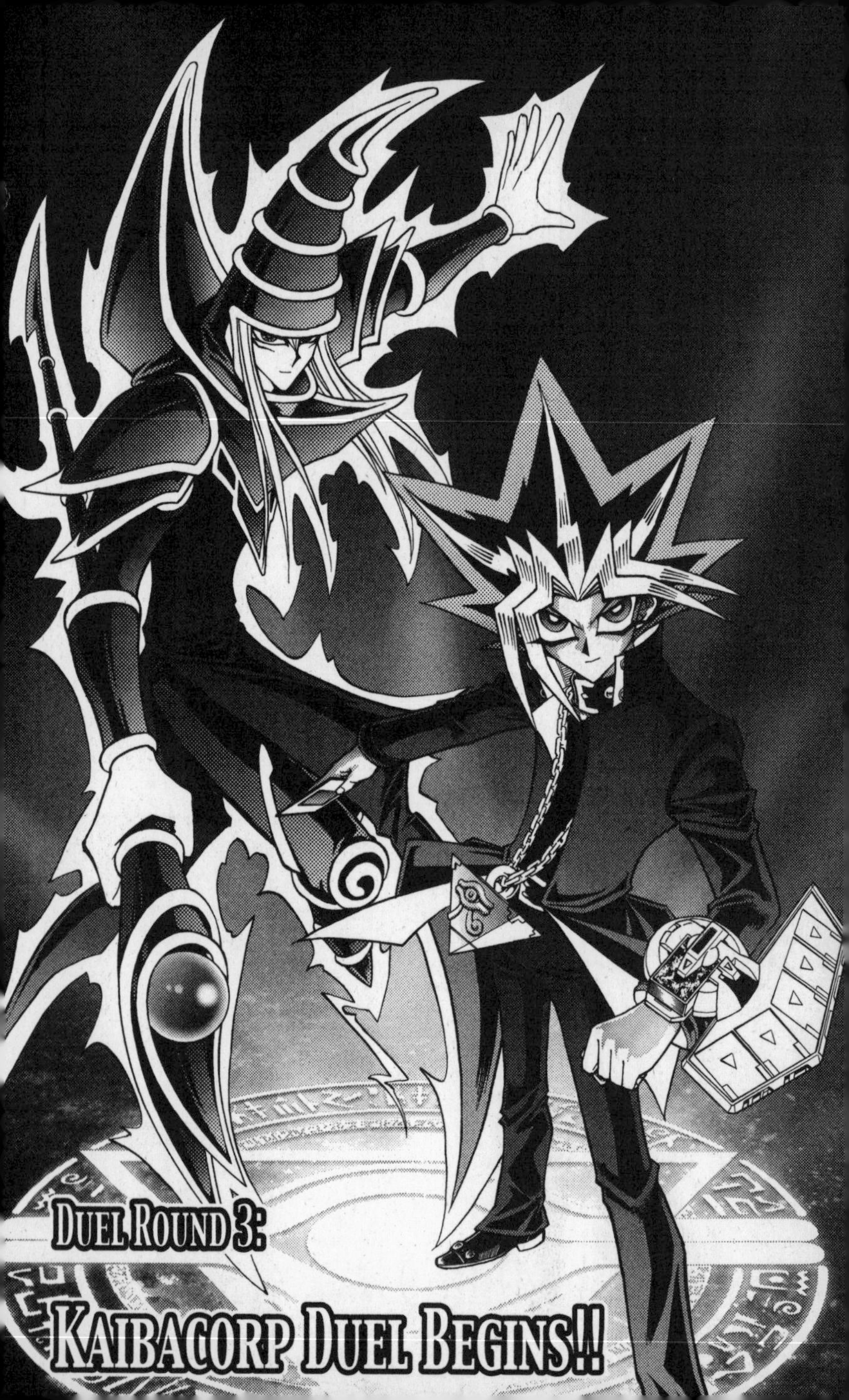
DUEL ROUND 3:
KAIBACORP DUEL BEGINS!!

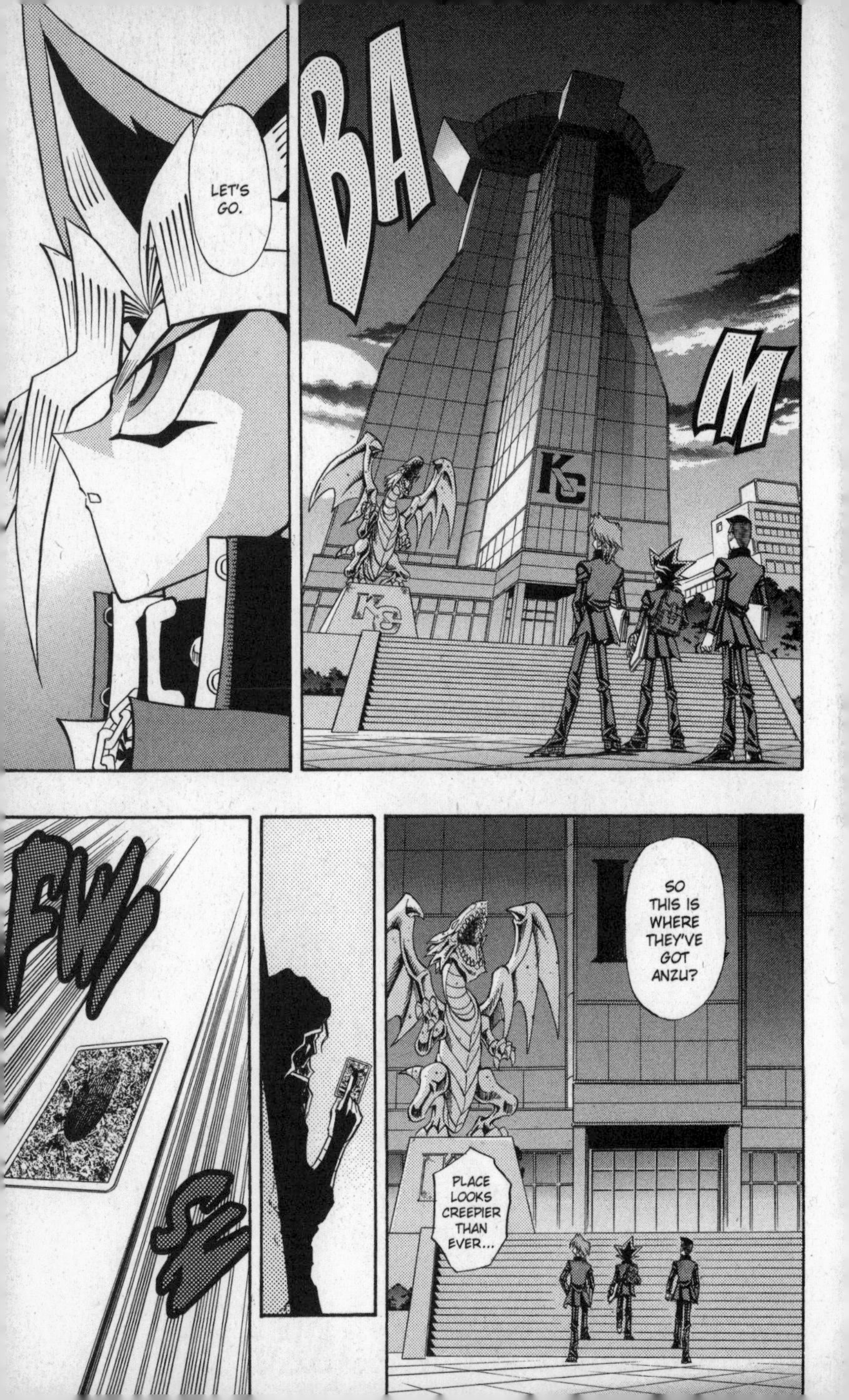
BA
M
LET'S GO.
SO THIS IS WHERE THEY'VE GOT ANZU?
PLACE LOOKS CREEPIER THAN EVER...
FW
SH

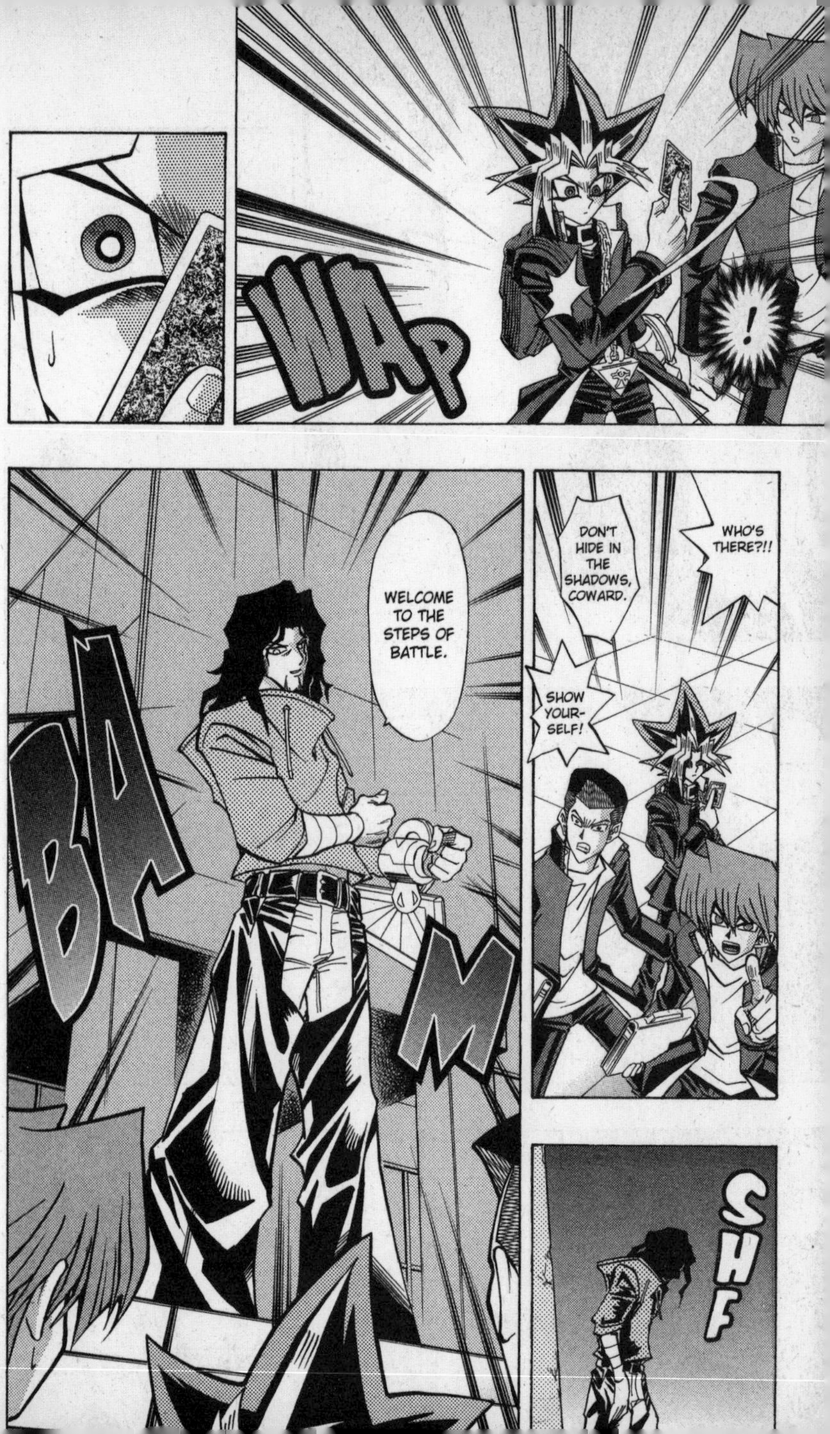
WAP
!
WHO'S THERE?!!
DON'T HIDE IN THE SHADOWS, COWARD.
SHOW YOUR-SELF!
SHF
BAM
WELCOME TO THE STEPS OF BATTLE.

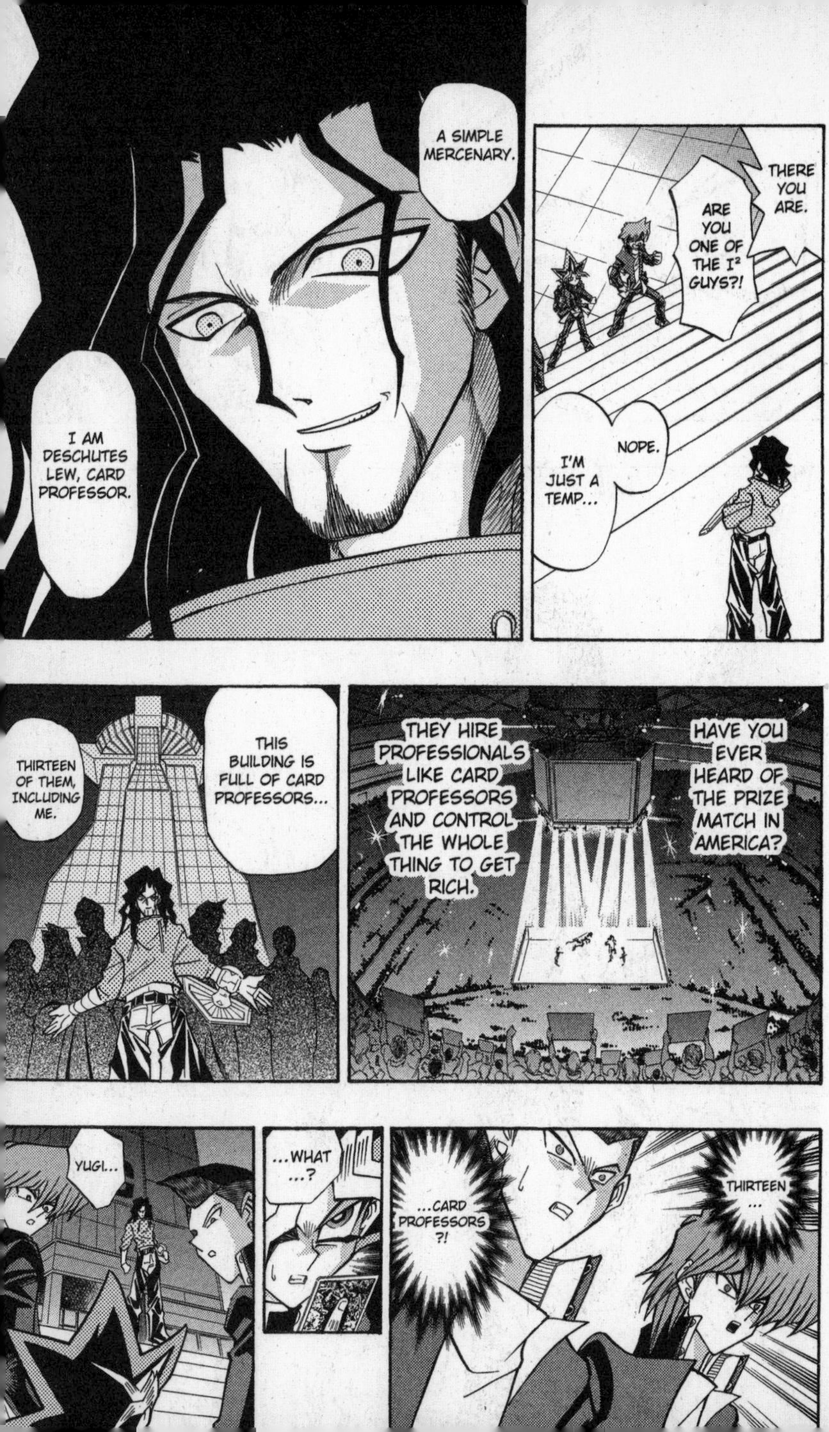
THERE YOU ARE.
ARE YOU ONE OF THE I^2 GUYS?!
NOPE.
I'M JUST A TEMP...
A SIMPLE MERCENARY.
I AM DESCHUTES LEW, CARD PROFESSOR.
HAVE YOU EVER HEARD OF THE PRIZE MATCH IN AMERICA?
THEY HIRE PROFESSIONALS LIKE CARD PROFESSORS AND CONTROL THE WHOLE THING TO GET RICH.
THIS BUILDING IS FULL OF CARD PROFESSORS...
THIRTEEN OF THEM, INCLUDING ME.
THIRTEEN...
...CARD PROFESSORS?!
...WHAT...?
YUGI...

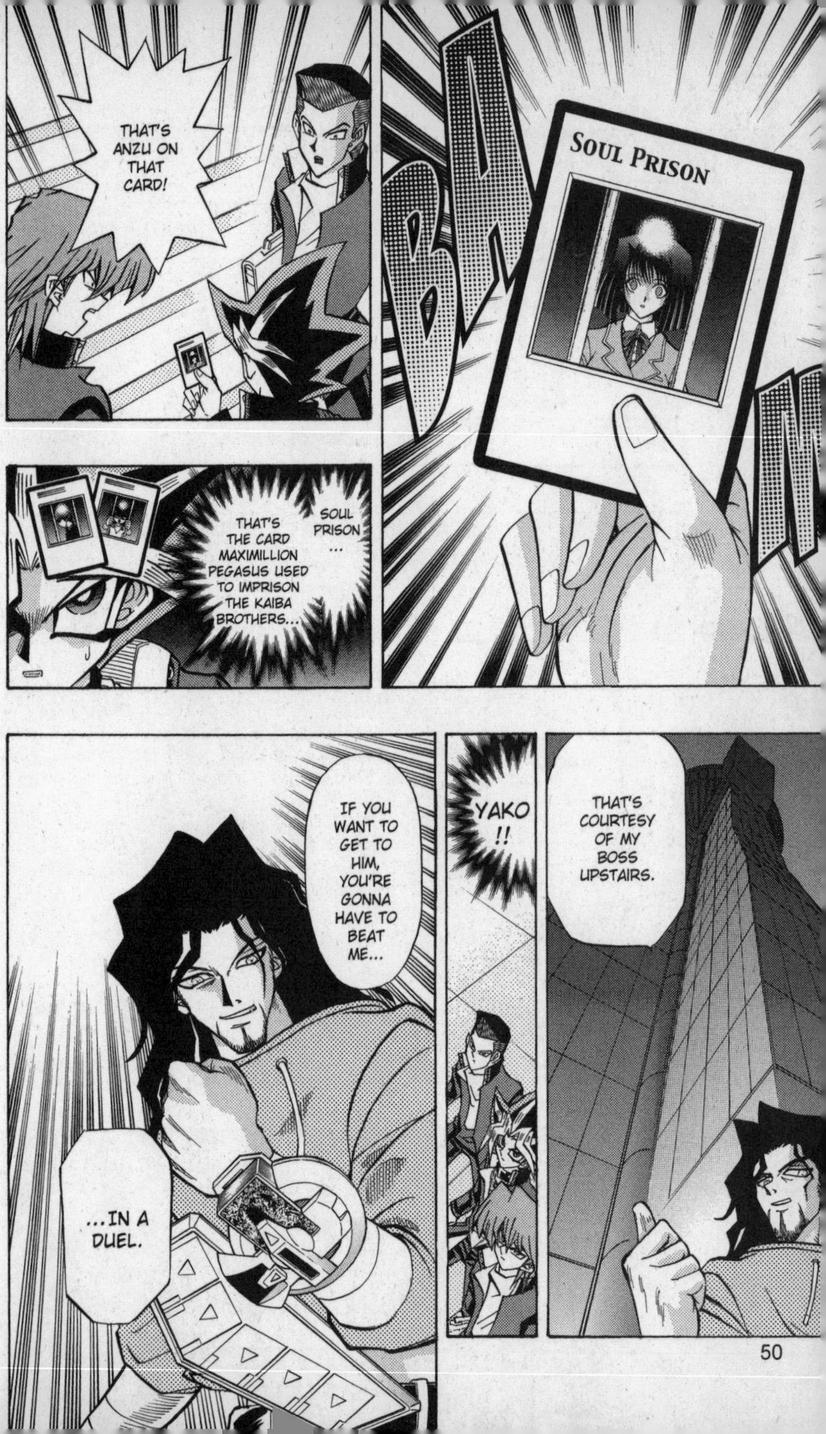
BAM
SOUL PRISON
THAT'S ANZU ON THAT CARD!
SOUL PRISON ...
THAT'S THE CARD MAXIMILLION PEGASUS USED TO IMPRISON THE KAIBA BROTHERS...
THAT'S COURTESY OF MY BOSS UPSTAIRS.
YAKO !!
IF YOU WANT TO GET TO HIM, YOU'RE GONNA HAVE TO BEAT ME...
...IN A DUEL.

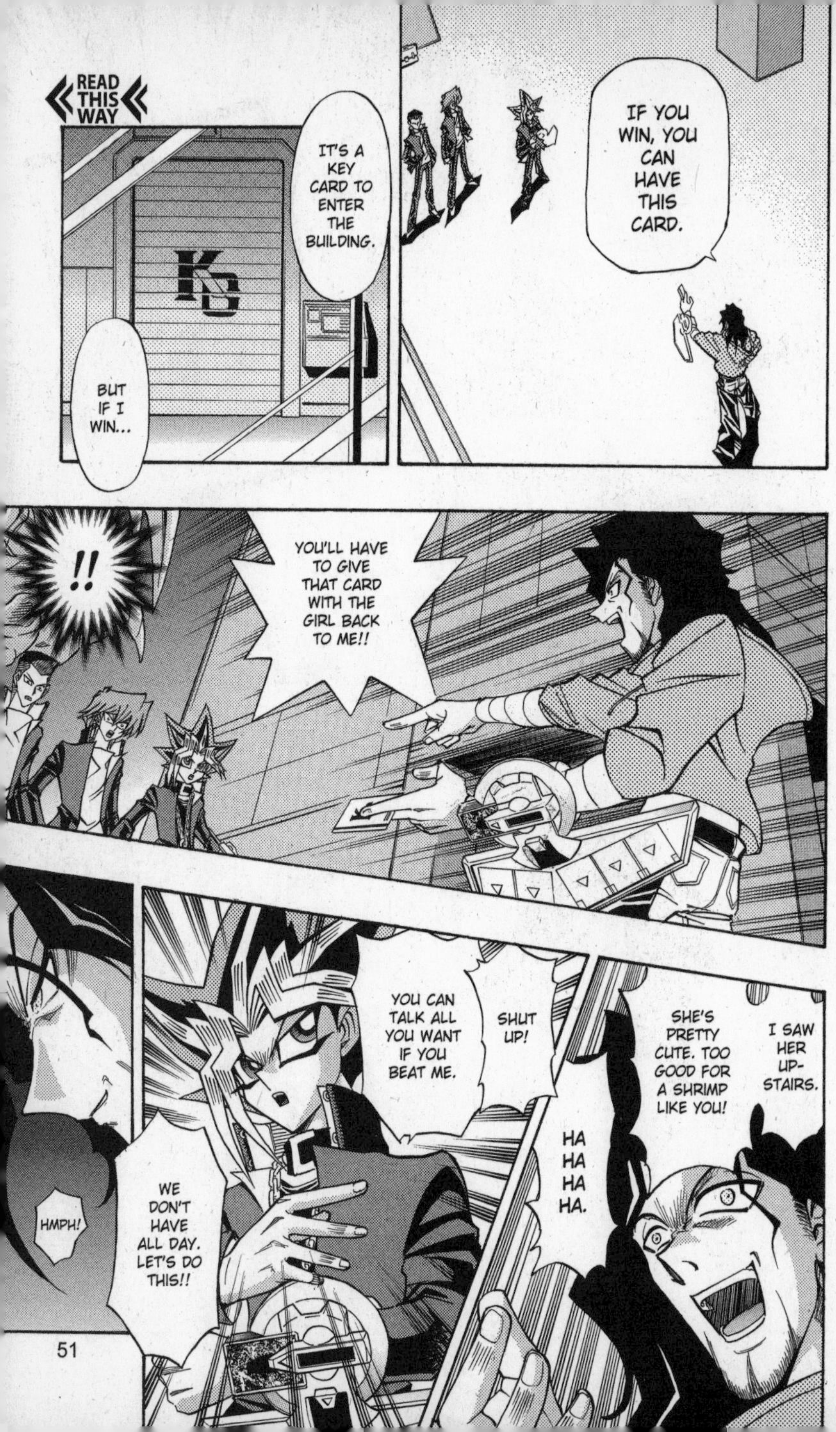
READ THIS WAY
IF YOU WIN, YOU CAN HAVE THIS CARD.
IT'S A KEY CARD TO ENTER THE BUILDING.
BUT IF I WIN...
YOU'LL HAVE TO GIVE THAT CARD WITH THE GIRL BACK TO ME!!
!!
I SAW HER UP-STAIRS.
SHE'S PRETTY CUTE. TOO GOOD FOR A SHRIMP LIKE YOU!
HA HA HA HA.
SHUT UP!
YOU CAN TALK ALL YOU WANT IF YOU BEAT ME.
WE DON'T HAVE ALL DAY. LET'S DO THIS!!
HMPH!

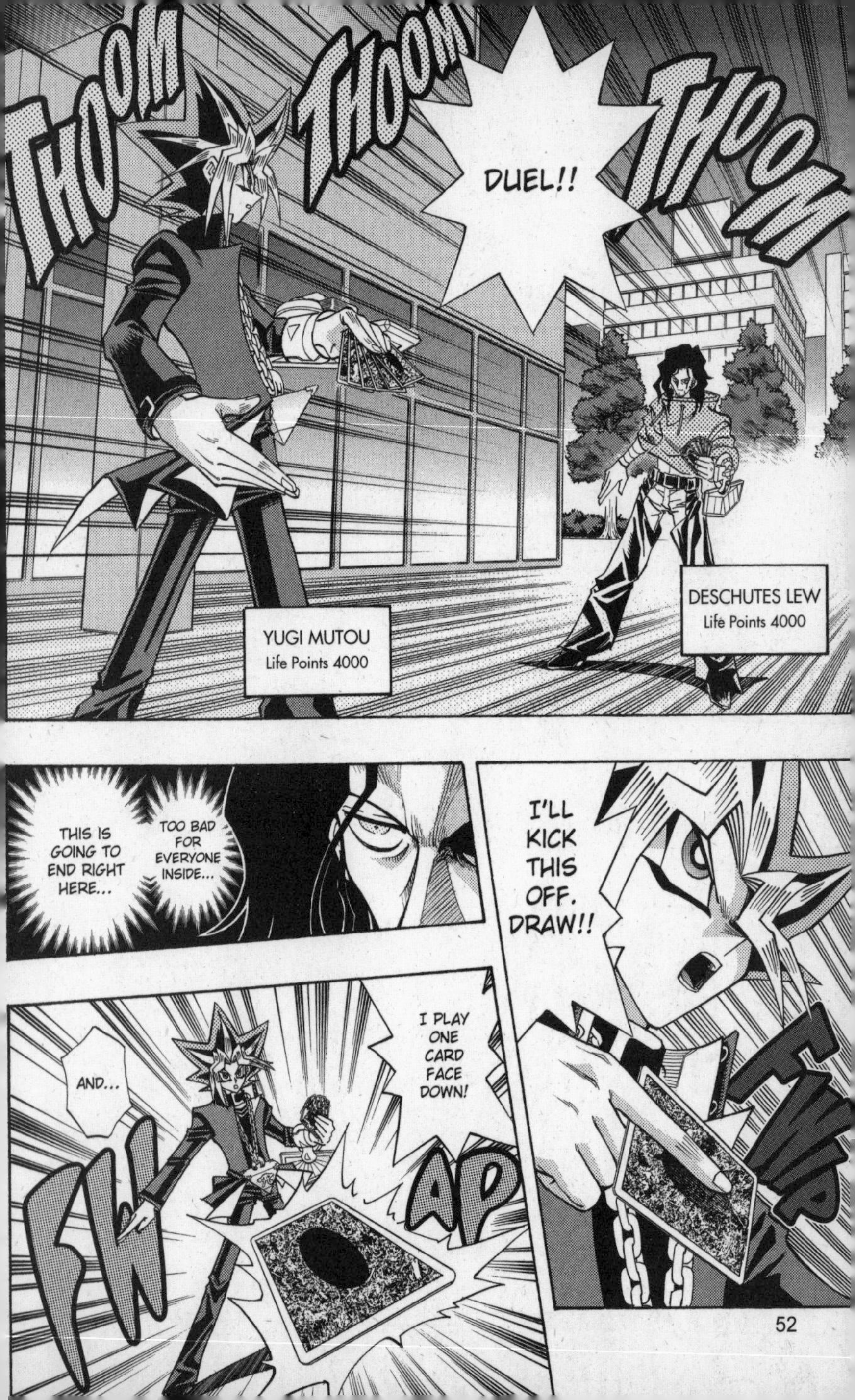
THOOM
THOOM
THOOM
DUEL!!
DESCHUTES LEW
Life Points 4000
YUGI MUTOU
Life Points 4000
I'LL KICK THIS OFF. DRAW!!
TOO BAD FOR EVERYONE INSIDE...
THIS IS GOING TO END RIGHT HERE...
I PLAY ONE CARD FACE DOWN!
AND...

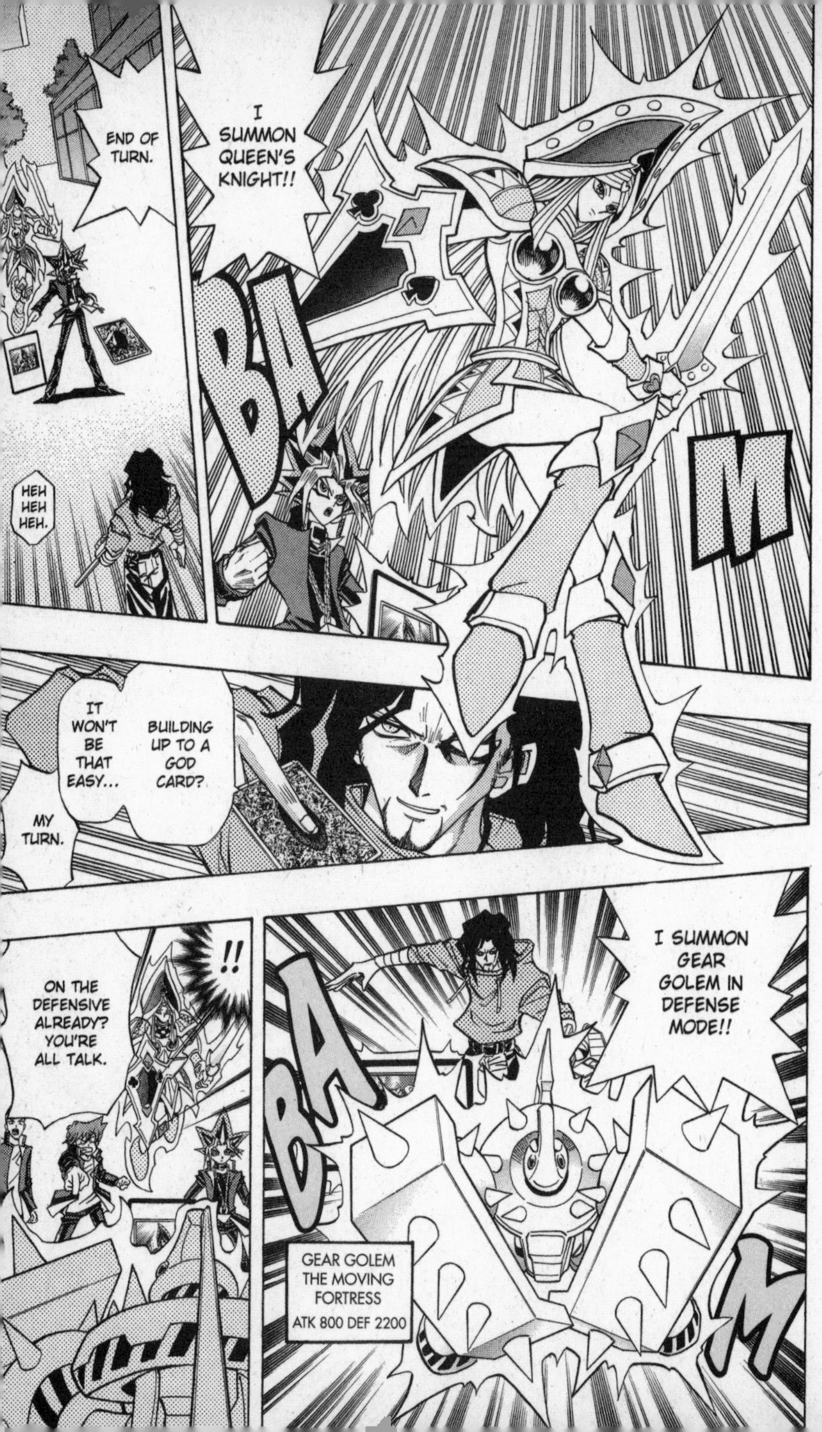
I SUMMON QUEEN'S KNIGHT!!
BAM
END OF TURN.
HEH HEH HEH.
BUILDING UP TO A GOD CARD?
IT WON'T BE THAT EASY...
MY TURN.
I SUMMON GEAR GOLEM IN DEFENSE MODE!!
BAM
GEAR GOLEM THE MOVING FORTRESS
ATK 800 DEF 2200
!!
ON THE DEFENSIVE ALREADY? YOU'RE ALL TALK.

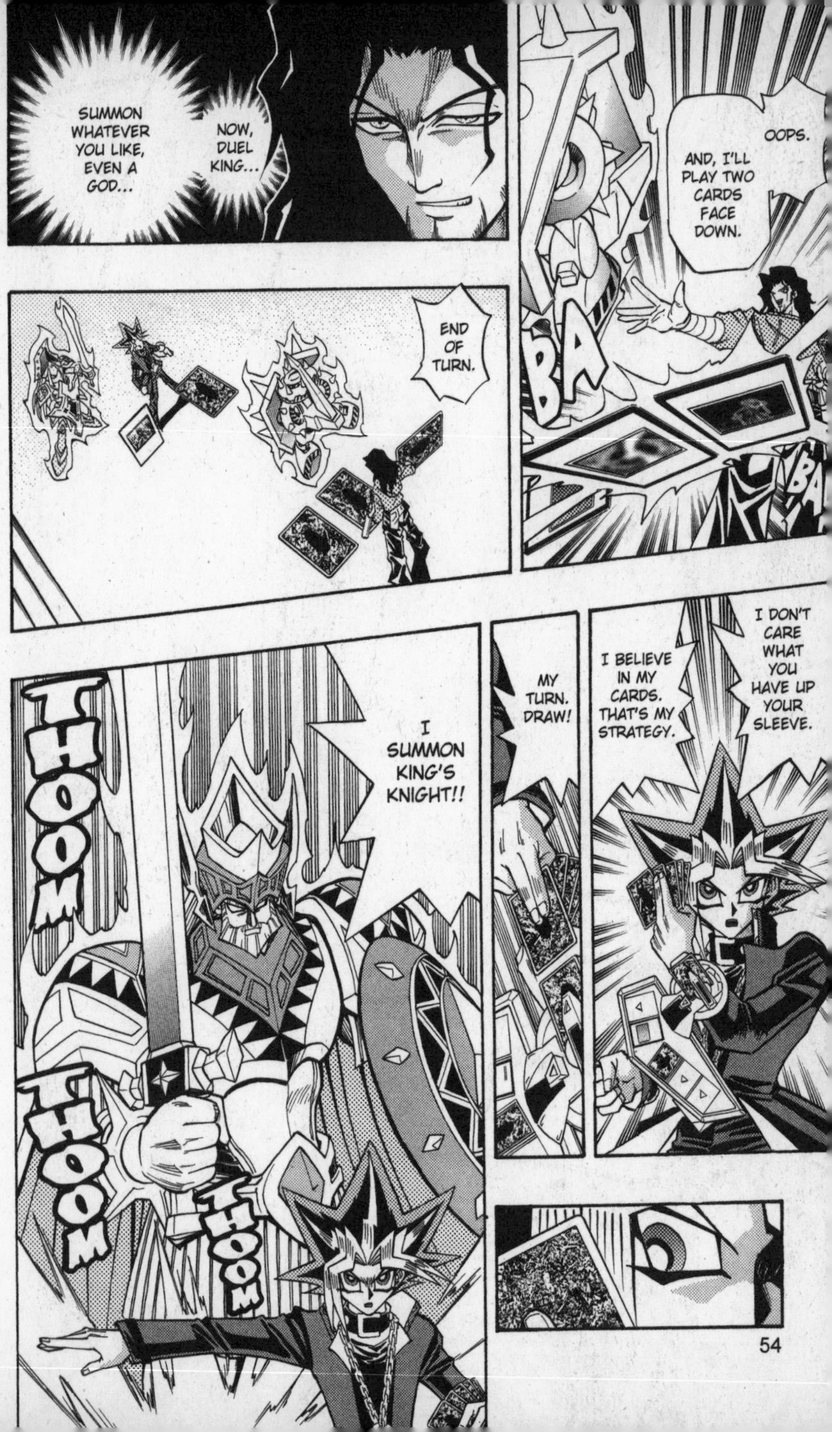
OOPS.
AND, I'LL PLAY TWO CARDS FACE DOWN.
BA
BA
NOW, DUEL KING...
SUMMON WHATEVER YOU LIKE, EVEN A GOD...
END OF TURN.
I DON'T CARE WHAT YOU HAVE UP YOUR SLEEVE.
I BELIEVE IN MY CARDS. THAT'S MY STRATEGY.
MY TURN. DRAW!
I SUMMON KING'S KNIGHT!!
THOOM
THOOM
THOOM

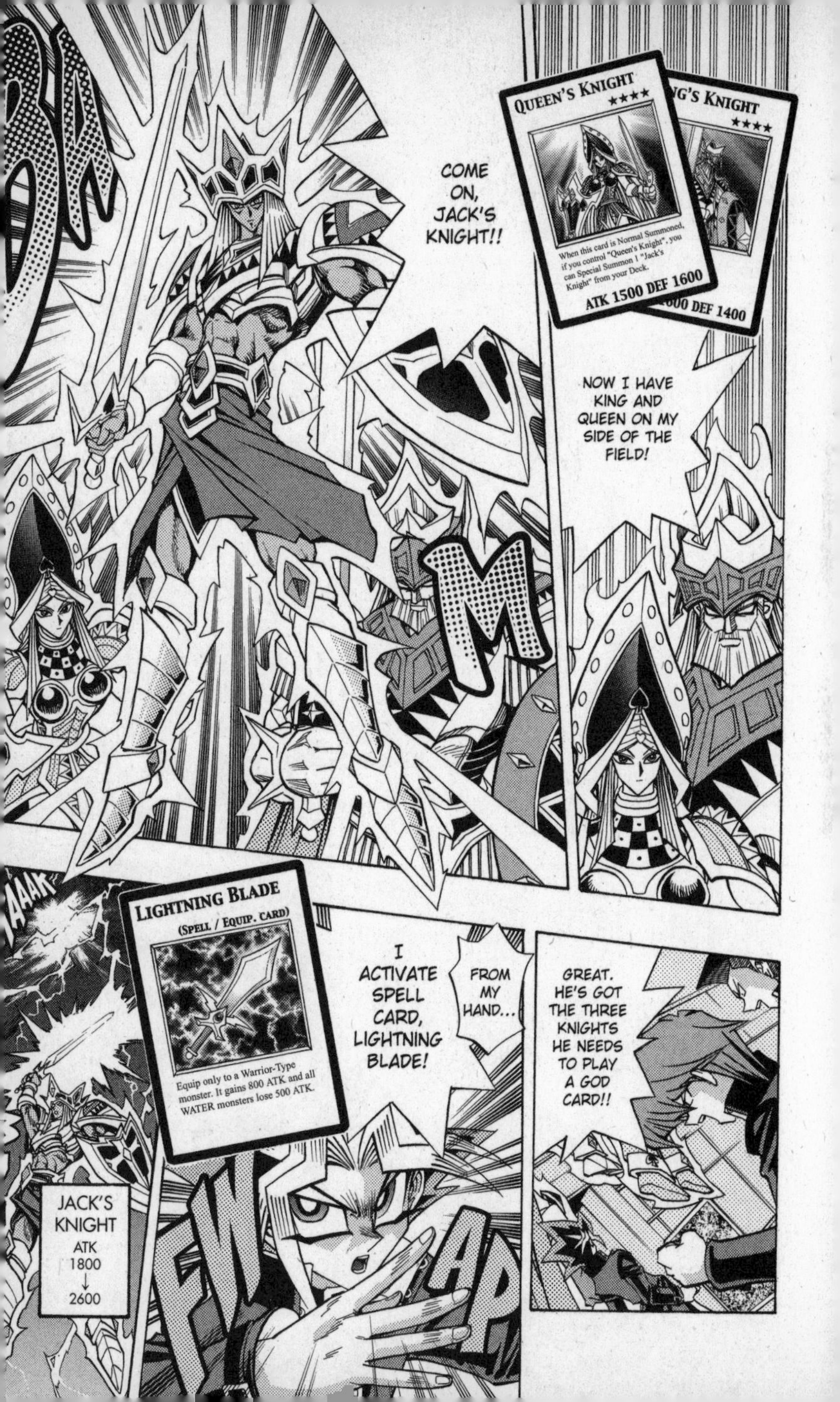

QUEEN'S KNIGHT
★★★★
When this card is Normal Summoned, if you control "Queen's Knight", you can Special Summon 1 "Jack's Knight" from your Deck.
ATK 1500 DEF 1600
NOW I HAVE KING AND QUEEN ON MY SIDE OF THE FIELD!
COME ON, JACK'S KNIGHT!!
M
GREAT. HE'S GOT THE THREE KNIGHTS HE NEEDS TO PLAY A GOD CARD!!
FROM MY HAND...
I ACTIVATE SPELL CARD, LIGHTNING BLADE!
LIGHTNING BLADE
(SPELL / EQUIP. CARD)
Equip only to a Warrior-Type monster. It gains 800 ATK and all WATER monsters lose 500 ATK.
JACK'S KNIGHT
ATK
1800
↓
2600

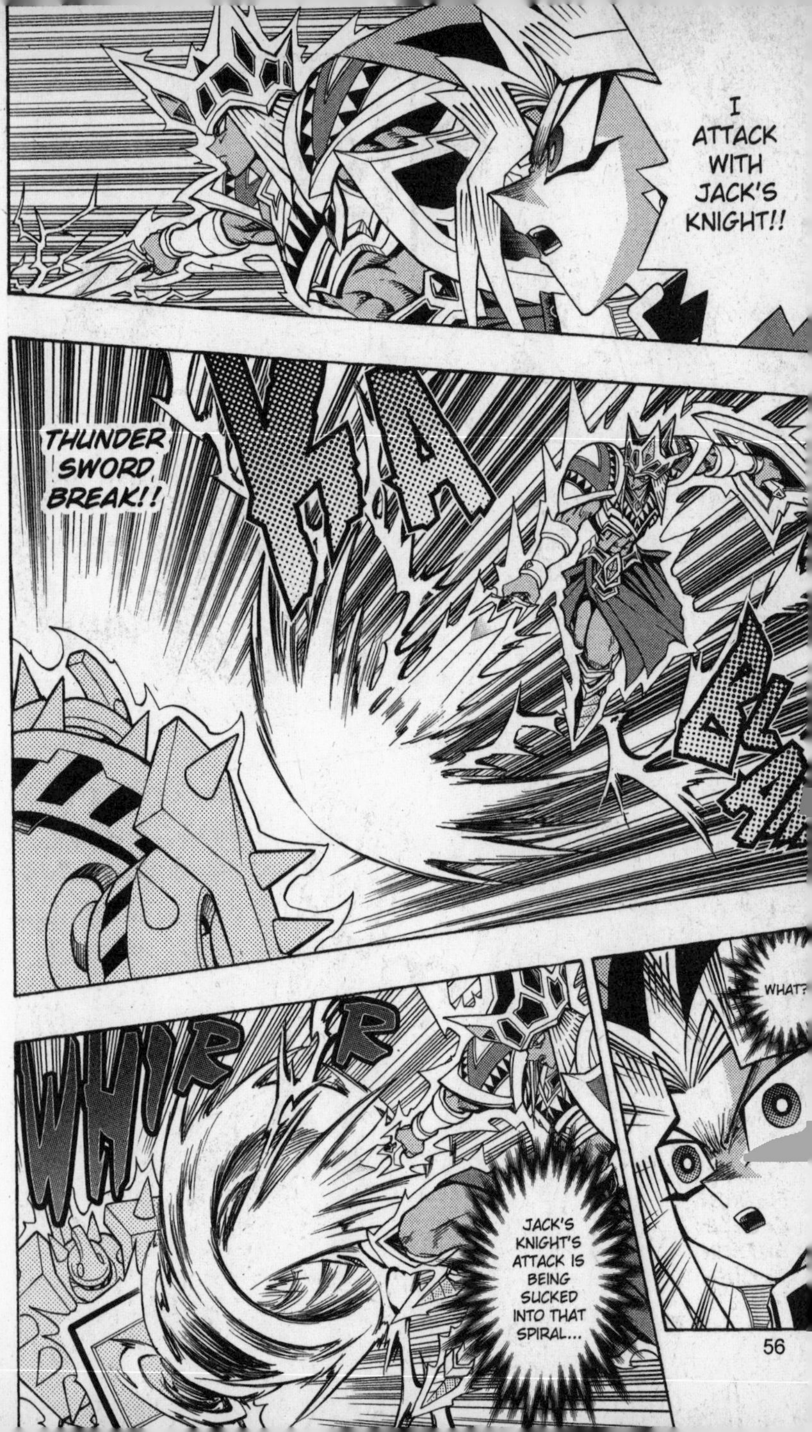
I ATTACK WITH JACK'S KNIGHT!!
THUNDER SWORD BREAK!!
WHAT?
WHIRR
JACK'S KNIGHT'S ATTACK IS BEING SUCKED INTO THAT SPIRAL...

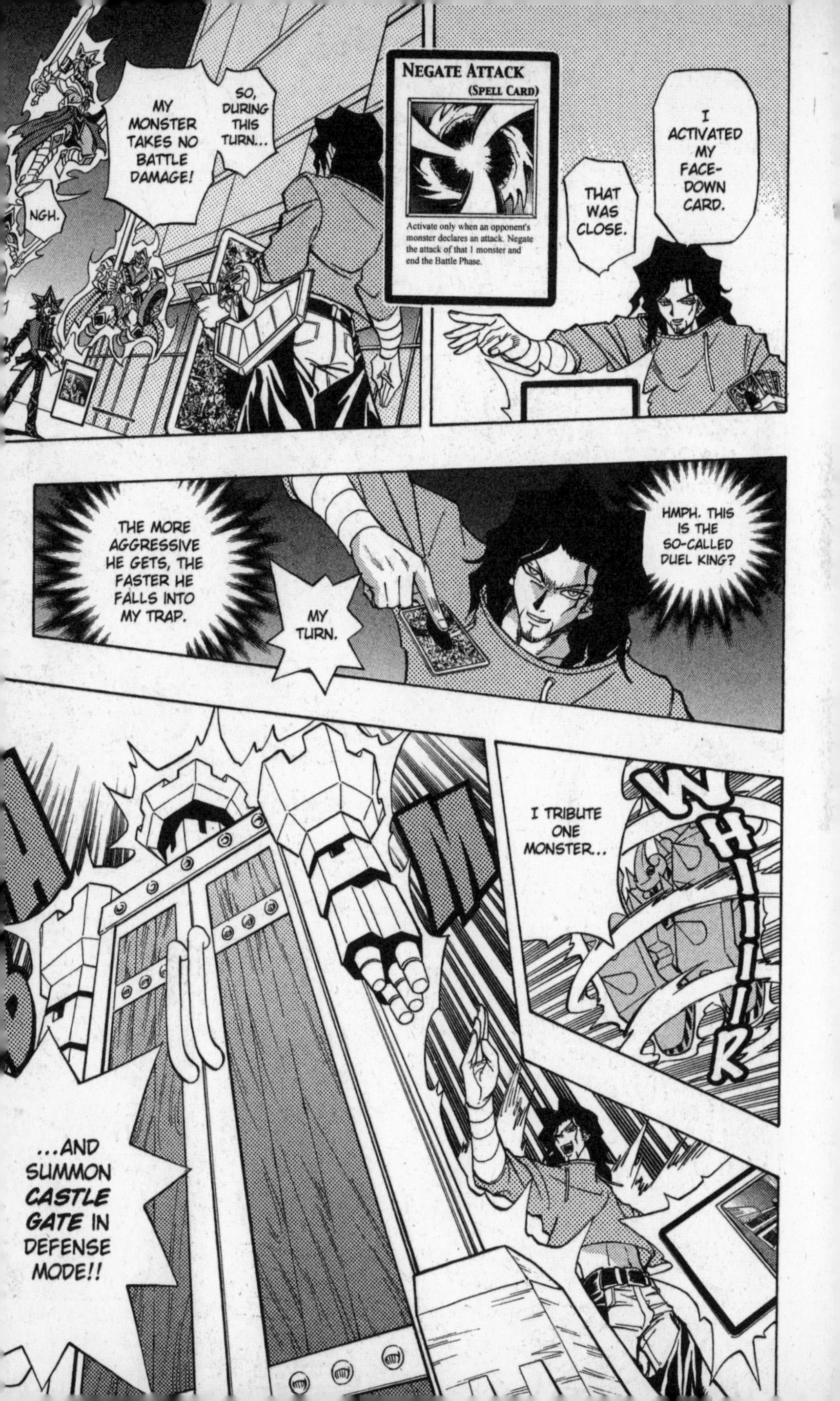
I ACTIVATED MY FACE-DOWN CARD.
THAT WAS CLOSE.
NEGATE ATTACK
(SPELL CARD)
Activate only when an opponent's monster declares an attack. Negate the attack of that 1 monster and end the Battle Phase.
SO, DURING THIS TURN...
MY MONSTER TAKES NO BATTLE DAMAGE!
NGH.
HMPH. THIS IS THE SO-CALLED DUEL KING?
MY TURN.
THE MORE AGGRESSIVE HE GETS, THE FASTER HE FALLS INTO MY TRAP.
WHHIIIR
I TRIBUTE ONE MONSTER...
...AND SUMMON CASTLE GATE IN DEFENSE MODE!!

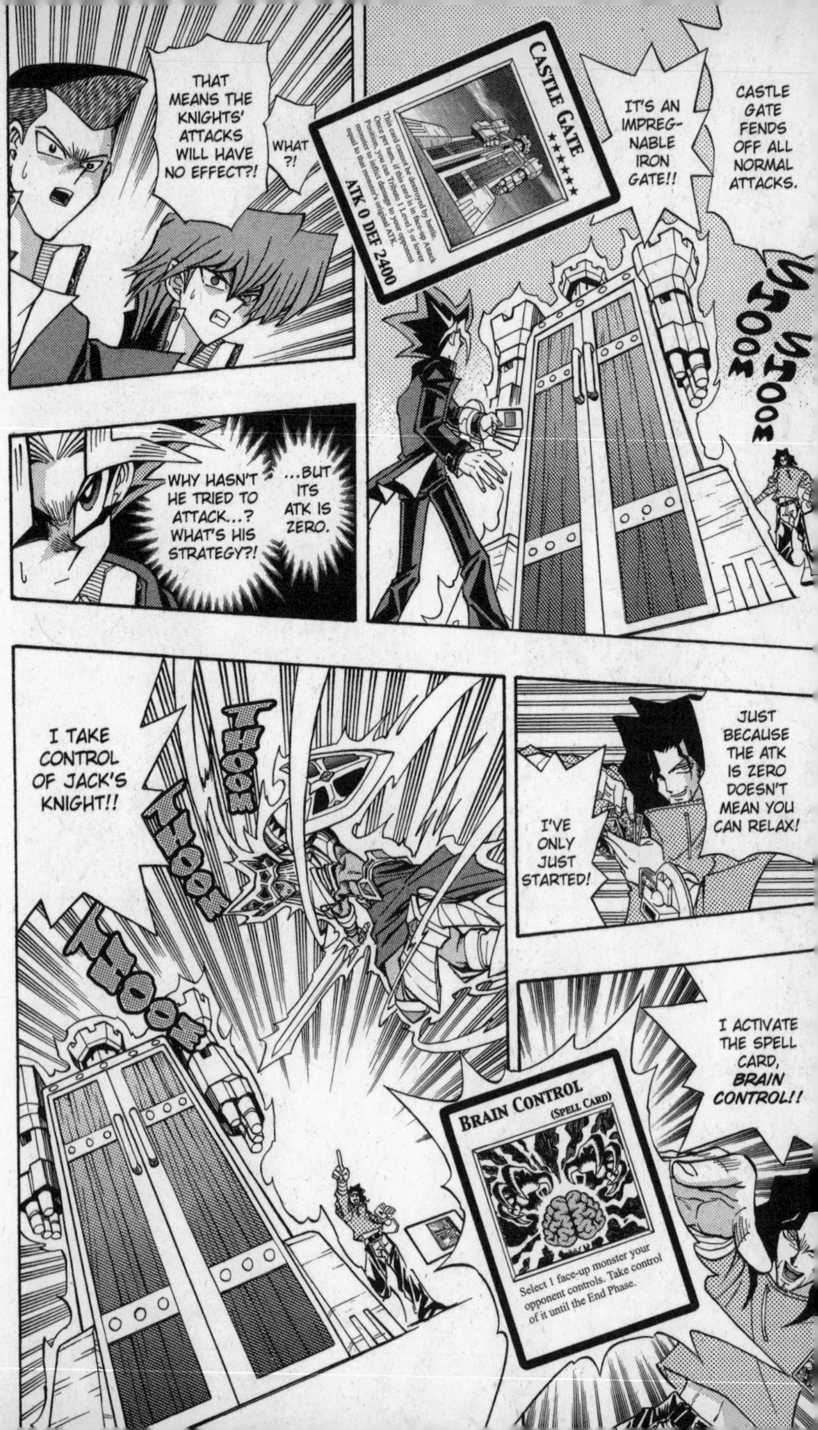

CASTLE GATE FENDS OFF ALL NORMAL ATTACKS.
IT'S AN IMPREG-NABLE IRON GATE!!
CASTLE GATE
★★★★★★
This card cannot be destroyed by battle. Once per turn, if this card is in face-up Attack Position, you can Tribute 1 Level 5 or lower monster to inflict damage to your opponent equal to that monster's original ATK.
ATK 0 DEF 2400
STOOM
STOOM
THAT MEANS THE KNIGHTS' ATTACKS WILL HAVE NO EFFECT?!
WHAT ?!
...BUT ITS ATK IS ZERO.
WHY HASN'T HE TRIED TO ATTACK...? WHAT'S HIS STRATEGY?!
JUST BECAUSE THE ATK IS ZERO DOESN'T MEAN YOU CAN RELAX!
I'VE ONLY JUST STARTED!
I ACTIVATE THE SPELL CARD, BRAIN CONTROL!!
BRAIN CONTROL
(SPELL CARD)
Select 1 face-up monster your opponent controls. Take control of it until the End Phase.
I TAKE CONTROL OF JACK'S KNIGHT!!
THOOM
THOOM

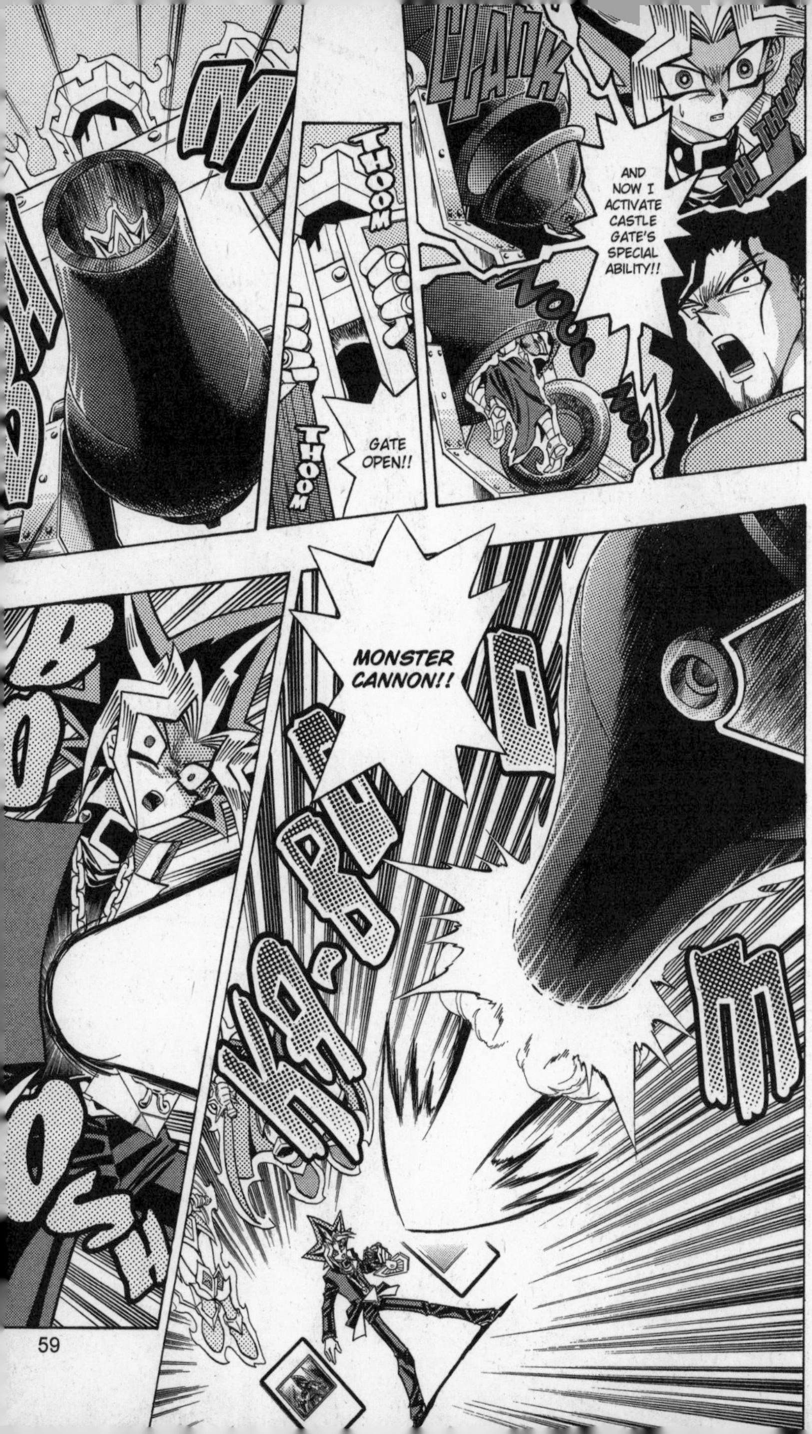
CLANK
TH-THUMP
AND NOW I ACTIVATE CASTLE GATE'S SPECIAL ABILITY!!
THOOM
GATE OPEN!!
THOOM
MONSTER CANNON!!

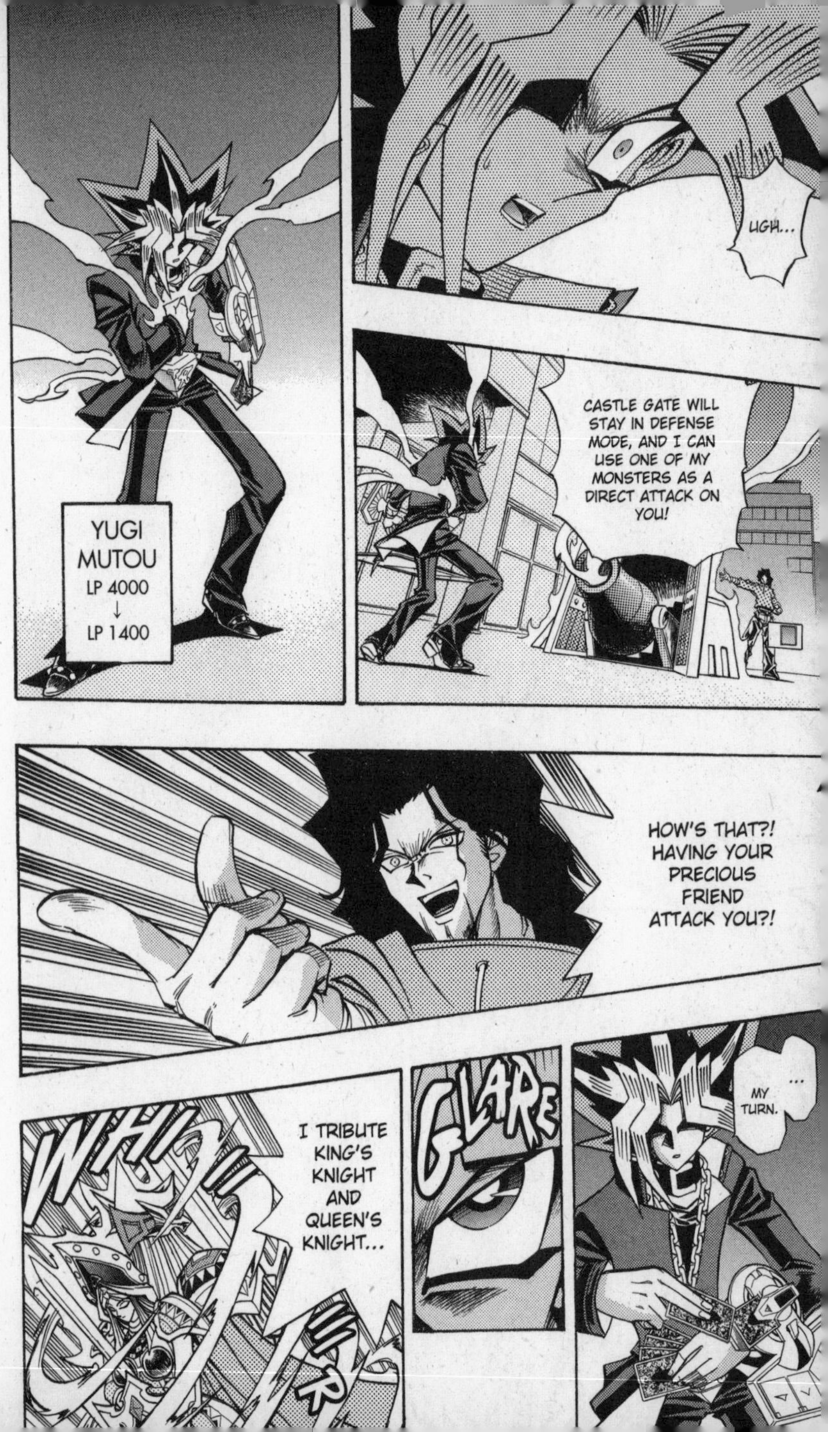
UGH...
CASTLE GATE WILL STAY IN DEFENSE MODE, AND I CAN USE ONE OF MY MONSTERS AS A DIRECT ATTACK ON YOU!
YUGI MUTOU
LP 4000
↓
LP 1400
HOW'S THAT?! HAVING YOUR PRECIOUS FRIEND ATTACK YOU?!
... MY TURN.
GLARE
I TRIBUTE KING'S KNIGHT AND QUEEN'S KNIGHT...

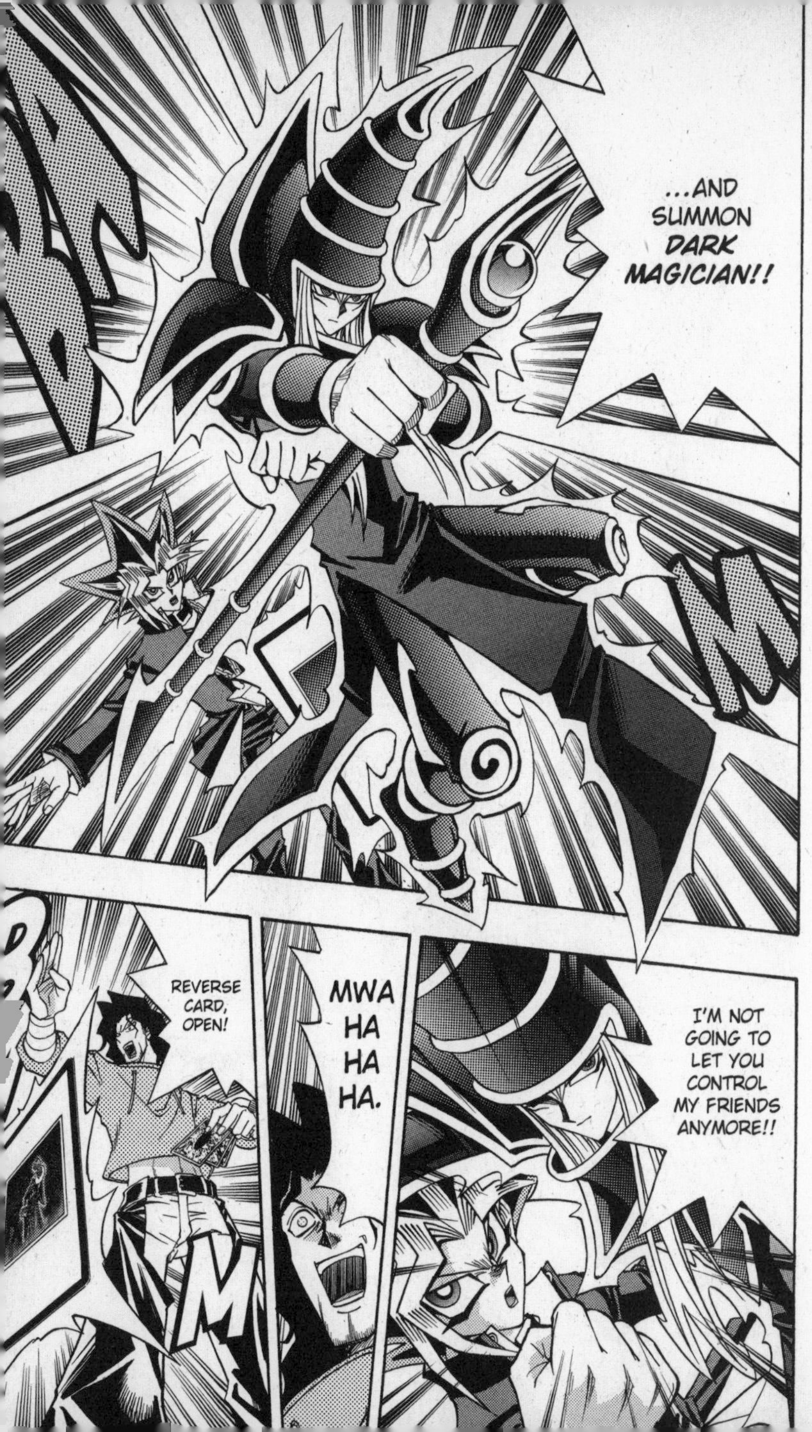
...AND SUMMON DARK MAGICIAN!!
I'M NOT GOING TO LET YOU CONTROL MY FRIENDS ANYMORE!!
MWA HA HA HA.
REVERSE CARD, OPEN!

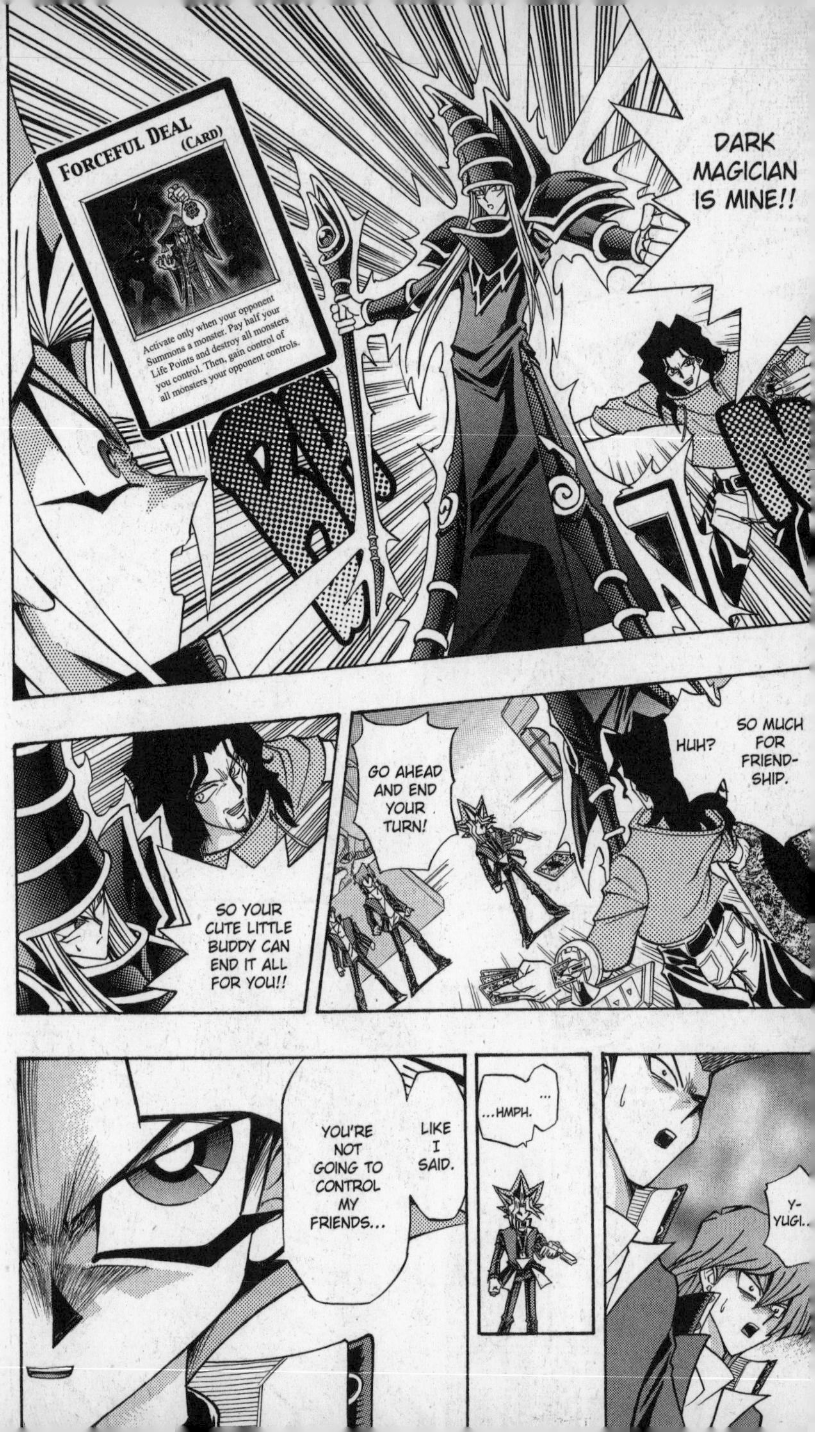
DARK MAGICIAN IS MINE!!
FORCEFUL DEAL
(CARD)
Activate only when your opponent Summons a monster. Pay half your Life Points and destroy all monsters you control. Then, gain control of all monsters your opponent controls.
SO MUCH FOR FRIEND-SHIP.
HUH?
GO AHEAD AND END YOUR TURN!
SO YOUR CUTE LITTLE BUDDY CAN END IT ALL FOR YOU!!
Y-YUGI..
...
...HMPH.
LIKE I SAID.
YOU'RE NOT GOING TO CONTROL MY FRIENDS...

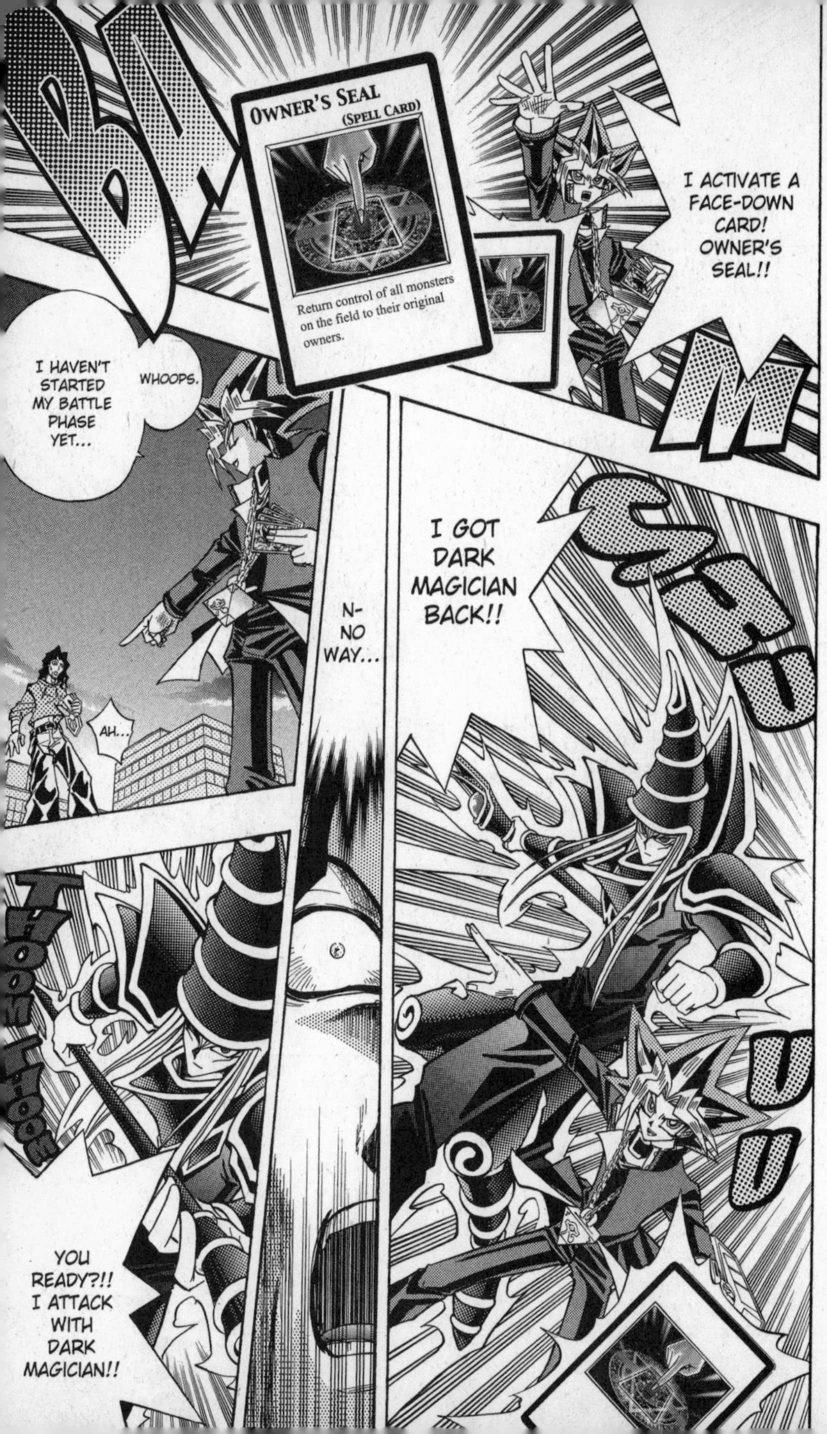
I ACTIVATE A FACE-DOWN CARD! OWNER'S SEAL!!
OWNER'S SEAL
(SPELL CARD)
Return control of all monsters on the field to their original owners.
WHOOPS.
I HAVEN'T STARTED MY BATTLE PHASE YET...
AH...
I GOT DARK MAGICIAN BACK!!
N- NO WAY...
YOU READY?!! I ATTACK WITH DARK MAGICIAN!!

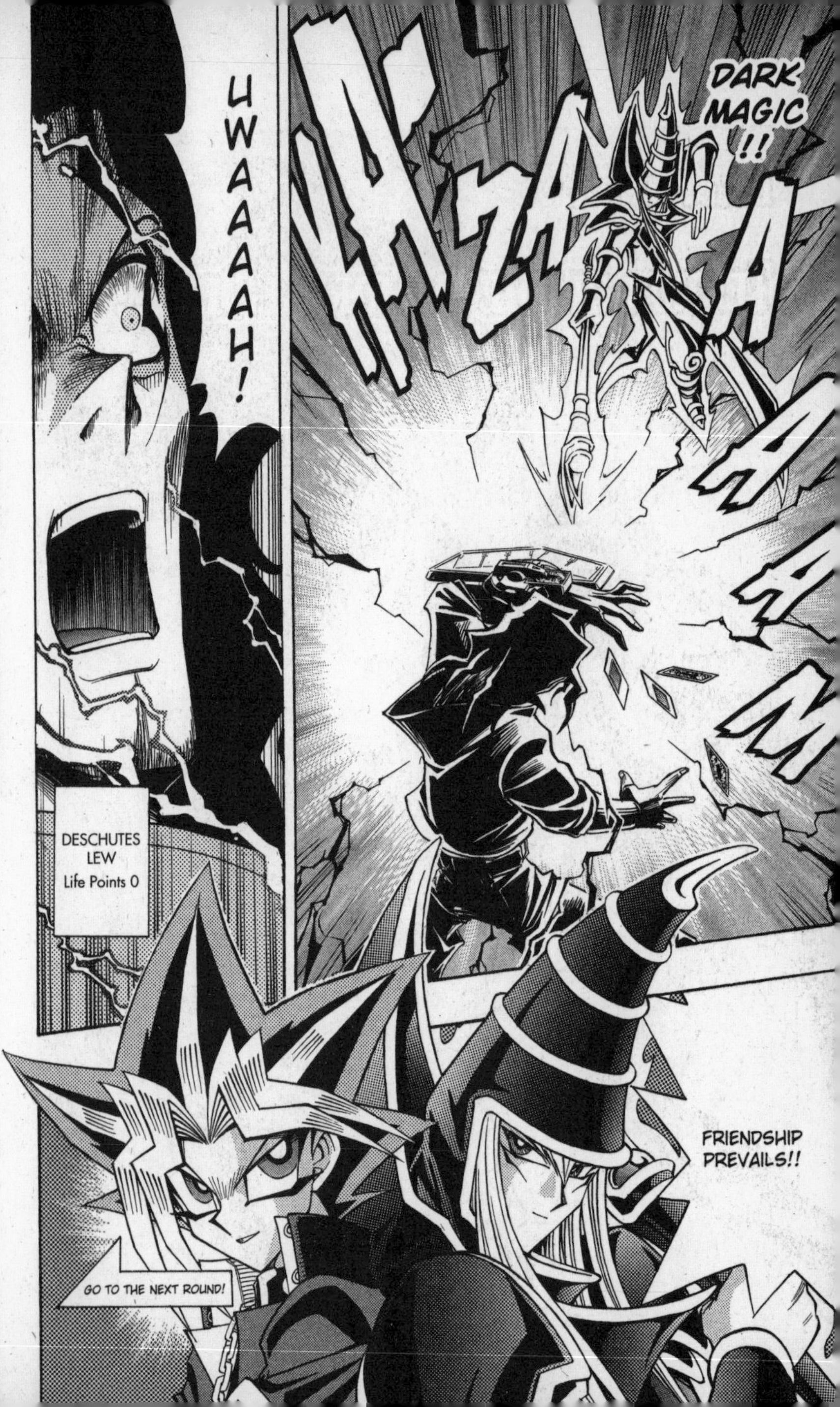

DARK MAGIC!!
UWAAAAAH!
DESCHUTES LEW
Life Points 0
FRIENDSHIP PREVAILS!!
GO TO THE NEXT ROUND!

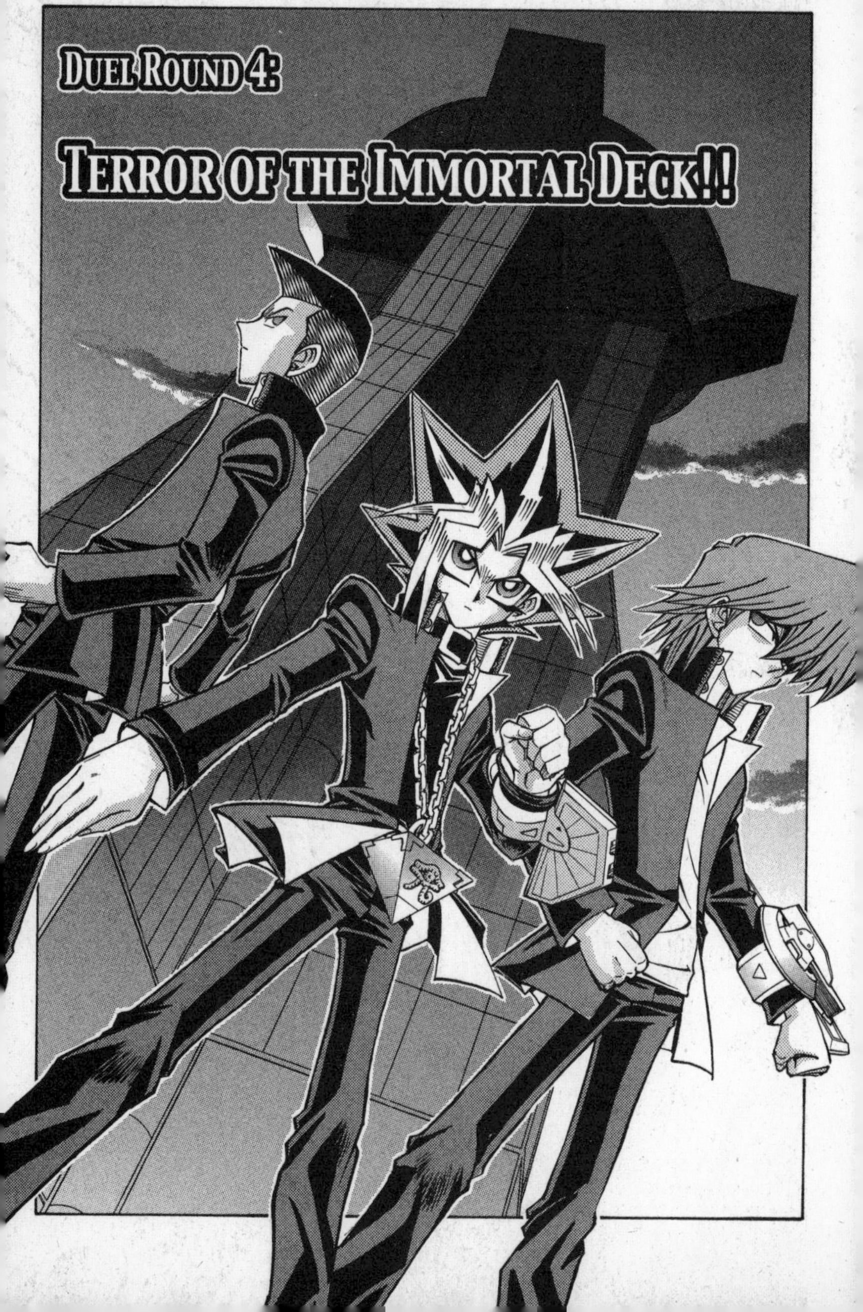
DUEL ROUND 4:
TERROR OF THE IMMORTAL DECK!!

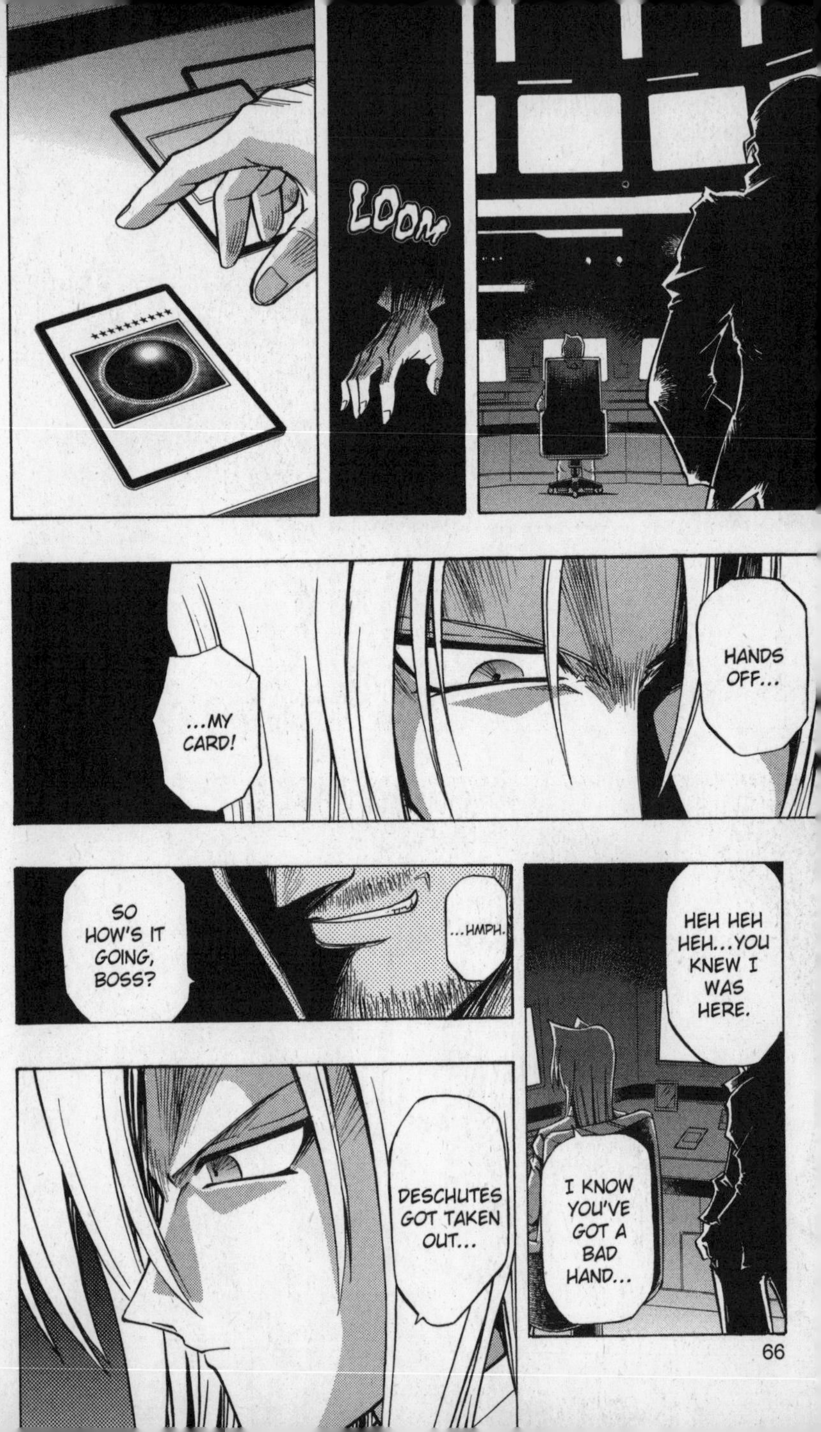
LOOM
HANDS OFF...
...MY CARD!
HEH HEH HEH...YOU KNEW I WAS HERE.
I KNOW YOU'VE GOT A BAD HAND...
...HMPH.
SO HOW'S IT GOING, BOSS?
DESCHUTES GOT TAKEN OUT...

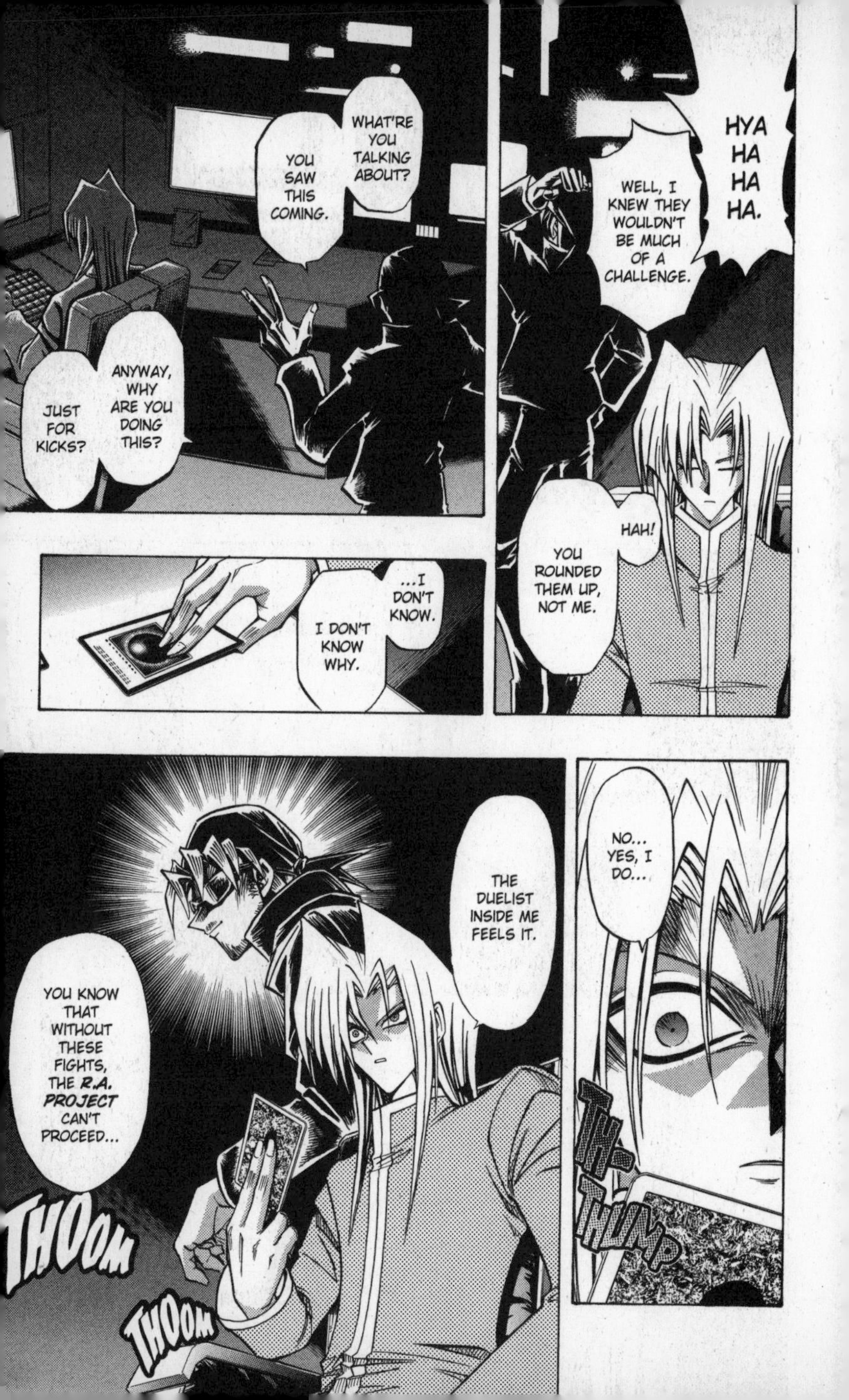
HYA HA HA HA.
WELL, I KNEW THEY WOULDN'T BE MUCH OF A CHALLENGE.
HAH!
YOU ROUNDED THEM UP, NOT ME.
WHAT'RE YOU TALKING ABOUT?
YOU SAW THIS COMING.
ANYWAY, WHY ARE YOU DOING THIS?
JUST FOR KICKS?
...I DON'T KNOW.
I DON'T KNOW WHY.
NO... YES, I DO...
TH-THUMP
THE DUELIST INSIDE ME FEELS IT.
YOU KNOW THAT WITHOUT THESE FIGHTS, THE *R.A. PROJECT* CAN'T PROCEED...
THOOM
THOOM

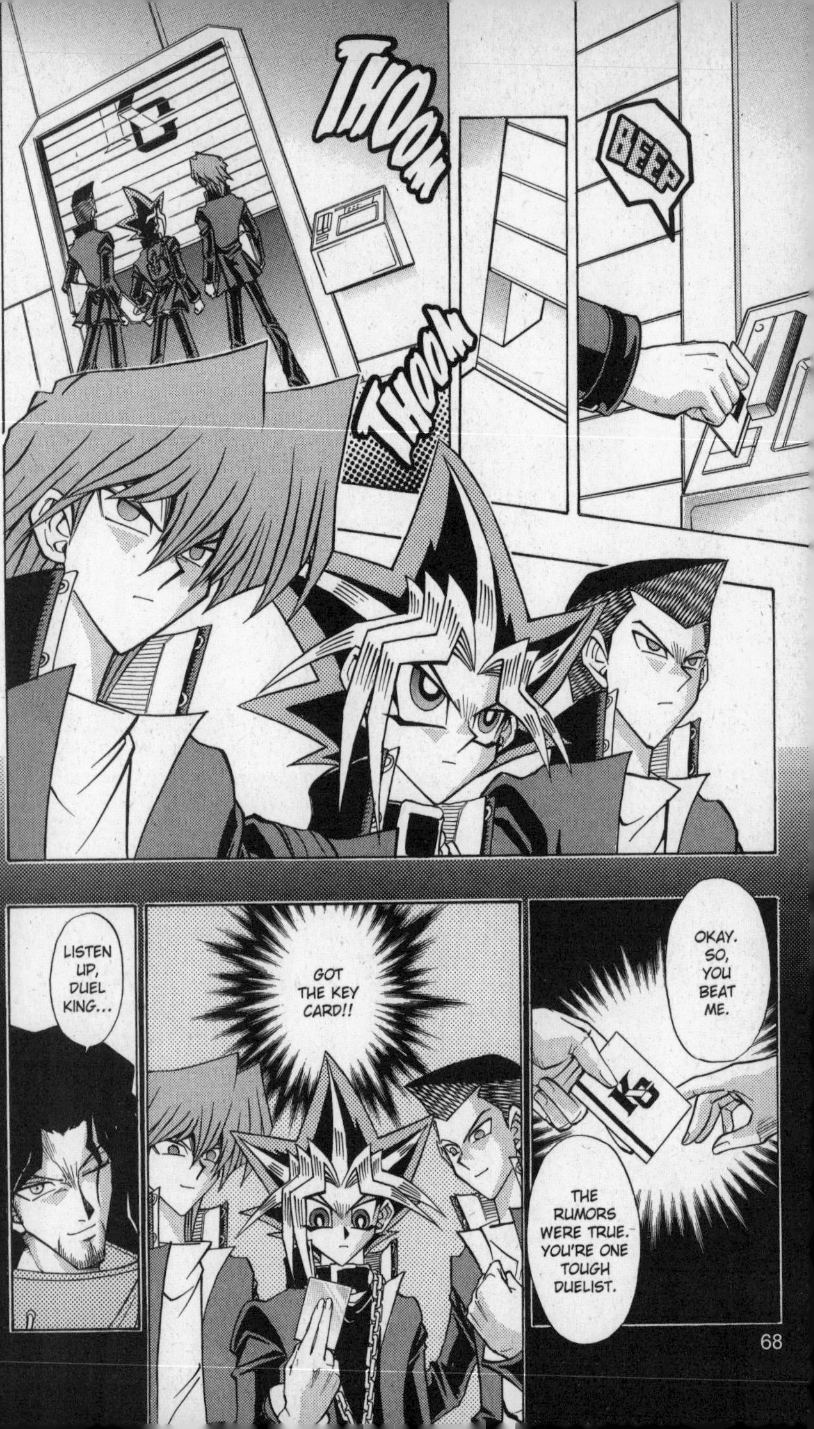
BEEP
THOOM
THOOM
OKAY. SO, YOU BEAT ME.
THE RUMORS WERE TRUE. YOU'RE ONE TOUGH DUELIST.
GOT THE KEY CARD!!
LISTEN UP, DUEL KING...

READ THIS WAY

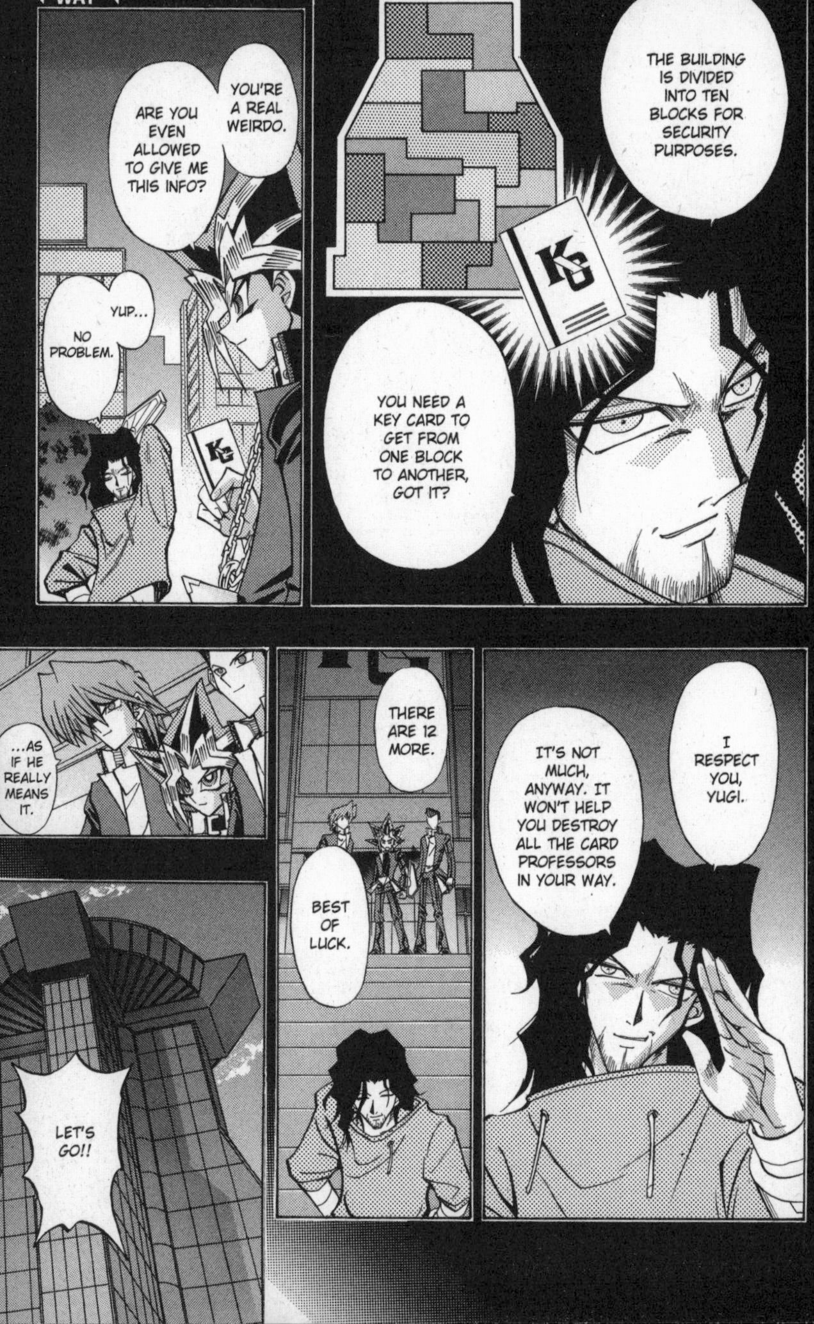
THE BUILDING IS DIVIDED INTO TEN BLOCKS FOR SECURITY PURPOSES.
YOU NEED A KEY CARD TO GET FROM ONE BLOCK TO ANOTHER, GOT IT?
YOU'RE A REAL WEIRDO.
ARE YOU EVEN ALLOWED TO GIVE ME THIS INFO?
YUP... NO PROBLEM.
I RESPECT YOU, YUGI.
IT'S NOT MUCH, ANYWAY. IT WON'T HELP YOU DESTROY ALL THE CARD PROFESSORS IN YOUR WAY.
THERE ARE 12 MORE.
BEST OF LUCK.
...AS IF HE REALLY MEANS IT.
LET'S GO!!

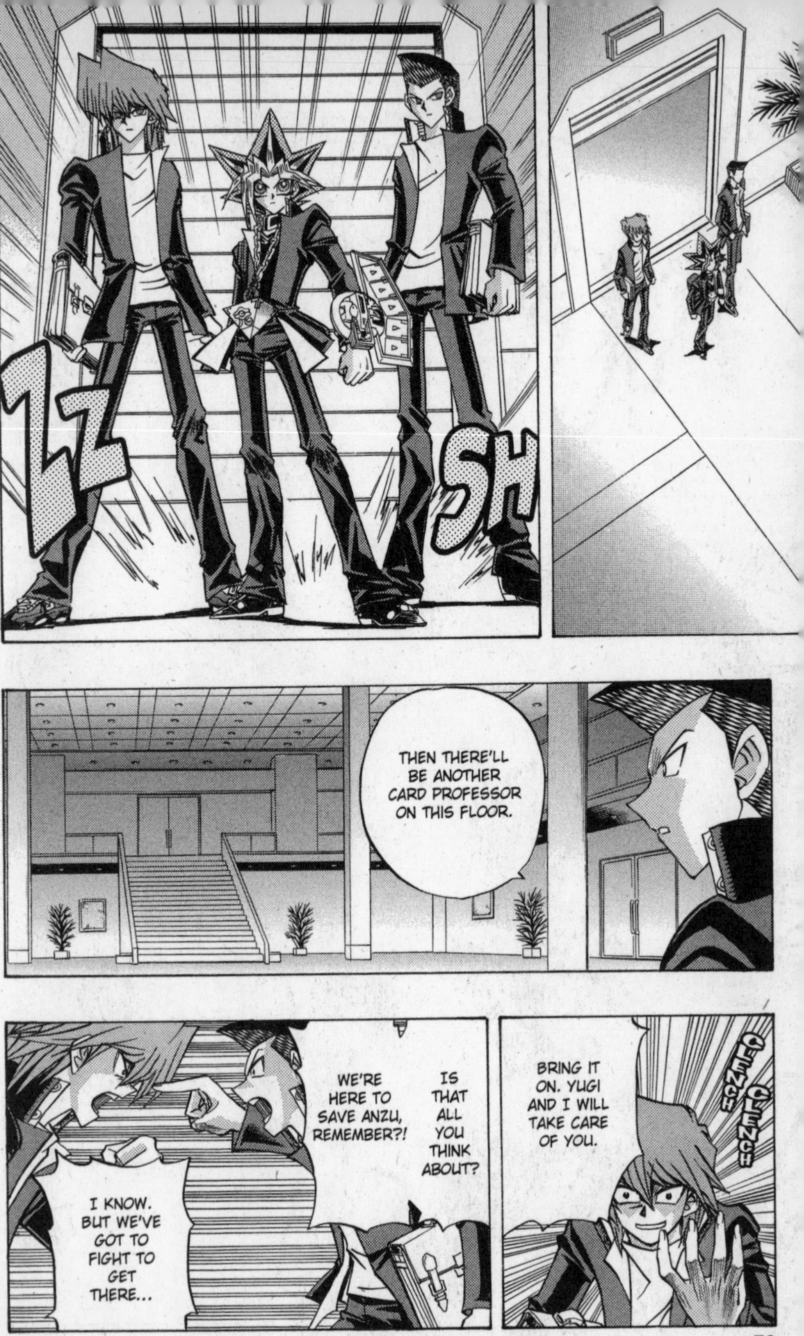
SH
ZZ
THEN THERE'LL BE ANOTHER CARD PROFESSOR ON THIS FLOOR.
CLENCH
CLENCH
BRING IT ON. YUGI AND I WILL TAKE CARE OF YOU.
IS THAT ALL YOU THINK ABOUT?
WE'RE HERE TO SAVE ANZU, REMEMBER?!
I KNOW. BUT WE'VE GOT TO FIGHT TO GET THERE...

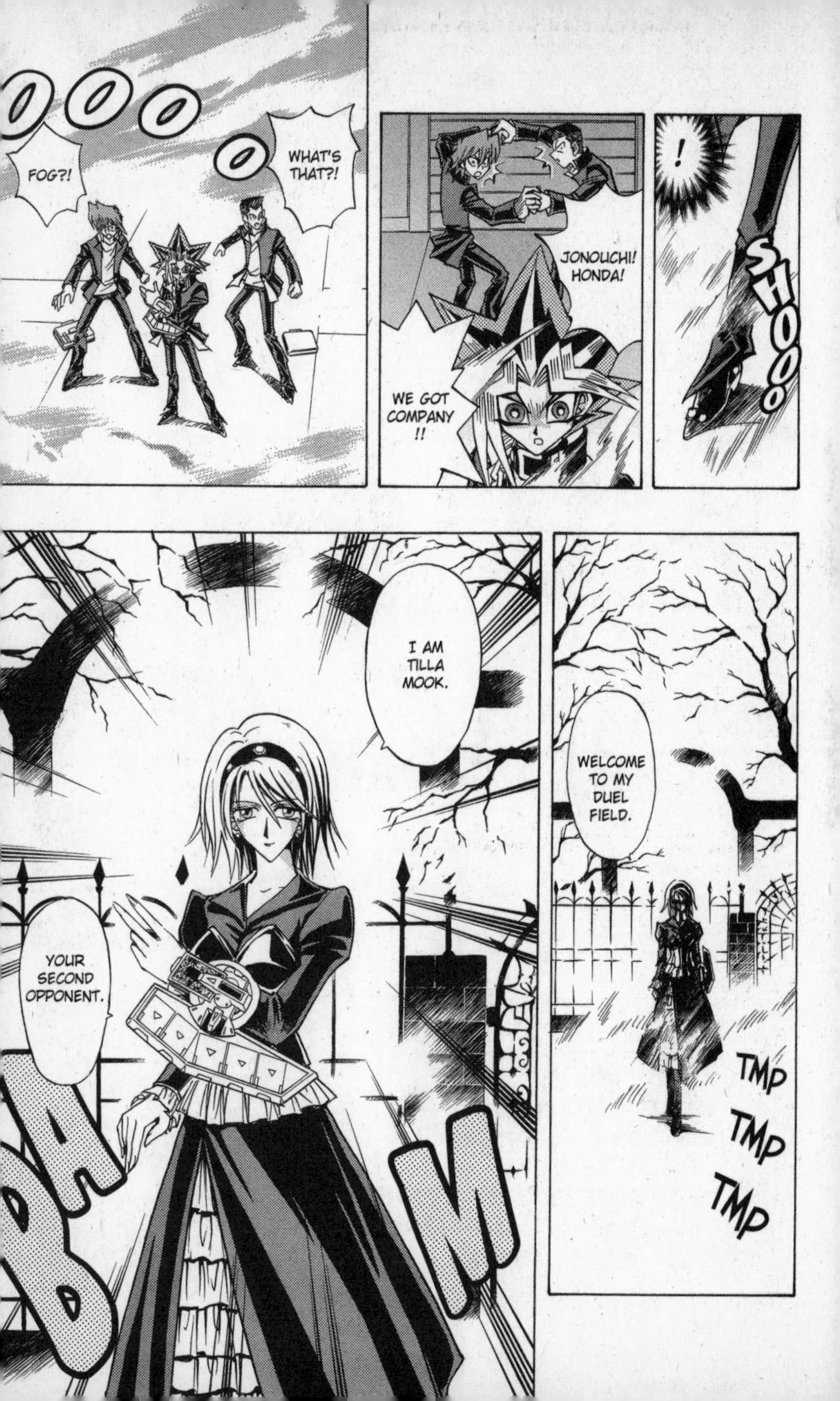
!
SHOOO
JONOUCHI! HONDA!
WE GOT COMPANY !!
OOOO
WHAT'S THAT?!
FOG?!
WELCOME TO MY DUEL FIELD.
TMP
TMP
TMP
I AM TILLA MOOK.
YOUR SECOND OPPONENT.
BAM

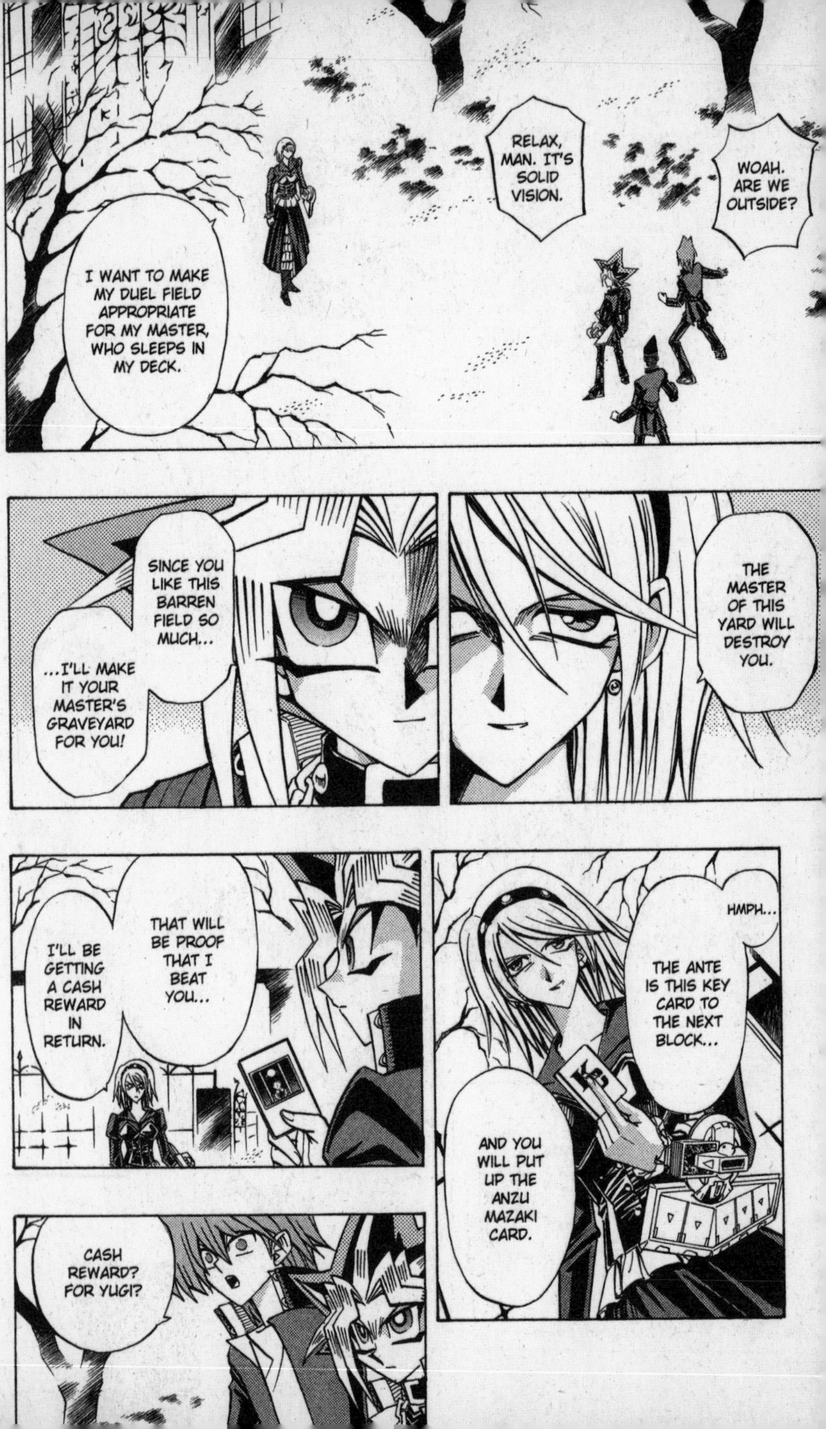
WOAH. ARE WE OUTSIDE?
RELAX, MAN. IT'S SOLID VISION.
I WANT TO MAKE MY DUEL FIELD APPROPRIATE FOR MY MASTER, WHO SLEEPS IN MY DECK.
THE MASTER OF THIS YARD WILL DESTROY YOU.
SINCE YOU LIKE THIS BARREN FIELD SO MUCH...
...I'LL MAKE IT YOUR MASTER'S GRAVEYARD FOR YOU!
HMPH...
THE ANTE IS THIS KEY CARD TO THE NEXT BLOCK...
AND YOU WILL PUT UP THE ANZU MAZAKI CARD.
THAT WILL BE PROOF THAT I BEAT YOU...
I'LL BE GETTING A CASH REWARD IN RETURN.
CASH REWARD? FOR YUGI?

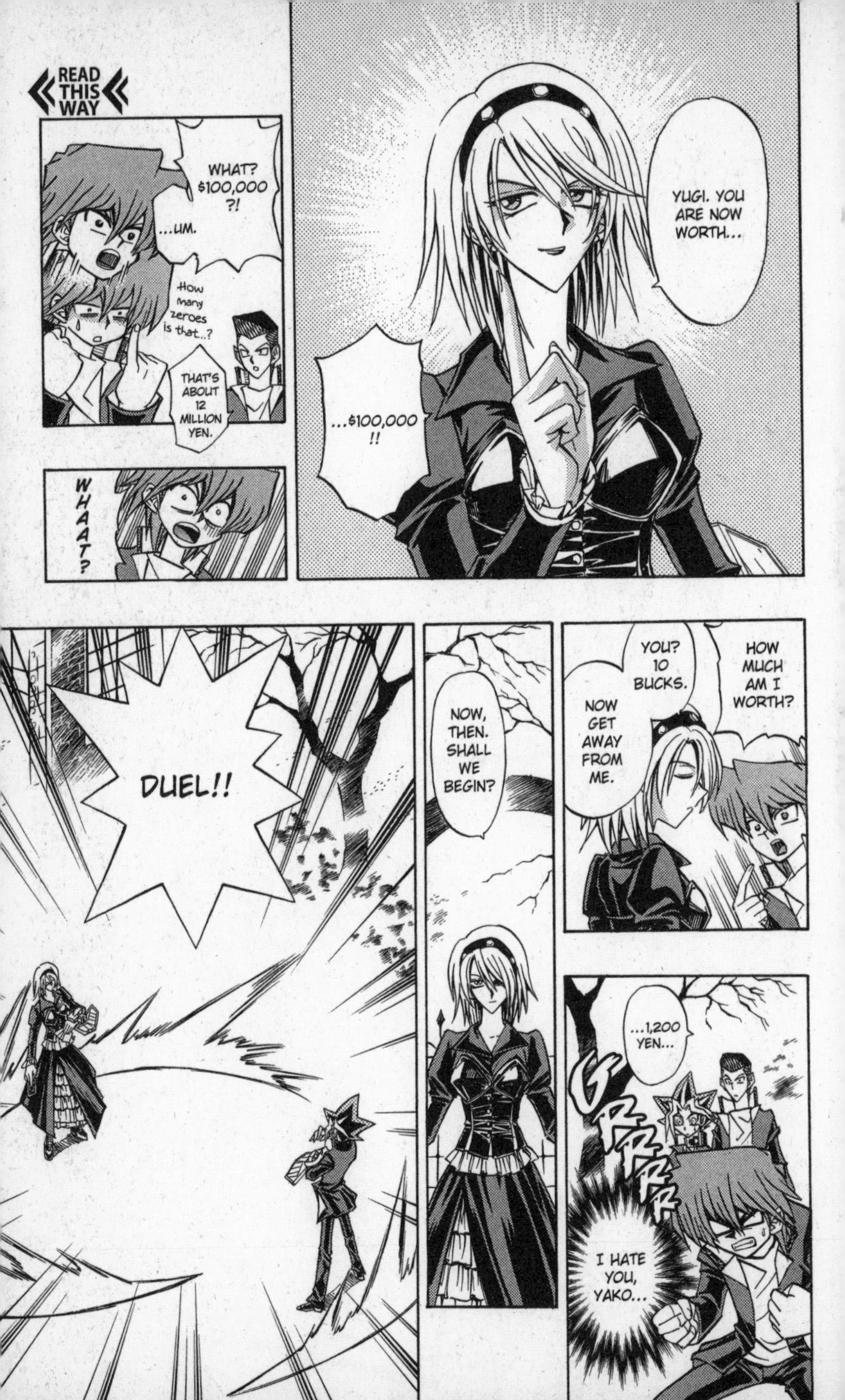
READ THIS WAY
YUGI. YOU ARE NOW WORTH...
...$100,000!!
WHAT? $100,000?!
...UM.
How many zeroes is that..?
THAT'S ABOUT 12 MILLION YEN.
WHAAAT?
HOW MUCH AM I WORTH?
YOU? 10 BUCKS.
NOW GET AWAY FROM ME.
...1,200 YEN...
GRRRR
I HATE YOU, YAKO...
NOW, THEN. SHALL WE BEGIN?
DUEL!!

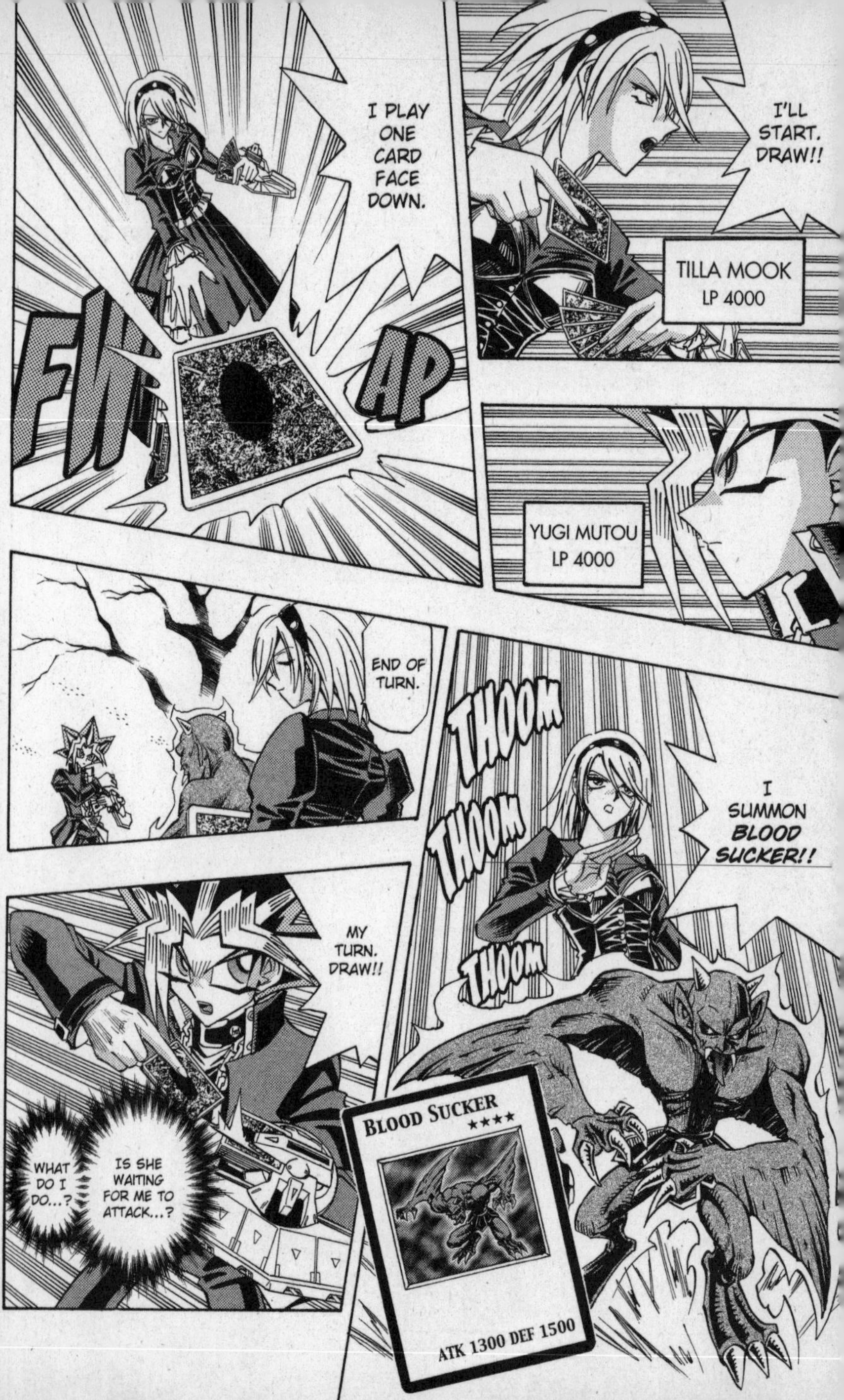
I'LL START. DRAW!!
TILLA MOOK
LP 4000
YUGI MUTOU
LP 4000
I PLAY ONE CARD FACE DOWN.
FWAP
THOOM
THOOM
THOOM
I SUMMON BLOOD SUCKER!!
BLOOD SUCKER ★★★★
ATK 1300 DEF 1500
END OF TURN.
MY TURN. DRAW!!
IS SHE WAITING FOR ME TO ATTACK...?
WHAT DO I DO...?

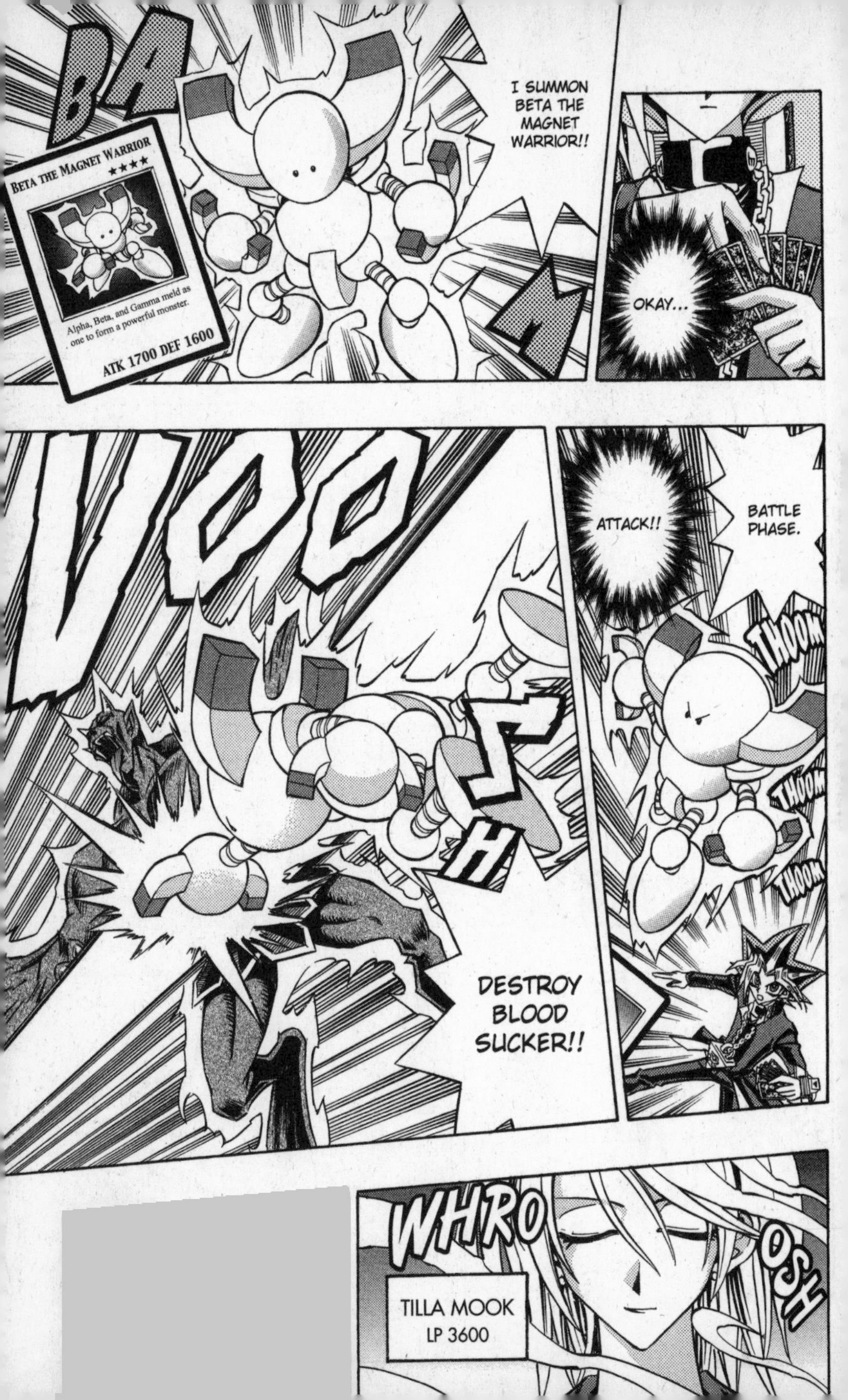
OKAY...
BA
M
I SUMMON BETA THE MAGNET WARRIOR!!
BETA THE MAGNET WARRIOR ★★★★
Alpha, Beta, and Gamma meld as one to form a powerful monster.
ATK 1700 DEF 1600
BATTLE PHASE.
ATTACK!!
THOOM
THOOM
THOOM
VOO
SH
DESTROY BLOOD SUCKER!!
WHRO
OSH
TILLA MOOK
LP 3600

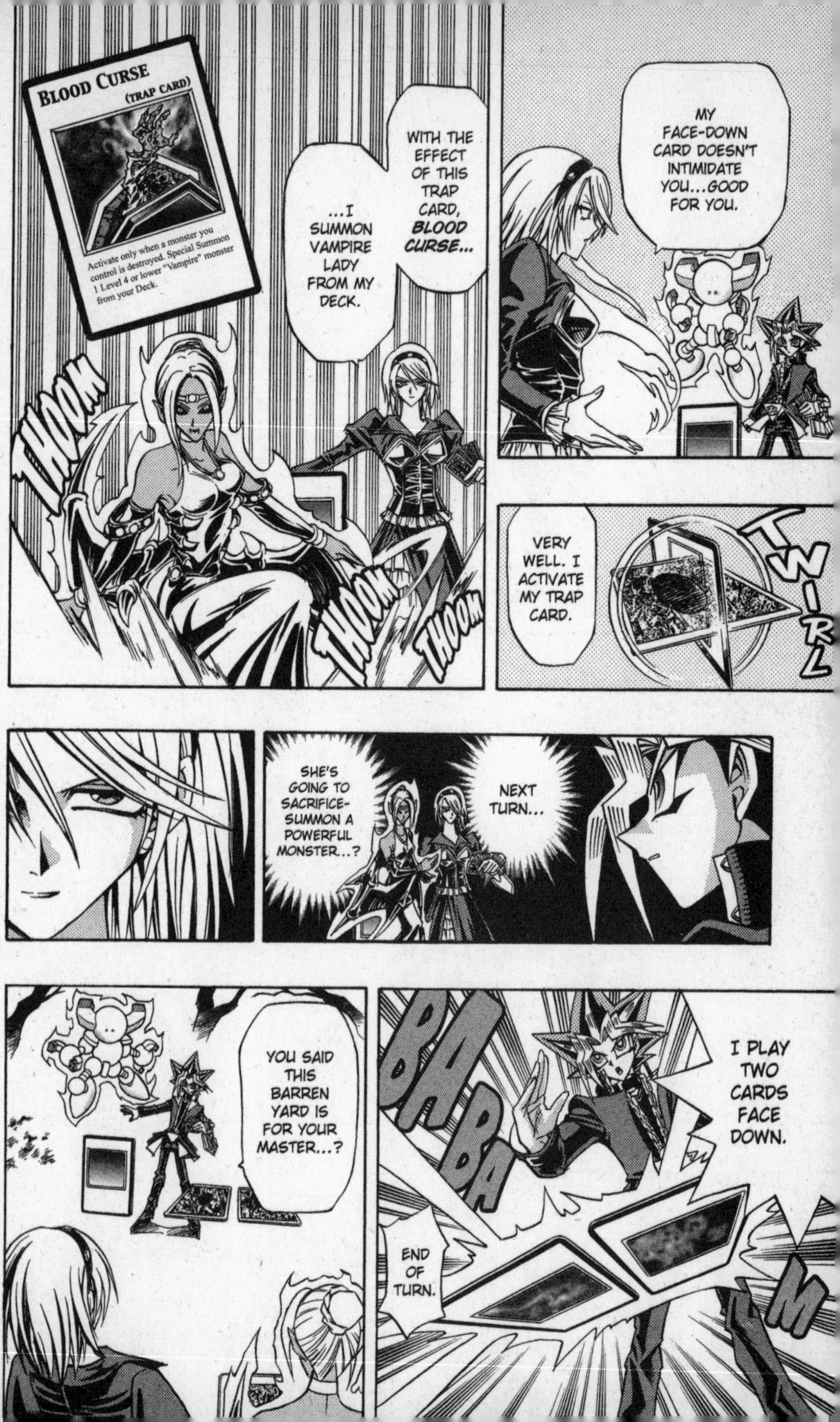
MY FACE-DOWN CARD DOESN'T INTIMIDATE YOU...GOOD FOR YOU.
VERY WELL. I ACTIVATE MY TRAP CARD.
TWIRL
WITH THE EFFECT OF THIS TRAP CARD, BLOOD CURSE...
...I SUMMON VAMPIRE LADY FROM MY DECK.
BLOOD CURSE
(TRAP CARD)
Activate only when a monster you control is destroyed. Special Summon 1 Level 4 or lower "Vampire" monster from your Deck.
THOOM
THOOM
THOOM
NEXT TURN...
SHE'S GOING TO SACRIFICE-SUMMON A POWERFUL MONSTER...?
I PLAY TWO CARDS FACE DOWN.
BA BA
END OF TURN.
YOU SAID THIS BARREN YARD IS FOR YOUR MASTER...?

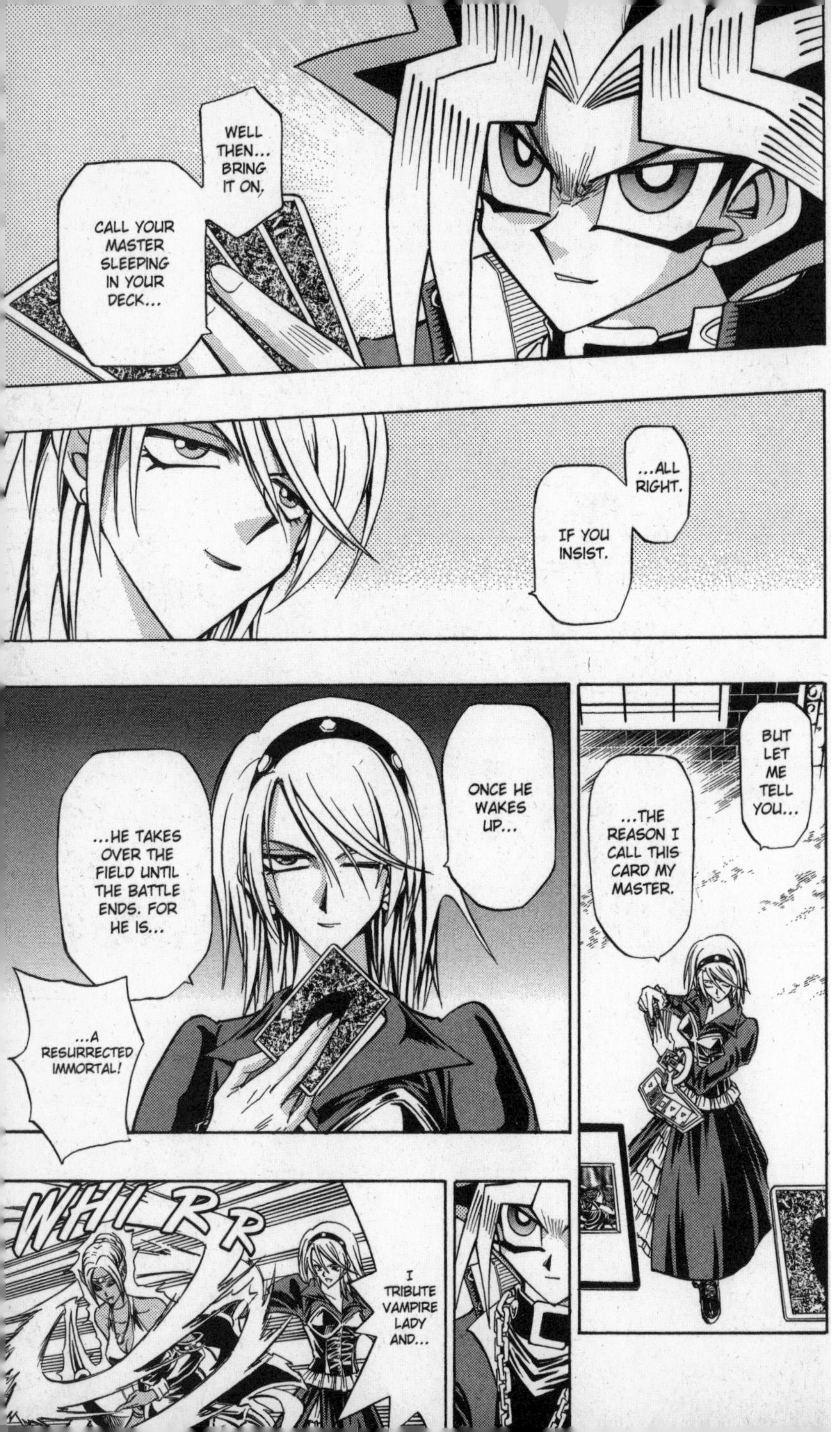
WELL THEN... BRING IT ON,
CALL YOUR MASTER SLEEPING IN YOUR DECK...
...ALL RIGHT.
IF YOU INSIST.
BUT LET ME TELL YOU...
...THE REASON I CALL THIS CARD MY MASTER.
ONCE HE WAKES UP...
...HE TAKES OVER THE FIELD UNTIL THE BATTLE ENDS. FOR HE IS...
...A RESURRECTED IMMORTAL!
WHIRR
I TRIBUTE VAMPIRE LADY AND...

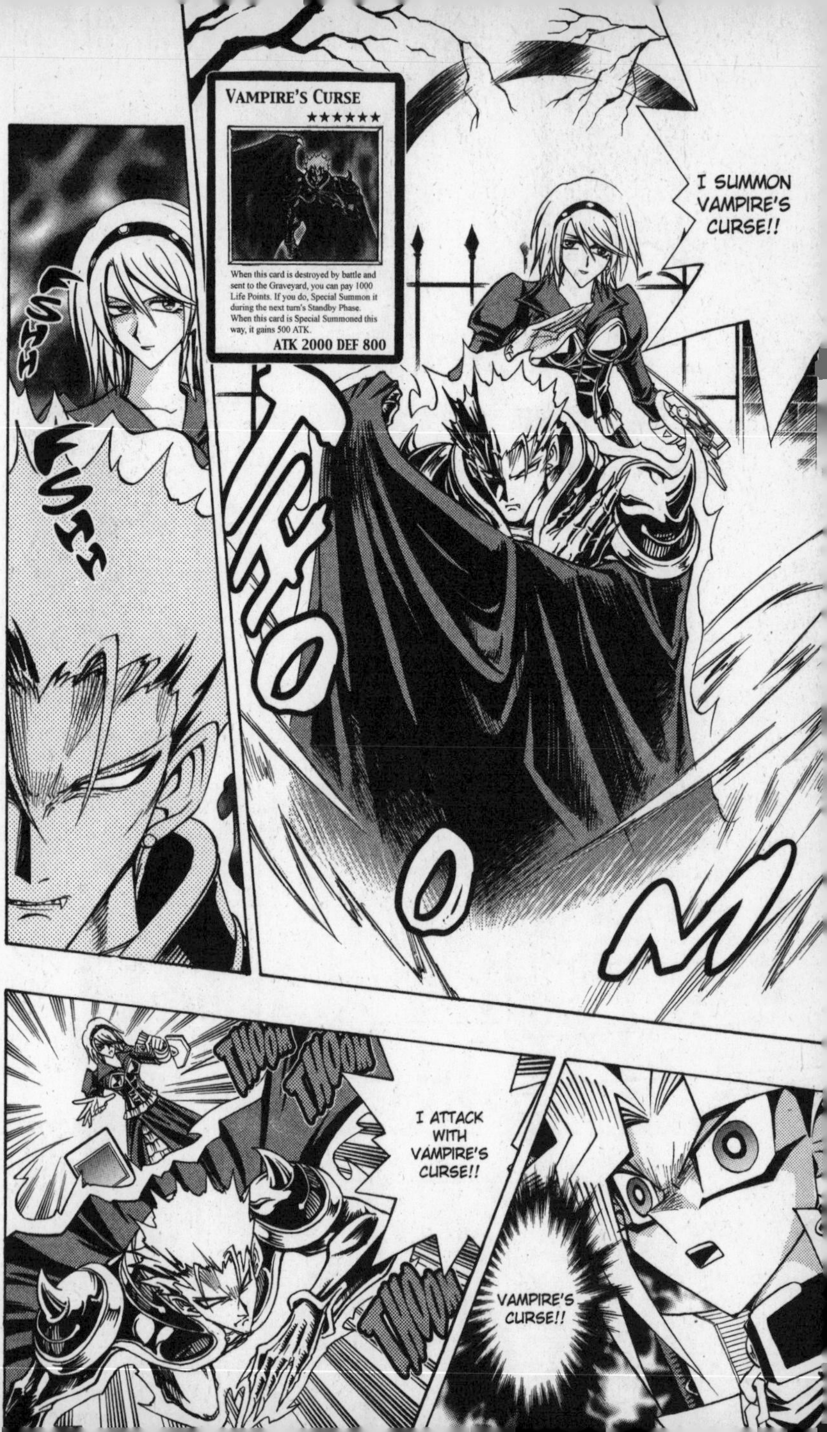

VAMPIRE'S CURSE
★★★★★★
When this card is destroyed by battle and sent to the Graveyard, you can pay 1000 Life Points. If you do, Special Summon it during the next turn's Standby Phase. When this card is Special Summoned this way, it gains 500 ATK.
ATK 2000 DEF 800
I SUMMON VAMPIRE'S CURSE!!
VAMPIRE'S CURSE!!
I ATTACK WITH VAMPIRE'S CURSE!!
THOOM THOOM

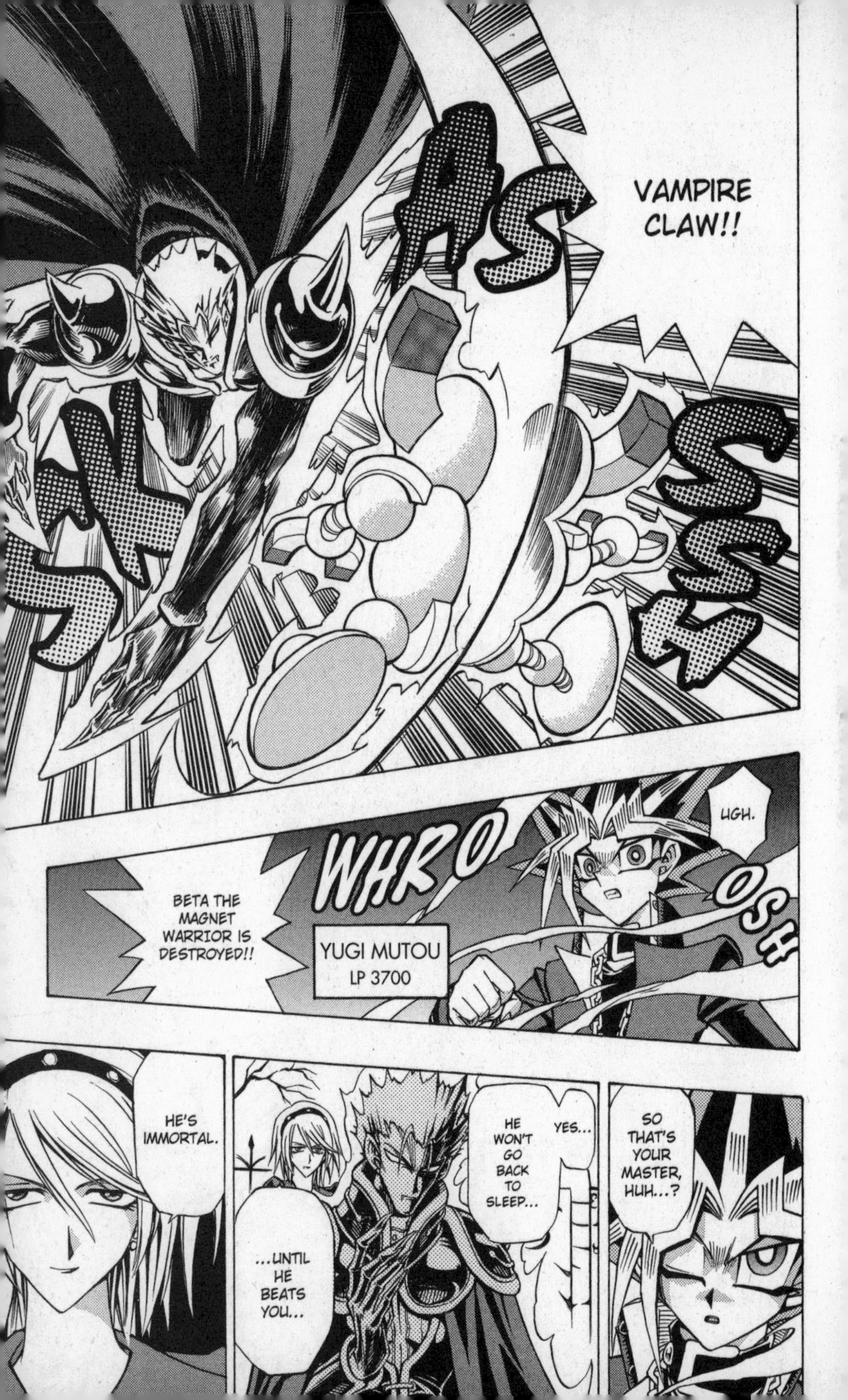
VAMPIRE CLAW!!
UGH.
WHROOSH
BETA THE MAGNET WARRIOR IS DESTROYED!!
YUGI MUTOU
LP 3700
SO THAT'S YOUR MASTER, HUH...?
YES...
HE WON'T GO BACK TO SLEEP...
...UNTIL HE BEATS YOU...
HE'S IMMORTAL.

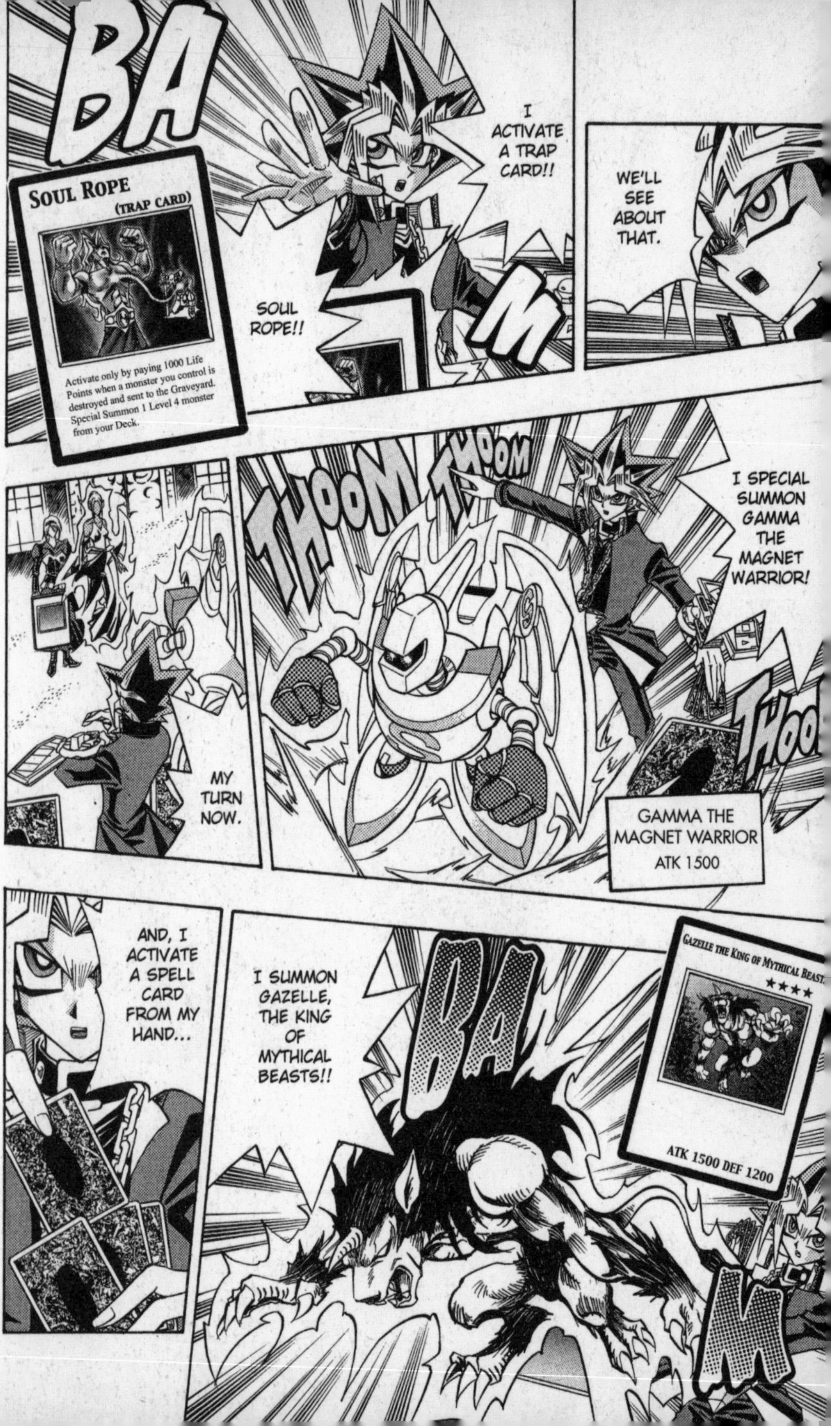
WE'LL SEE ABOUT THAT.
I ACTIVATE A TRAP CARD!!
BA
SOUL ROPE!!
M
SOUL ROPE
(TRAP CARD)
Activate only by paying 1000 Life Points when a monster you control is destroyed and sent to the Graveyard. Special Summon 1 Level 4 monster from your Deck.
I SPECIAL SUMMON GAMMA THE MAGNET WARRIOR!
THOOM
THOOM
THOO
GAMMA THE MAGNET WARRIOR
ATK 1500
MY TURN NOW.
GAZELLE THE KING OF MYTHICAL BEASTS
★★★★
ATK 1500 DEF 1200
I SUMMON GAZELLE, THE KING OF MYTHICAL BEASTS!!
BA
M
AND, I ACTIVATE A SPELL CARD FROM MY HAND...

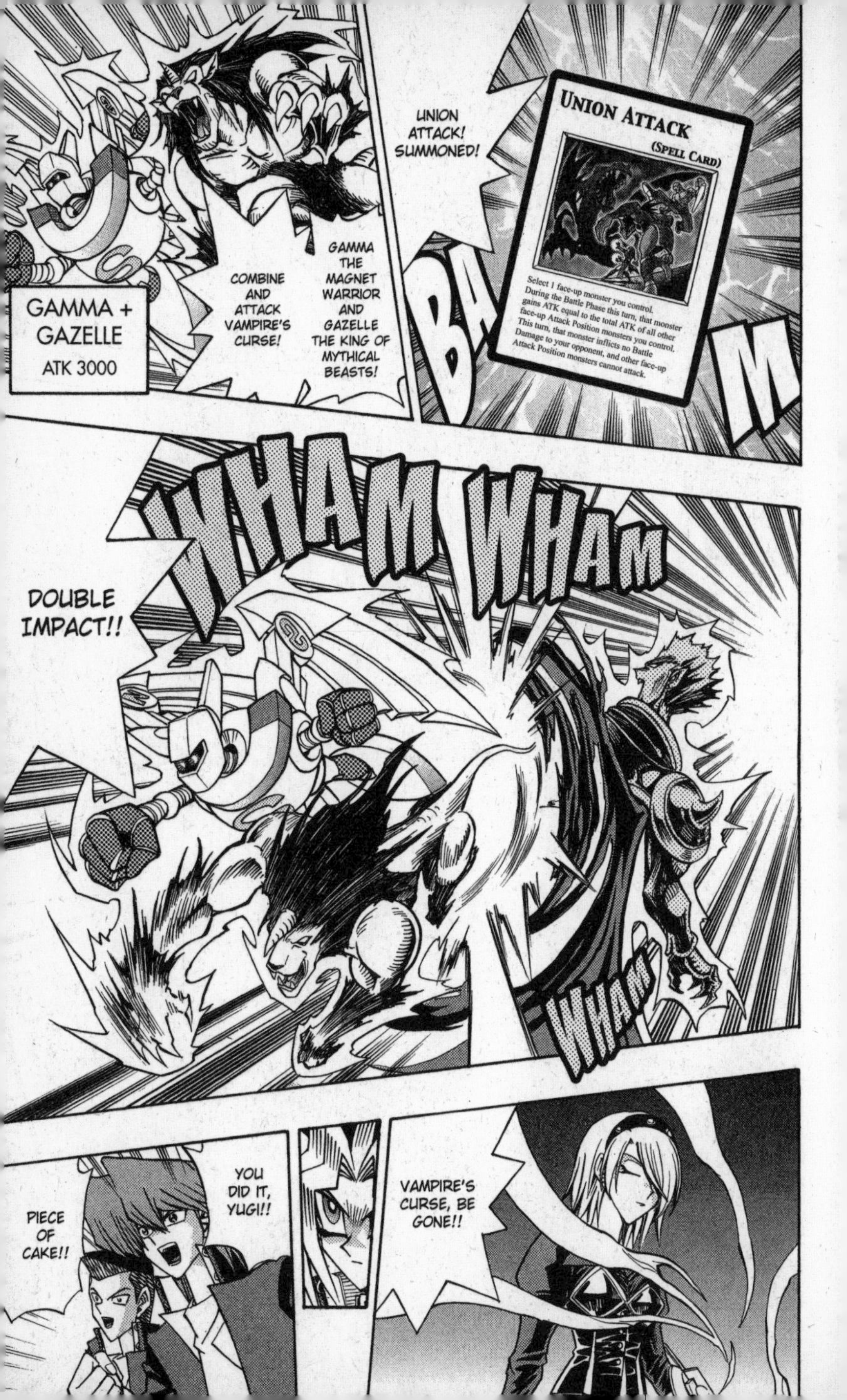
UNION ATTACK! SUMMONED!
UNION ATTACK
(SPELL CARD)
Select 1 face-up monster you control. During the Battle Phase this turn, that monster gains ATK equal to the total ATK of all other face-up Attack Position monsters you control. This turn, that monster inflicts no Battle Damage to your opponent, and other face-up Attack Position monsters cannot attack.
BAM
GAMMA THE MAGNET WARRIOR AND GAZELLE THE KING OF MYTHICAL BEASTS!
COMBINE AND ATTACK VAMPIRE'S CURSE!
GAMMA + GAZELLE
ATK 3000
WHAM WHAM
DOUBLE IMPACT!!
WHAM
VAMPIRE'S CURSE, BE GONE!!
YOU DID IT, YUGI!!
PIECE OF CAKE!!

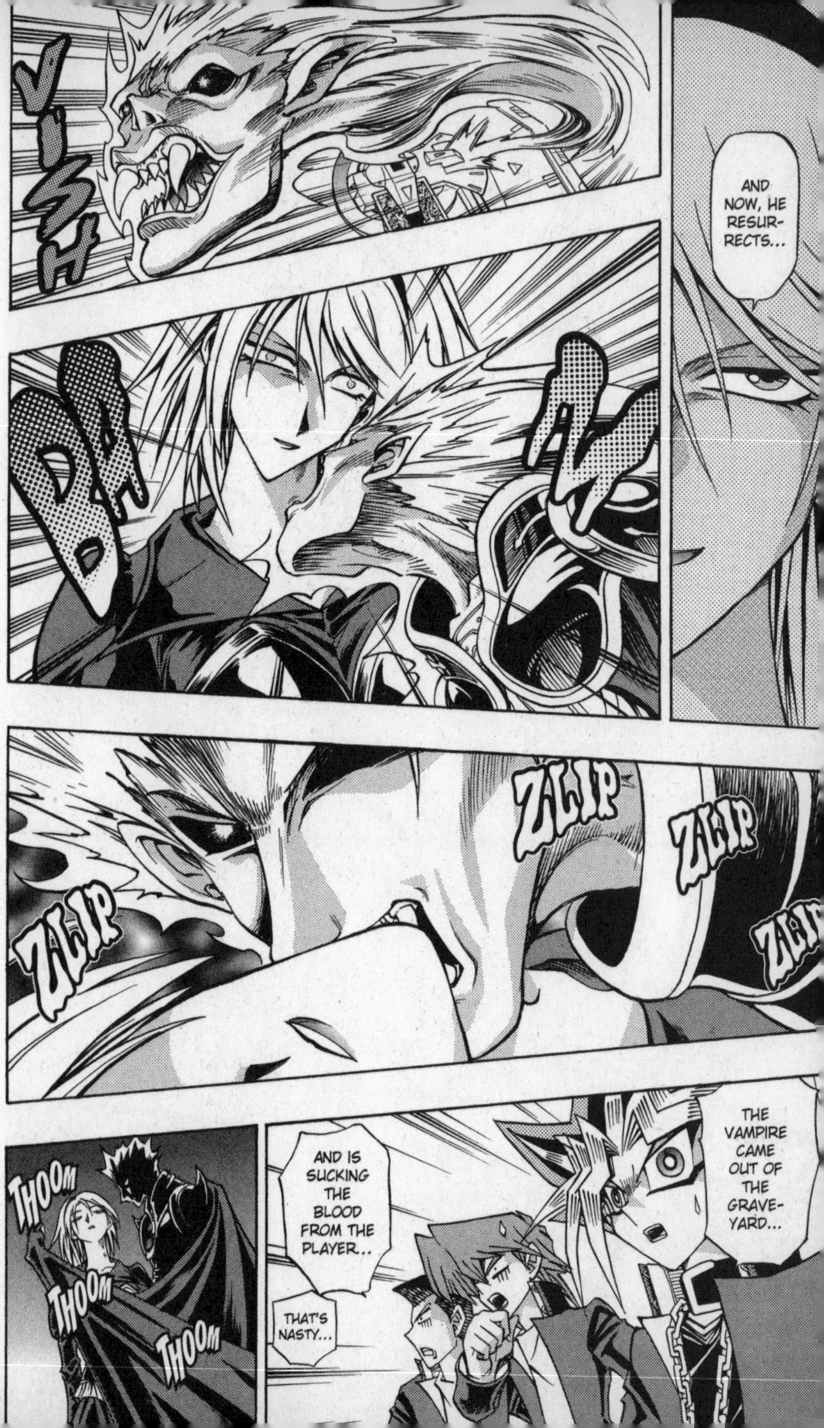
AND NOW, HE RESURRECTS...
VISH
ZLIP
ZLIP
ZLIP
THE VAMPIRE CAME OUT OF THE GRAVEYARD...
AND IS SUCKING THE BLOOD FROM THE PLAYER...
THAT'S NASTY...
THOOM
THOOM
THOOM

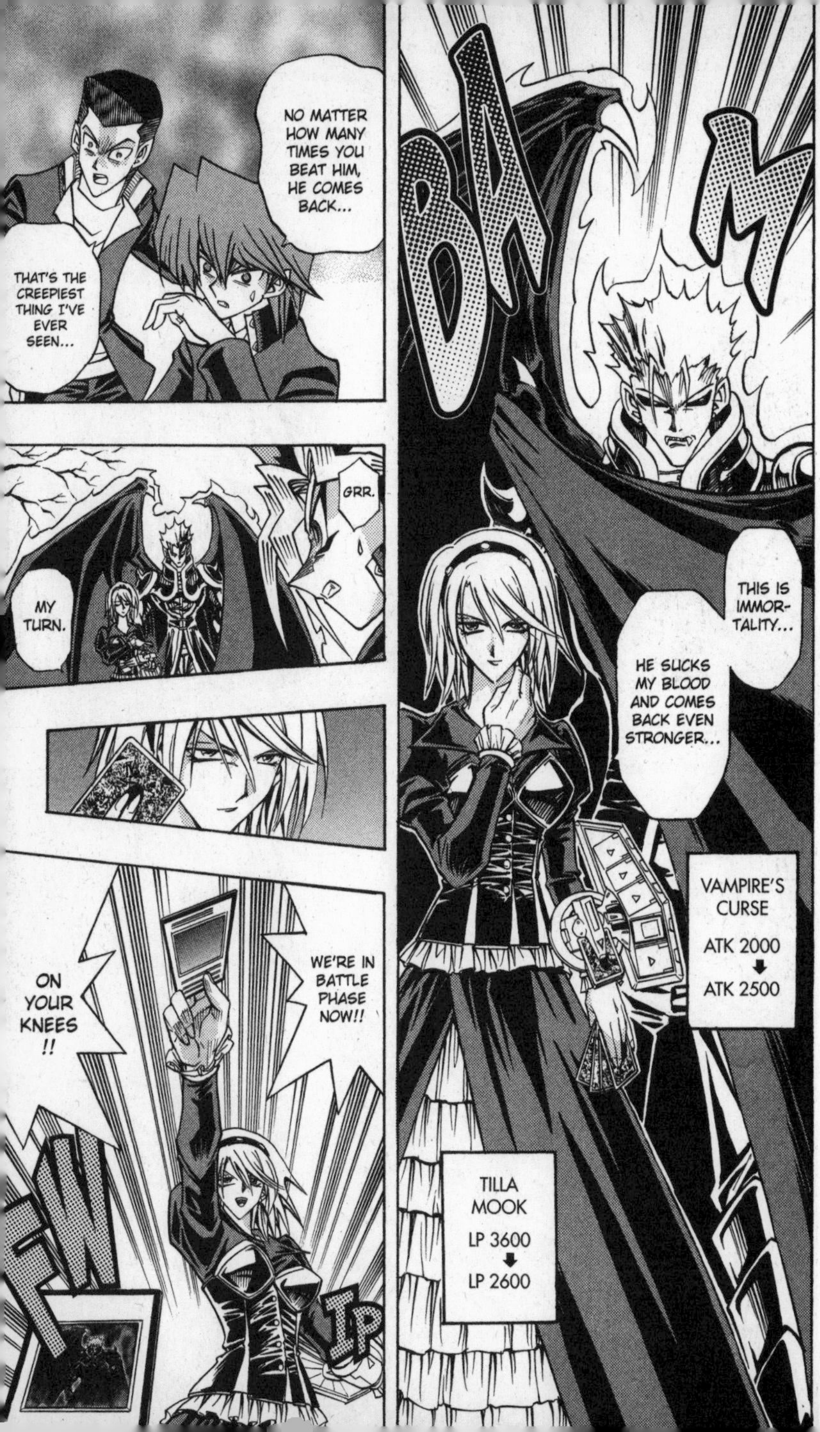
BAM
THIS IS IMMORTALITY...
HE SUCKS MY BLOOD AND COMES BACK EVEN STRONGER...
VAMPIRE'S CURSE
ATK 2000
ATK 2500
TILLA MOOK
LP 3600
LP 2600
NO MATTER HOW MANY TIMES YOU BEAT HIM, HE COMES BACK...
THAT'S THE CREEPIEST THING I'VE EVER SEEN...
GRR.
MY TURN.
WE'RE IN BATTLE PHASE NOW!!
ON YOUR KNEES!!
FW
IP

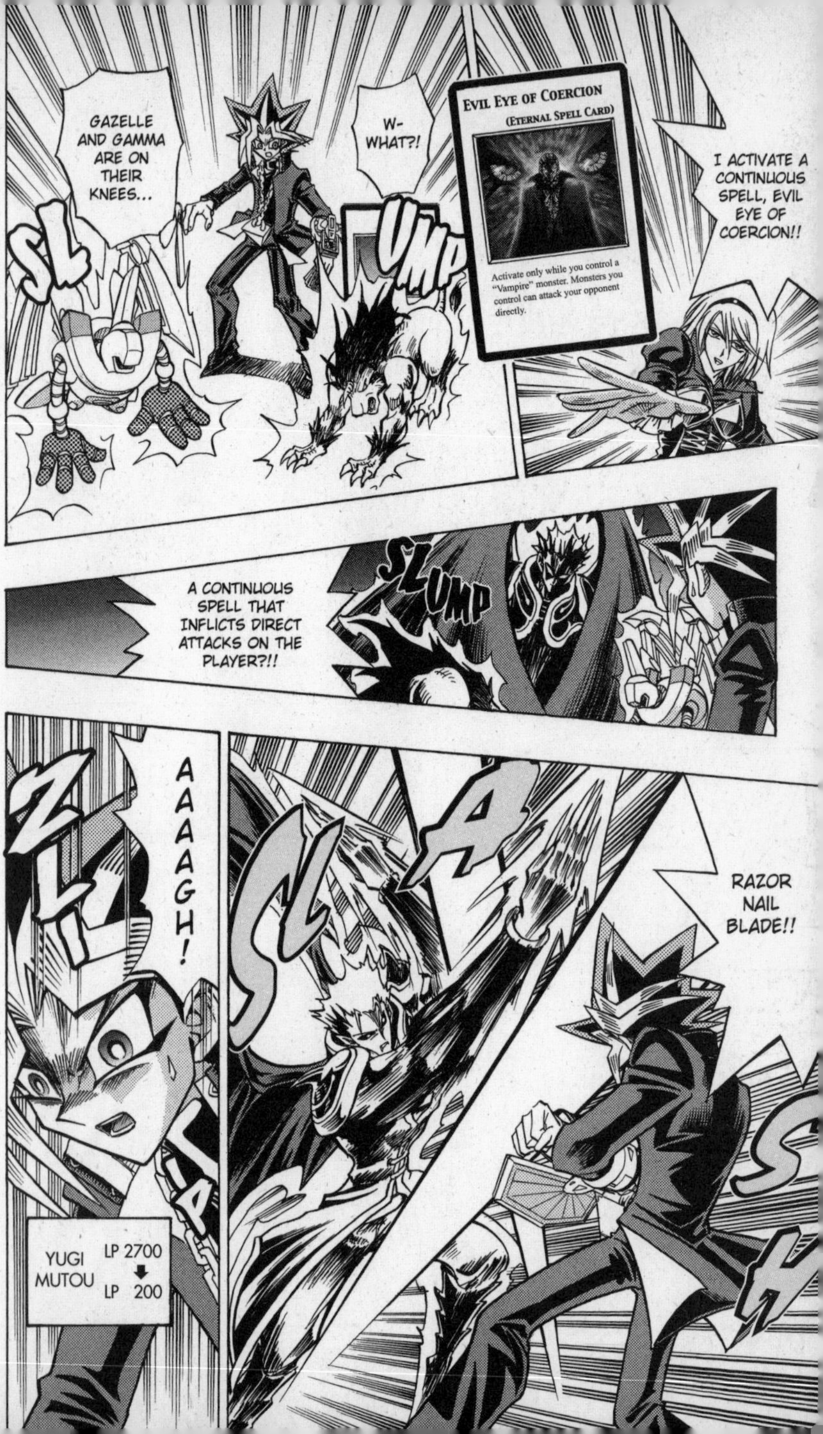
EVIL EYE OF COERCION
(ETERNAL SPELL CARD)
Activate only while you control a "Vampire" monster. Monsters you control can attack your opponent directly.
I ACTIVATE A CONTINUOUS SPELL, EVIL EYE OF COERCION!!
W- WHAT?!
UMP
GAZELLE AND GAMMA ARE ON THEIR KNEES...
SL
SLUMP
A CONTINUOUS SPELL THAT INFLICTS DIRECT ATTACKS ON THE PLAYER?!!
RAZOR NAIL BLADE!!
SH
SLA
AAAAAGH!
YUGI MUTOU LP 2700 ➡ LP 200

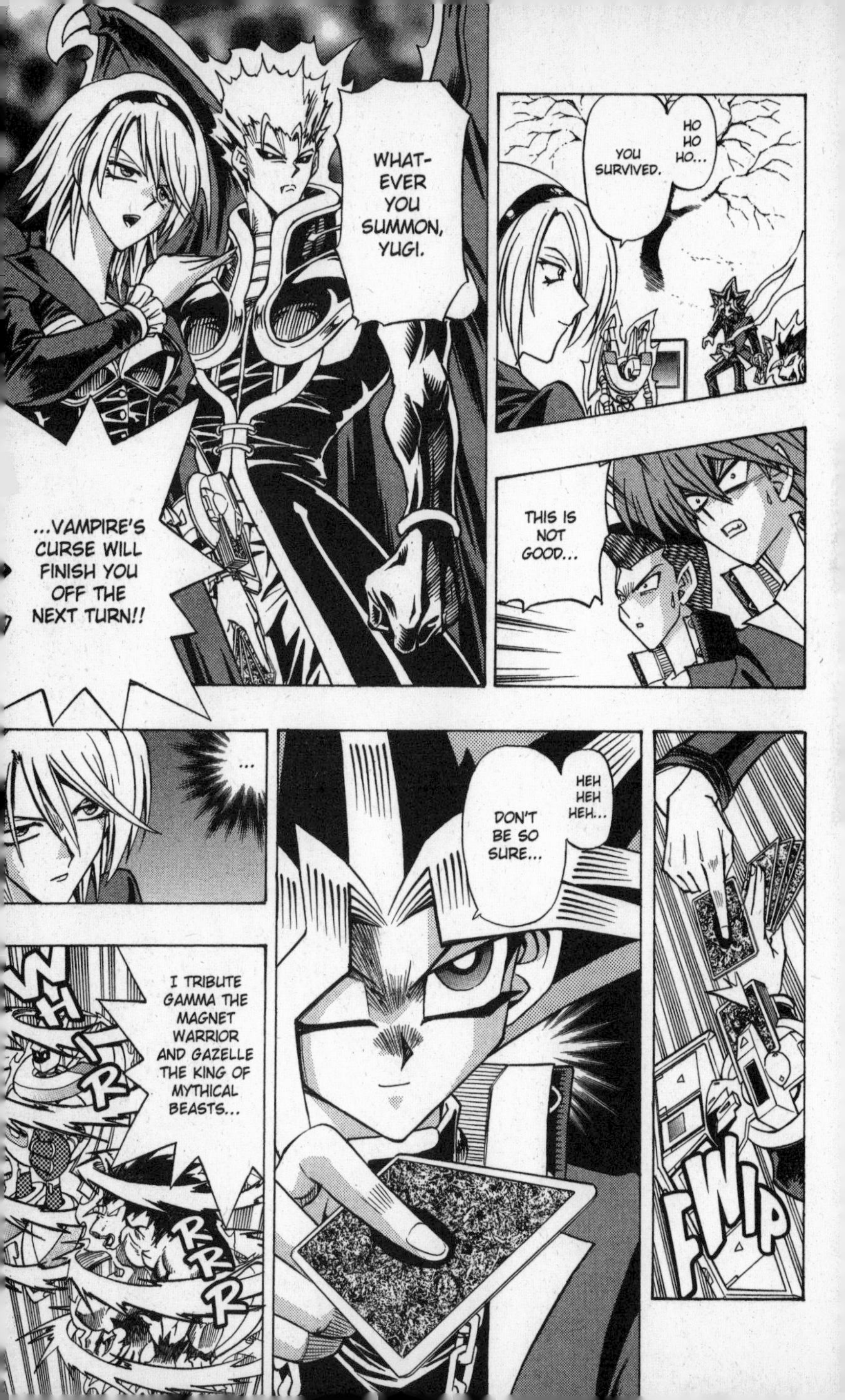
HO HO HO...
YOU SURVIVED.
THIS IS NOT GOOD...
WHATEVER YOU SUMMON, YUGI.
...VAMPIRE'S CURSE WILL FINISH YOU OFF THE NEXT TURN!!
FWIP
HEH HEH HEH...
DON'T BE SO SURE...
...
I TRIBUTE GAMMA THE MAGNET WARRIOR AND GAZELLE THE KING OF MYTHICAL BEASTS...
WHIRRRR

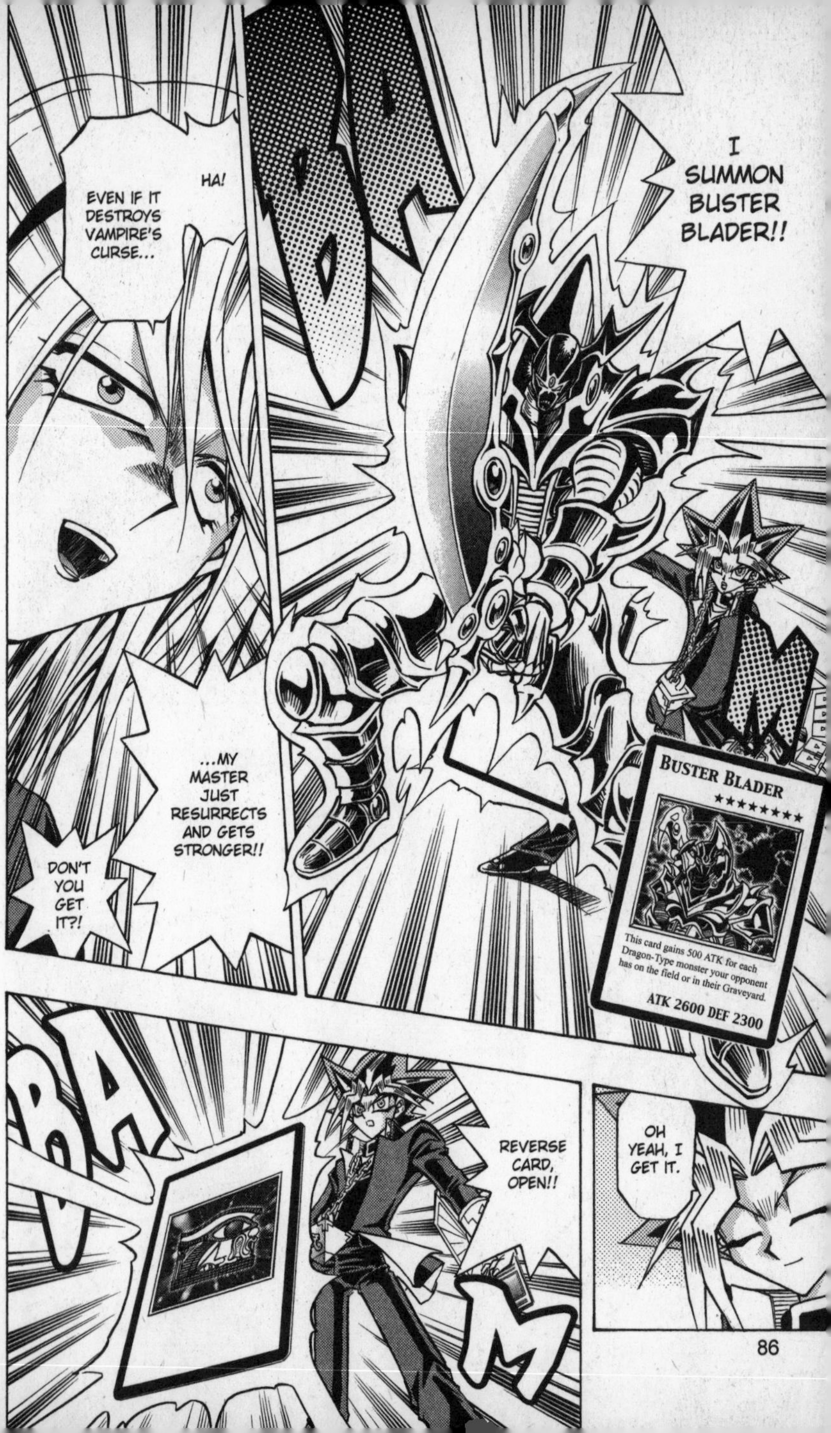
I SUMMON BUSTER BLADER!!
BUSTER BLADER
This card gains 500 ATK for each Dragon-Type monster your opponent has on the field or in their Graveyard.
ATK 2600 DEF 2300
HA!
EVEN IF IT DESTROYS VAMPIRE'S CURSE...
...MY MASTER JUST RESURRECTS AND GETS STRONGER!!
DON'T YOU GET IT?!
OH YEAH, I GET IT.
REVERSE CARD, OPEN!!

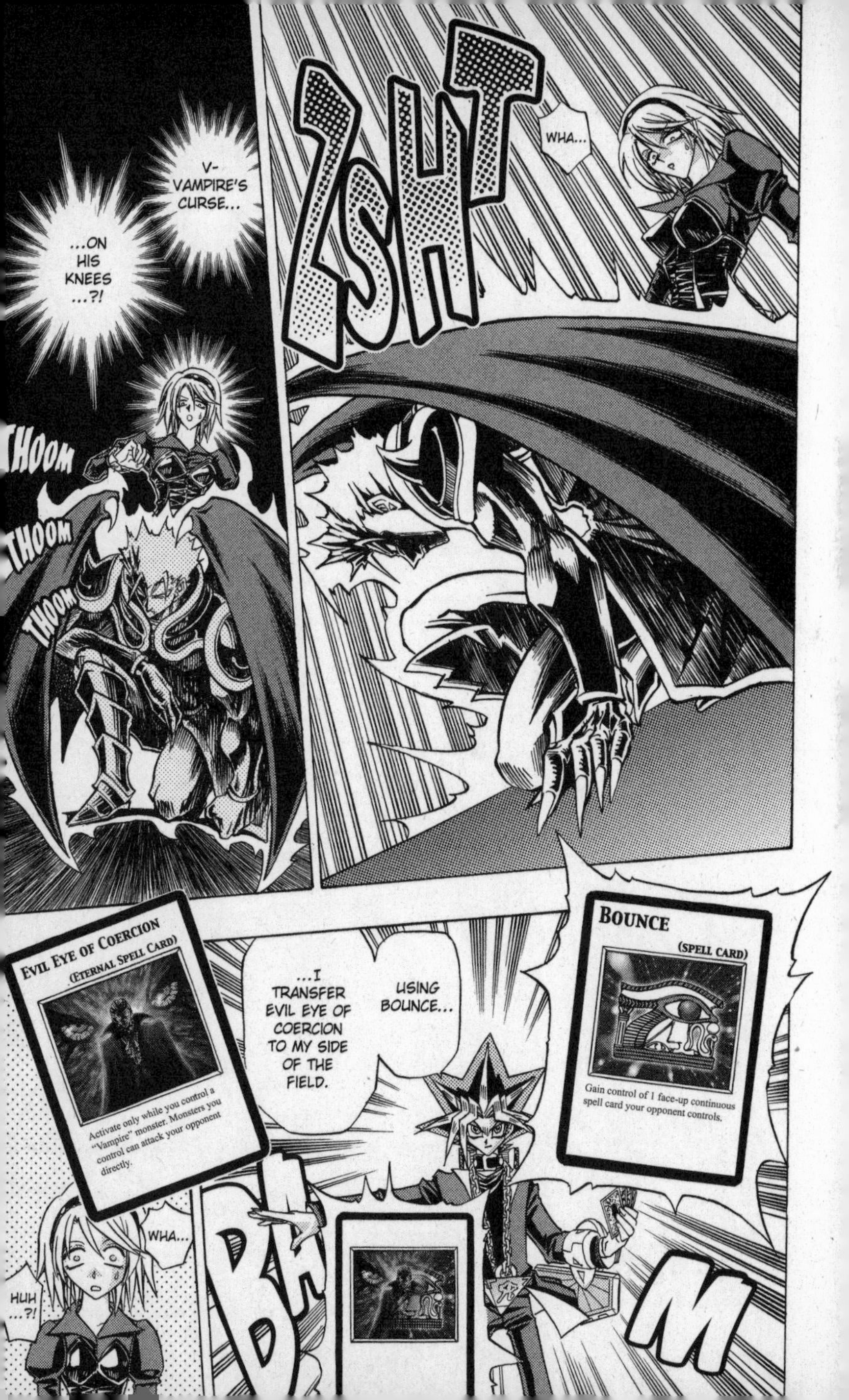

ZSHT
WHA...
V- VAMPIRE'S CURSE...
...ON HIS KNEES ...?!
THOOM
THOOM
THOOM
BOUNCE
(SPELL CARD)
Gain control of 1 face-up continuous spell card your opponent controls.
USING BOUNCE...
...I TRANSFER EVIL EYE OF COERCION TO MY SIDE OF THE FIELD.
EVIL EYE OF COERCION
EVIL EYE OF COERCION
(ETERNAL SPELL CARD)
Activate only while you control a "Vampire" monster. Monsters you control can attack your opponent directly.
WHA...
HUH ...?!

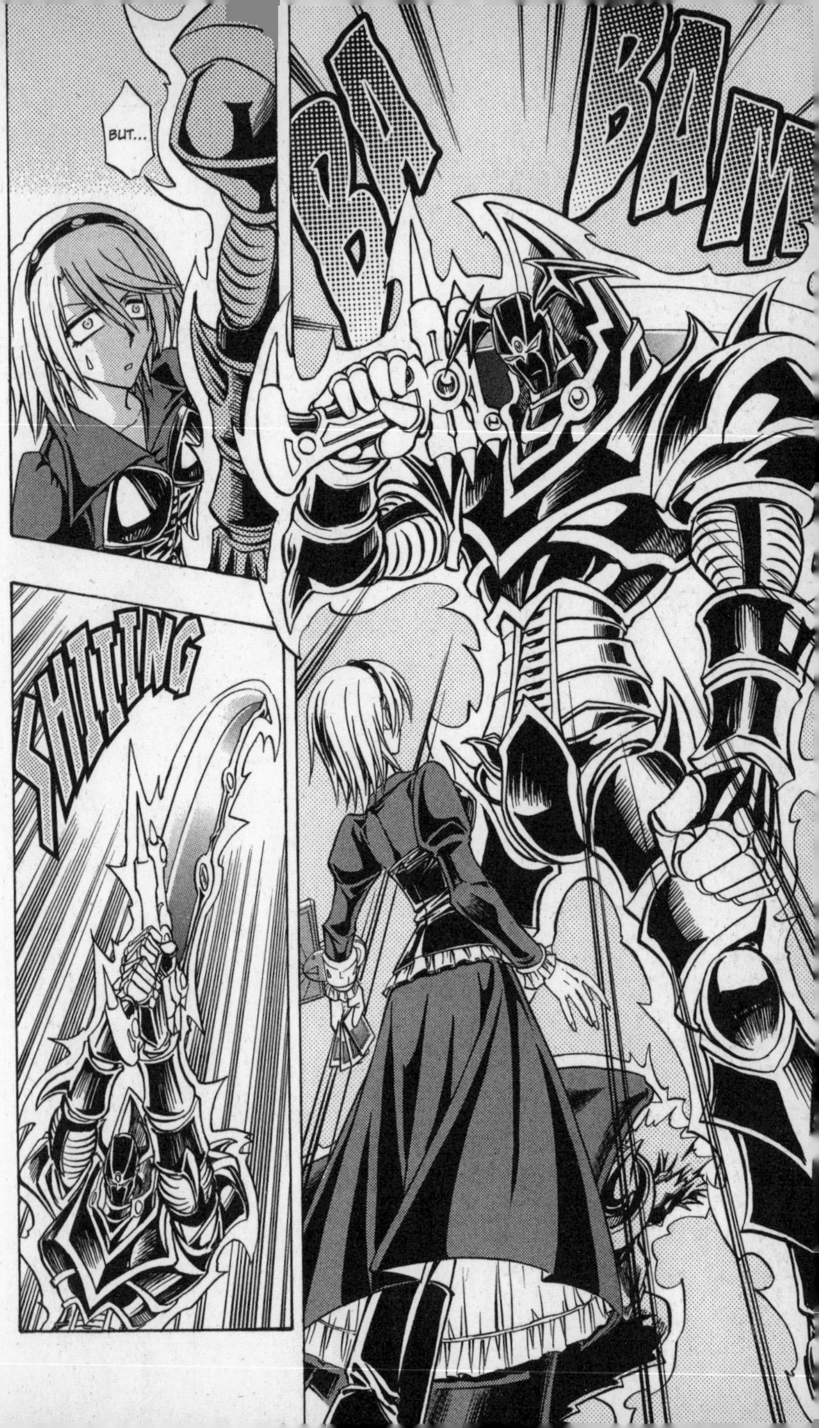
BA
BAM
BUT...
SHIIIING

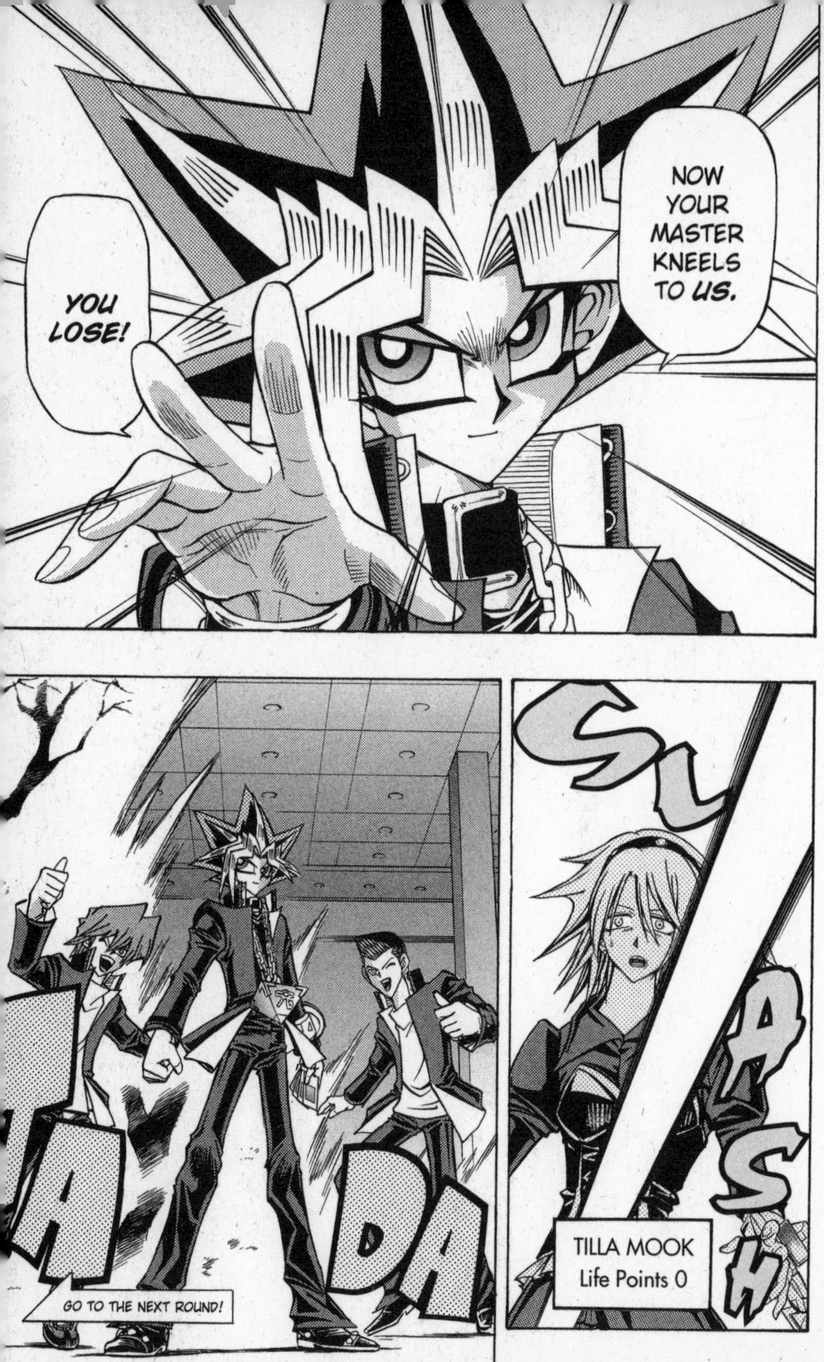
NOW YOUR MASTER KNEELS TO US.
YOU LOSE!
SLASH
TILLA MOOK
Life Points 0
TA DA
GO TO THE NEXT ROUND!

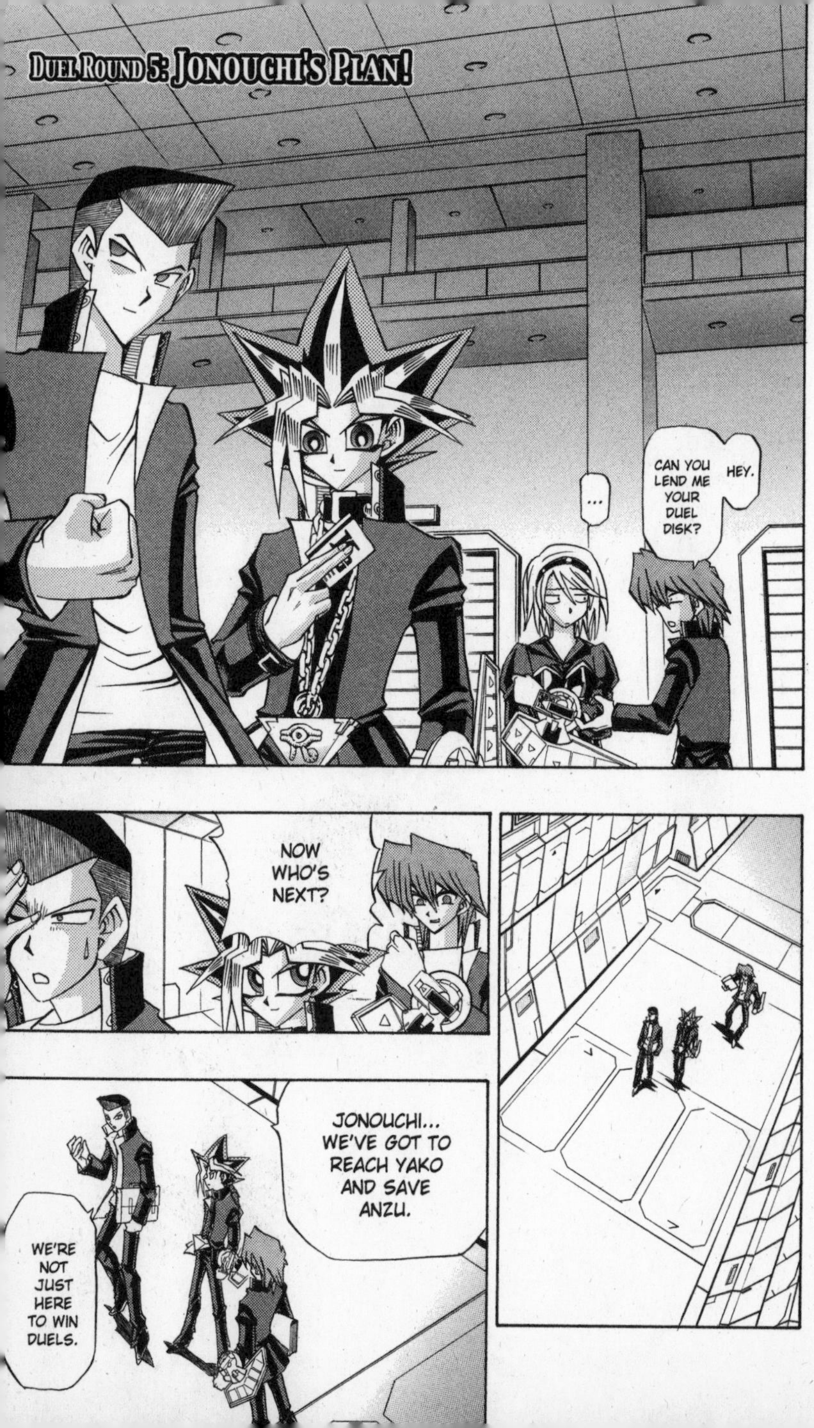
DUEL ROUND 5: JONOUCHI'S PLAN!
HEY.
CAN YOU LEND ME YOUR DUEL DISK?
...
NOW WHO'S NEXT?
JONOUCHI... WE'VE GOT TO REACH YAKO AND SAVE ANZU.
WE'RE NOT JUST HERE TO WIN DUELS.

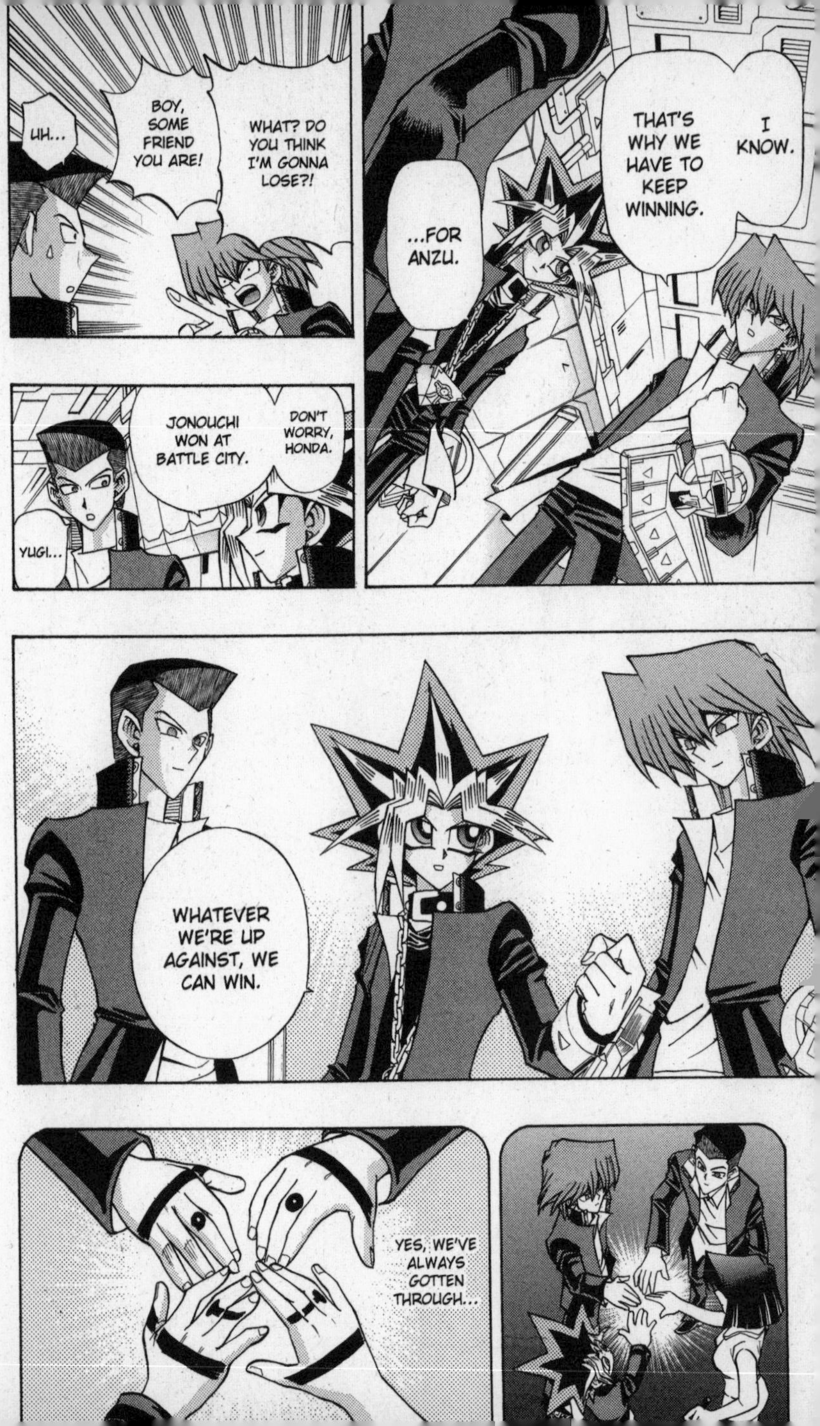
I KNOW.
THAT'S WHY WE HAVE TO KEEP WINNING.
...FOR ANZU.
WHAT? DO YOU THINK I'M GONNA LOSE?!
BOY, SOME FRIEND YOU ARE!
UH...
DON'T WORRY, HONDA.
JONOUCHI WON AT BATTLE CITY.
YUGI...
WHATEVER WE'RE UP AGAINST, WE CAN WIN.
YES, WE'VE ALWAYS GOTTEN THROUGH...

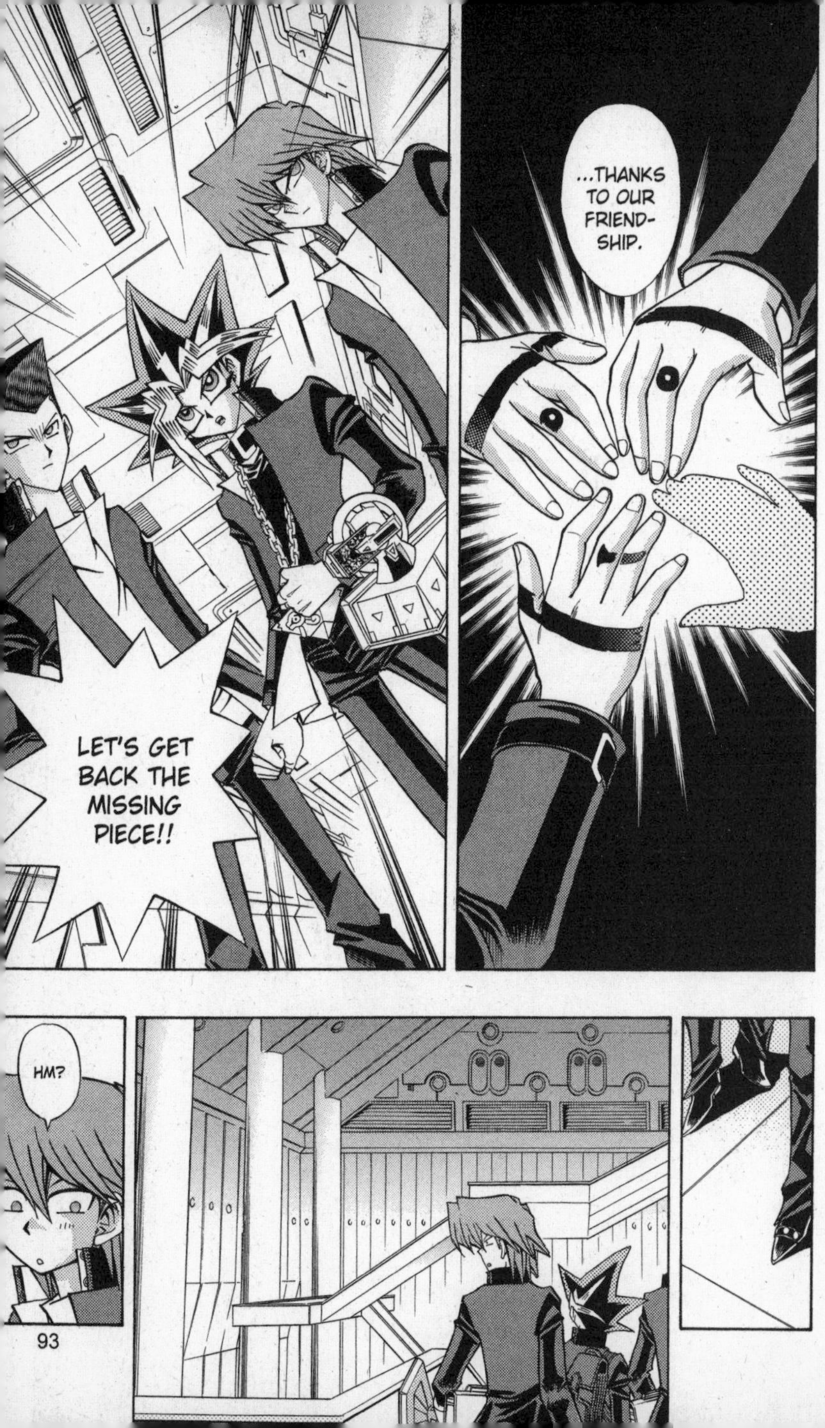
...THANKS TO OUR FRIEND-SHIP.
LET'S GET BACK THE MISSING PIECE!!
HM?

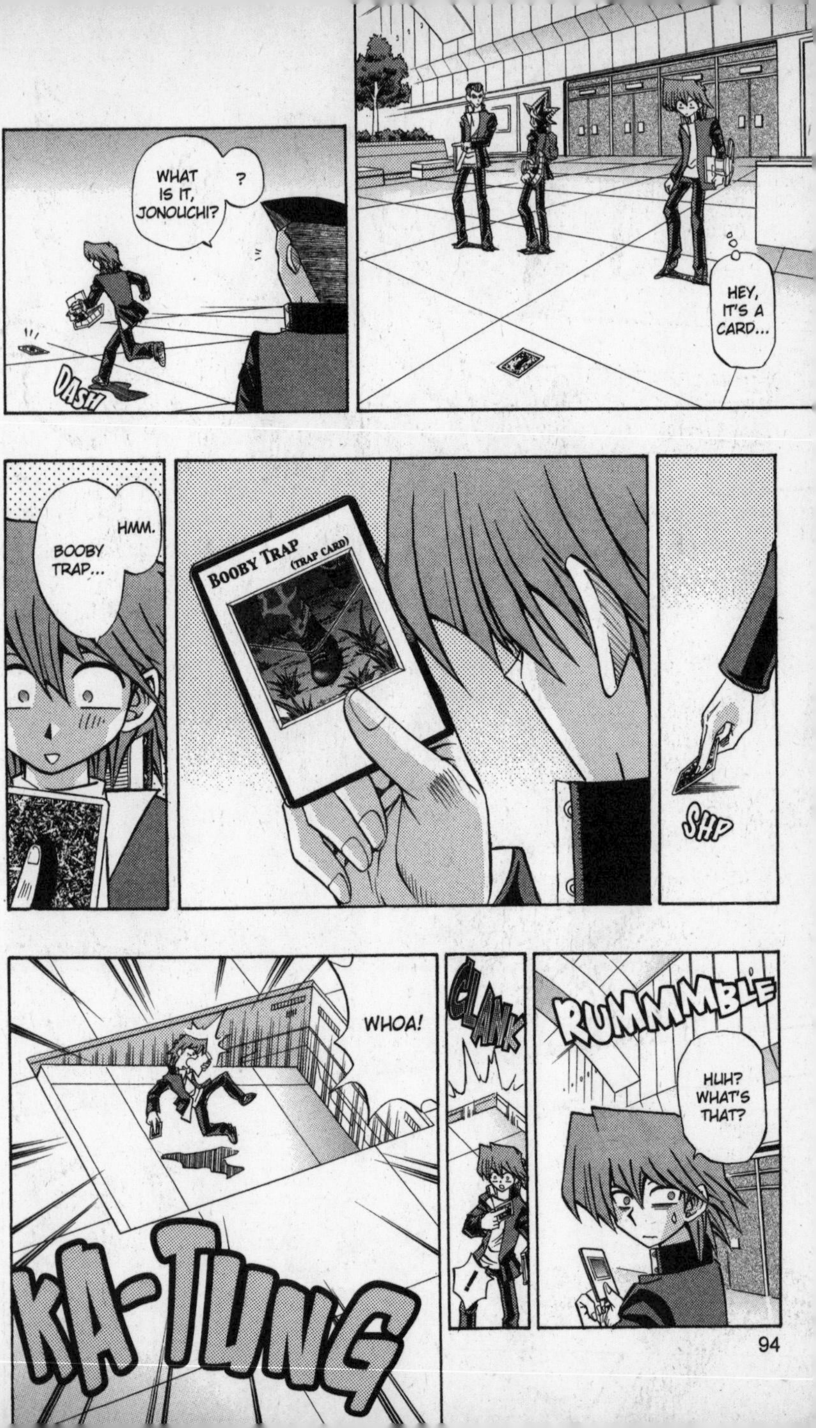
HEY, IT'S A CARD...
?
WHAT IS IT, JONOUCHI?
DASH
SHP
BOOBY TRAP (TRAP CARD)
HMM.
BOOBY TRAP...
RUMMMBLE
HUH? WHAT'S THAT?
CLANK
!
WHOA!
KA-TUNG

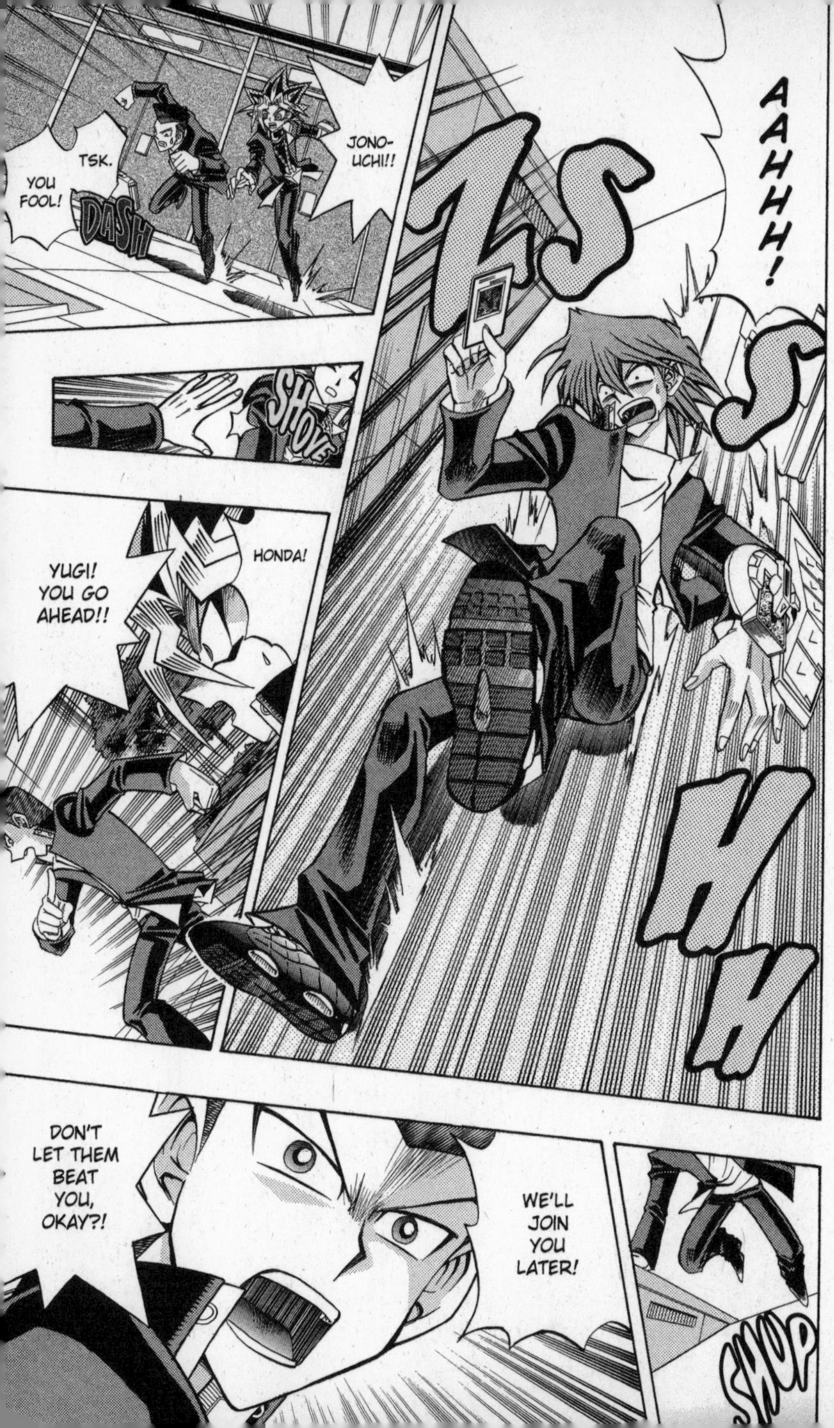
AAHHHH!
JONO-UCHI!!
TSK.
YOU FOOL!
DASH
SHOVE
HONDA!
YUGI! YOU GO AHEAD!!
SHUP
DON'T LET THEM BEAT YOU, OKAY?!
WE'LL JOIN YOU LATER!

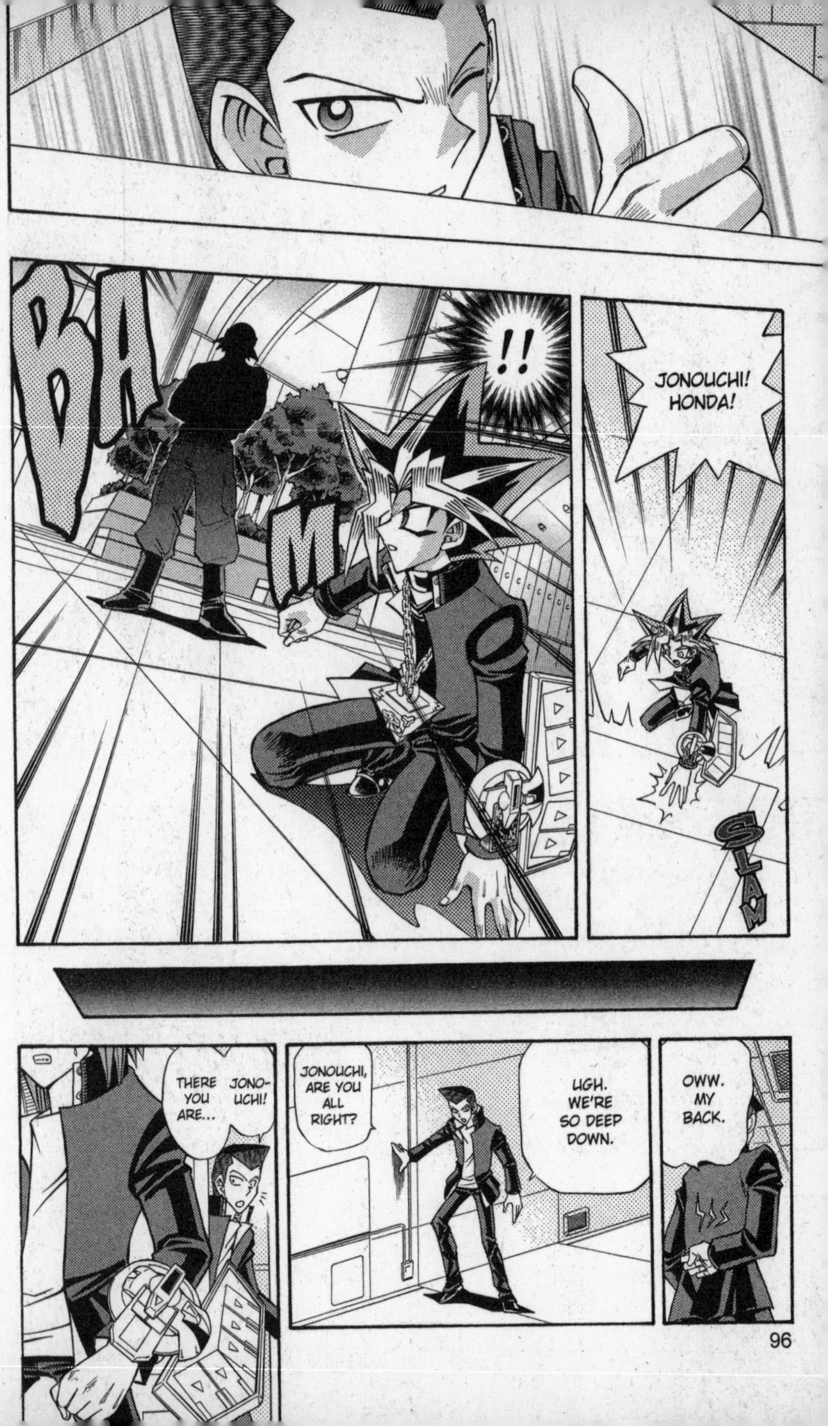
JONOUCHI! HONDA!
SLAM
!!
BAM
OWW. MY BACK.
UGH. WE'RE SO DEEP DOWN.
JONOUCHI, ARE YOU ALL RIGHT?
JONO-UCHI!
THERE YOU ARE...

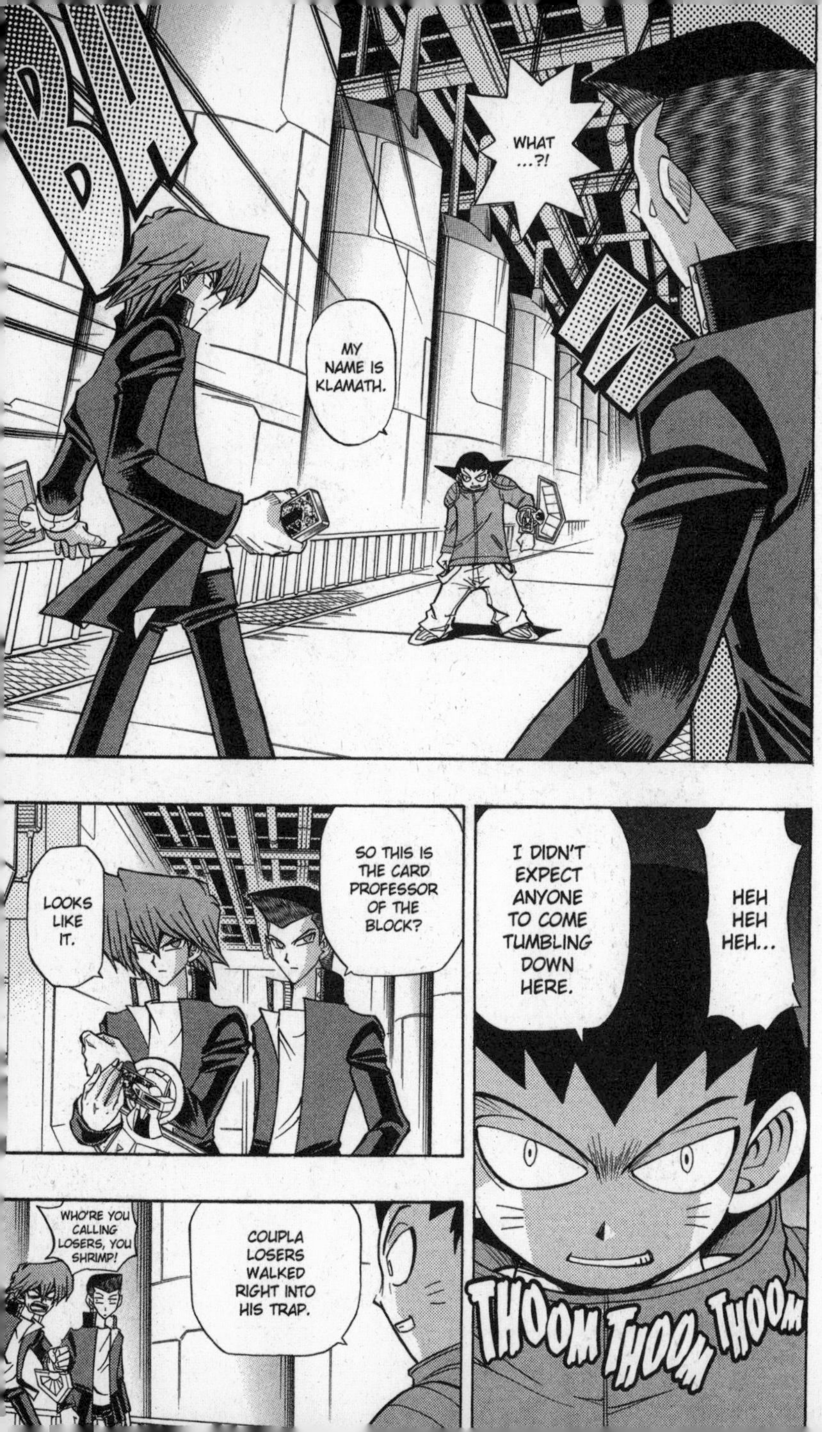
WHAT ...?!
MY NAME IS KLAMATH.
HEH HEH HEH...
I DIDN'T EXPECT ANYONE TO COME TUMBLING DOWN HERE.
THOOM THOOM THOOM
SO THIS IS THE CARD PROFESSOR OF THE BLOCK?
LOOKS LIKE IT.
COUPLA LOSERS WALKED RIGHT INTO HIS TRAP.
WHO'RE YOU CALLING LOSERS, YOU SHRIMP!

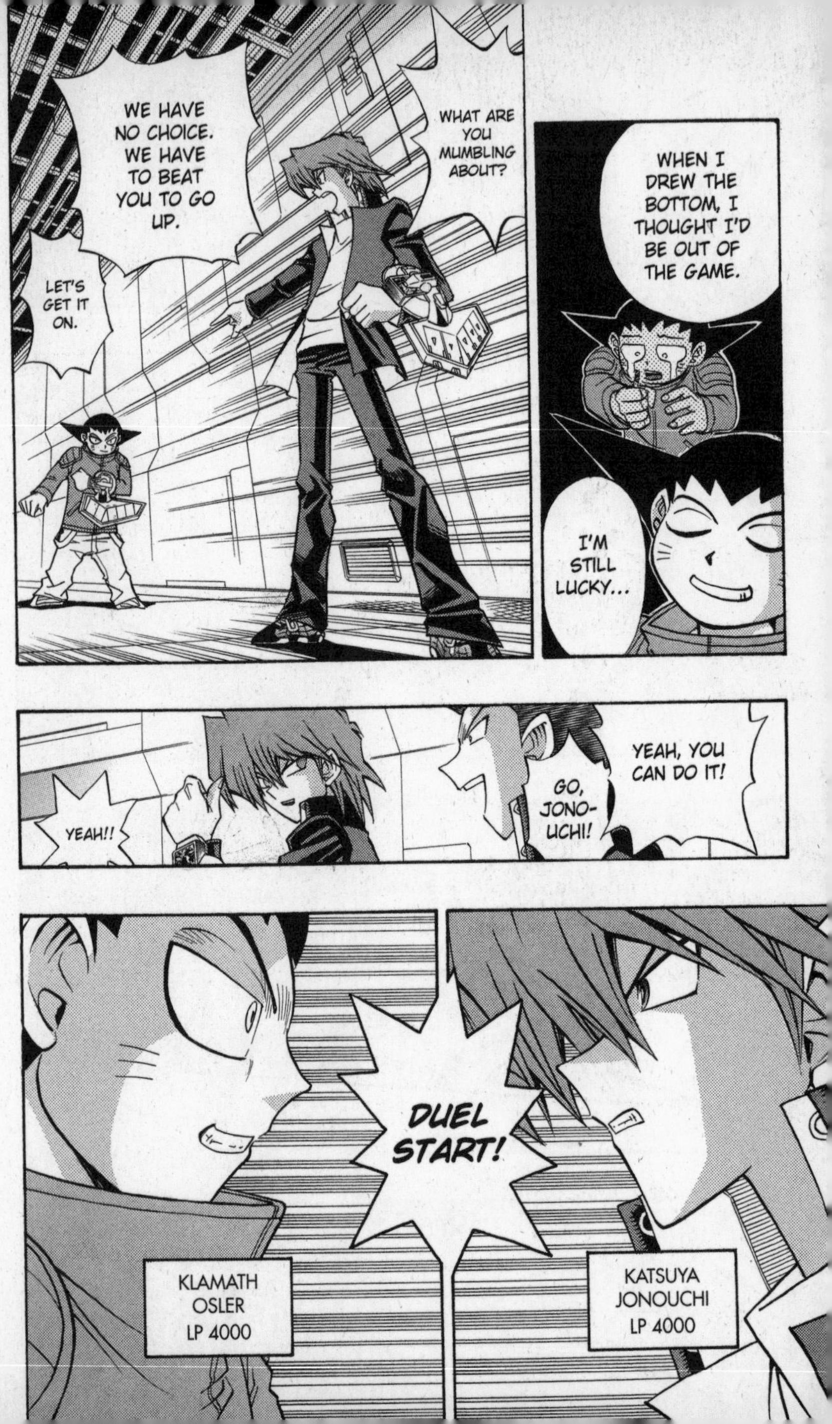
WHEN I DREW THE BOTTOM, I THOUGHT I'D BE OUT OF THE GAME.
I'M STILL LUCKY...
WHAT ARE YOU MUMBLING ABOUT?
WE HAVE NO CHOICE. WE HAVE TO BEAT YOU TO GO UP.
LET'S GET IT ON.
YEAH, YOU CAN DO IT!
GO, JONOUCHI!
YEAH!!
KATSUYA JONOUCHI LP 4000
DUEL START!
KLAMATH OSLER LP 4000

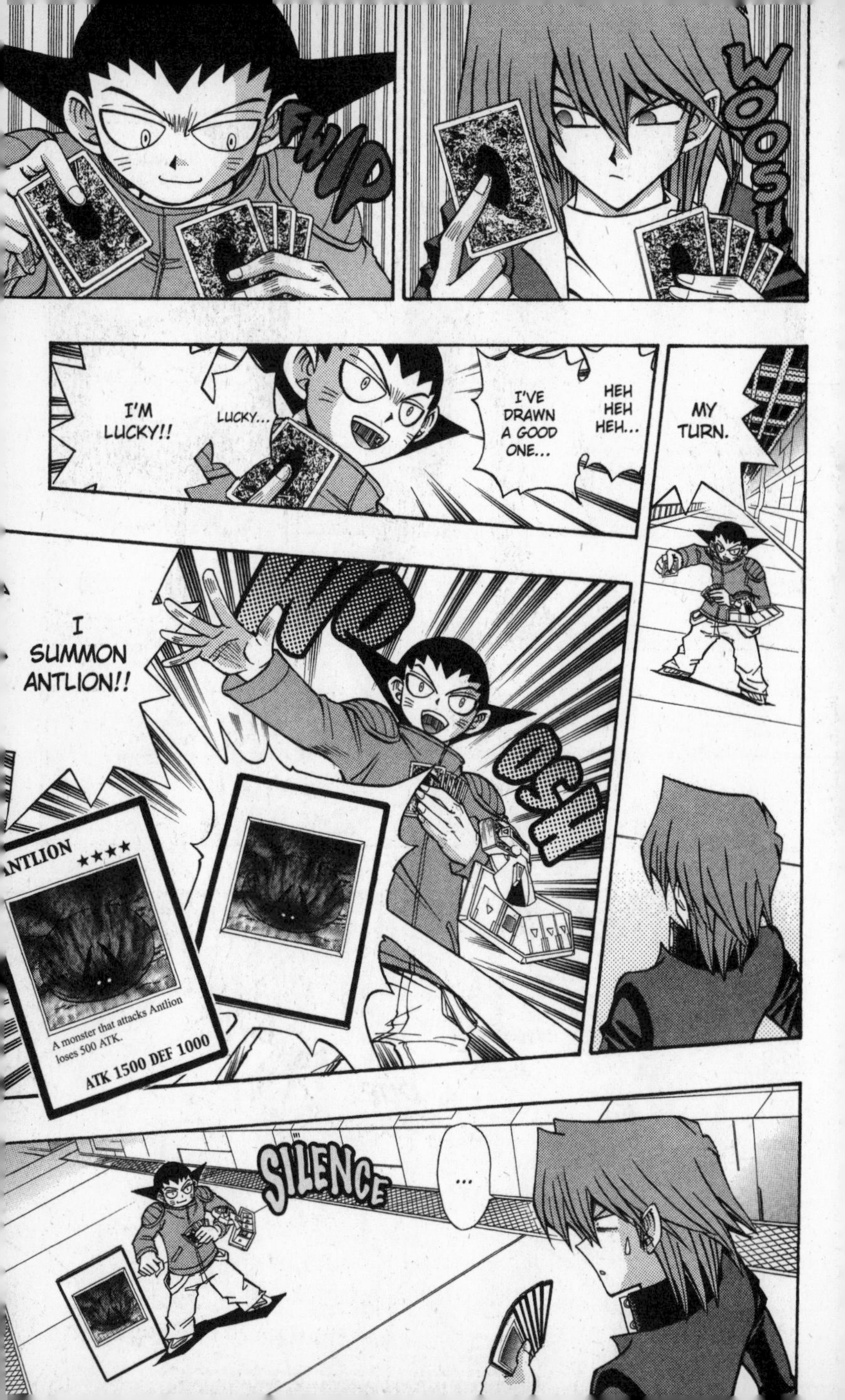
WOOSH
FWIP
MY TURN.
HEH HEH HEH...
I'VE DRAWN A GOOD ONE...
LUCKY...
I'M LUCKY!!
I SUMMON ANTLION!!
ANTLION ★★★★
A monster that attacks Antlion loses 500 ATK.
ATK 1500 DEF 1000
...
SILENCE

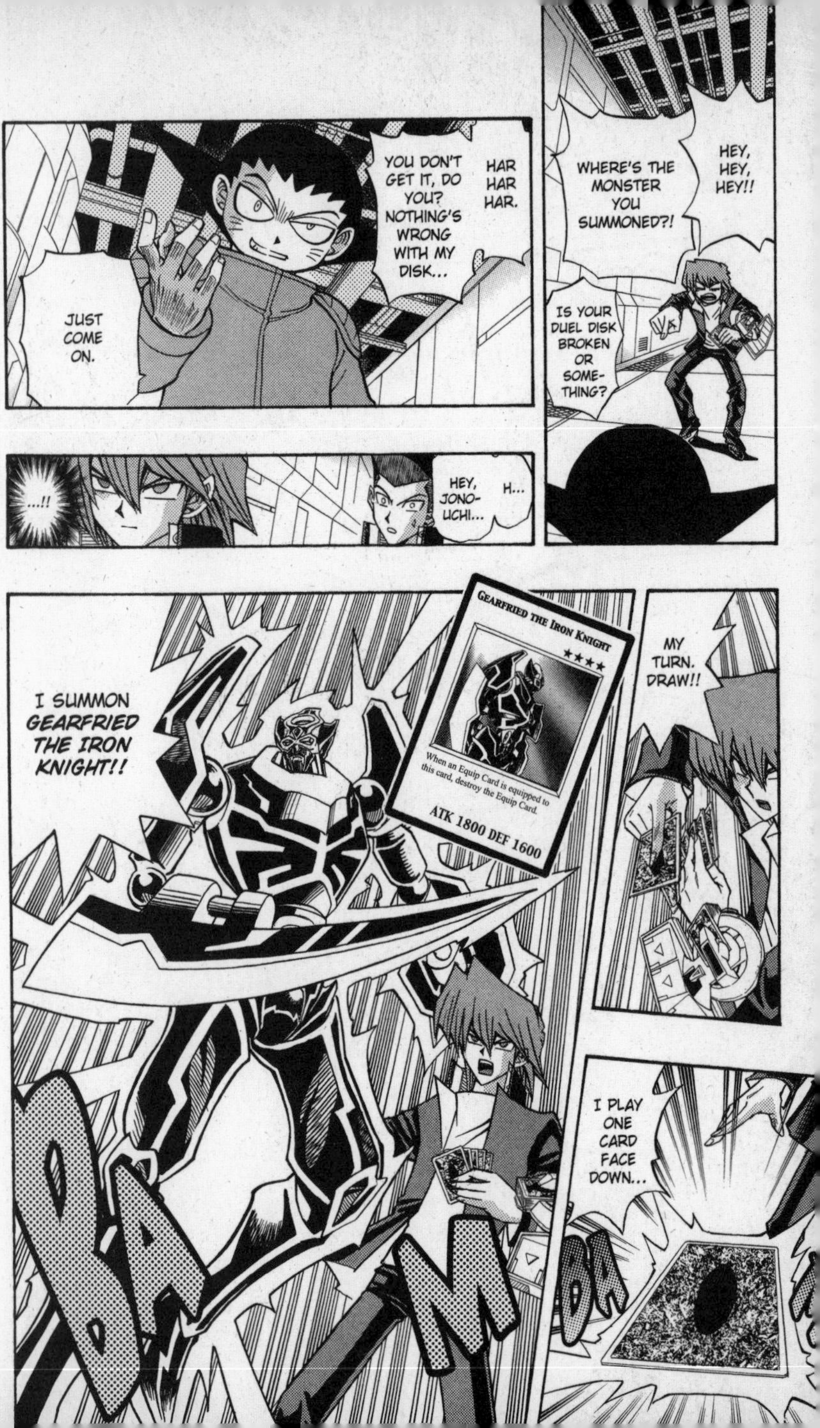
HEY, HEY, HEY!!
WHERE'S THE MONSTER YOU SUMMONED?!
IS YOUR DUEL DISK BROKEN OR SOME-THING?
HAR HAR HAR.
YOU DON'T GET IT, DO YOU? NOTHING'S WRONG WITH MY DISK...
JUST COME ON.
H...
HEY, JONO-UCHI...
...!!
MY TURN. DRAW!!
I PLAY ONE CARD FACE DOWN...
I SUMMON GEARFRIED THE IRON KNIGHT!!
GEARFRIED THE IRON KNIGHT
When an Equip Card is equipped to this card, destroy the Equip Card.
ATK 1800 DEF 1600
BAM

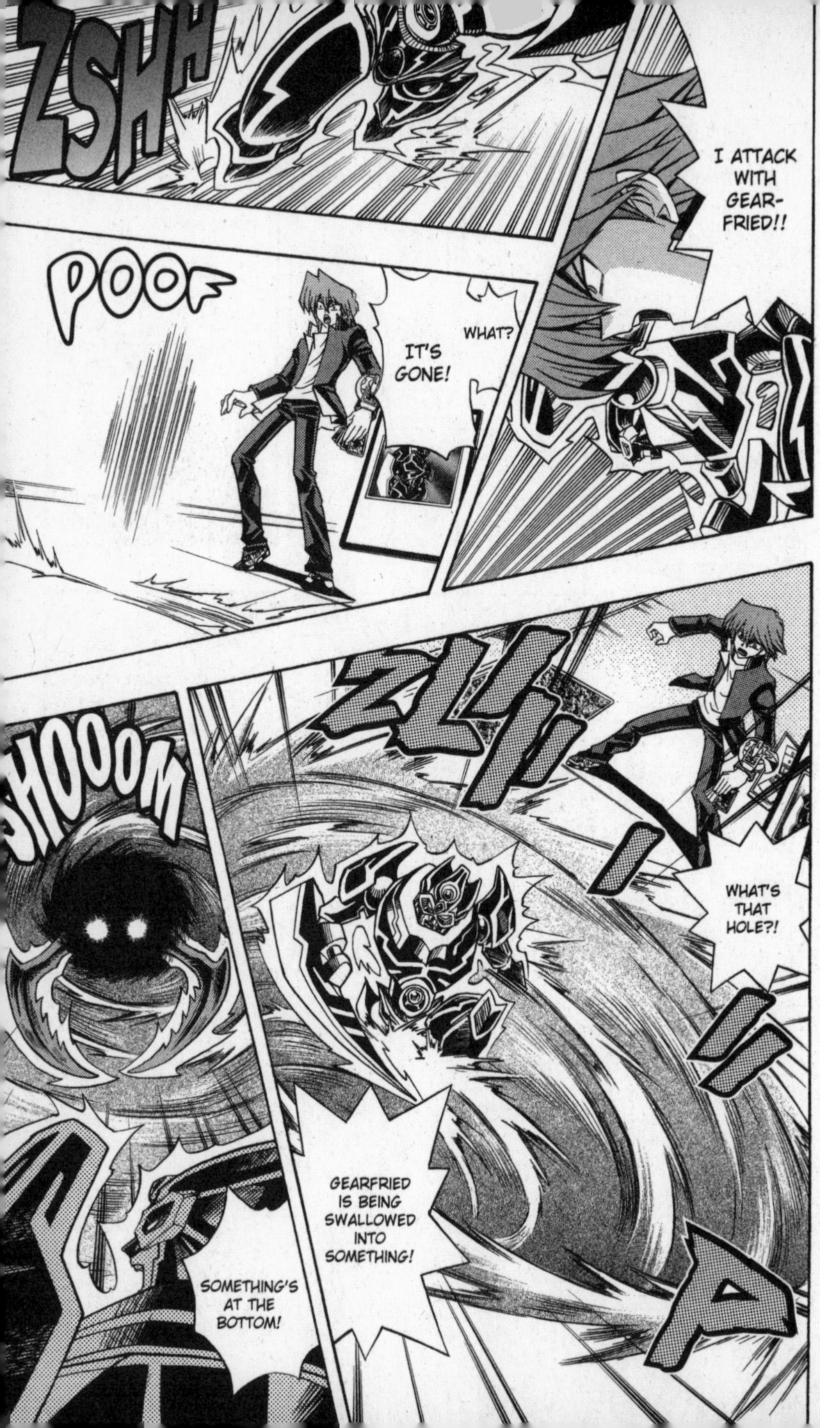
I ATTACK WITH GEAR-FRIED!!
ZSHH
POOF
WHAT?
IT'S GONE!
WHAT'S THAT HOLE?!
GEARFRIED IS BEING SWALLOWED INTO SOMETHING!
SHOOOM
SOMETHING'S AT THE BOTTOM!

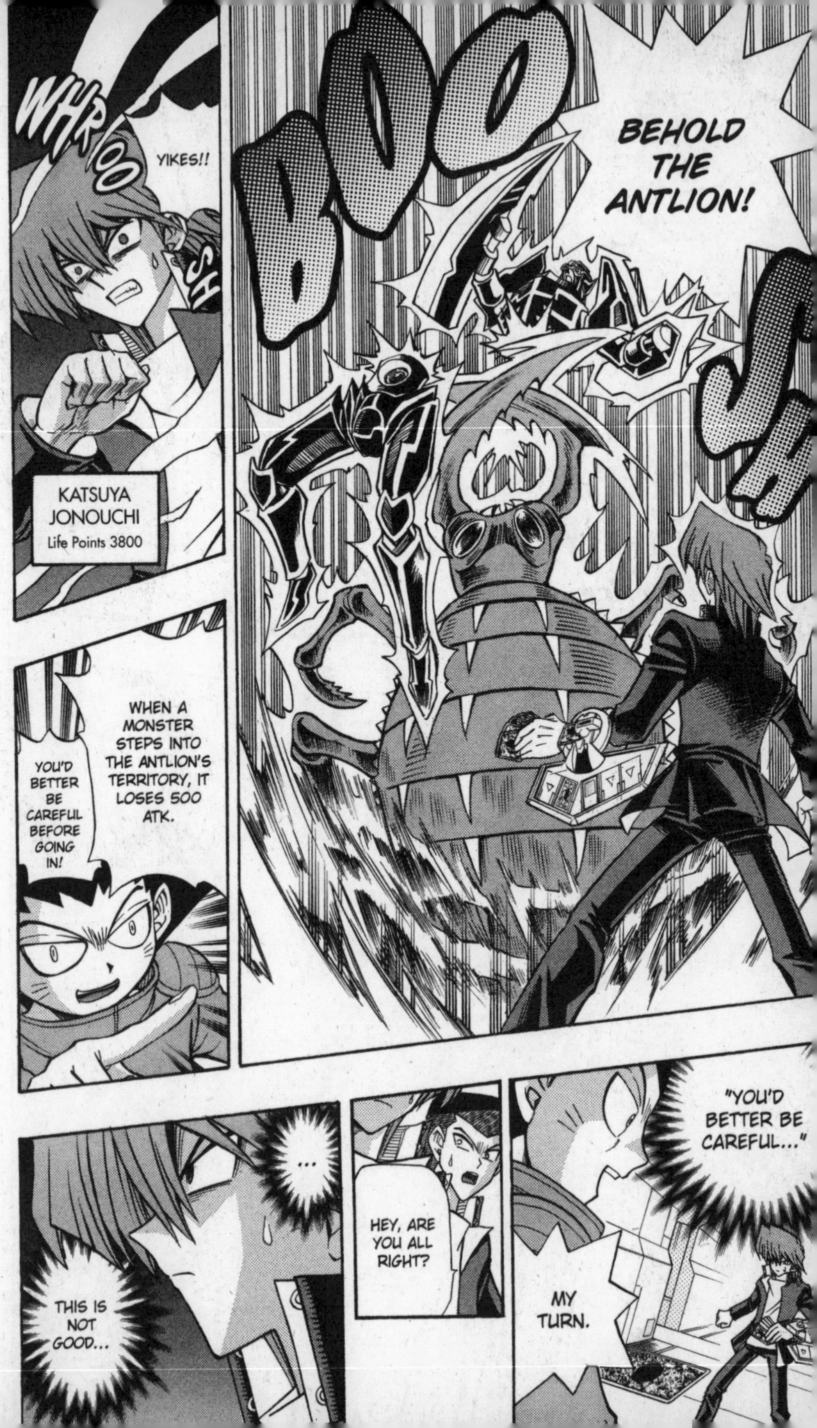

BOOOSH
BEHOLD THE ANTLION!
WHROOSH
YIKES!!
KATSUYA JONOUCHI
Life Points 3800
WHEN A MONSTER STEPS INTO THE ANTLION'S TERRITORY, IT LOSES 500 ATK.
YOU'D BETTER BE CAREFUL BEFORE GOING IN!
"YOU'D BETTER BE CAREFUL..."
MY TURN.
HEY, ARE YOU ALL RIGHT?
...
THIS IS NOT GOOD...

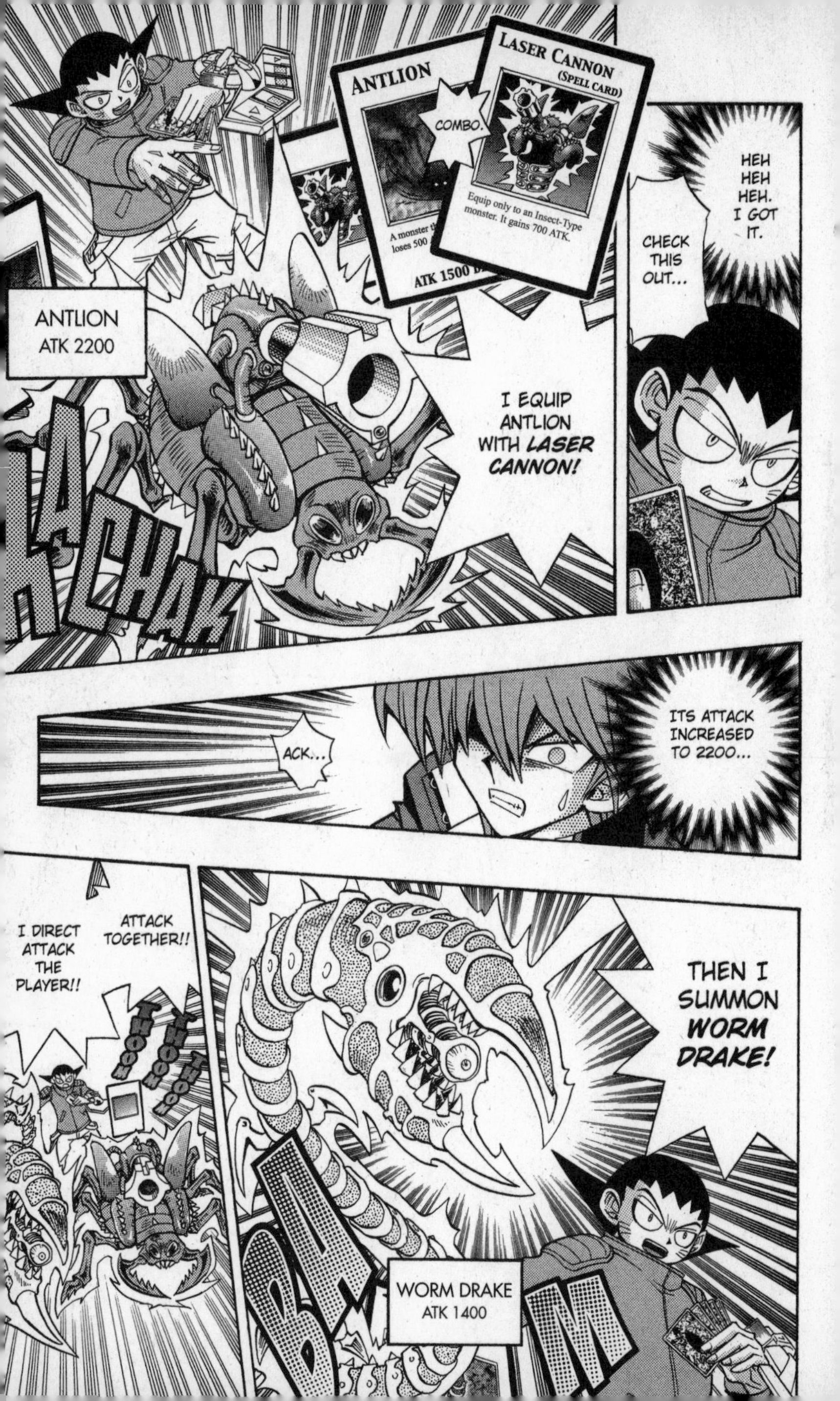
HEH HEH HEH. I GOT IT.
CHECK THIS OUT...
LASER CANNON
(SPELL CARD)
Equip only to an Insect-Type monster. It gains 700 ATK.
ANTLION
COMBO.
ATK 1500
I EQUIP ANTLION WITH LASER CANNON!
ANTLION
ATK 2200
CHAK CHAK
ITS ATTACK INCREASED TO 2200...
ACK...
THEN I SUMMON WORM DRAKE!
WORM DRAKE
ATK 1400
ATTACK TOGETHER!!
I DIRECT ATTACK THE PLAYER!!
THOOM THOOM THOOM

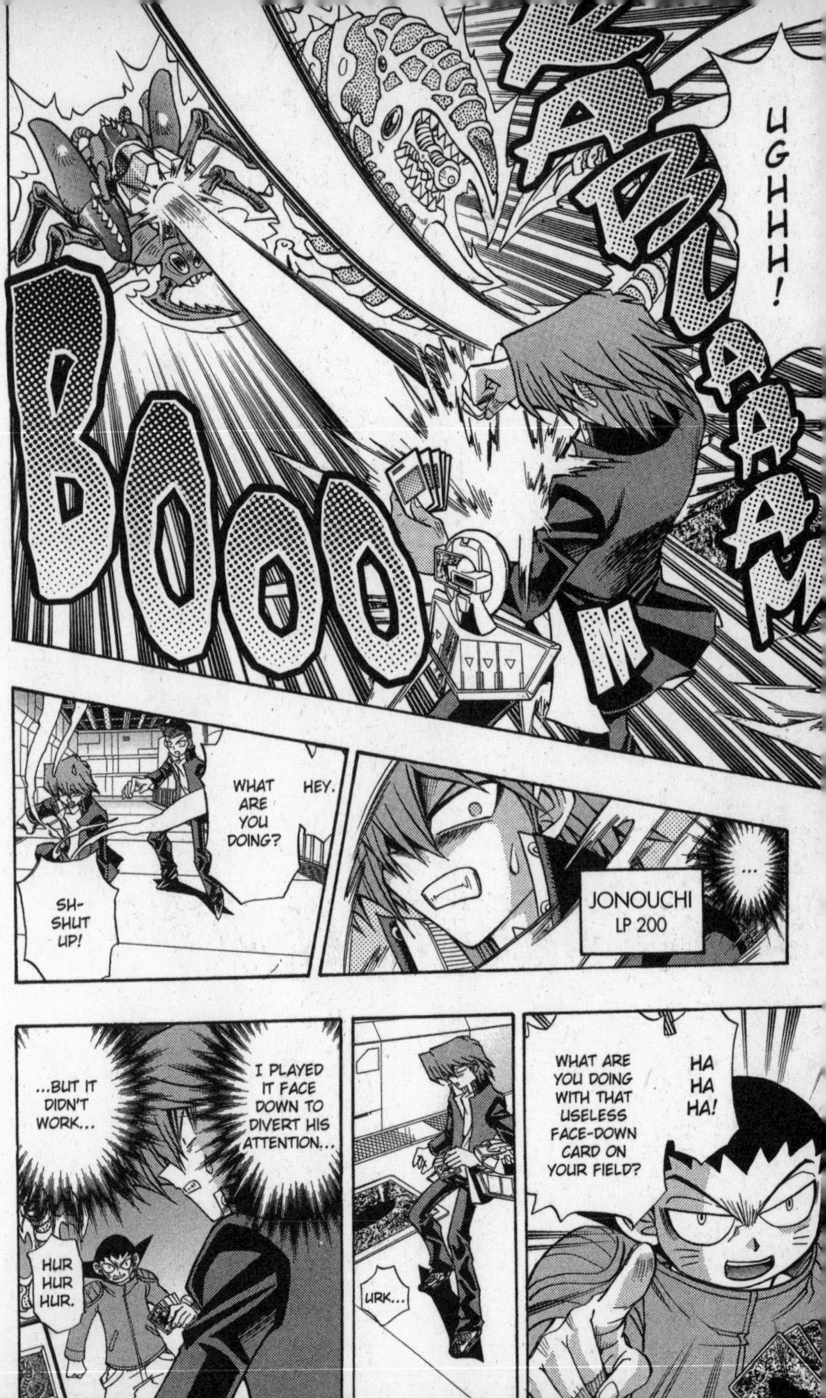
UGHHH!
BOOOOM
...
JONOUCHI LP 200
HEY.
WHAT ARE YOU DOING?
SH-SHUT UP!
HA HA HA!
WHAT ARE YOU DOING WITH THAT USELESS FACE-DOWN CARD ON YOUR FIELD?
URK...
I PLAYED IT FACE DOWN TO DIVERT HIS ATTENTION...
...BUT IT DIDN'T WORK...
HUR HUR HUR.

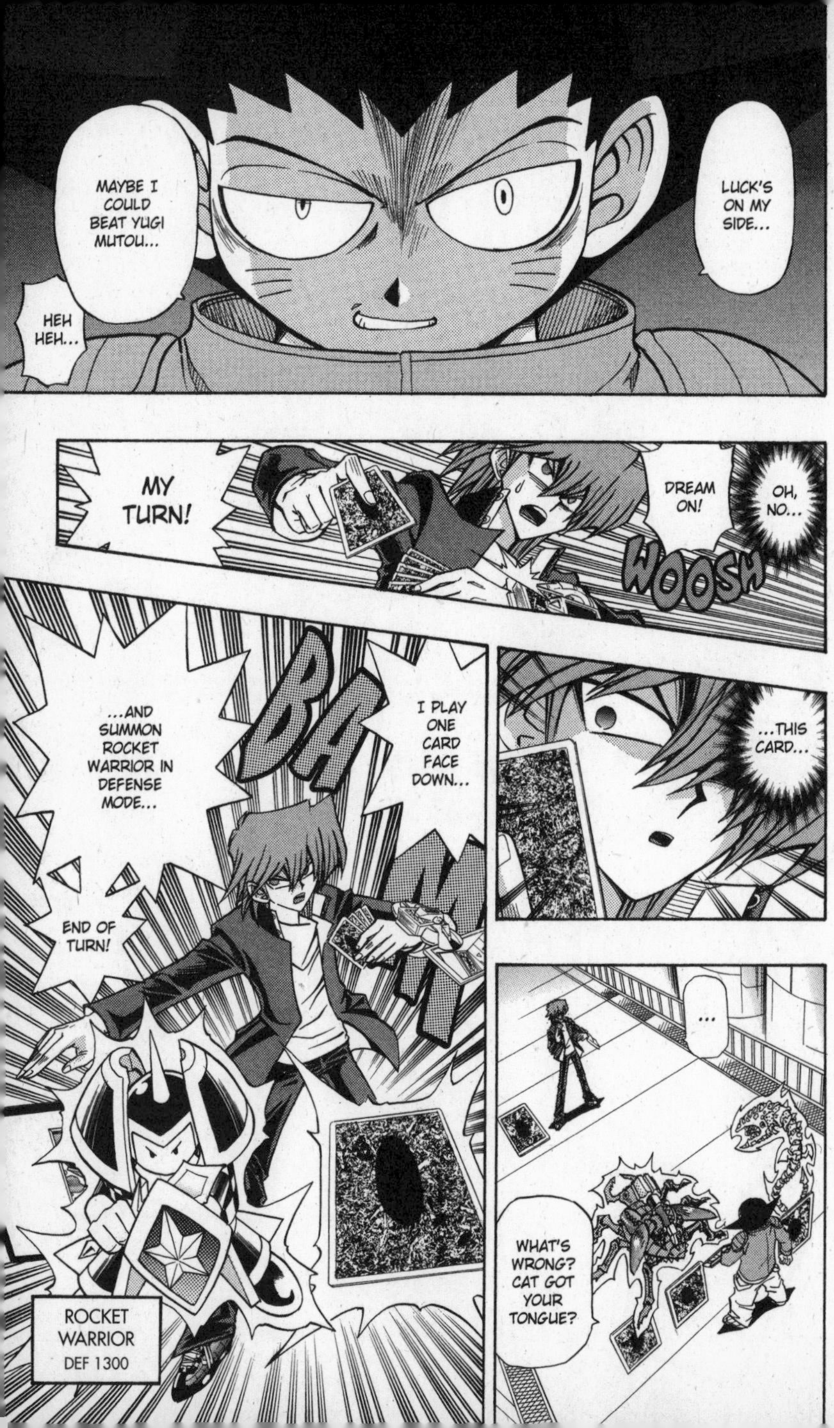

LUCK'S ON MY SIDE...
MAYBE I COULD BEAT YUGI MUTOU...
HEH HEH...
OH, NO...
DREAM ON!
WOOSH
MY TURN!
...THIS CARD...
...
WHAT'S WRONG? CAT GOT YOUR TONGUE?
BAM
I PLAY ONE CARD FACE DOWN...
...AND SUMMON ROCKET WARRIOR IN DEFENSE MODE...
END OF TURN!
ROCKET WARRIOR
DEF 1300

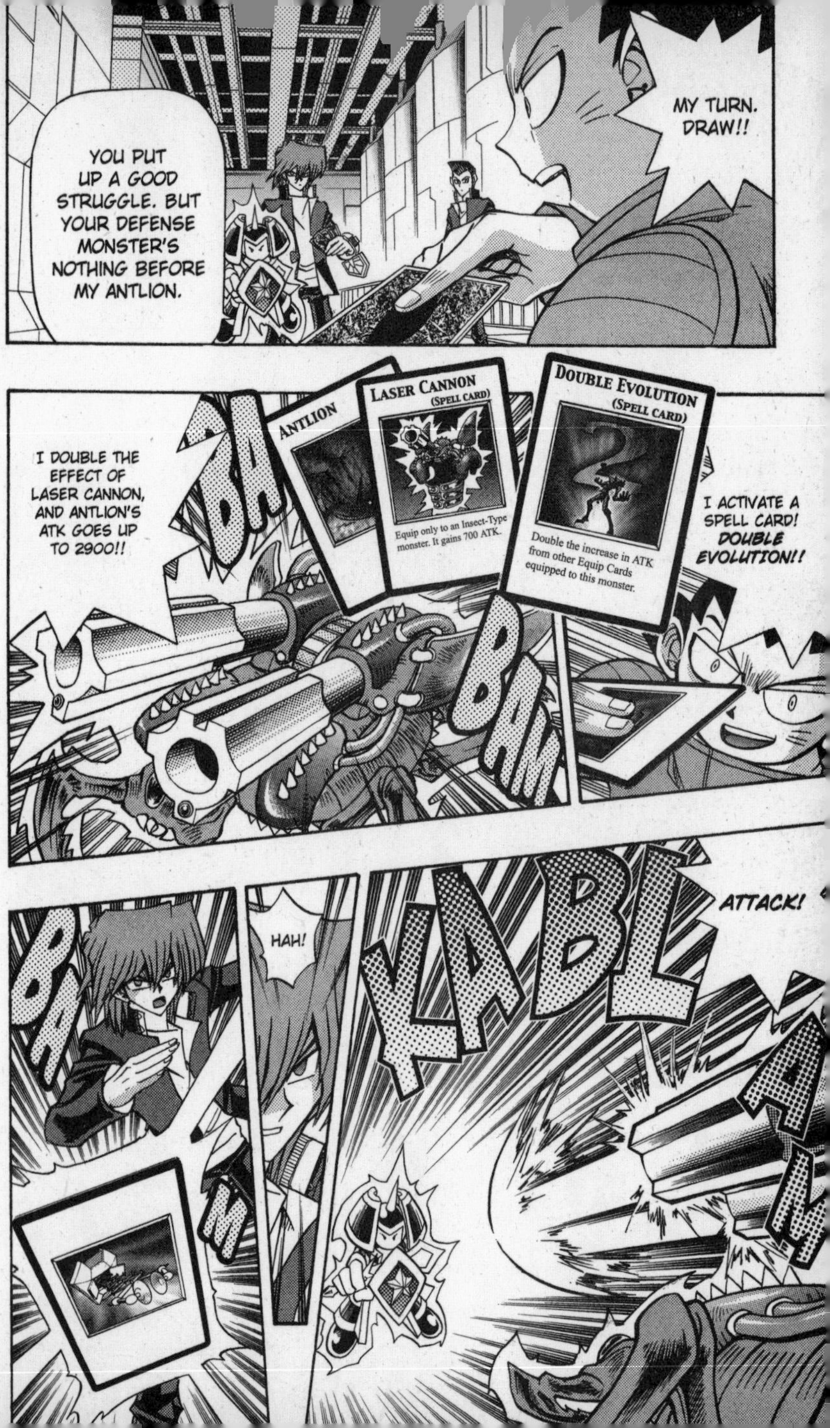
MY TURN. DRAW!!
YOU PUT UP A GOOD STRUGGLE. BUT YOUR DEFENSE MONSTER'S NOTHING BEFORE MY ANTLION.
I ACTIVATE A SPELL CARD! DOUBLE EVOLUTION!!
BAM
DOUBLE EVOLUTION
(SPELL CARD)
Double the increase in ATK from other Equip Cards equipped to this monster.
LASER CANNON
(SPELL CARD)
Equip only to an Insect-Type monster. It gains 700 ATK.
ANTLION
BA
I DOUBLE THE EFFECT OF LASER CANNON, AND ANTLION'S ATK GOES UP TO 2900!!
ATTACK!
KABLAM
HAH!
BAM

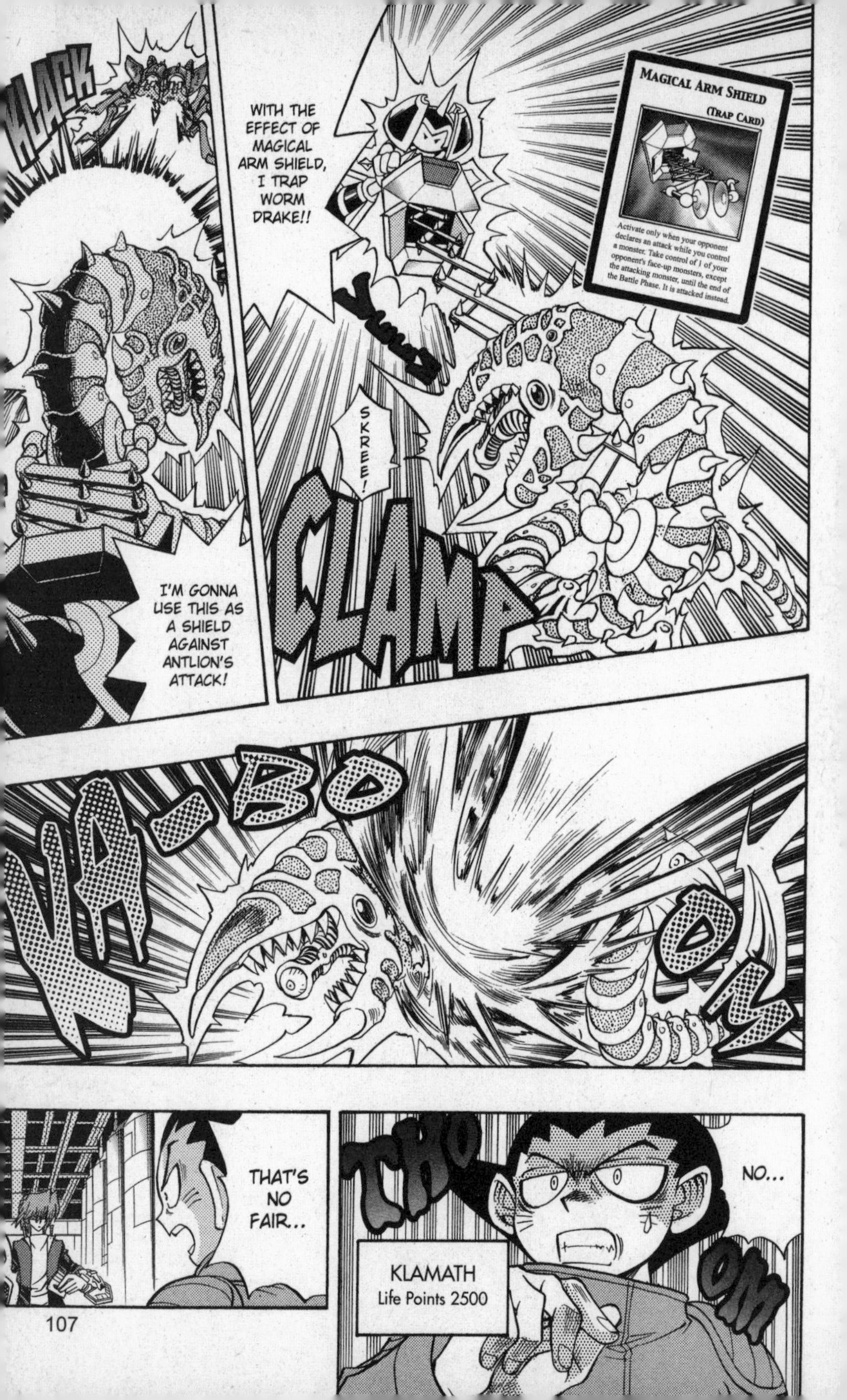
WITH THE EFFECT OF MAGICAL ARM SHIELD, I TRAP WORM DRAKE!!
MAGICAL ARM SHIELD
(TRAP CARD)
Activate only when your opponent declares an attack while you control a monster. Take control of 1 of your opponent's face-up monsters, except the attacking monster, until the end of the Battle Phase. It is attacked instead.
SKREE!
CLAMP
I'M GONNA USE THIS AS A SHIELD AGAINST ANTLION'S ATTACK!
THOOM
NO...
KLAMATH
Life Points 2500
THAT'S NO FAIR...

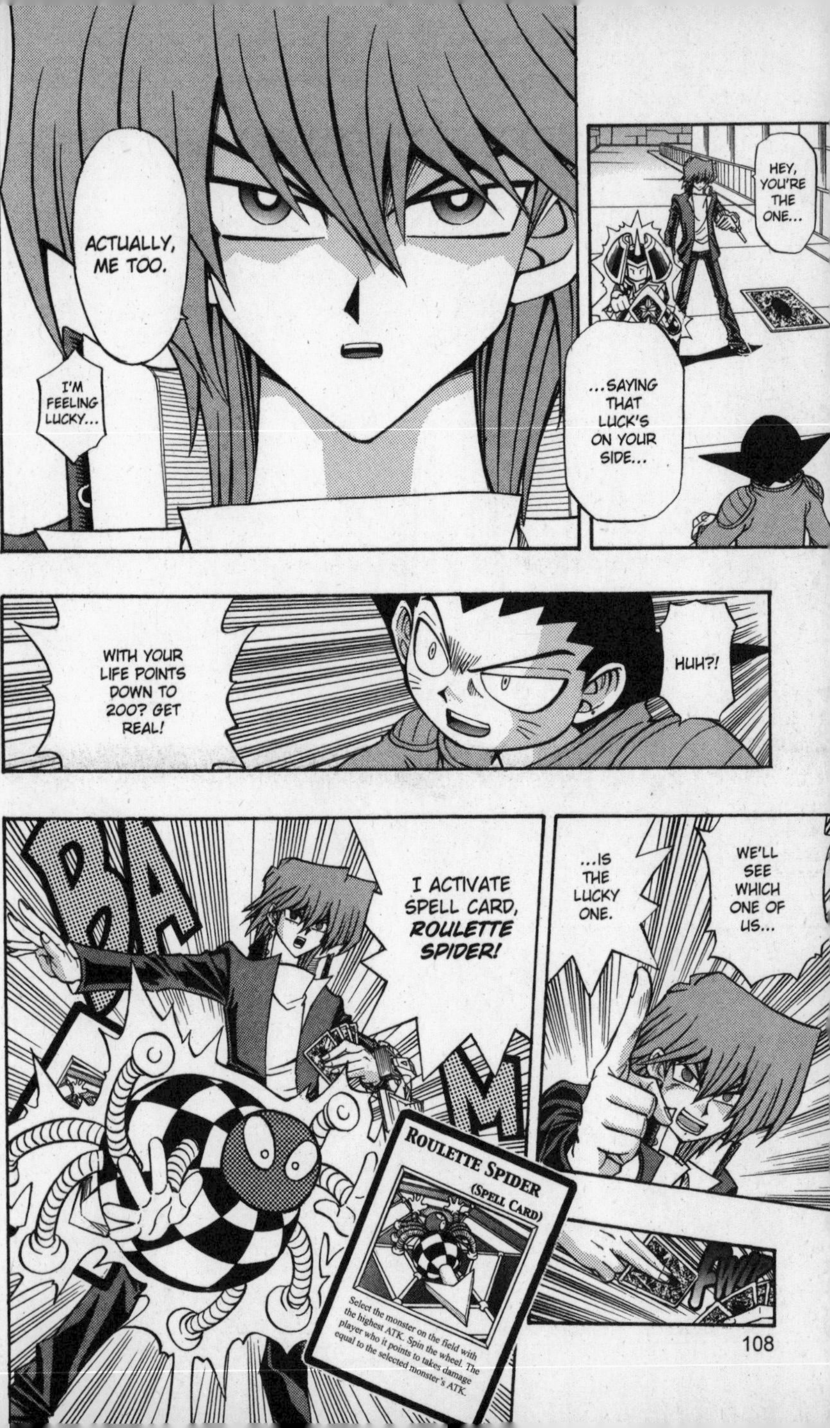
HEY, YOU'RE THE ONE...
...SAYING THAT LUCK'S ON YOUR SIDE...
ACTUALLY, ME TOO.
I'M FEELING LUCKY...
HUH?!
WITH YOUR LIFE POINTS DOWN TO 200? GET REAL!
WE'LL SEE WHICH ONE OF US...
...IS THE LUCKY ONE.
I ACTIVATE SPELL CARD, ROULETTE SPIDER!
BAM
ROULETTE SPIDER
(SPELL CARD)
Select the monster on the field with the highest ATK. Spin the wheel. The player who it points to takes damage equal to the selected monster's ATK.

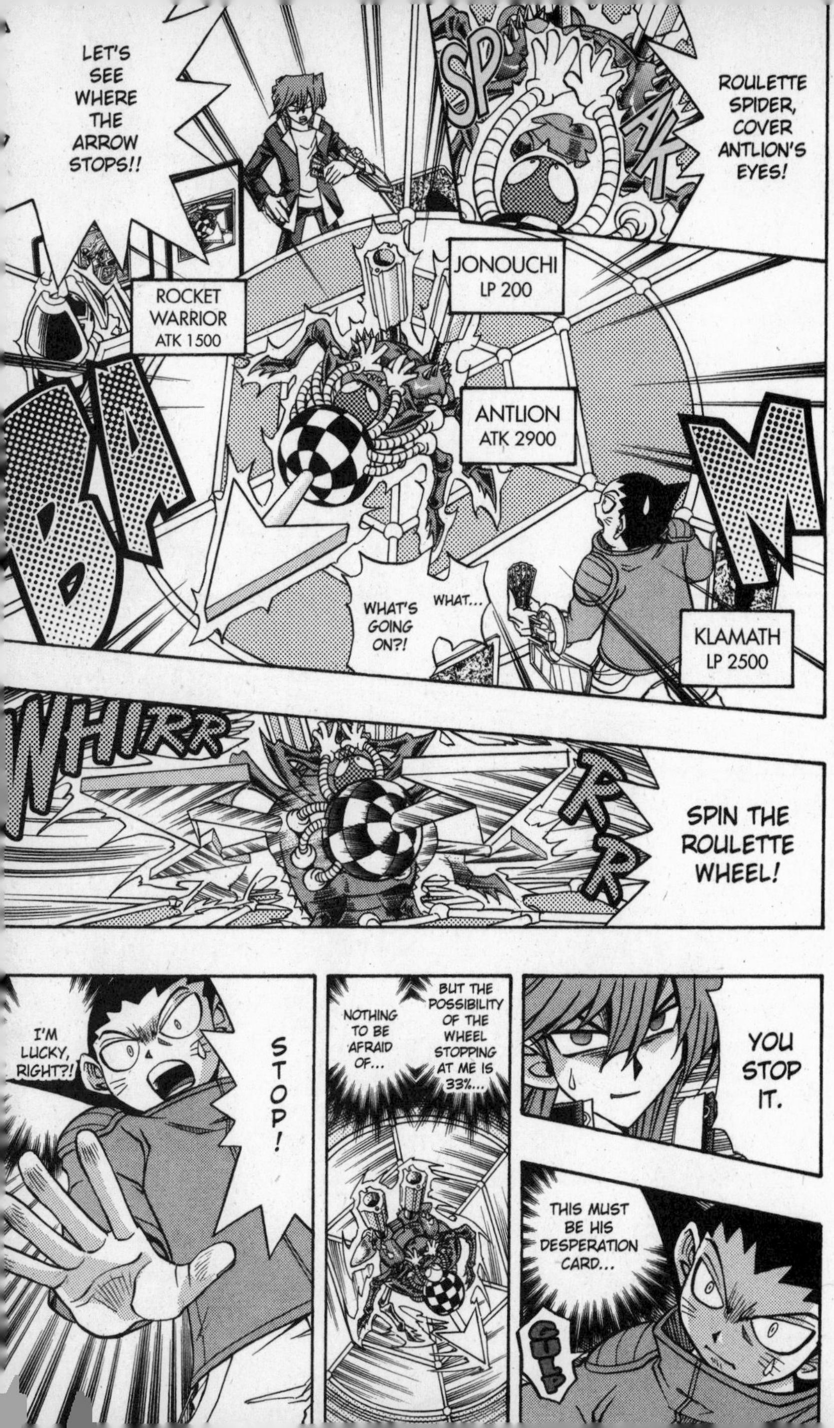
ROULETTE SPIDER, COVER ANTLION'S EYES!
LET'S SEE WHERE THE ARROW STOPS!!
BAM
JONOUCHI LP 200
ROCKET WARRIOR ATK 1500
ANTLION ATK 2900
WHAT...
WHAT'S GOING ON?!
KLAMATH LP 2500
SPIN THE ROULETTE WHEEL!
TRR
WHIRR
YOU STOP IT.
THIS MUST BE HIS DESPERATION CARD...
BUT THE POSSIBILITY OF THE WHEEL STOPPING AT ME IS 33%...
NOTHING TO BE AFRAID OF...
STOP!
I'M LUCKY, RIGHT?!

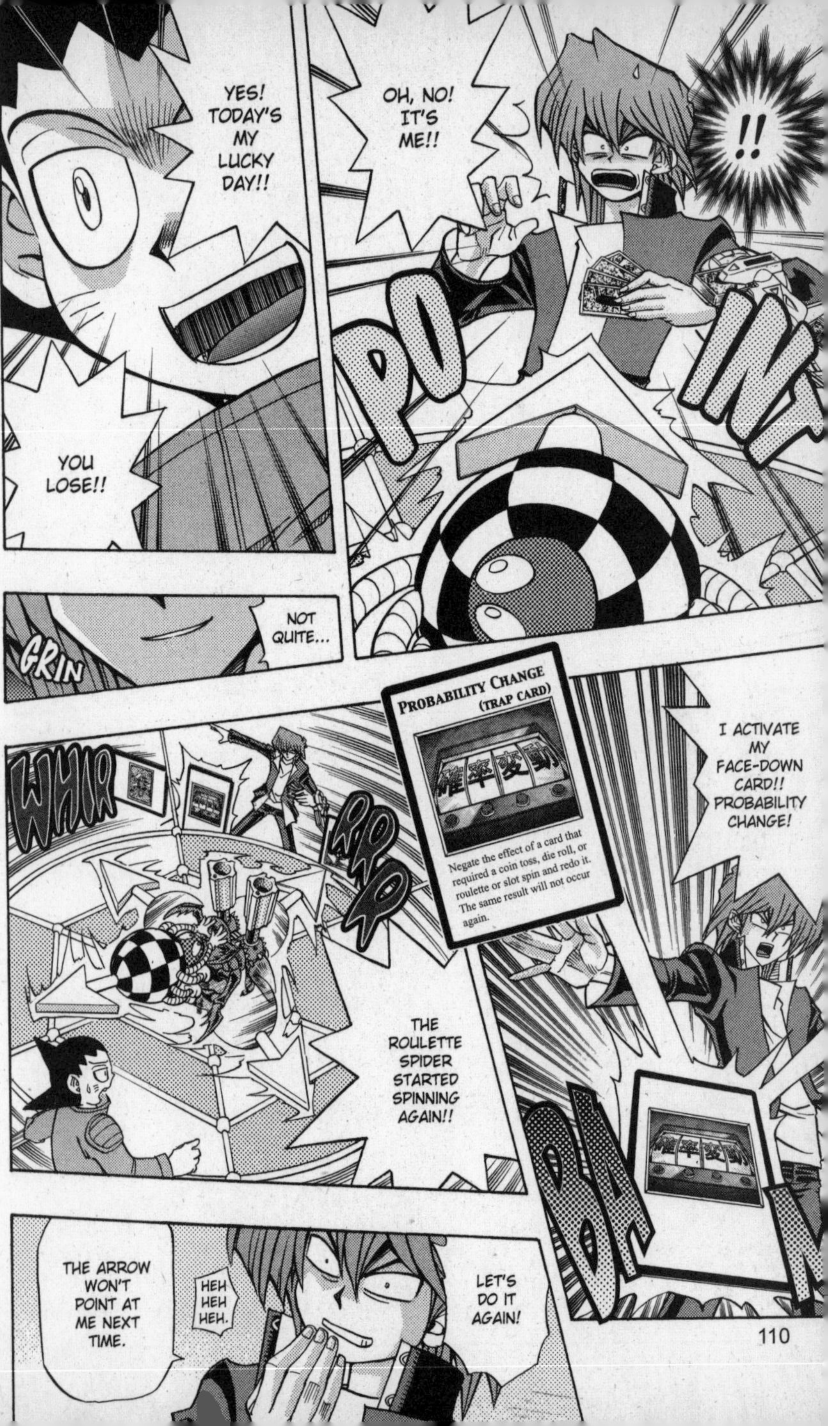
OH, NO! IT'S ME!!
!!
POINT
YES! TODAY'S MY LUCKY DAY!!
YOU LOSE!!
NOT QUITE...
GRIN
I ACTIVATE MY FACE-DOWN CARD!! PROBABILITY CHANGE!
PROBABILITY CHANGE
(TRAP CARD)
確率変動
Negate the effect of a card that required a coin toss, die roll, or roulette or slot spin and redo it. The same result will not occur again.
BAM
WHIRRR
THE ROULETTE SPIDER STARTED SPINNING AGAIN!!
LET'S DO IT AGAIN!
HEH HEH HEH.
THE ARROW WON'T POINT AT ME NEXT TIME.

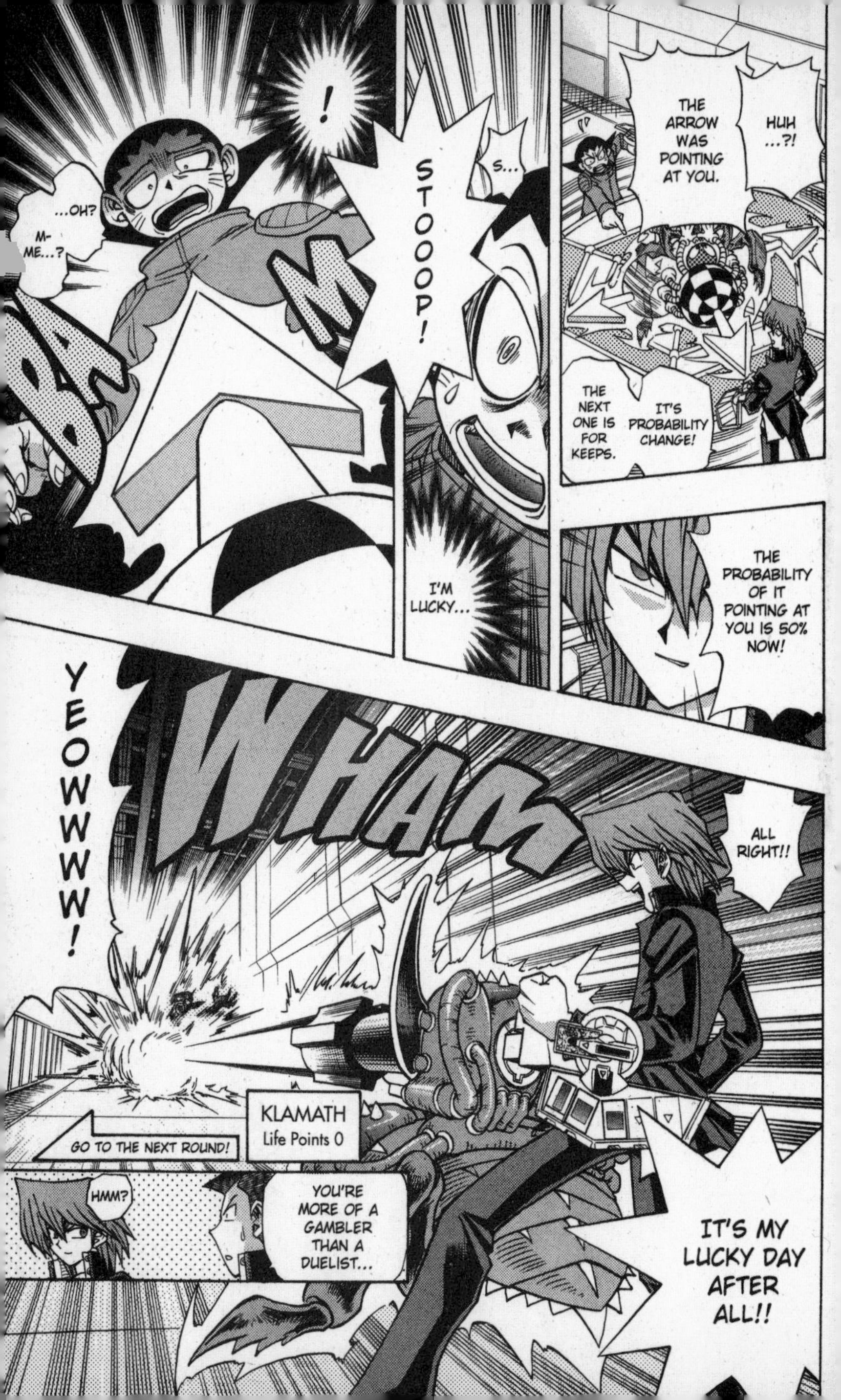

HUH ...?!
THE ARROW WAS POINTING AT YOU.
IT'S PROBABILITY CHANGE!
THE NEXT ONE IS FOR KEEPS.
THE PROBABILITY OF IT POINTING AT YOU IS 50% NOW!
S...
STOOOP!
I'M LUCKY...
!
...OH?
M-ME...?
ALL RIGHT!!
WHAM
YEOWWWWW!
IT'S MY LUCKY DAY AFTER ALL!!
KLAMATH
Life Points 0
GO TO THE NEXT ROUND!
YOU'RE MORE OF A GAMBLER THAN A DUELIST...
HMM?

Duel Round 6:

Marvelous Armed Division!!

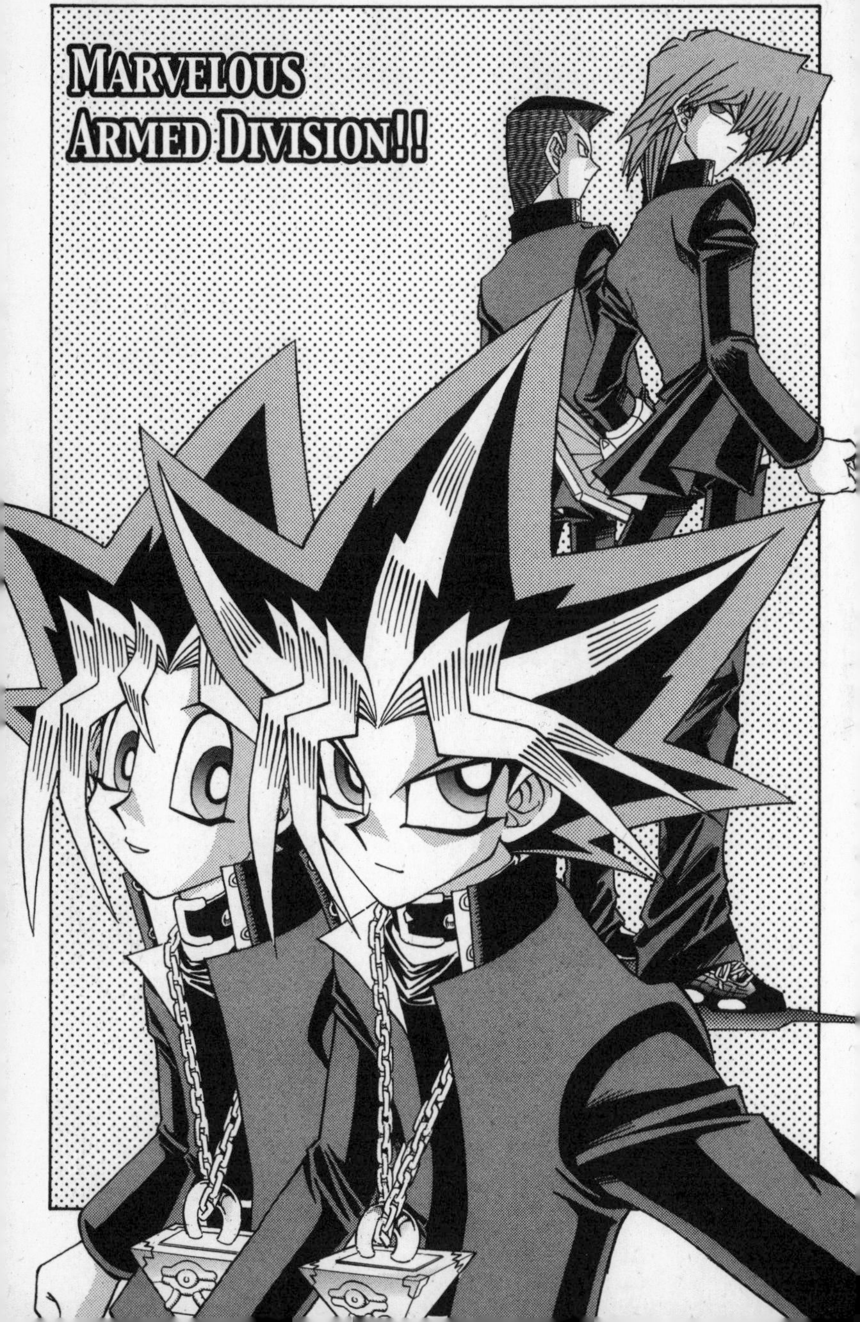

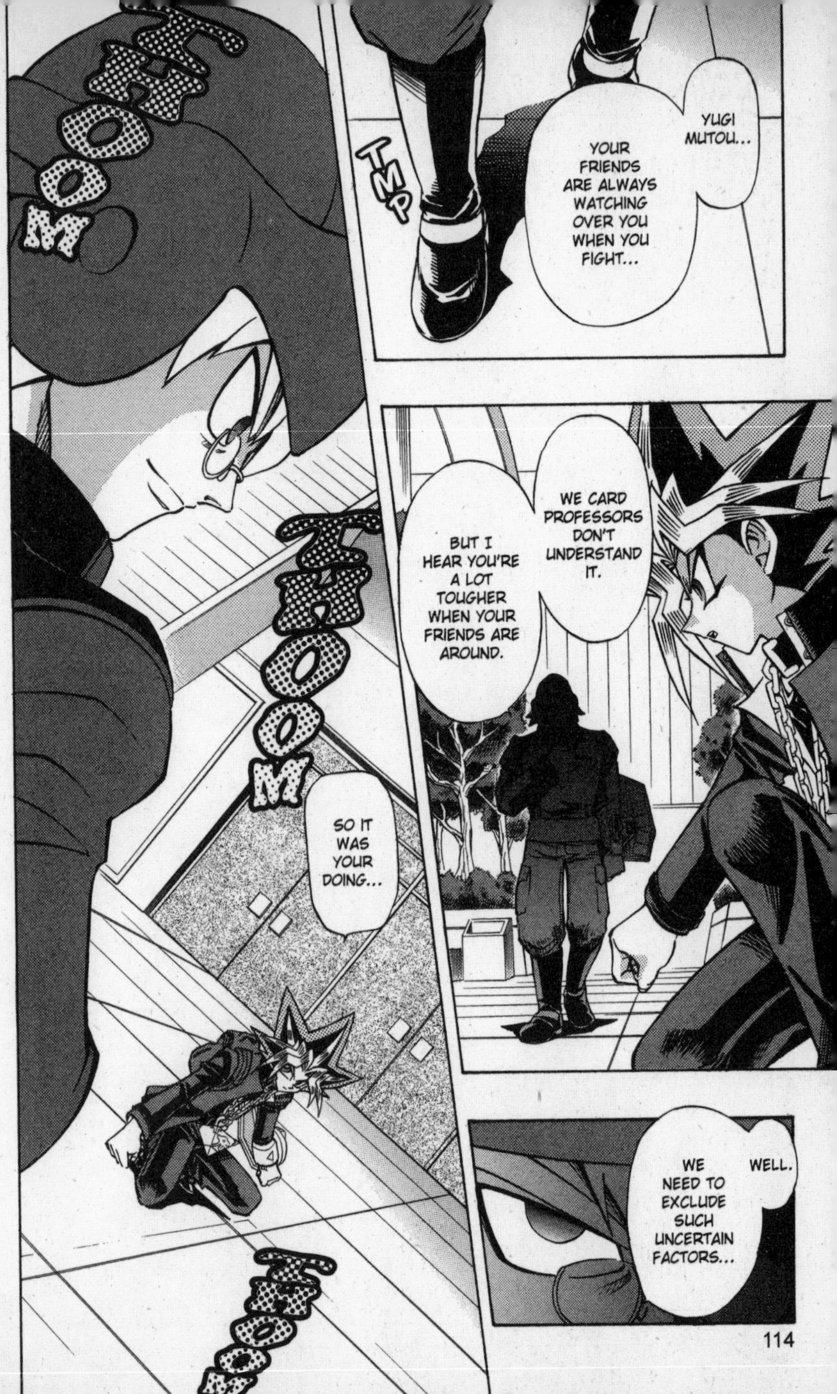
YUGI MUTOU...
YOUR FRIENDS ARE ALWAYS WATCHING OVER YOU WHEN YOU FIGHT...
TMP
WE CARD PROFESSORS DON'T UNDERSTAND IT.
BUT I HEAR YOU'RE A LOT TOUGHER WHEN YOUR FRIENDS ARE AROUND.
WELL.
WE NEED TO EXCLUDE SUCH UNCERTAIN FACTORS...
THOOM
THOOM
SO IT WAS YOUR DOING...
THOOM

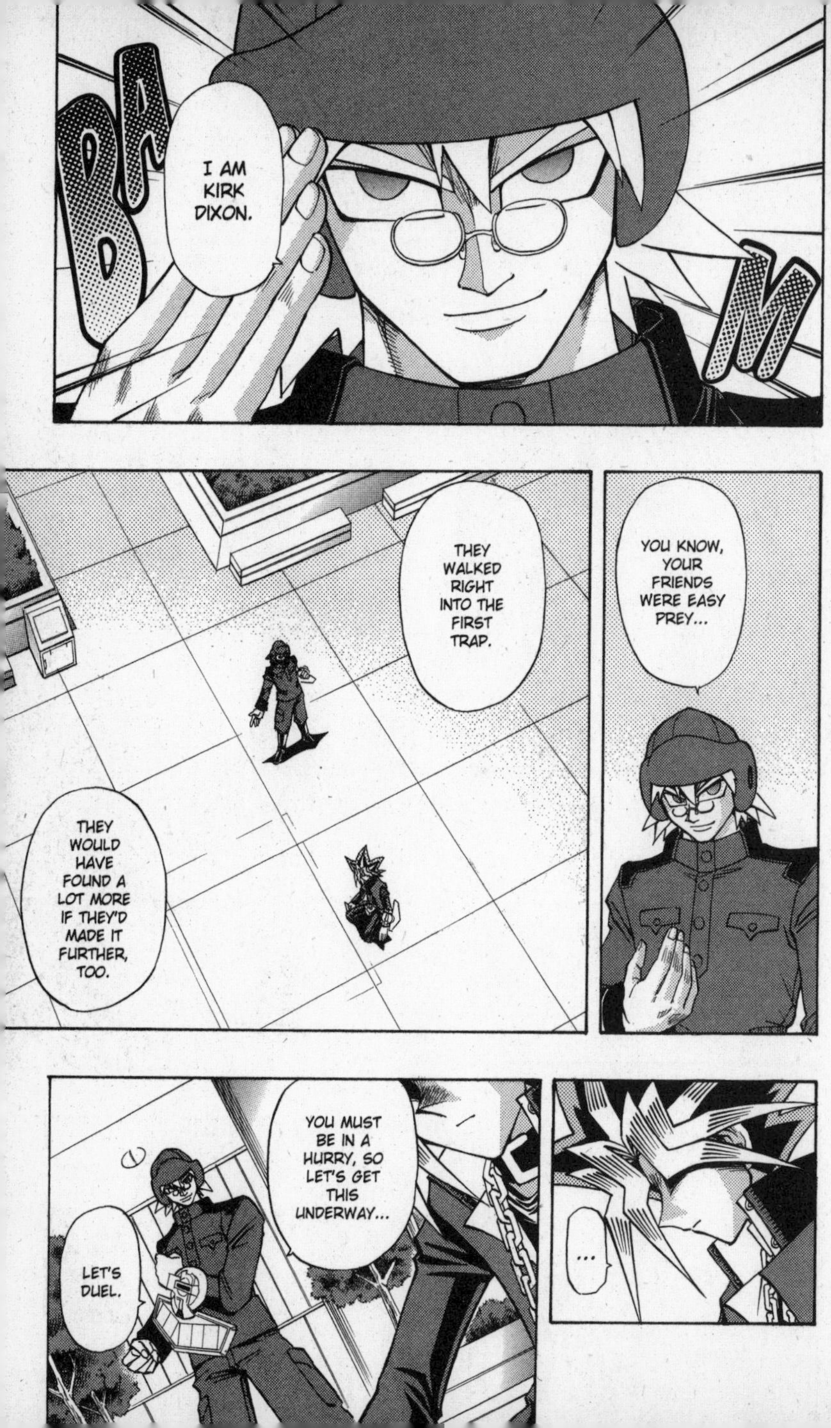
BAD
I AM KIRK DIXON.
M
YOU KNOW, YOUR FRIENDS WERE EASY PREY...
THEY WALKED RIGHT INTO THE FIRST TRAP.
THEY WOULD HAVE FOUND A LOT MORE IF THEY'D MADE IT FURTHER, TOO.
...
YOU MUST BE IN A HURRY, SO LET'S GET THIS UNDERWAY...
LET'S DUEL.

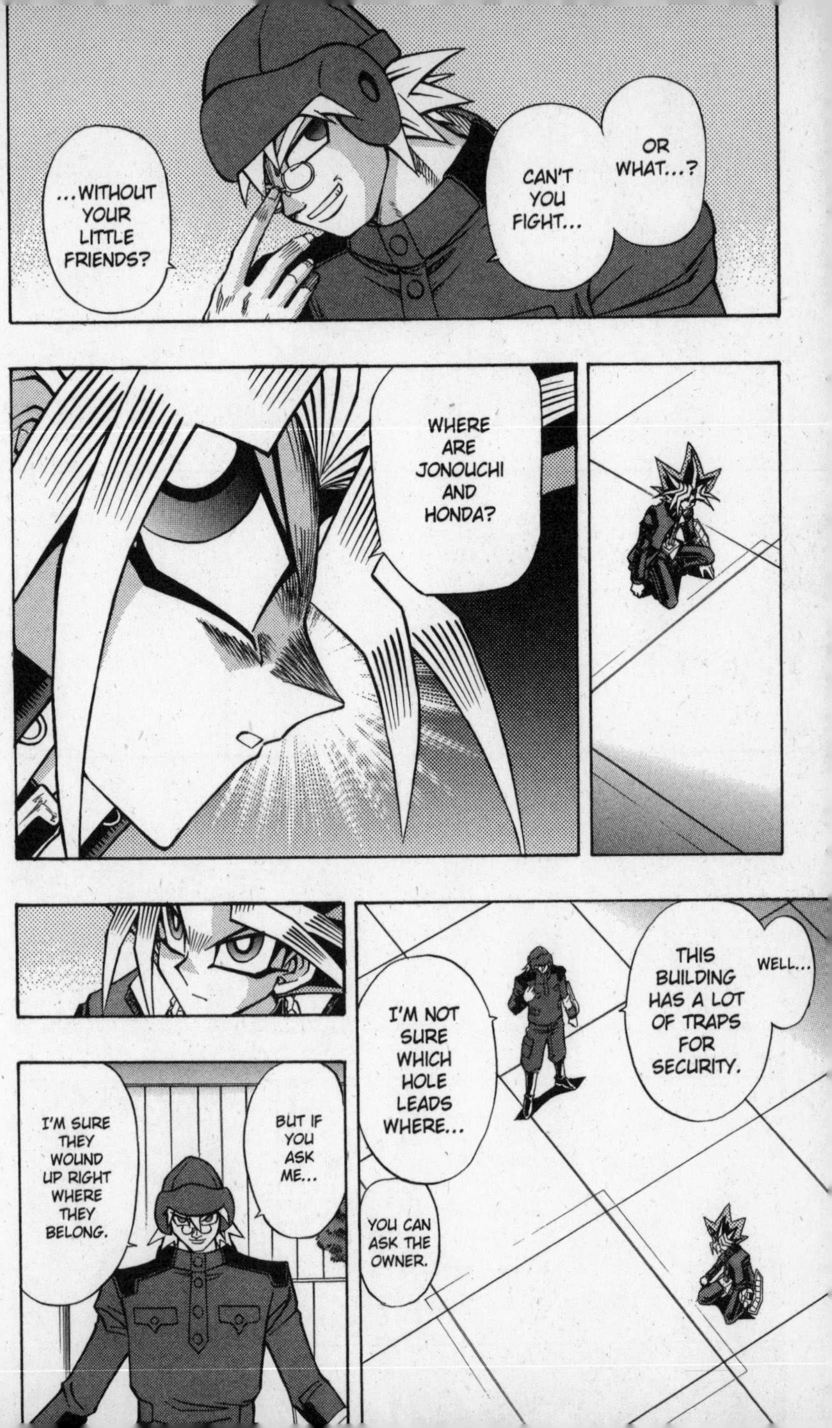
CAN'T YOU FIGHT...
OR WHAT...?
...WITHOUT YOUR LITTLE FRIENDS?
WHERE ARE JONOUCHI AND HONDA?
WELL...
THIS BUILDING HAS A LOT OF TRAPS FOR SECURITY.
I'M NOT SURE WHICH HOLE LEADS WHERE...
YOU CAN ASK THE OWNER.
BUT IF YOU ASK ME...
I'M SURE THEY WOUND UP RIGHT WHERE THEY BELONG.

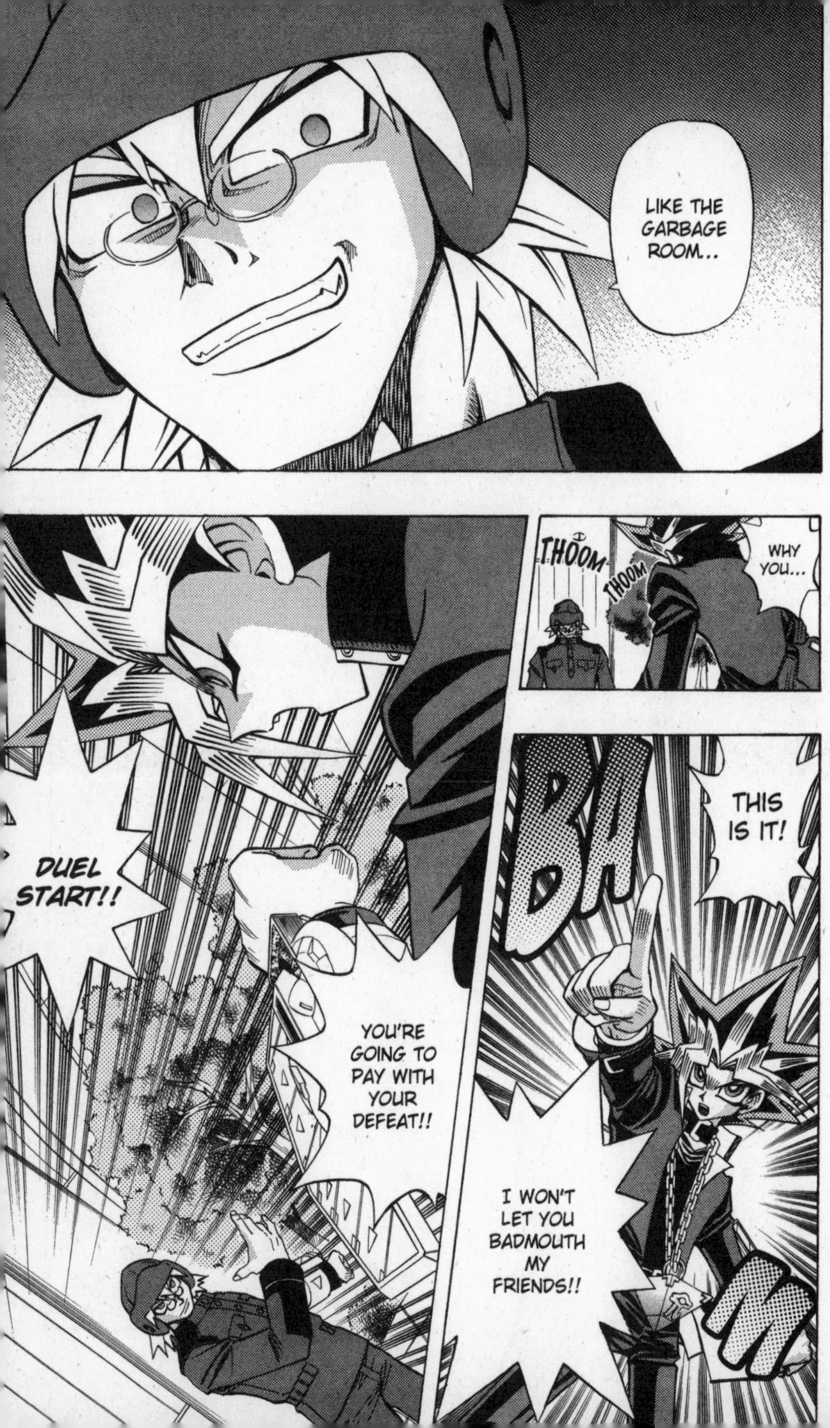
LIKE THE GARBAGE ROOM...
THOOM
THOOM
WHY YOU...
THIS IS IT!
BA
I WON'T LET YOU BADMOUTH MY FRIENDS!!
YOU'RE GOING TO PAY WITH YOUR DEFEAT!!
DUEL START!!

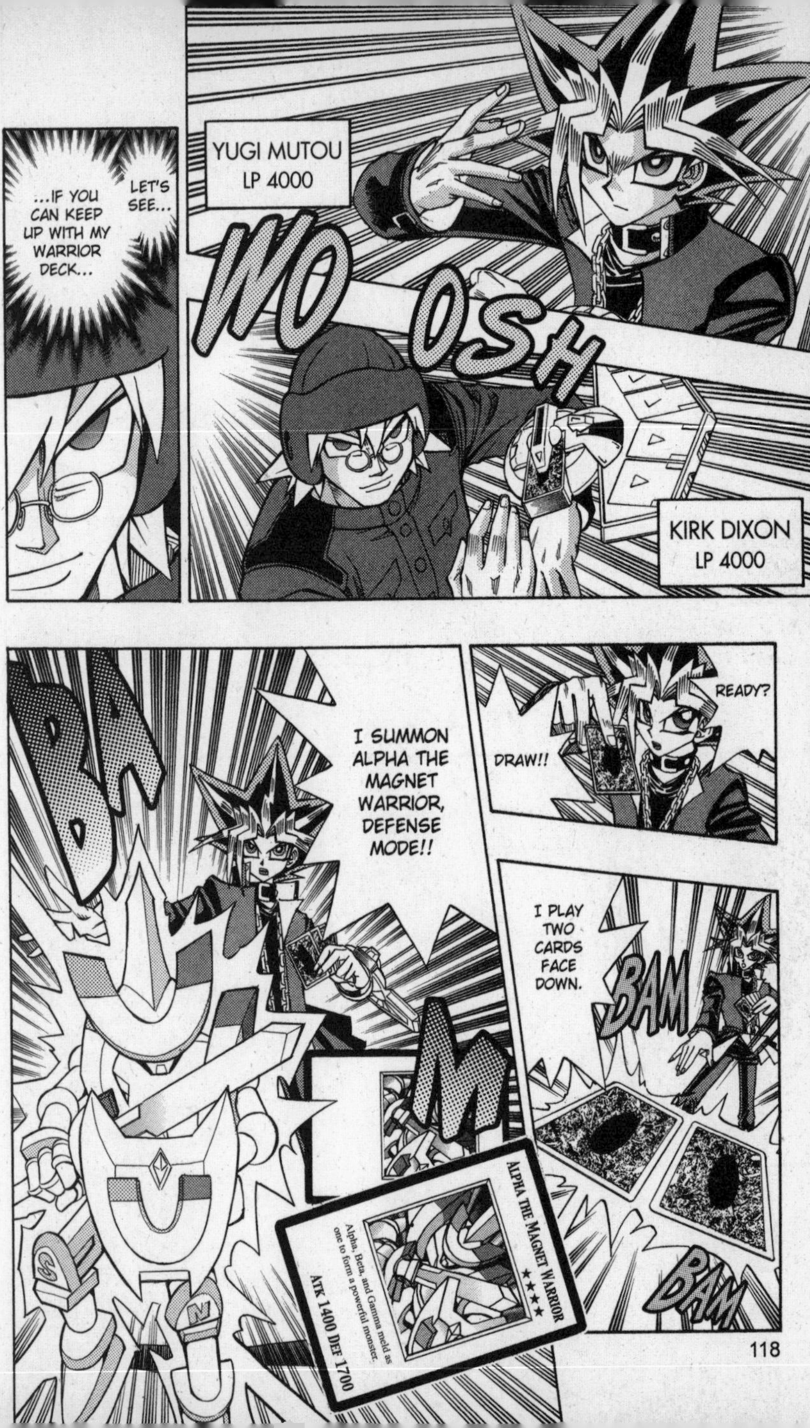
YUGI MUTOU
LP 4000
WOOSH
KIRK DIXON
LP 4000
LET'S SEE...
...IF YOU CAN KEEP UP WITH MY WARRIOR DECK...
READY?
DRAW!!
I PLAY TWO CARDS FACE DOWN.
BAM
BAM
I SUMMON ALPHA THE MAGNET WARRIOR, DEFENSE MODE!!
ALPHA THE MAGNET WARRIOR
Alpha, Beta, and Gamma meld as one to form a powerful monster.
ATK 1400 DEF 1700

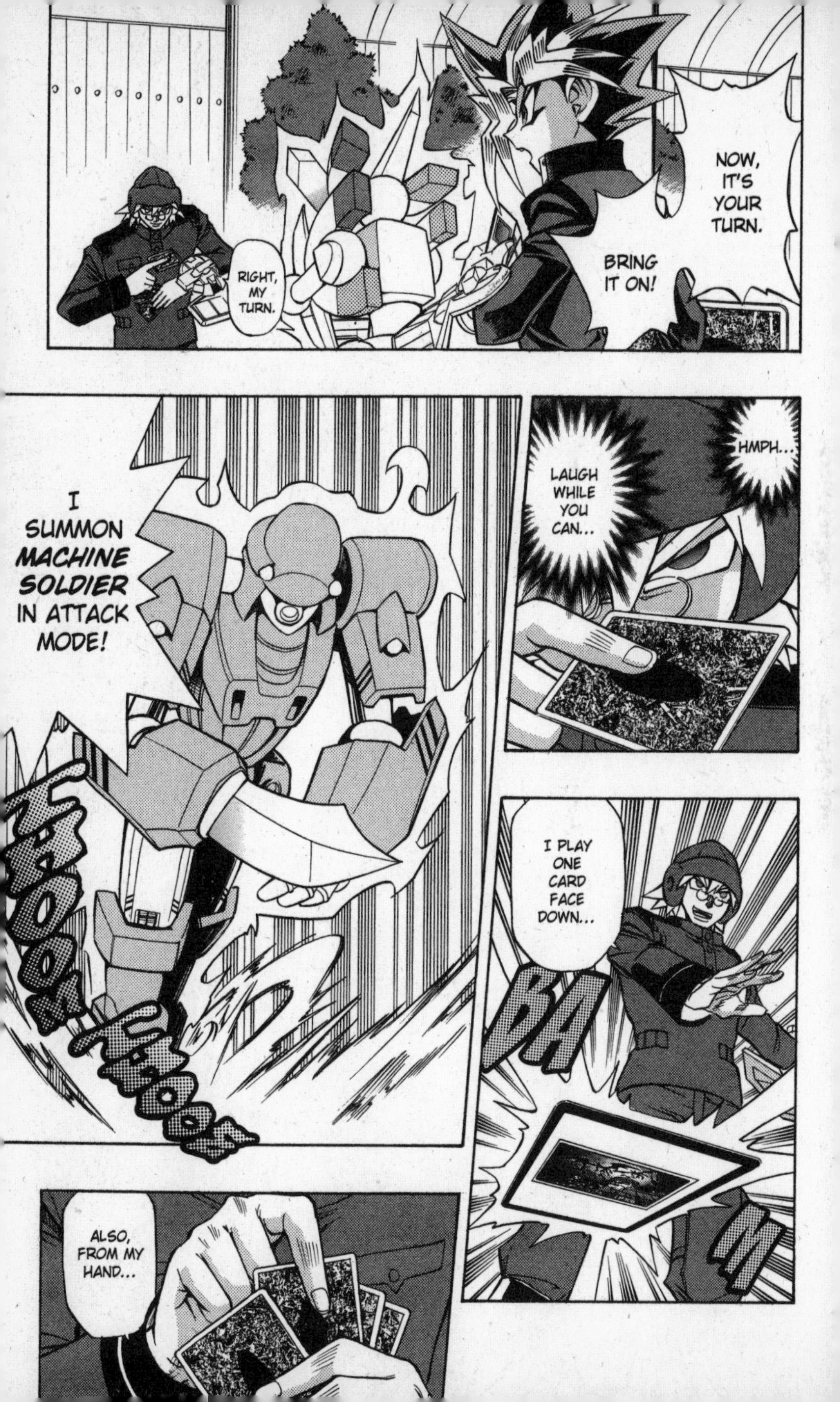
NOW, IT'S YOUR TURN.
BRING IT ON!
RIGHT, MY TURN.
HMPH...
LAUGH WHILE YOU CAN...
I PLAY ONE CARD FACE DOWN...
BAM
I SUMMON MACHINE SOLDIER IN ATTACK MODE!
WHOOM WHOOM
ALSO, FROM MY HAND...

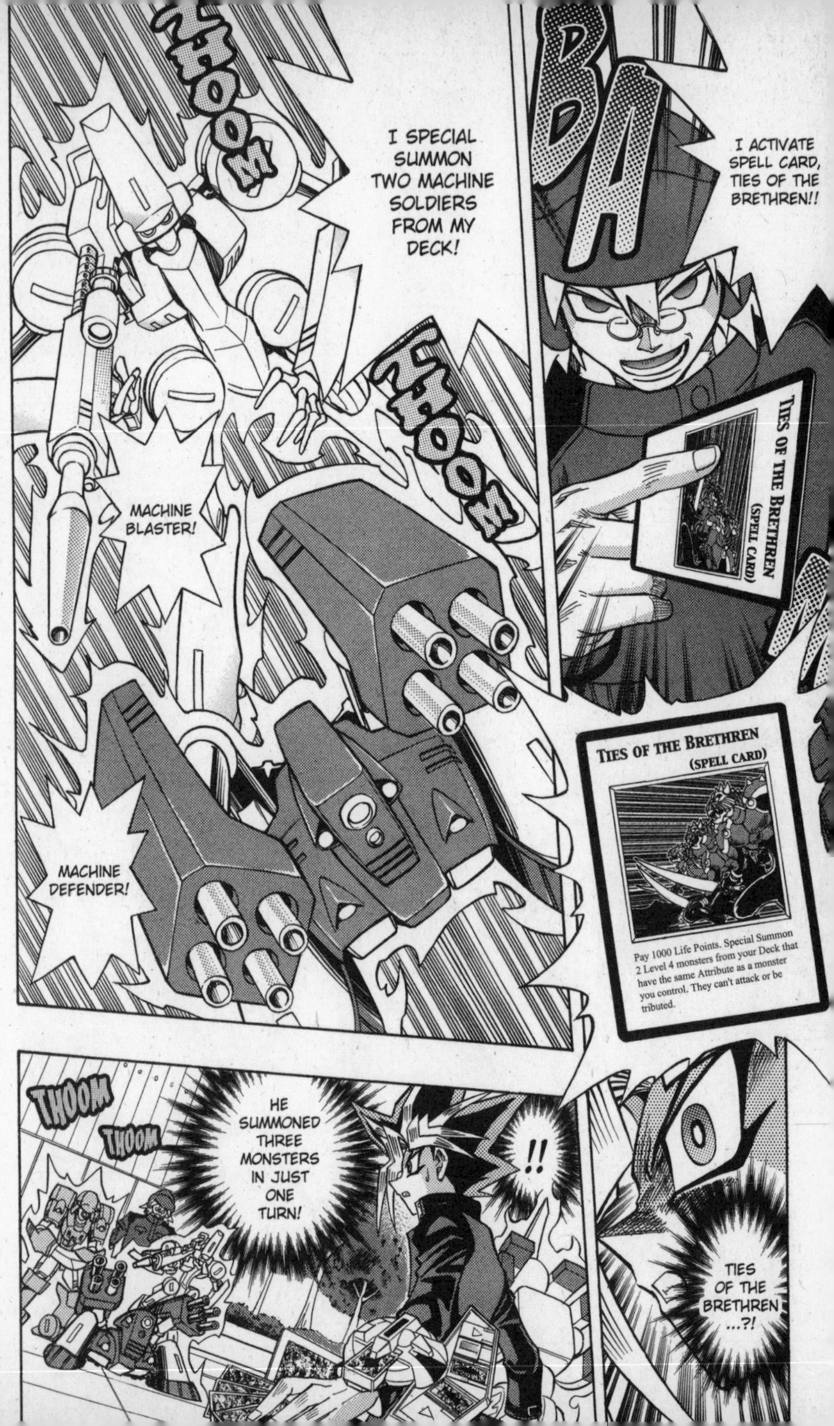
BA
I ACTIVATE SPELL CARD, TIES OF THE BRETHREN!!
TIES OF THE BRETHREN
(SPELL CARD)
TIES OF THE BRETHREN
(SPELL CARD)
Pay 1000 Life Points. Special Summon 2 Level 4 monsters from your Deck that have the same Attribute as a monster you control. They can't attack or be tributed.
WHOOM
I SPECIAL SUMMON TWO MACHINE SOLDIERS FROM MY DECK!
WHOOM
MACHINE BLASTER!
MACHINE DEFENDER!
TIES OF THE BRETHREN ...?!
!!
HE SUMMONED THREE MONSTERS IN JUST ONE TURN!
THOOM
THOOM

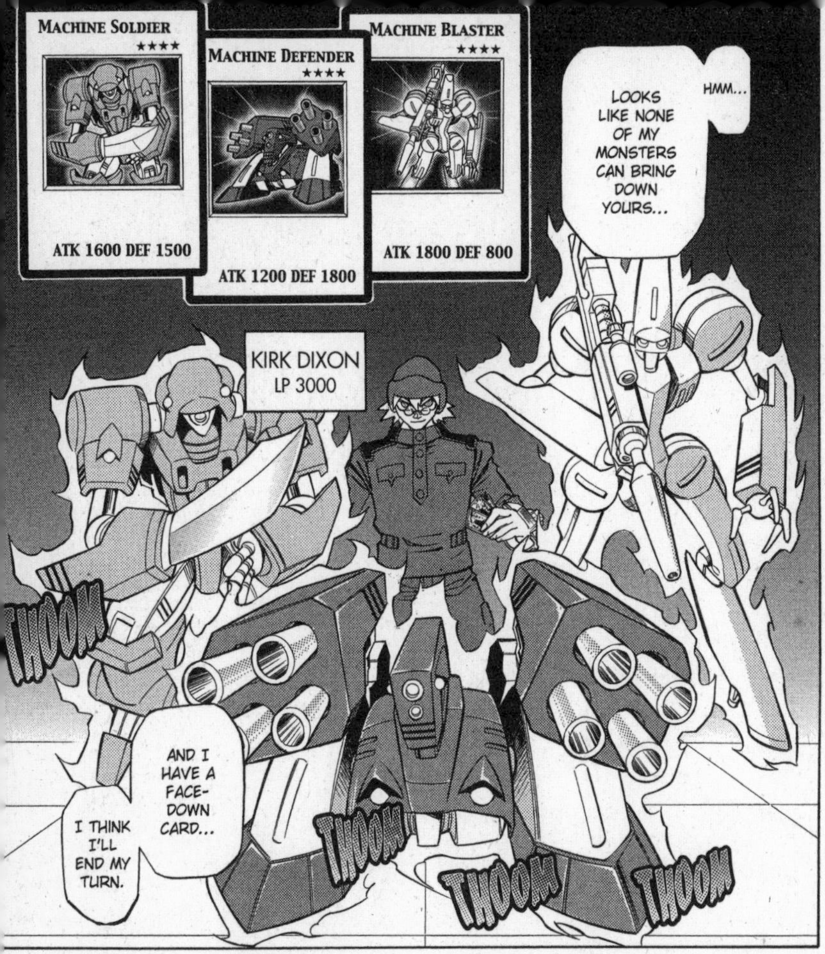
HMM...
LOOKS LIKE NONE OF MY MONSTERS CAN BRING DOWN YOURS...
MACHINE BLASTER
ATK 1800 DEF 800
MACHINE DEFENDER
ATK 1200 DEF 1800
MACHINE SOLDIER
ATK 1600 DEF 1500
KIRK DIXON
LP 3000
THOOM
THOOM
THOOM
THOOM
AND I HAVE A FACE-DOWN CARD...
I THINK I'LL END MY TURN.

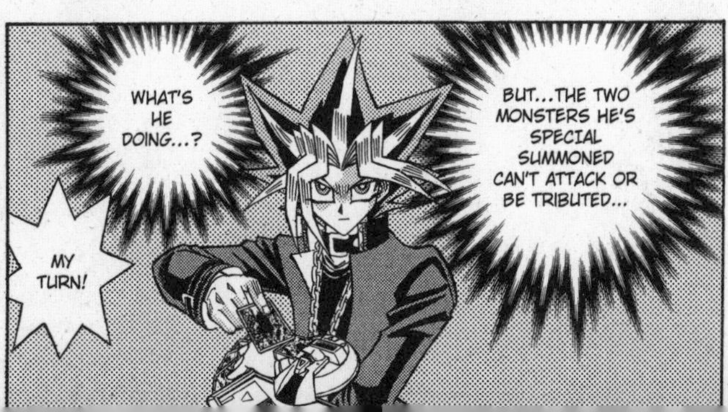
BUT...THE TWO MONSTERS HE'S SPECIAL SUMMONED CAN'T ATTACK OR BE TRIBUTED...
WHAT'S HE DOING...?
MY TURN!

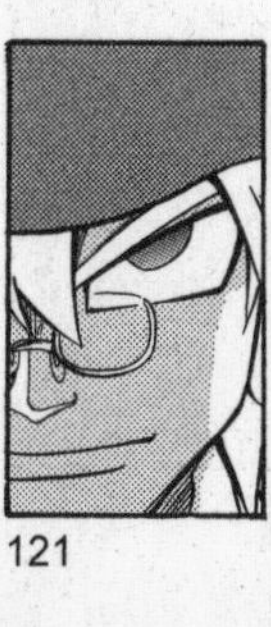

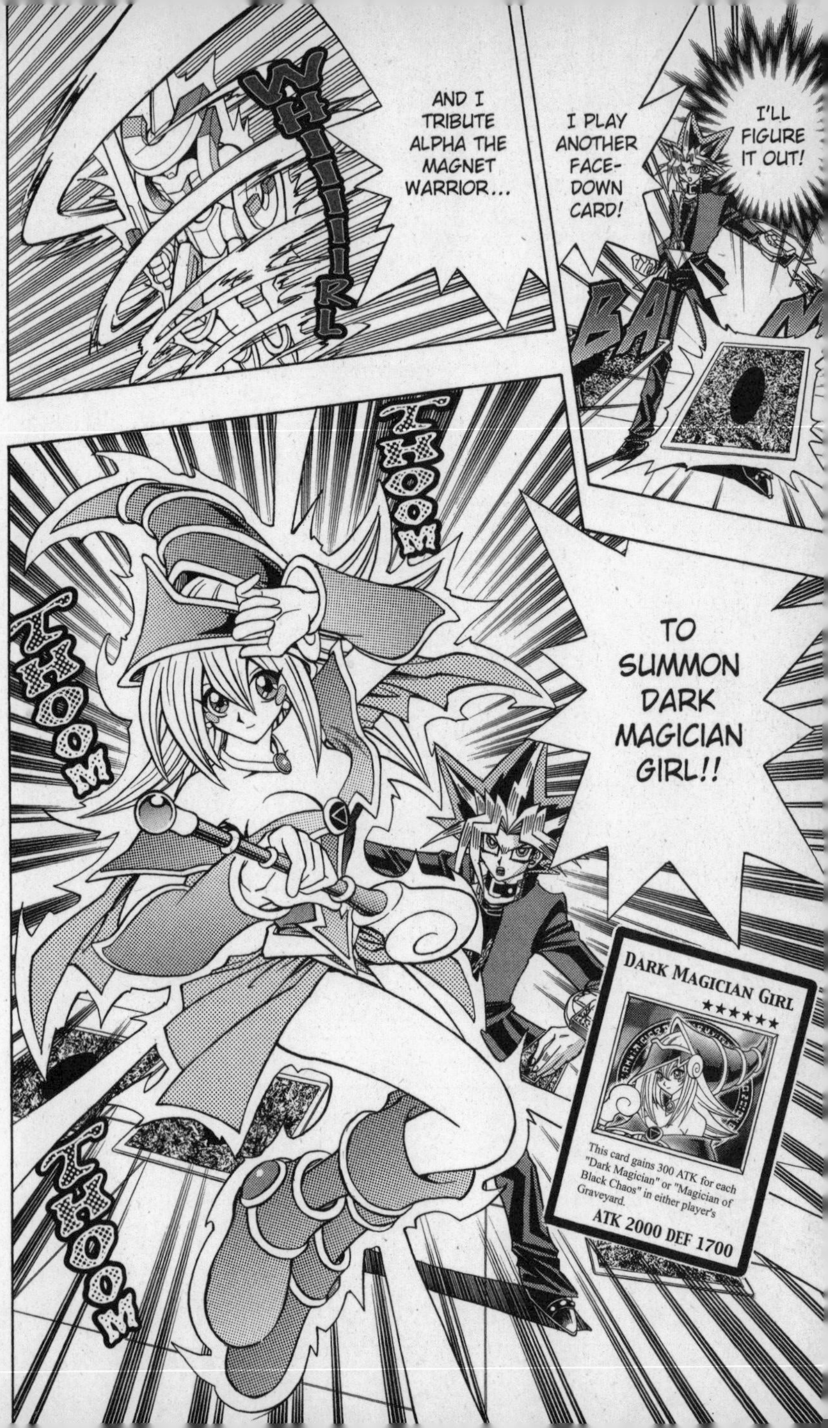
I'LL FIGURE IT OUT!
I PLAY ANOTHER FACE-DOWN CARD!
BAM
AND I TRIBUTE ALPHA THE MAGNET WARRIOR...
WHIIIIIIRL
THOOM
TO SUMMON DARK MAGICIAN GIRL!!
THOOM
DARK MAGICIAN GIRL
★★★★★★
This card gains 300 ATK for each "Dark Magician" or "Magician of Black Chaos" in either player's Graveyard.
ATK 2000 DEF 1700
THOOM

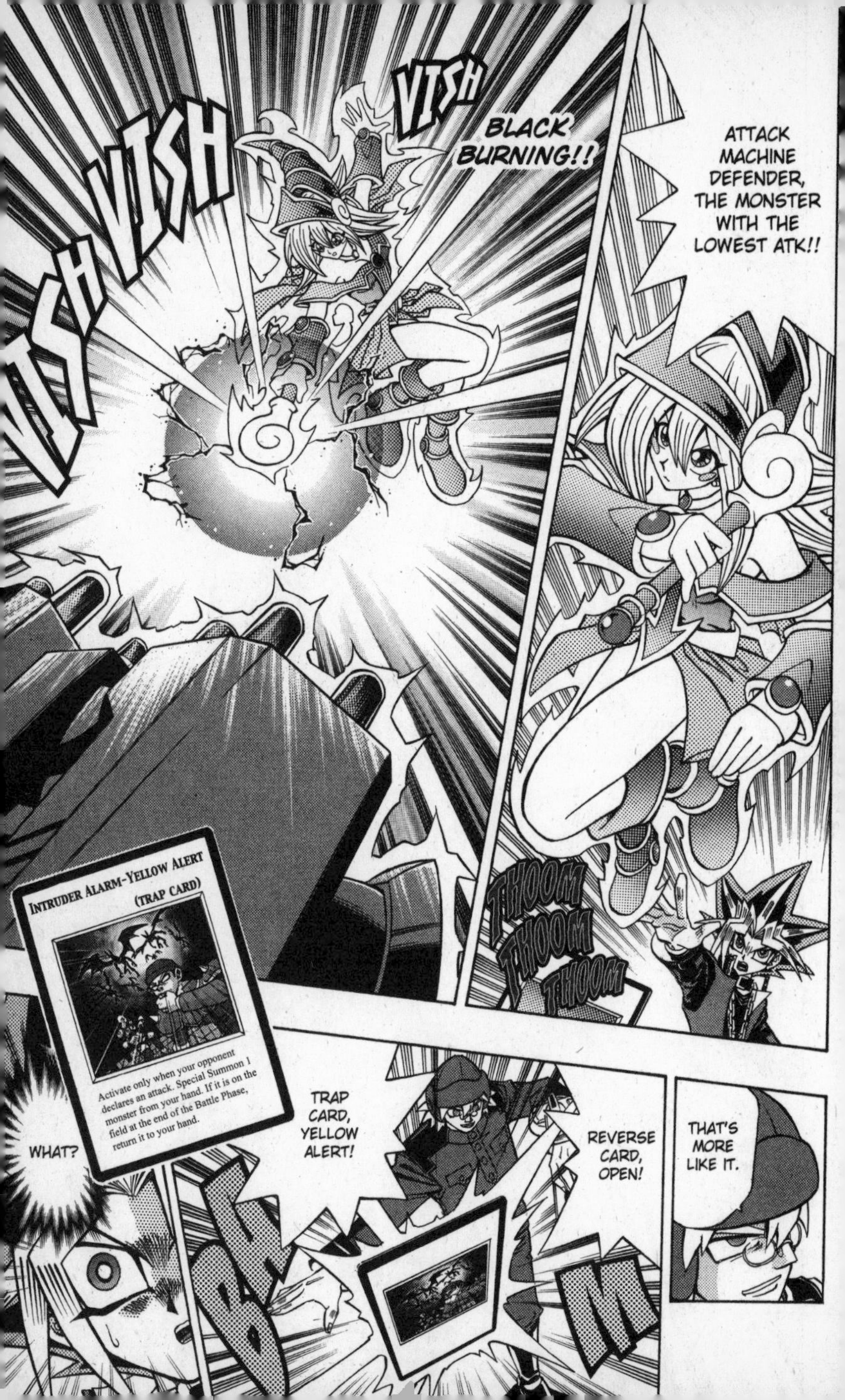
ATTACK MACHINE DEFENDER, THE MONSTER WITH THE LOWEST ATK!!
THOOM THOOM THOOM
VISH
BLACK BURNING!!
VISH VISH VISH
THAT'S MORE LIKE IT.
REVERSE CARD, OPEN!
TRAP CARD, YELLOW ALERT!
INTRUDER ALARM-YELLOW ALERT
(TRAP CARD)
Activate only when your opponent declares an attack. Special Summon 1 monster from your hand. If it is on the field at the end of the Battle Phase, return it to your hand.
WHAT?

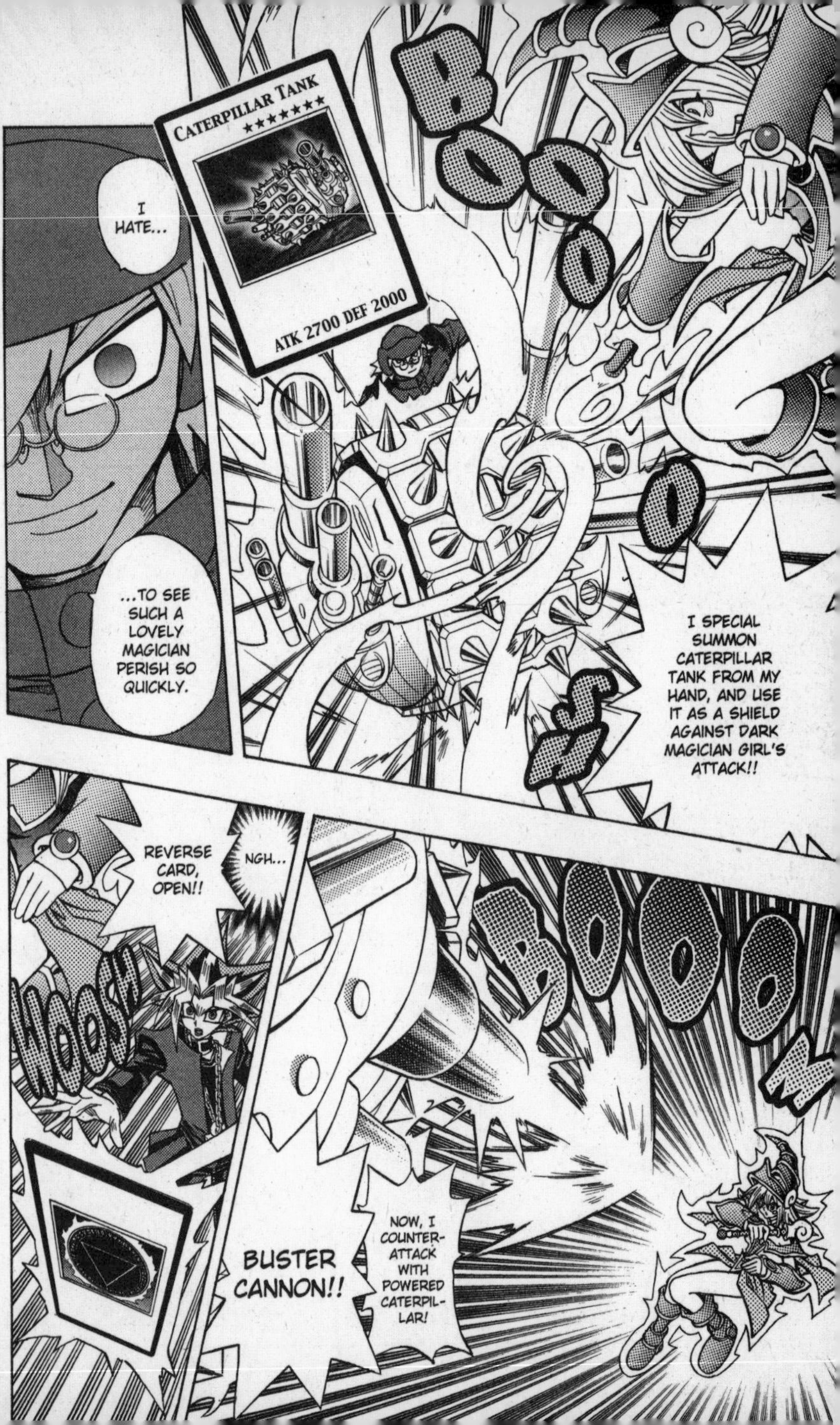
BOOOO
I SPECIAL SUMMON CATERPILLAR TANK FROM MY HAND, AND USE IT AS A SHIELD AGAINST DARK MAGICIAN GIRL'S ATTACK!!
CATERPILLAR TANK
ATK 2700 DEF 2000
I HATE...
...TO SEE SUCH A LOVELY MAGICIAN PERISH SO QUICKLY.
BOOOOM
NOW, I COUNTER-ATTACK WITH POWERED CATERPIL-LAR!
BUSTER CANNON!!
NGH...
REVERSE CARD, OPEN!!
WHOOSH

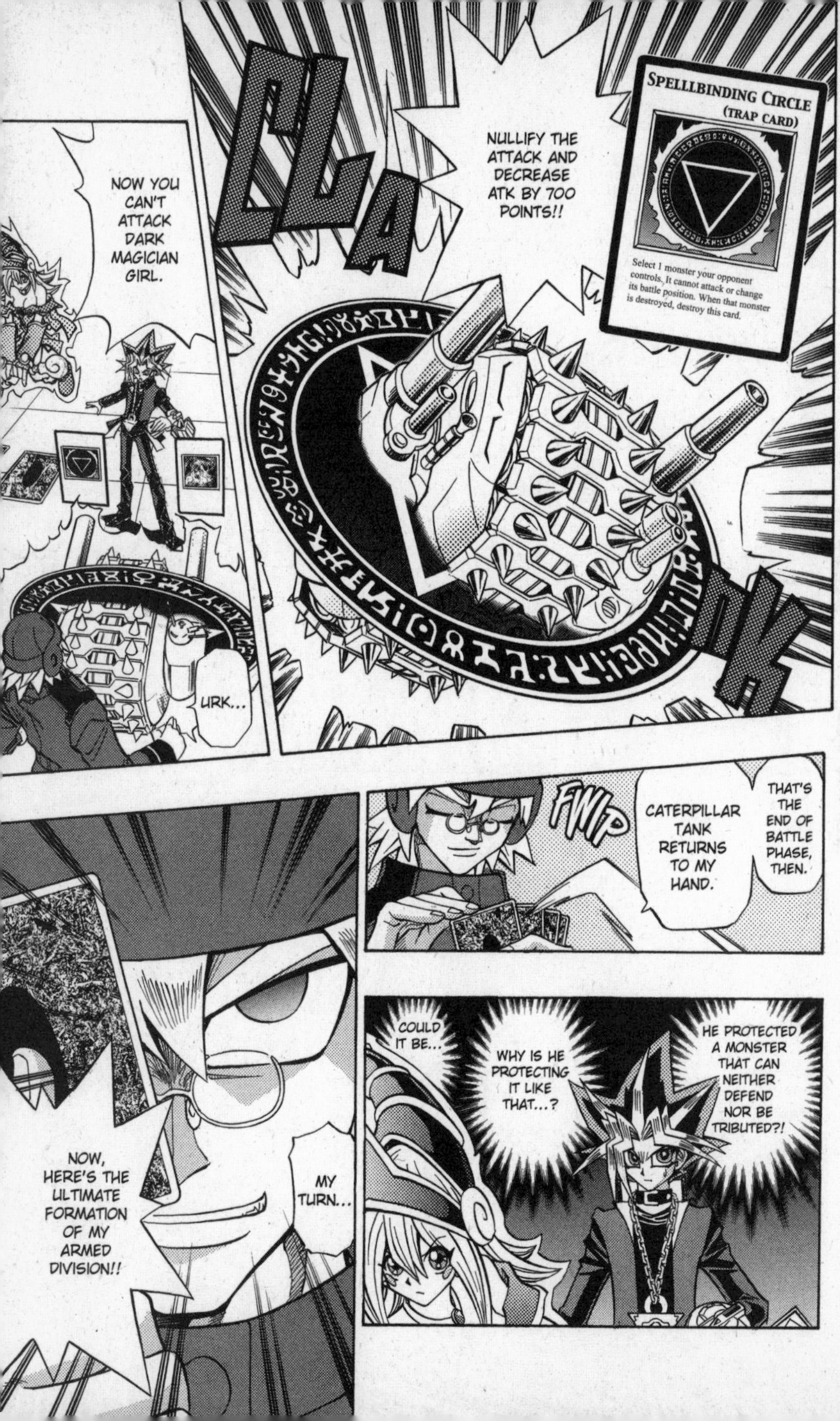

SPELLLBINDING CIRCLE
(TRAP CARD)
Select 1 monster your opponent controls. It cannot attack or change its battle position. When that monster is destroyed, destroy this card.
NULLIFY THE ATTACK AND DECREASE ATK BY 700 POINTS!!
CLA
K
NOW YOU CAN'T ATTACK DARK MAGICIAN GIRL.
URK...
THAT'S THE END OF BATTLE PHASE, THEN.
CATERPILLAR TANK RETURNS TO MY HAND.
FWIP
HE PROTECTED A MONSTER THAT CAN NEITHER DEFEND NOR BE TRIBUTED?!
WHY IS HE PROTECTING IT LIKE THAT...?
COULD IT BE...
MY TURN...
NOW, HERE'S THE ULTIMATE FORMATION OF MY ARMED DIVISION!!

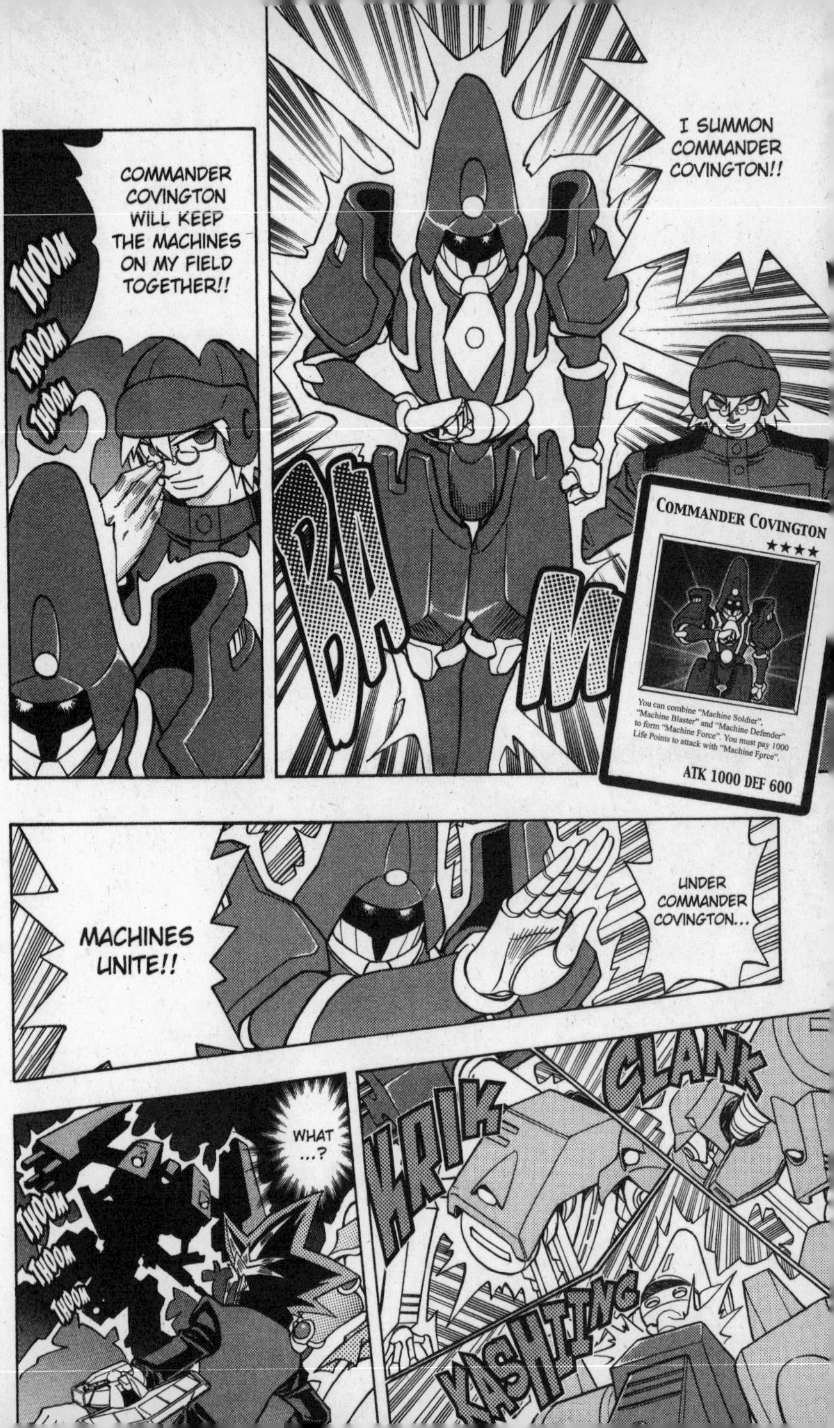
I SUMMON COMMANDER COVINGTON!!
BAM
COMMANDER COVINGTON
You can combine “Machine Soldier”, “Machine Blaster” and “Machine Defender” to form “Machine Force”. You must pay 1000 Life Points to attack with “Machine Fprce”.
ATK 1000 DEF 600
COMMANDER COVINGTON WILL KEEP THE MACHINES ON MY FIELD TOGETHER!!
THOOM
THOOM
THOOM
UNDER COMMANDER COVINGTON...
MACHINES UNITE!!
CLANK
KRIK
KASHTING
WHAT ...?
THOOM
THOOM
THOOM

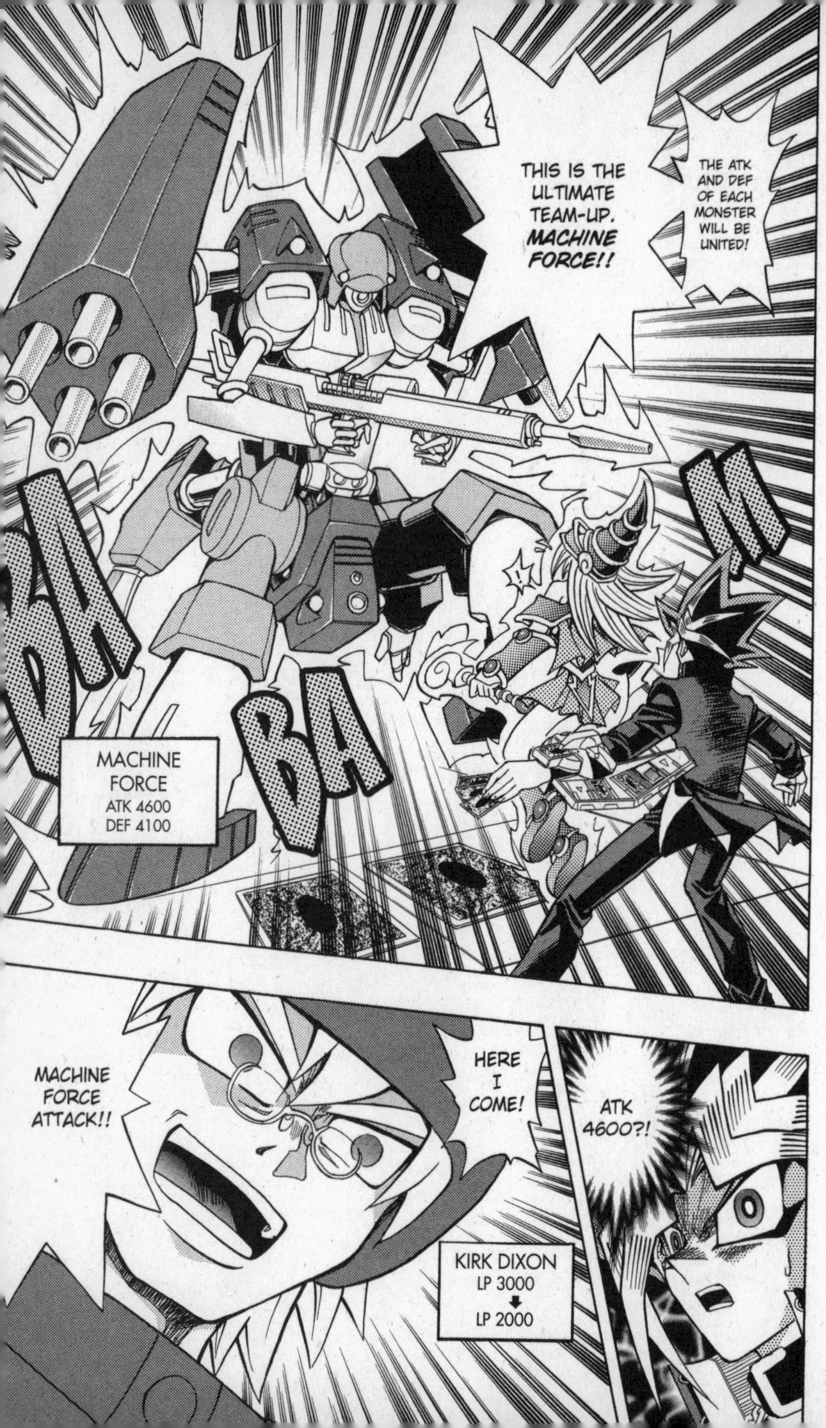
THE ATK AND DEF OF EACH MONSTER WILL BE UNITED!
THIS IS THE ULTIMATE TEAM-UP. MACHINE FORCE!!
M
BA
BA
MACHINE FORCE
ATK 4600
DEF 4100
ATK 4600?!
KIRK DIXON
LP 3000
LP 2000
HERE I COME!
MACHINE FORCE ATTACK!!

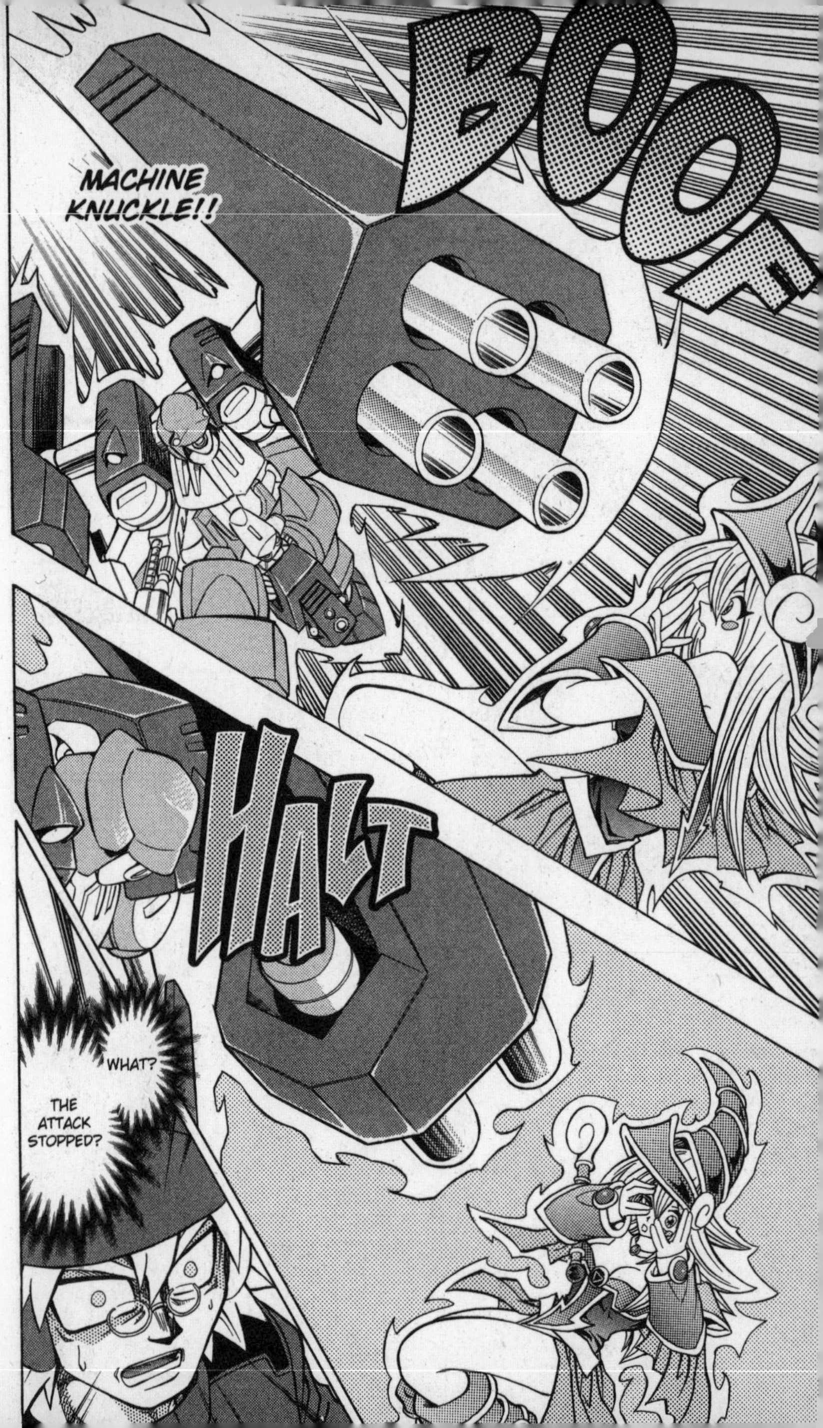
BOOOF
MACHINE KNUCKLE!!
HALT
WHAT?
THE ATTACK STOPPED?

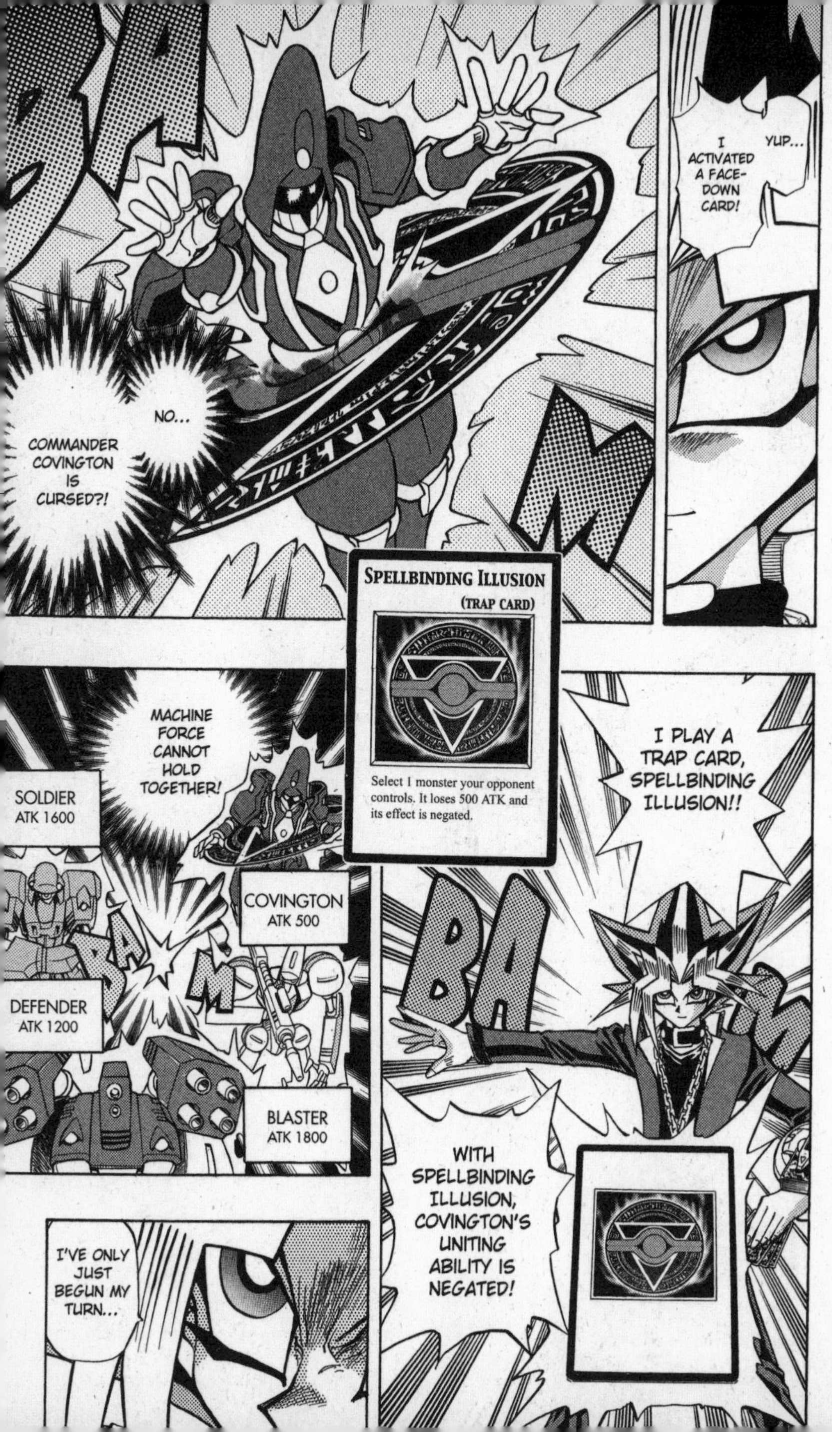
YUP...
I ACTIVATED A FACE-DOWN CARD!
NO...
COMMANDER COVINGTON IS CURSED?!
I PLAY A TRAP CARD, SPELLBINDING ILLUSION!!
SPELLBINDING ILLUSION
(TRAP CARD)
Select 1 monster your opponent controls. It loses 500 ATK and its effect is negated.
BA
WITH SPELLBINDING ILLUSION, COVINGTON'S UNITING ABILITY IS NEGATED!
MACHINE FORCE CANNOT HOLD TOGETHER!
SOLDIER
ATK 1600
COVINGTON
ATK 500
BA
M
DEFENDER
ATK 1200
BLASTER
ATK 1800
I'VE ONLY JUST BEGUN MY TURN...

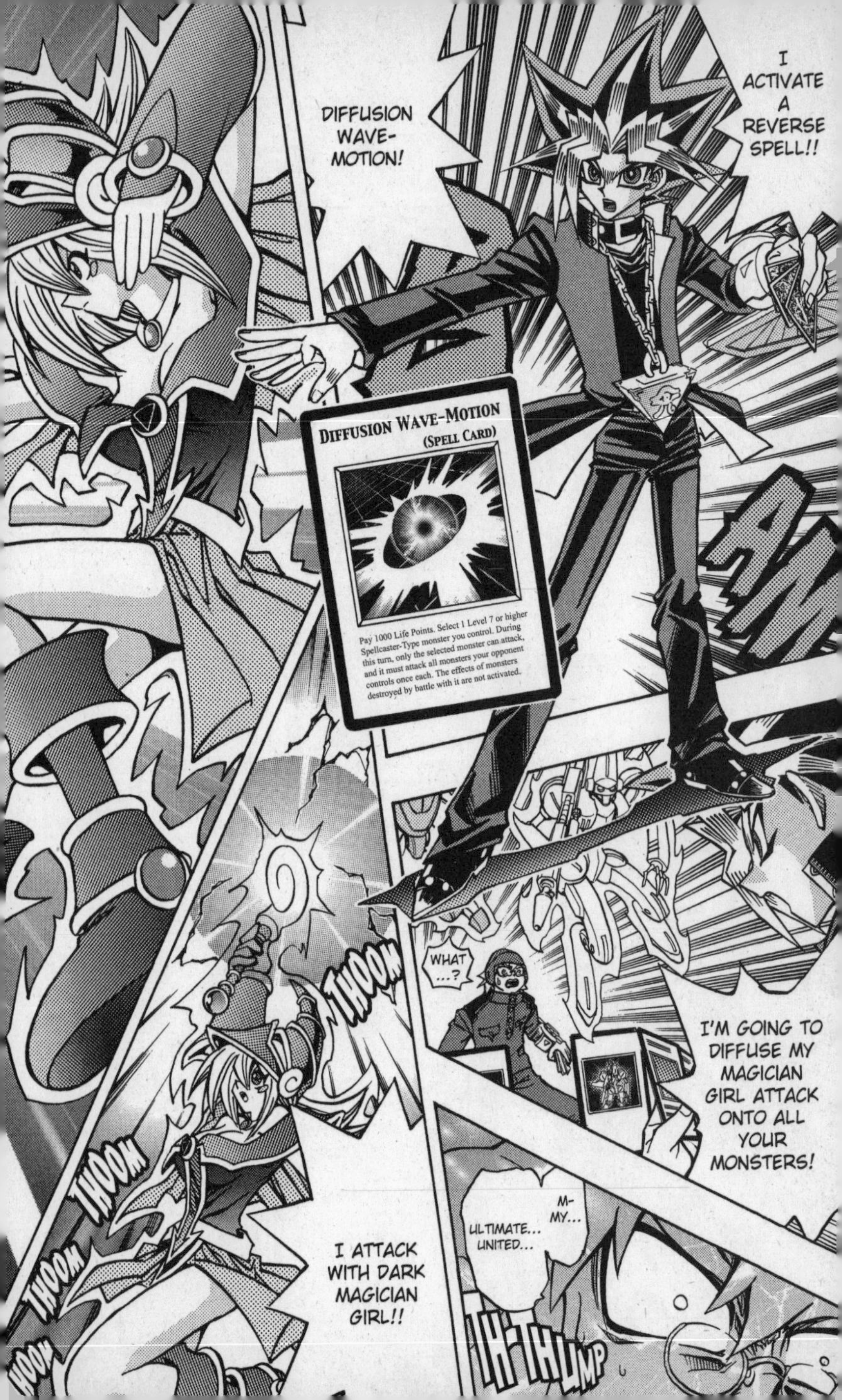
I ACTIVATE A REVERSE SPELL!!
DIFFUSION WAVE-MOTION!
DIFFUSION WAVE-MOTION
(SPELL CARD)
Pay 1000 Life Points. Select 1 Level 7 or higher Spellcaster-Type monster you control. During this turn, only the selected monster can attack, and it must attack all monsters your opponent controls once each. The effects of monsters destroyed by battle with it are not activated.
WHAT ...?
I'M GOING TO DIFFUSE MY MAGICIAN GIRL ATTACK ONTO ALL YOUR MONSTERS!
M-MY...
ULTIMATE... UNITED...
TH-THUMP
THOOM
I ATTACK WITH DARK MAGICIAN GIRL!!
THOOM
THOOM
THOOM

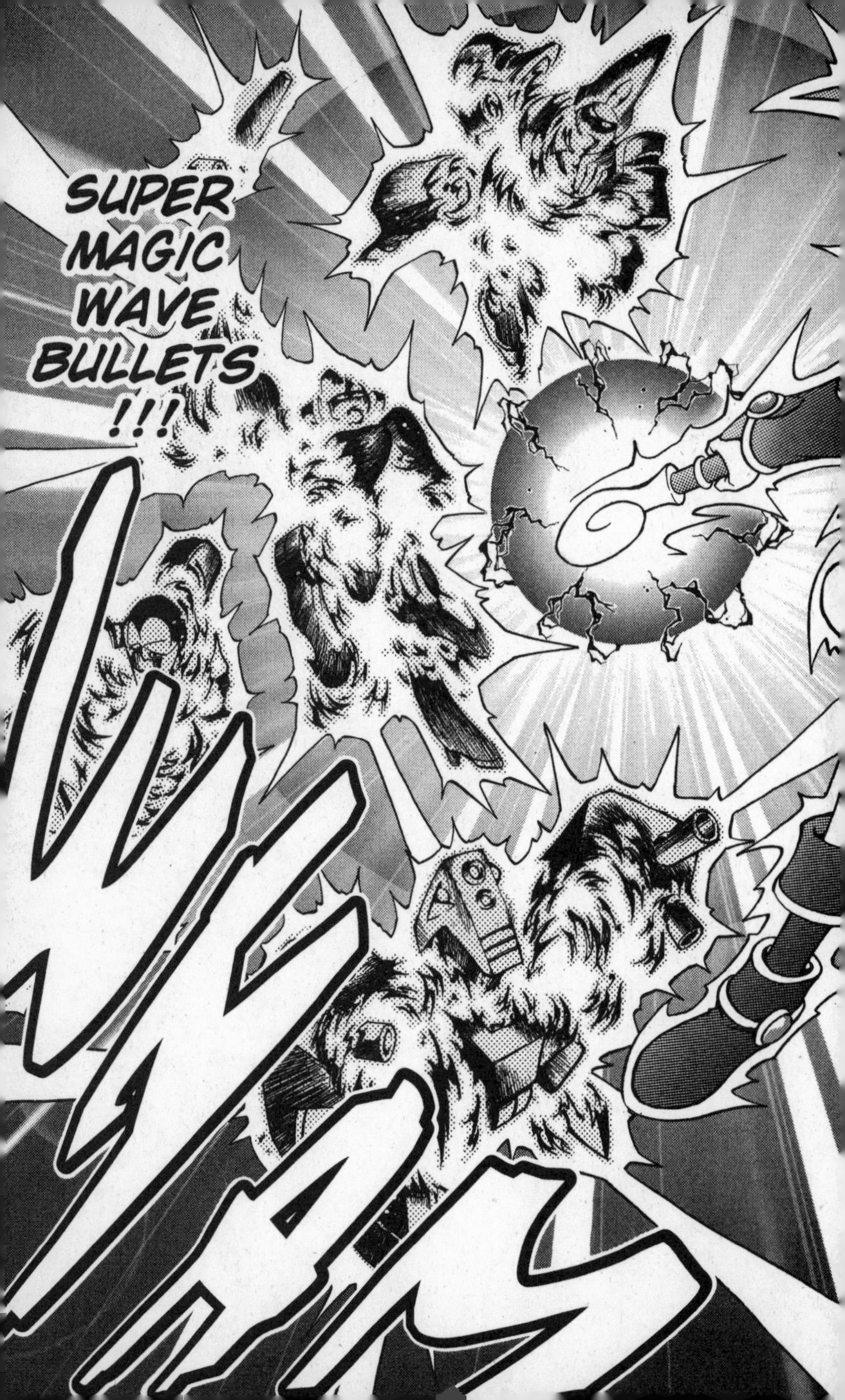
SUPER MAGIC WAVE BULLETS !!!

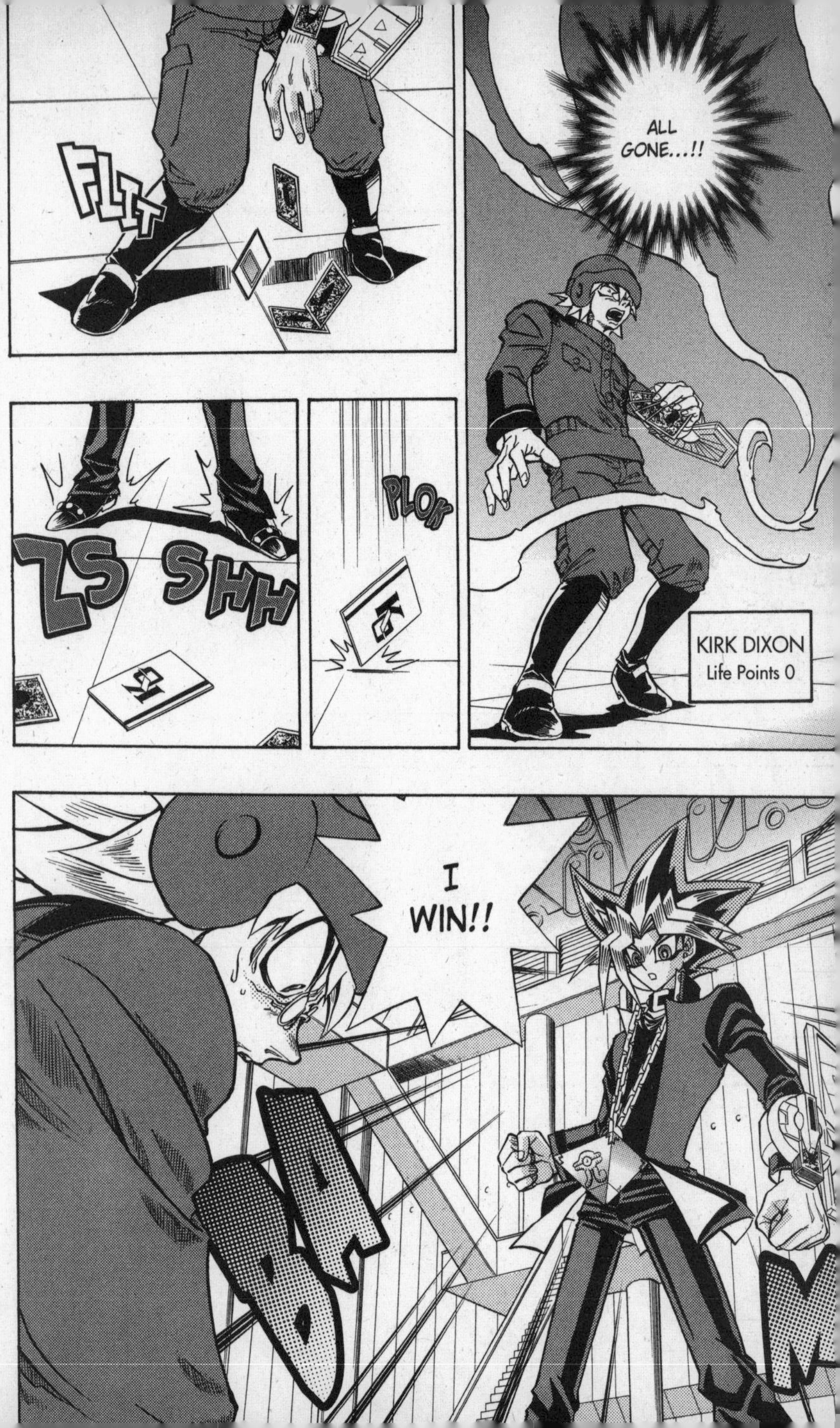
ALL GONE...!!
KIRK DIXON
Life Points 0
FLIT
PLOK
ZS SHH
I WIN!!

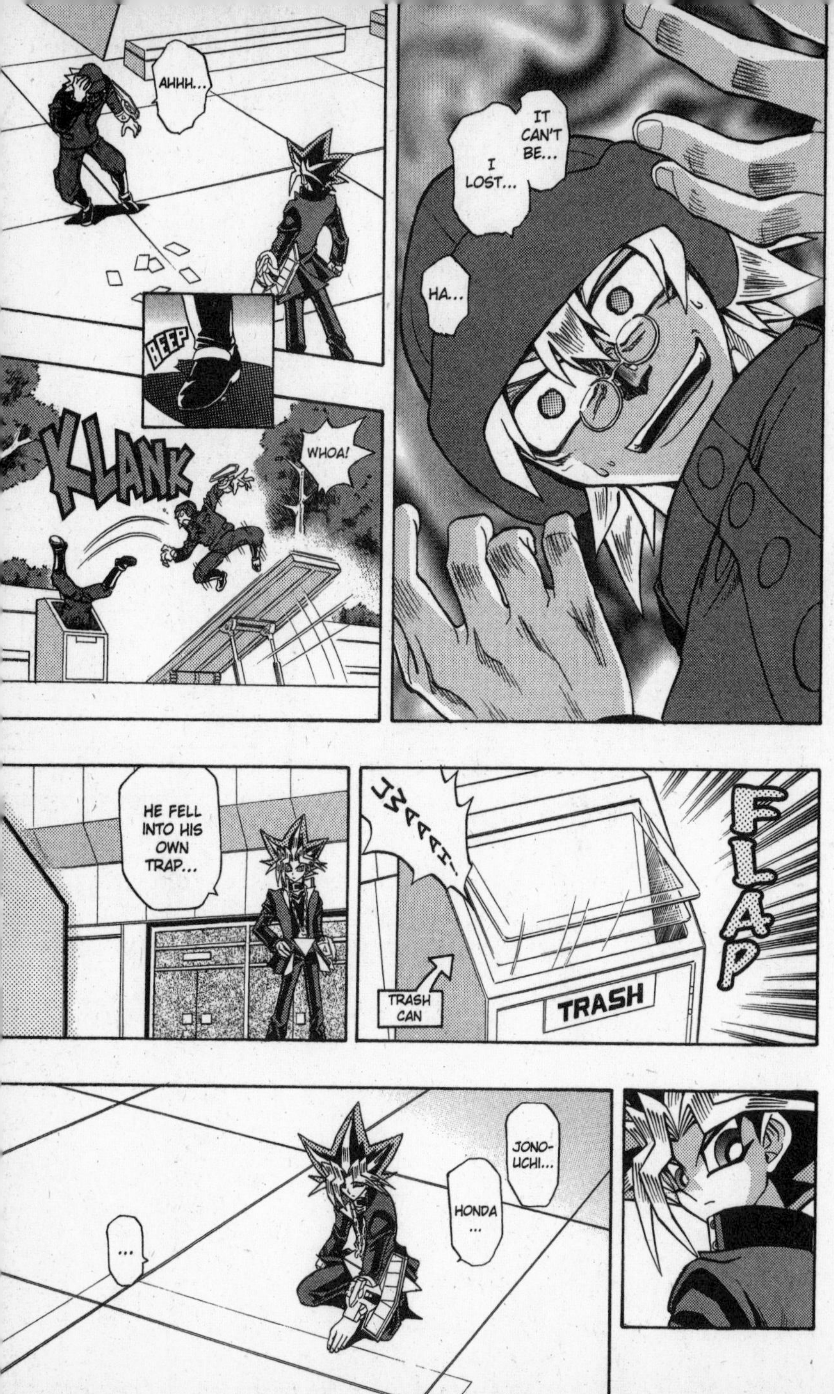
IT CAN'T BE...
I LOST...
HA...
AHHH...
BEEP
K-LANK
WHOA!
FLAP
TRASH
TRASH CAN
HE FELL INTO HIS OWN TRAP...
JONO-UCHI...
HONDA...
...

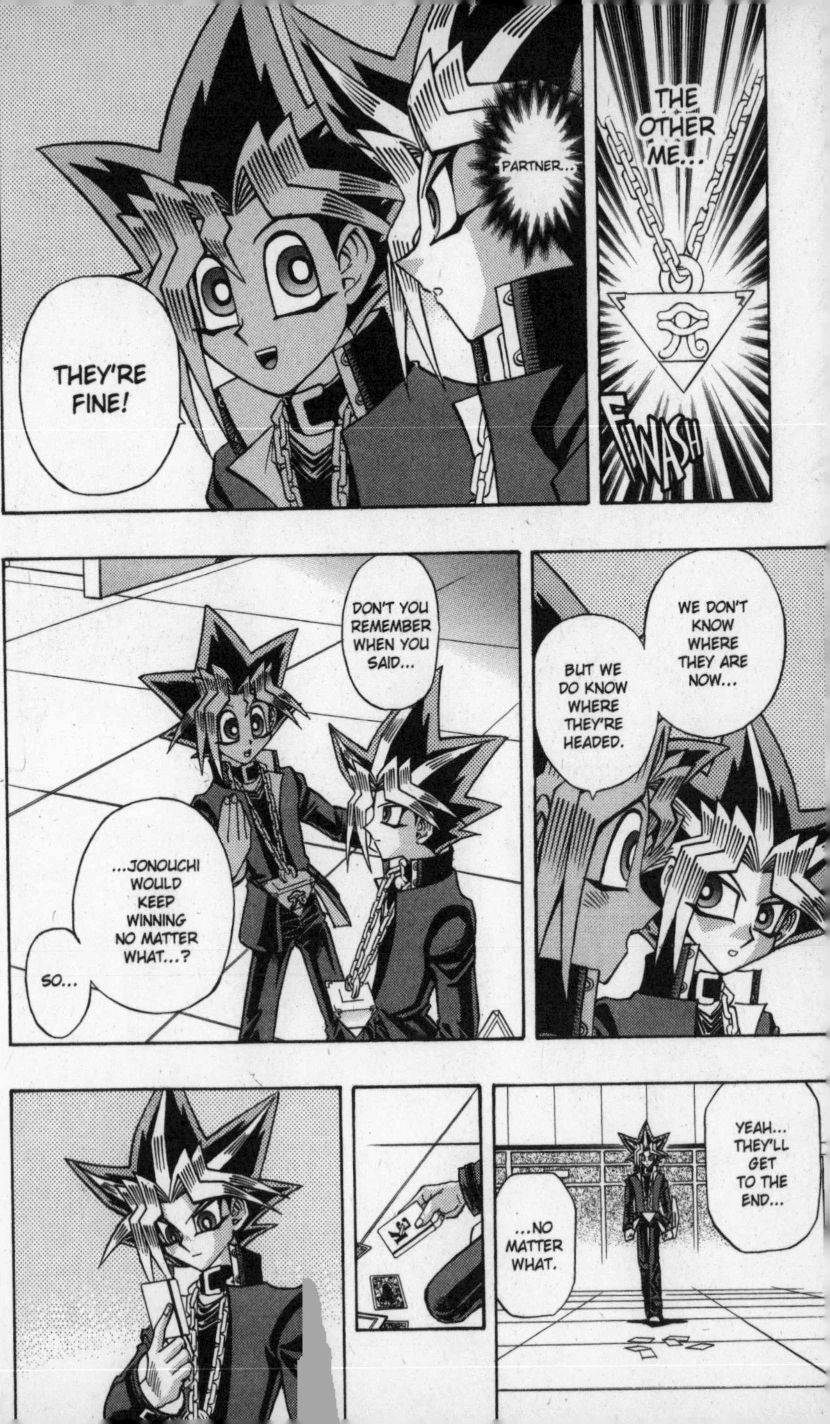
THE OTHER ME...
FWASH
PARTNER...
THEY'RE FINE!
WE DON'T KNOW WHERE THEY ARE NOW...
BUT WE DO KNOW WHERE THEY'RE HEADED.
DON'T YOU REMEMBER WHEN YOU SAID...
...JONOUCHI WOULD KEEP WINNING NO MATTER WHAT...?
SO...
YEAH... THEY'LL GET TO THE END...
...NO MATTER WHAT.

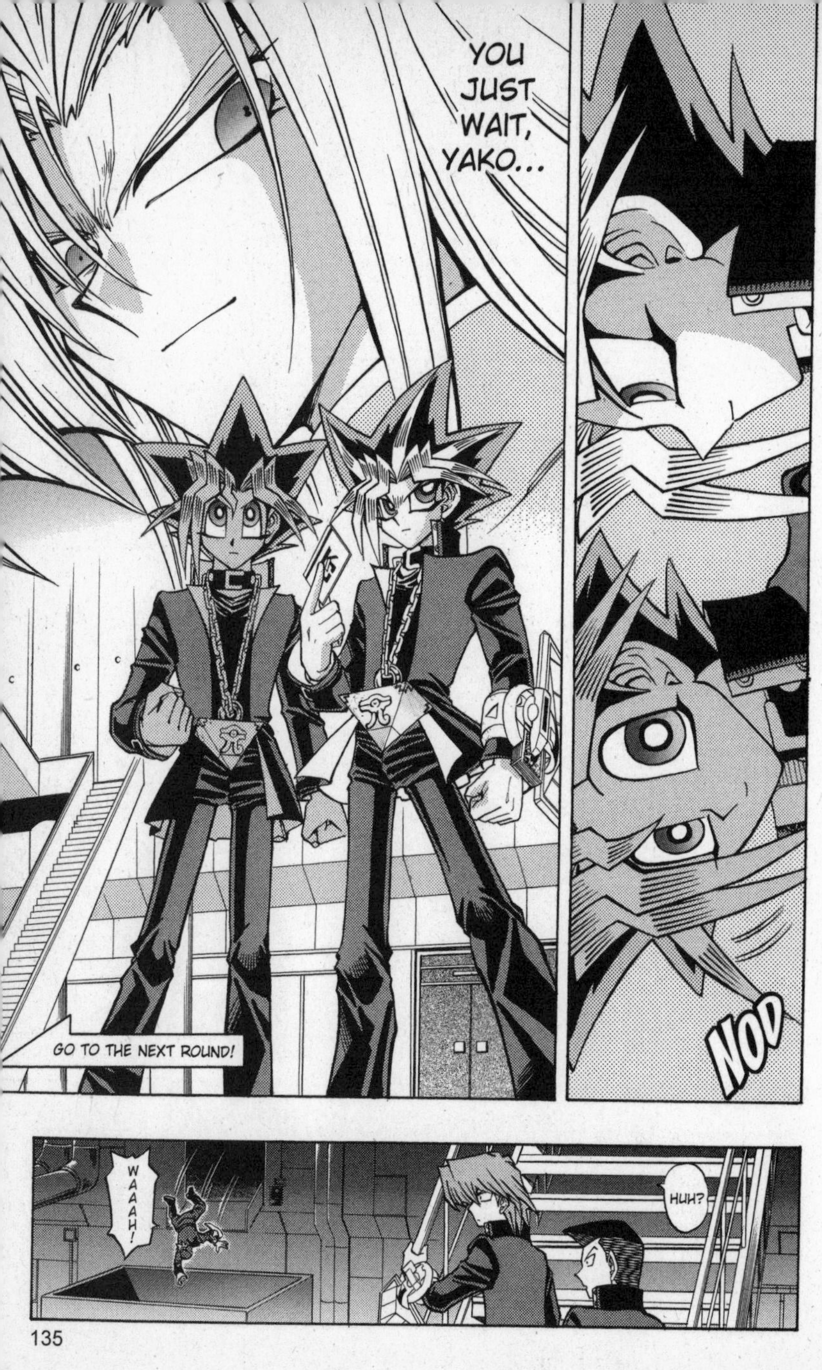
NOD
YOU JUST WAIT, YAKO...
GO TO THE NEXT ROUND!
HUH?
WAAAH!

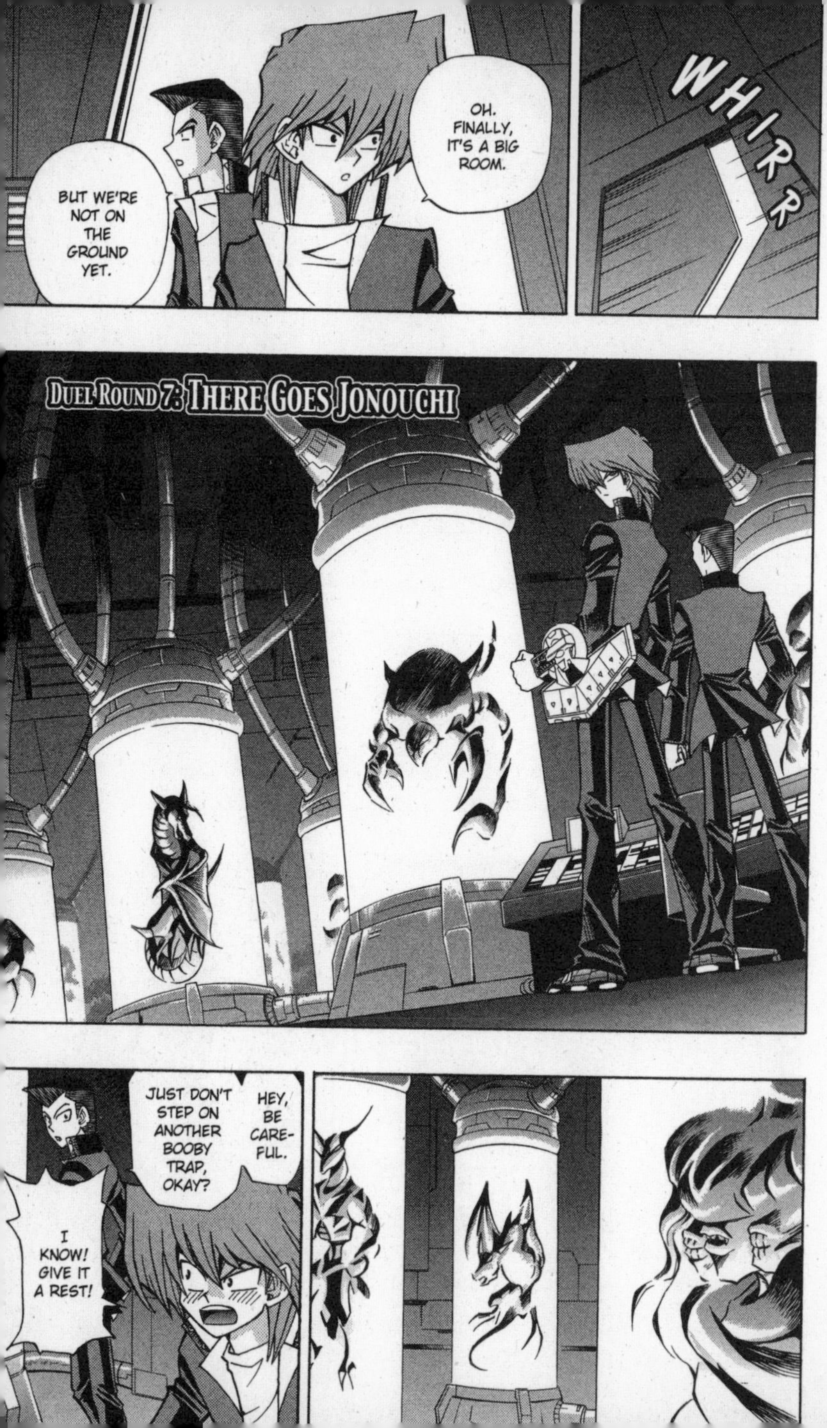
WHIRR
OH. FINALLY, IT'S A BIG ROOM.
BUT WE'RE NOT ON THE GROUND YET.
DUEL ROUND 7: THERE GOES JONOUCHI
HEY, BE CAREFUL.
JUST DON'T STEP ON ANOTHER BOOBY TRAP, OKAY?
I KNOW! GIVE IT A REST!

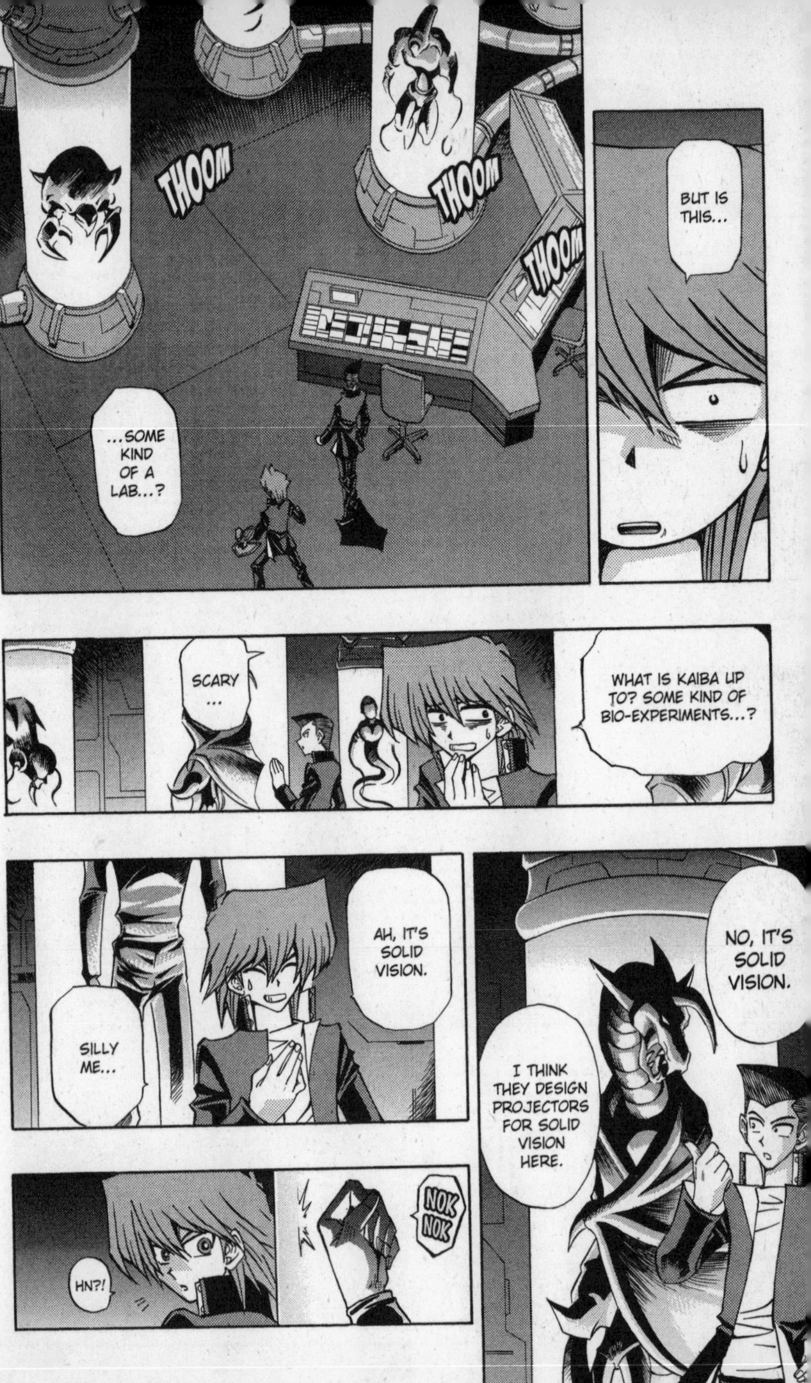
BUT IS THIS...
THOOM
THOOM
THOOM
...SOME KIND OF A LAB...?
WHAT IS KAIBA UP TO? SOME KIND OF BIO-EXPERIMENTS...?
SCARY ...
NO, IT'S SOLID VISION.
I THINK THEY DESIGN PROJECTORS FOR SOLID VISION HERE.
AH, IT'S SOLID VISION.
SILLY ME...
NOK NOK
HN?!

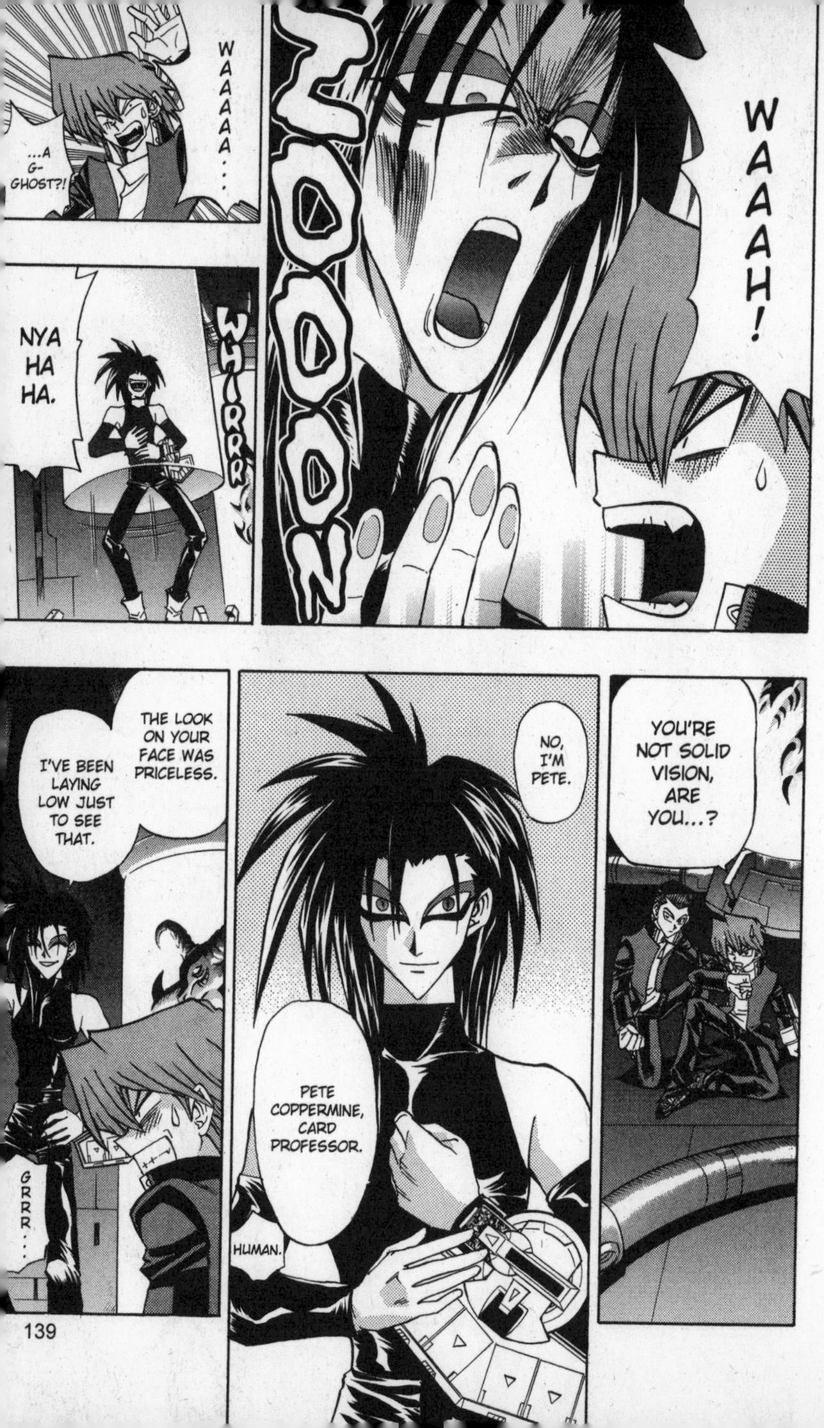
WAAAAH!
ZOOOON
WAAAAAA...
...A G-GHOST?!
NYA HA HA.
WHIRRR
YOU'RE NOT SOLID VISION, ARE YOU...?
NO, I'M PETE.
PETE COPPERMINE, CARD PROFESSOR.
HUMAN.
THE LOOK ON YOUR FACE WAS PRICELESS.
I'VE BEEN LAYING LOW JUST TO SEE THAT.
GRRR...

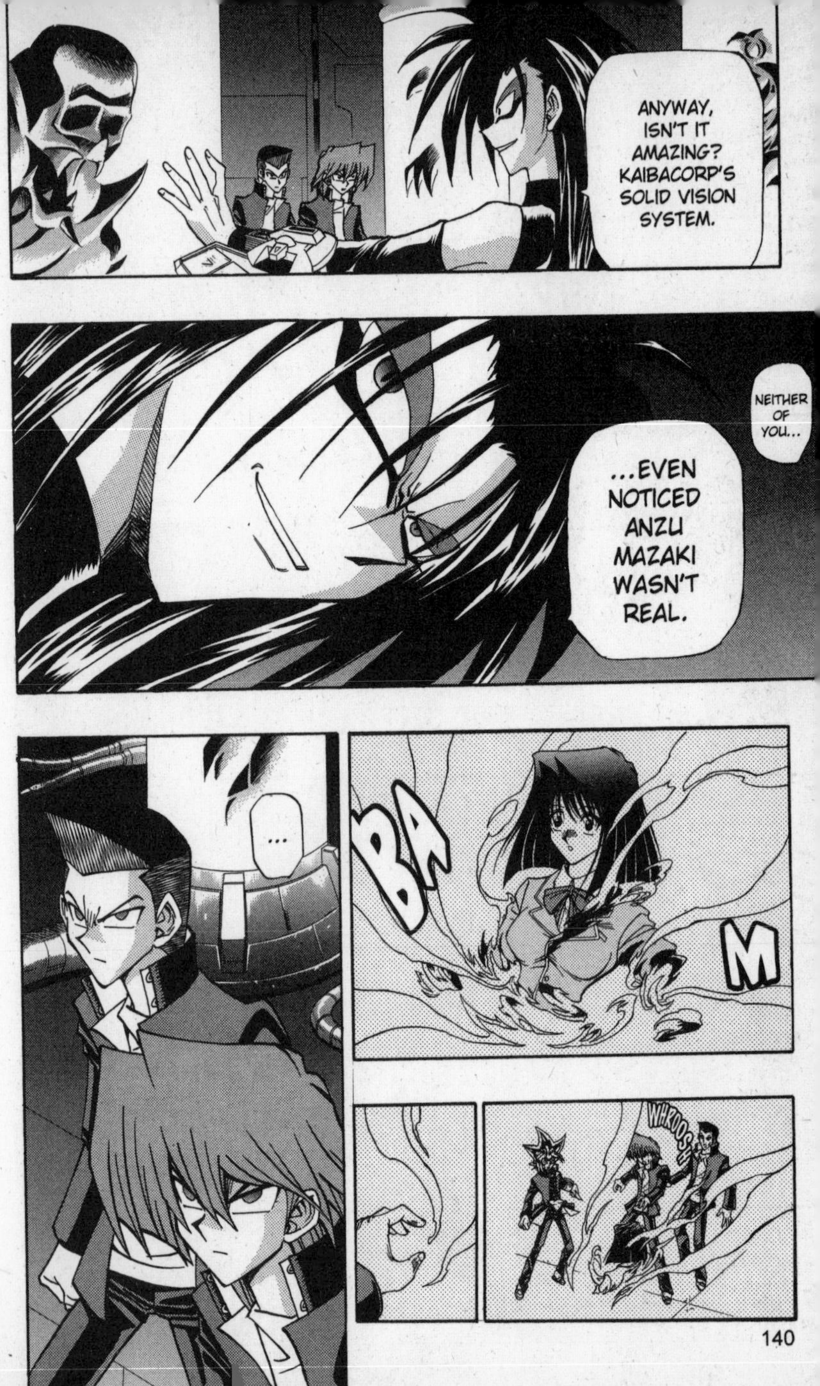
ANYWAY, ISN'T IT AMAZING? KAIBACORP'S SOLID VISION SYSTEM.
NEITHER OF YOU...
...EVEN NOTICED ANZU MAZAKI WASN'T REAL.
BA
M
WHOOSH
...

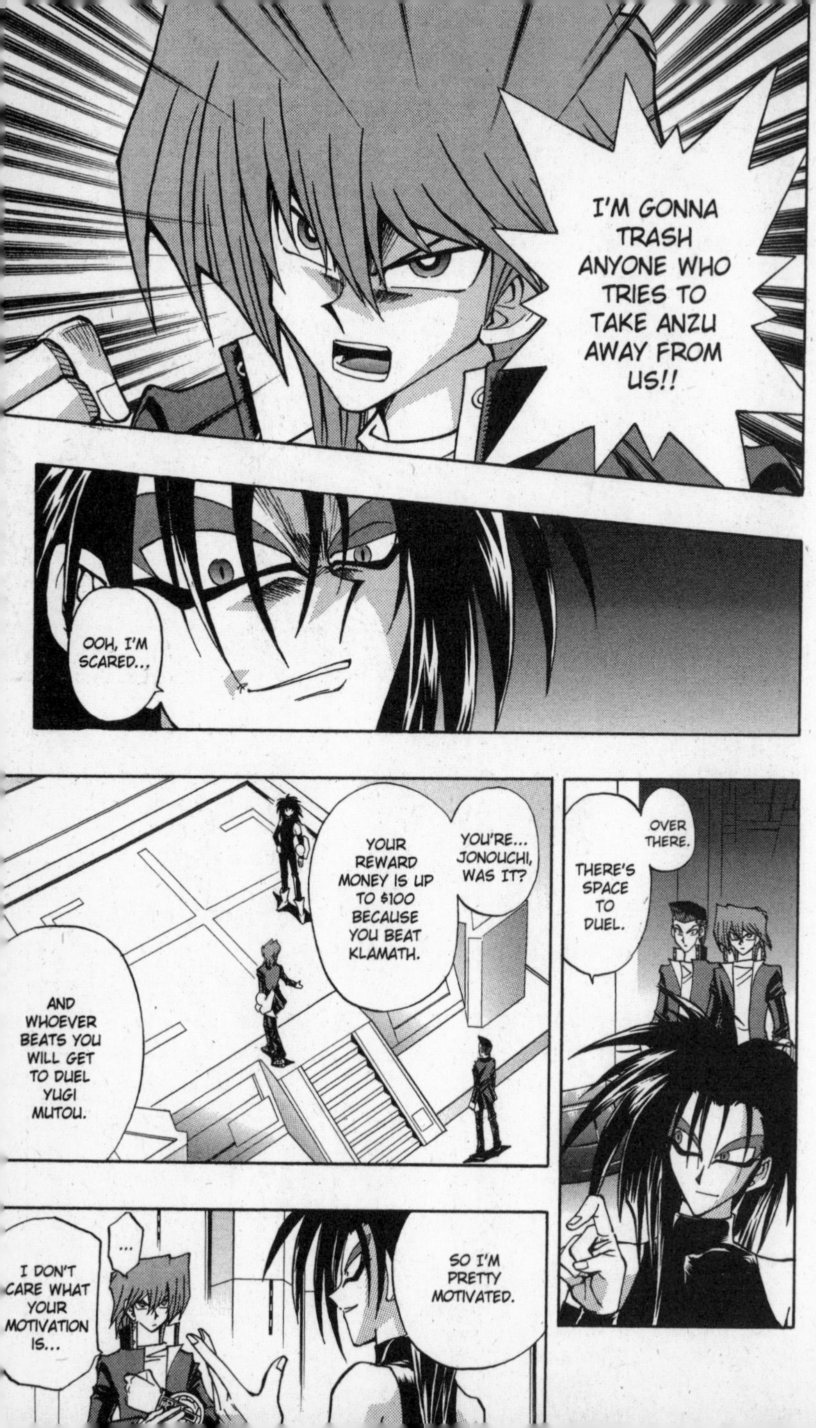
I'M GONNA TRASH ANYONE WHO TRIES TO TAKE ANZU AWAY FROM US!!
OOH, I'M SCARED...
OVER THERE.
THERE'S SPACE TO DUEL.
YOU'RE... JONOUCHI, WAS IT?
YOUR REWARD MONEY IS UP TO $100 BECAUSE YOU BEAT KLAMATH.
AND WHOEVER BEATS YOU WILL GET TO DUEL YUGI MUTOU.
SO I'M PRETTY MOTIVATED.
...
I DON'T CARE WHAT YOUR MOTIVATION IS...

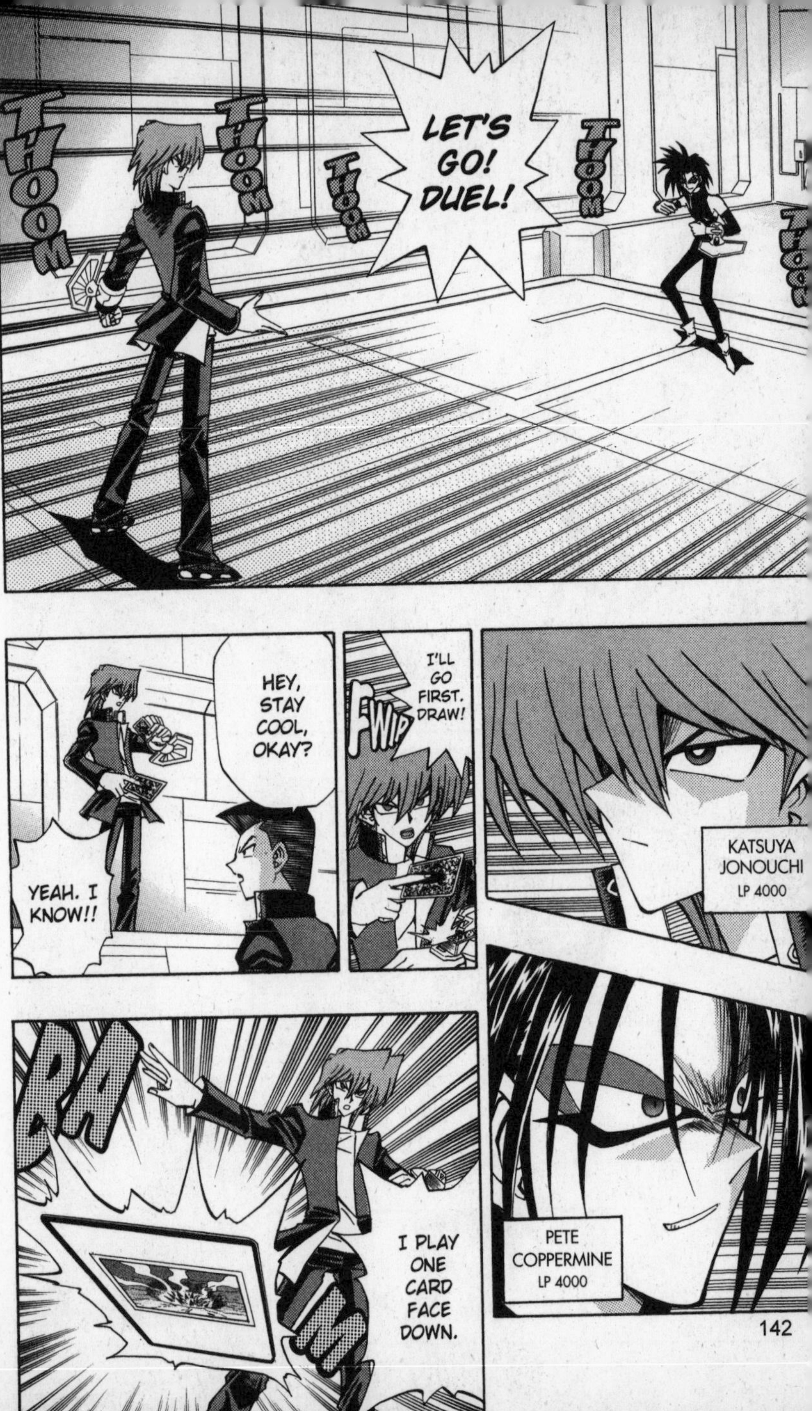
THOOM
THOOM
THOOM
LET'S GO! DUEL!
THOOM
THOOM
KATSUYA JONOUCHI
LP 4000
FWIP
I'LL GO FIRST. DRAW!
HEY, STAY COOL, OKAY?
YEAH. I KNOW!!
PETE COPPERMINE
LP 4000
BA
I PLAY ONE CARD FACE DOWN.

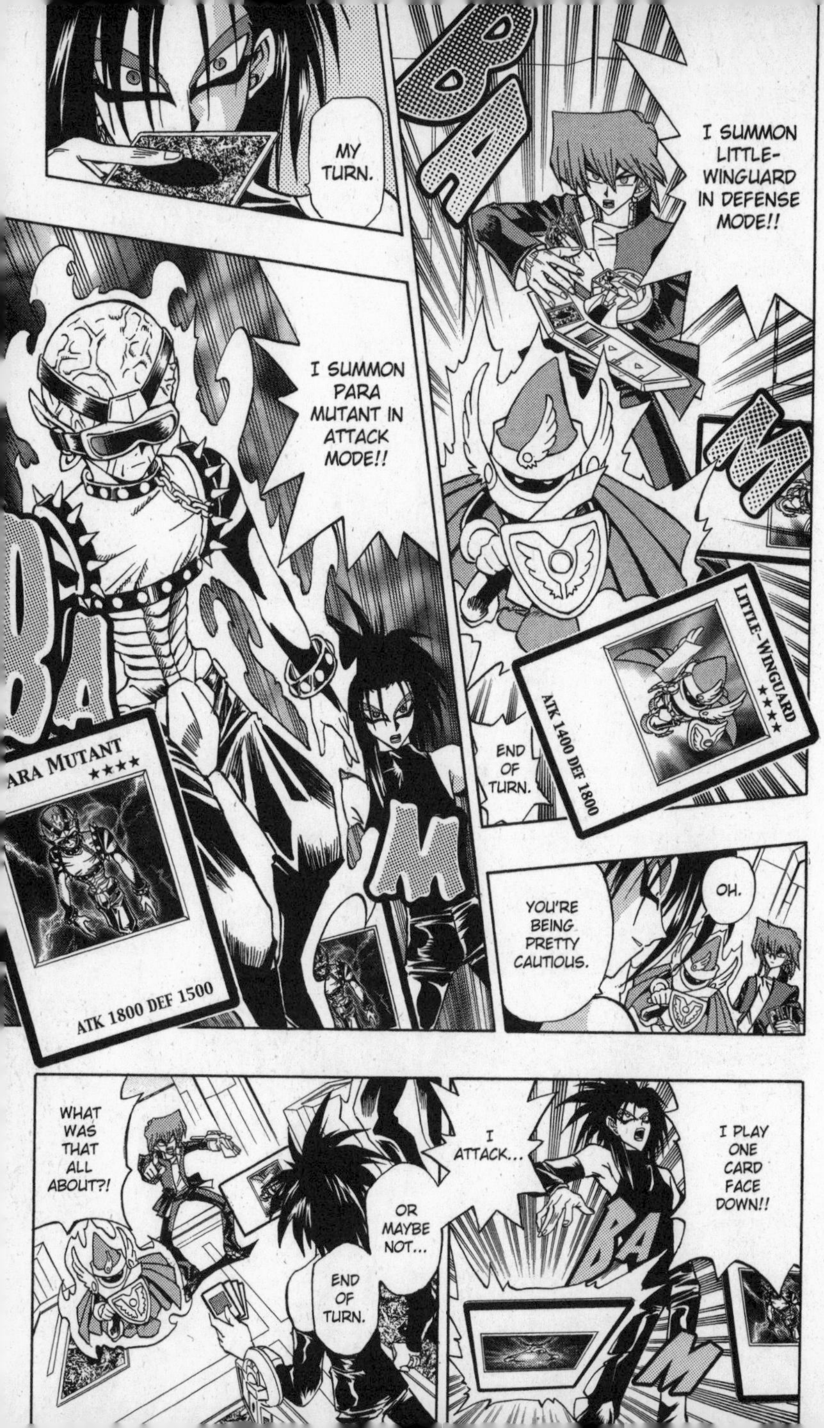
I SUMMON LITTLE-WINGUARD IN DEFENSE MODE!!
LITTLE-WINGUARD ★★★★
ATK 1400 DEF 1800
END OF TURN.
OH.
YOU'RE BEING PRETTY CAUTIOUS.
MY TURN.
I SUMMON PARA MUTANT IN ATTACK MODE!!
ARA MUTANT ★★★★
ATK 1800 DEF 1500
I PLAY ONE CARD FACE DOWN!!
I ATTACK...
OR MAYBE NOT...
END OF TURN.
WHAT WAS THAT ALL ABOUT?!

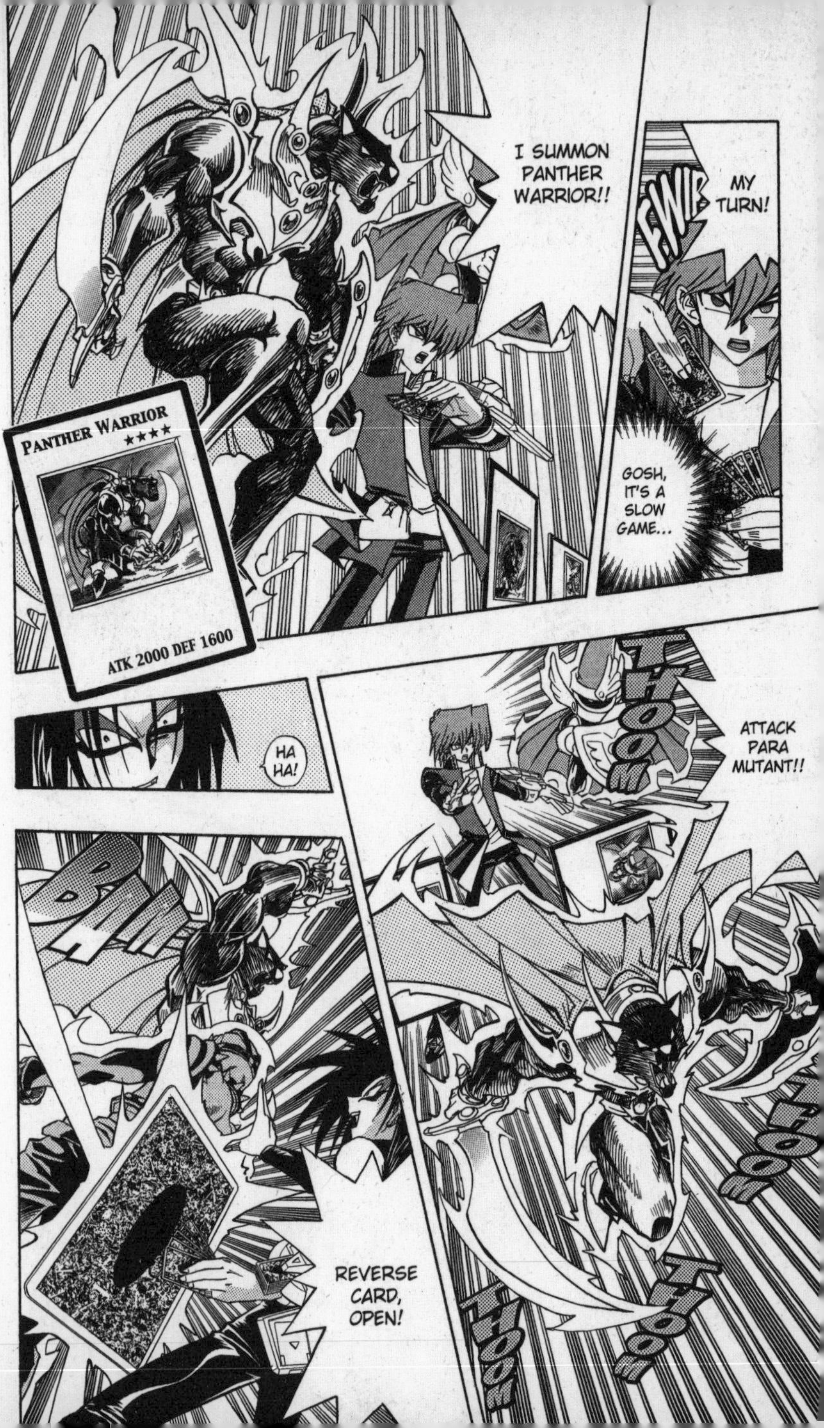
FWIP
MY TURN!
GOSH, IT'S A SLOW GAME...
I SUMMON PANTHER WARRIOR!!
PANTHER WARRIOR ★★★★
ATK 2000 DEF 1600
THOOM
ATTACK PARA MUTANT!!
HA HA!
THOOM
THOOM
BAM
REVERSE CARD, OPEN!

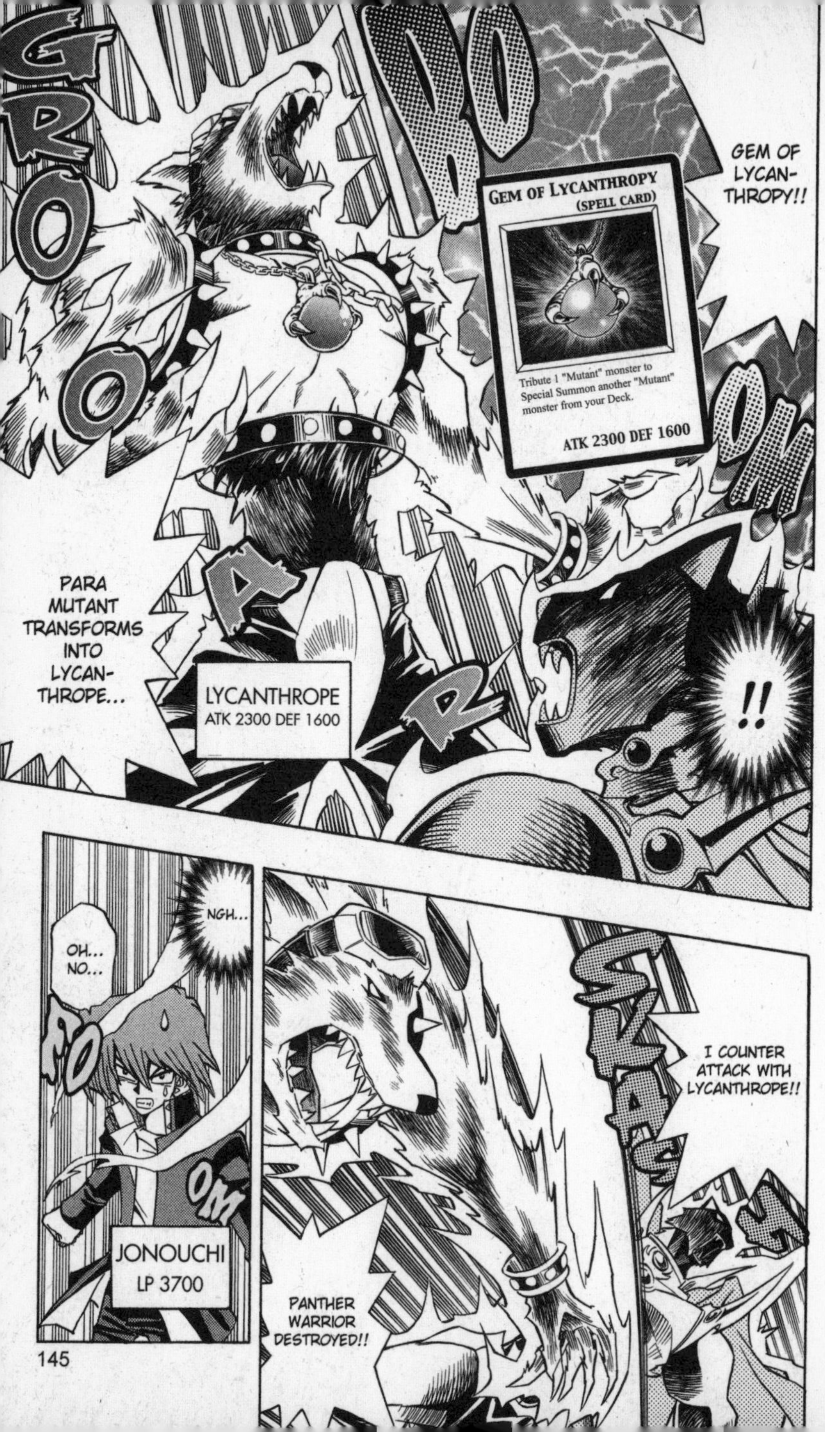
GEM OF LYCAN-THROPY!!
Gem of Lycanthropy
(spell card)
Tribute 1 "Mutant" monster to Special Summon another "Mutant" monster from your Deck.
ATK 2300 DEF 1600
PARA MUTANT TRANSFORMS INTO LYCAN-THROPE...
LYCANTHROPE
ATK 2300 DEF 1600
!!
I COUNTER ATTACK WITH LYCANTHROPE!!
PANTHER WARRIOR DESTROYED!!
NGH...
OH... NO...
JONOUCHI
LP 3700

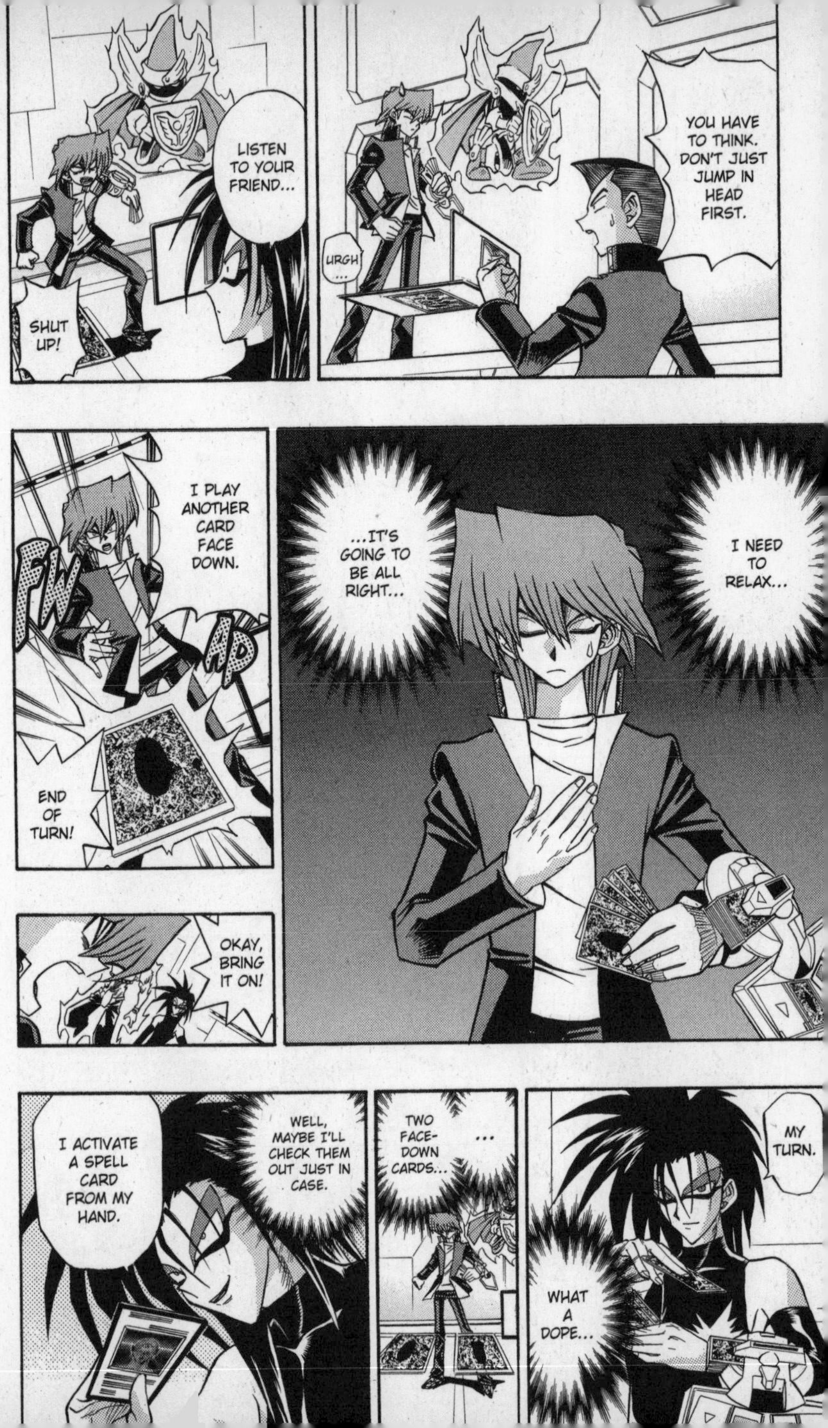
YOU HAVE TO THINK. DON'T JUST JUMP IN HEAD FIRST.
URGH...
LISTEN TO YOUR FRIEND...
SHUT UP!
I NEED TO RELAX...
...IT'S GOING TO BE ALL RIGHT...
I PLAY ANOTHER CARD FACE DOWN.
END OF TURN!
OKAY, BRING IT ON!
MY TURN.
WHAT A DOPE...
...
TWO FACE-DOWN CARDS...
WELL, MAYBE I'LL CHECK THEM OUT JUST IN CASE.
I ACTIVATE A SPELL CARD FROM MY HAND.

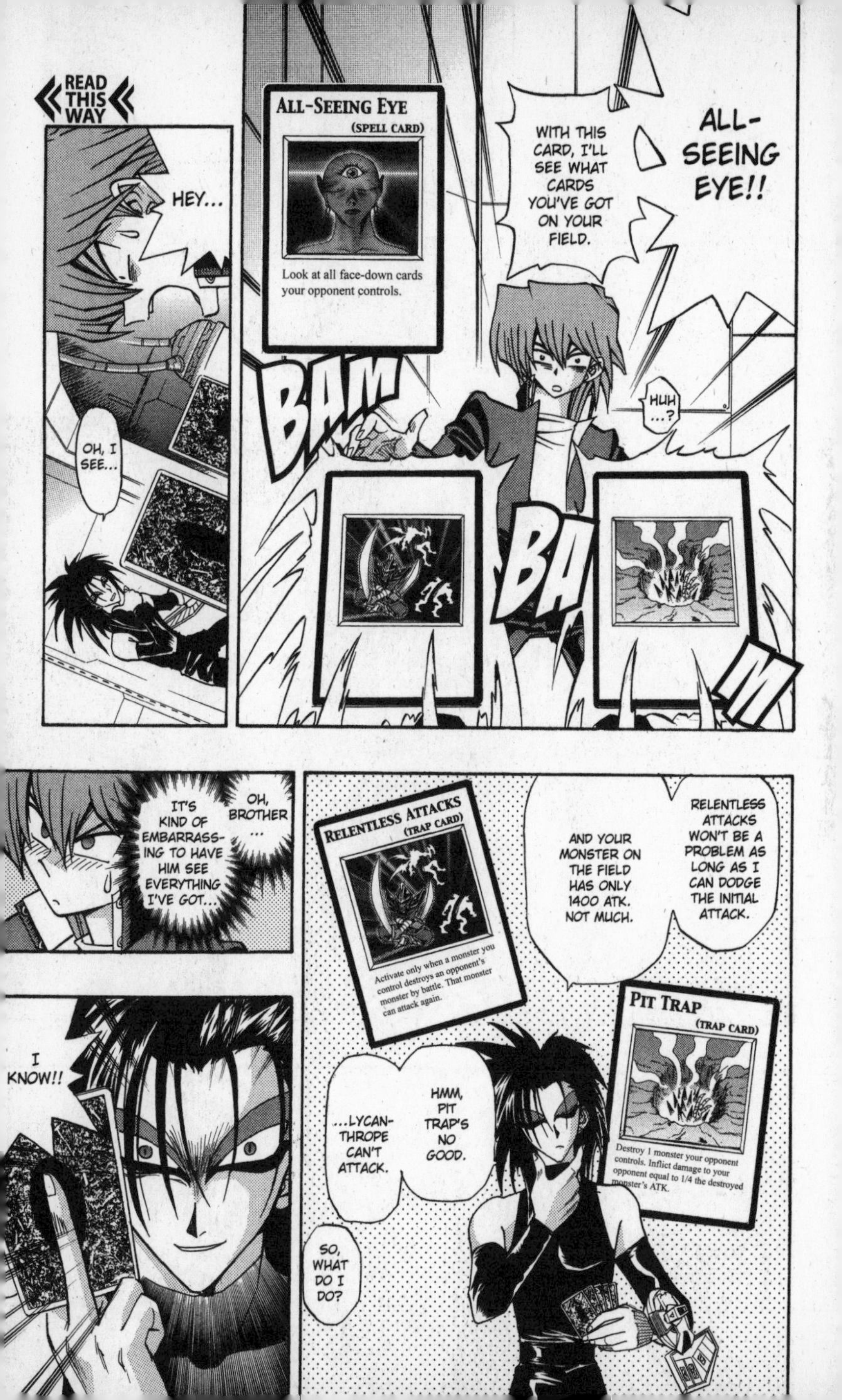

READ THIS WAY
ALL-SEEING EYE!!
WITH THIS CARD, I'LL SEE WHAT CARDS YOU'VE GOT ON YOUR FIELD.
ALL-SEEING EYE
(SPELL CARD)
Look at all face-down cards your opponent controls.
BAM
HUH ...?
BAM
HEY...
OH, I SEE...
RELENTLESS ATTACKS WON'T BE A PROBLEM AS LONG AS I CAN DODGE THE INITIAL ATTACK.
AND YOUR MONSTER ON THE FIELD HAS ONLY 1400 ATK. NOT MUCH.
RELENTLESS ATTACKS
(TRAP CARD)
Activate only when a monster you control destroys an opponent's monster by battle. That monster can attack again.
PIT TRAP
(TRAP CARD)
Destroy 1 monster your opponent controls. Inflict damage to your opponent equal to 1/4 the destroyed monster's ATK.
HMM, PIT TRAP'S NO GOOD.
...LYCANTHROPE CAN'T ATTACK.
SO, WHAT DO I DO?
OH, BROTHER...
IT'S KIND OF EMBARRASSING TO HAVE HIM SEE EVERYTHING I'VE GOT...
I KNOW!!

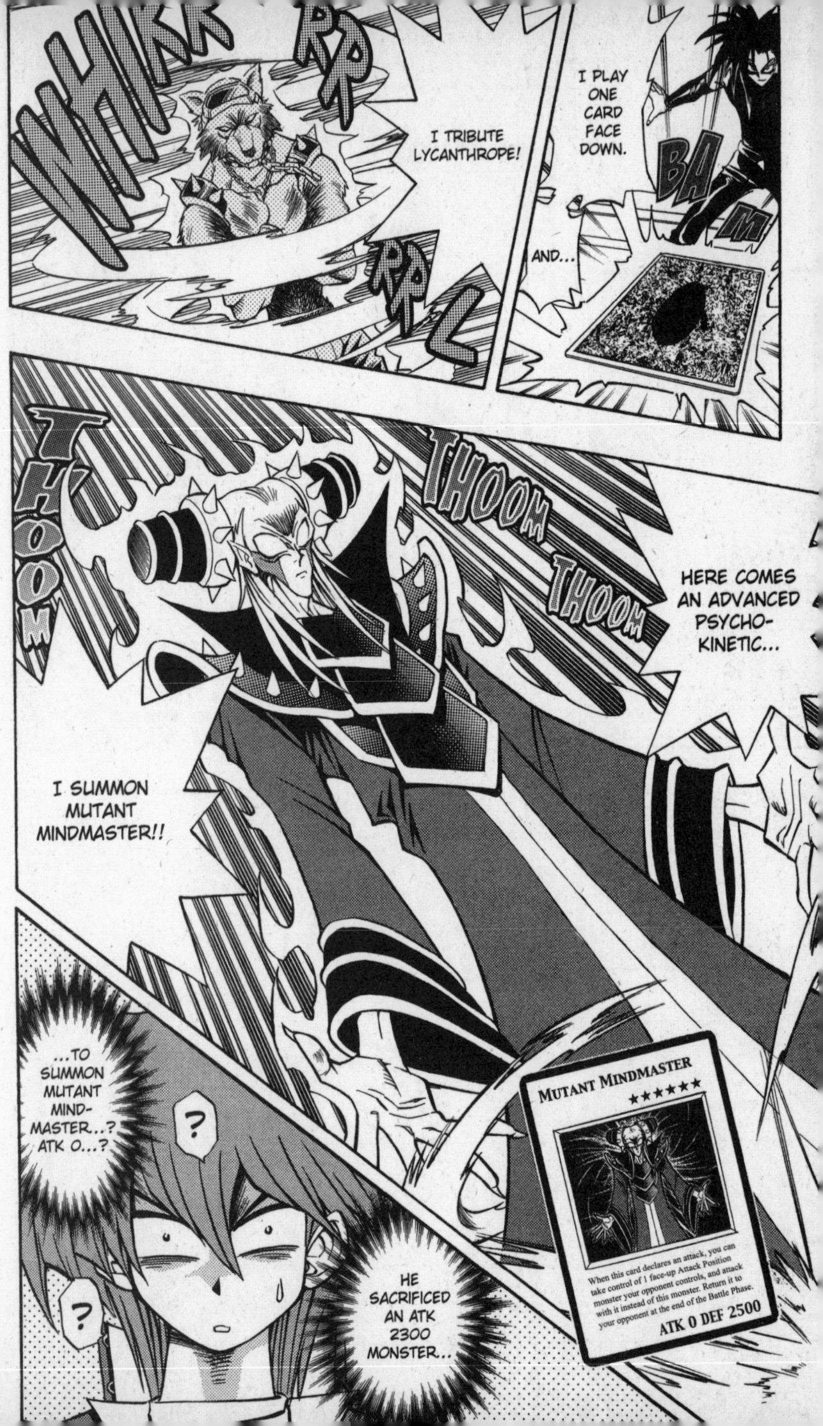
I PLAY ONE CARD FACE DOWN.
BAM
AND...
WHIRR
I TRIBUTE LYCANTHROPE!
RRRL
HERE COMES AN ADVANCED PSYCHO-KINETIC...
THOOM
THOOM
THOOM
I SUMMON MUTANT MINDMASTER!!
MUTANT MINDMASTER
When this card declares an attack, you can take control of 1 face-up Attack Position monster your opponent controls, and attack with it instead of this monster. Return it to your opponent at the end of the Battle Phase.
ATK 0 DEF 2500
HE SACRIFICED AN ATK 2300 MONSTER...
...TO SUMMON MUTANT MIND-MASTER..? ATK 0...?
?
?

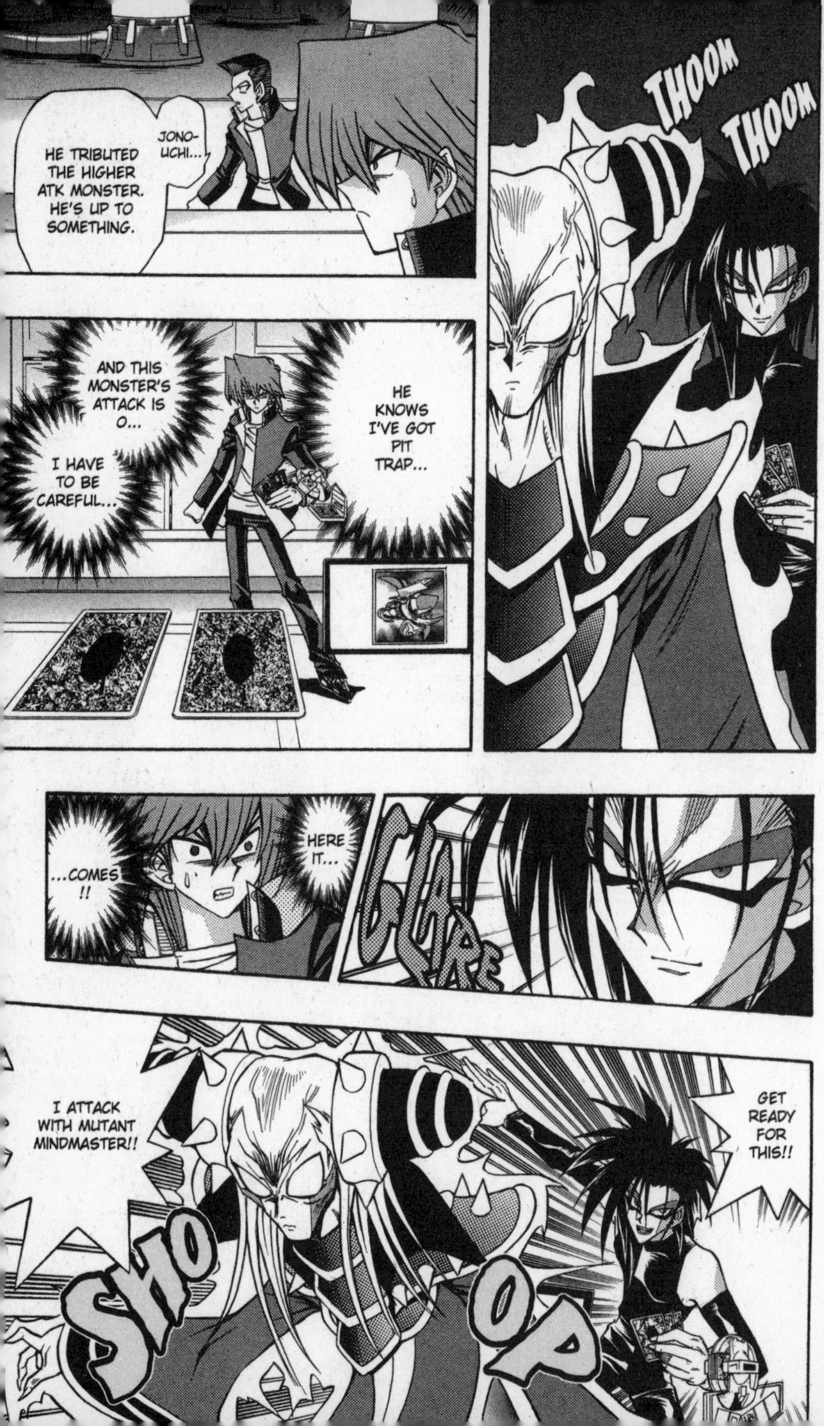
THOOM THOOM
JONO-UCHI...
HE TRIBUTED THE HIGHER ATK MONSTER. HE'S UP TO SOMETHING.
HE KNOWS I'VE GOT PIT TRAP...
AND THIS MONSTER'S ATTACK IS 0...
I HAVE TO BE CAREFUL...
GLARE
HERE IT...
...COMES!!
GET READY FOR THIS!!
I ATTACK WITH MUTANT MINDMASTER!!
SHOOP

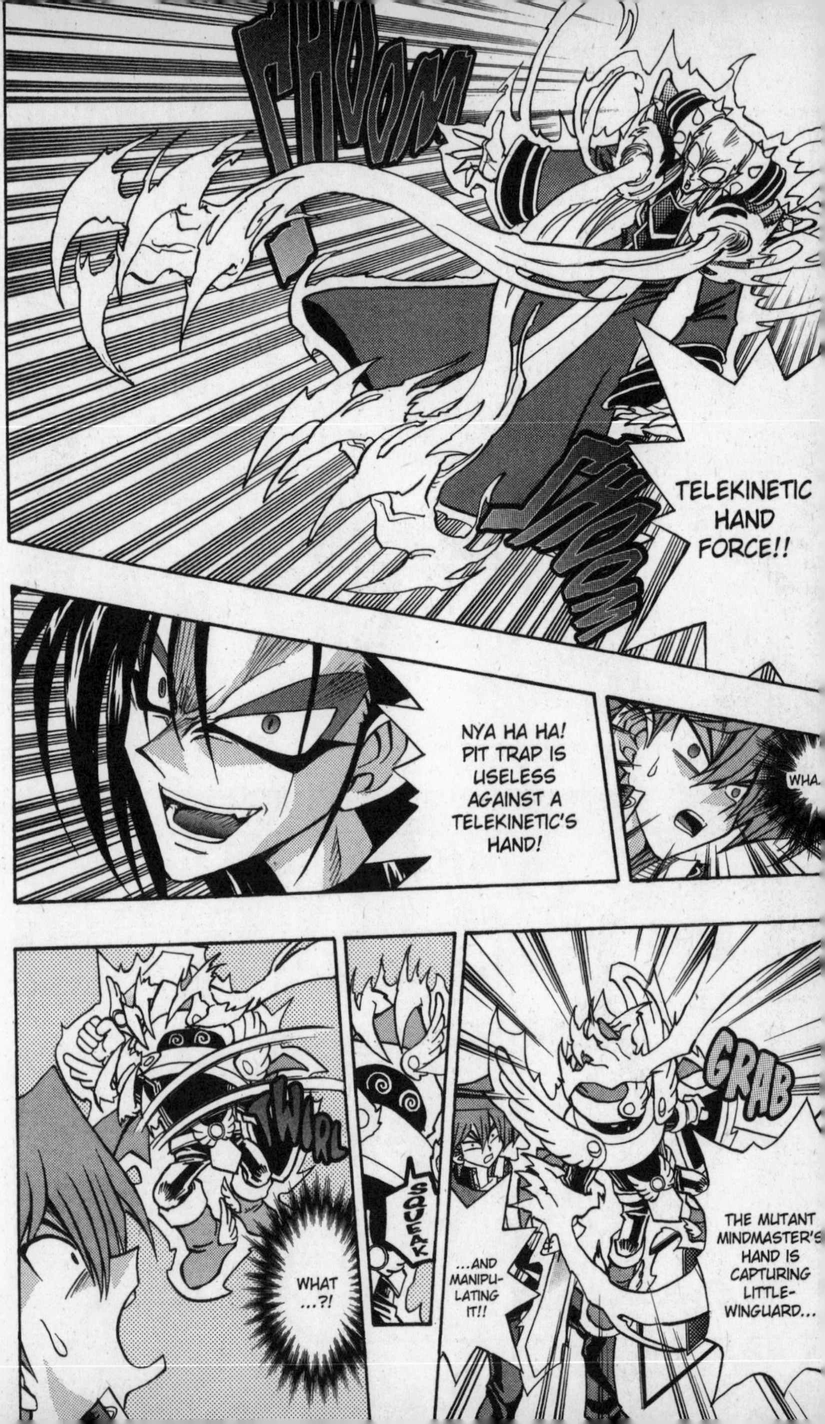
THOOM
THOOM
TELEKINETIC HAND FORCE!!
WHA...
NYA HA HA! PIT TRAP IS USELESS AGAINST A TELEKINETIC'S HAND!
GRAB
THE MUTANT MINDMASTER'S HAND IS CAPTURING LITTLE-WINGUARD...
...AND MANIPU-LATING IT!!
SQUEAK
TWIRL
WHAT ...?!

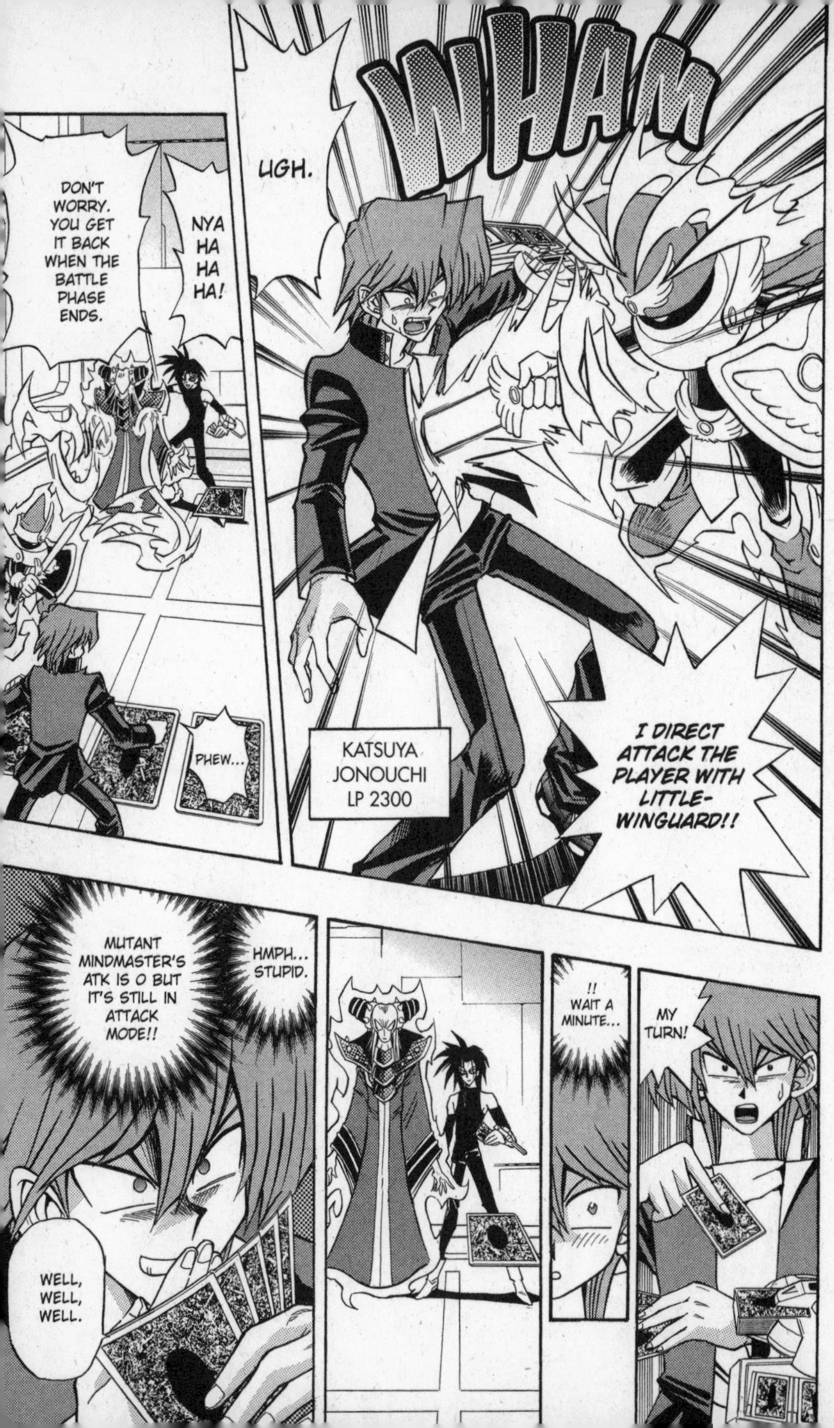
WHAM
UGH.
I DIRECT ATTACK THE PLAYER WITH LITTLE-WINGUARD!!
KATSUYA JONOUCHI LP 2300
NYA HA HA HA!
DON'T WORRY. YOU GET IT BACK WHEN THE BATTLE PHASE ENDS.
PHEW...
MY TURN!
!! WAIT A MINUTE...
HMPH... STUPID.
MUTANT MINDMASTER'S ATK IS 0 BUT IT'S STILL IN ATTACK MODE!!
WELL, WELL, WELL.

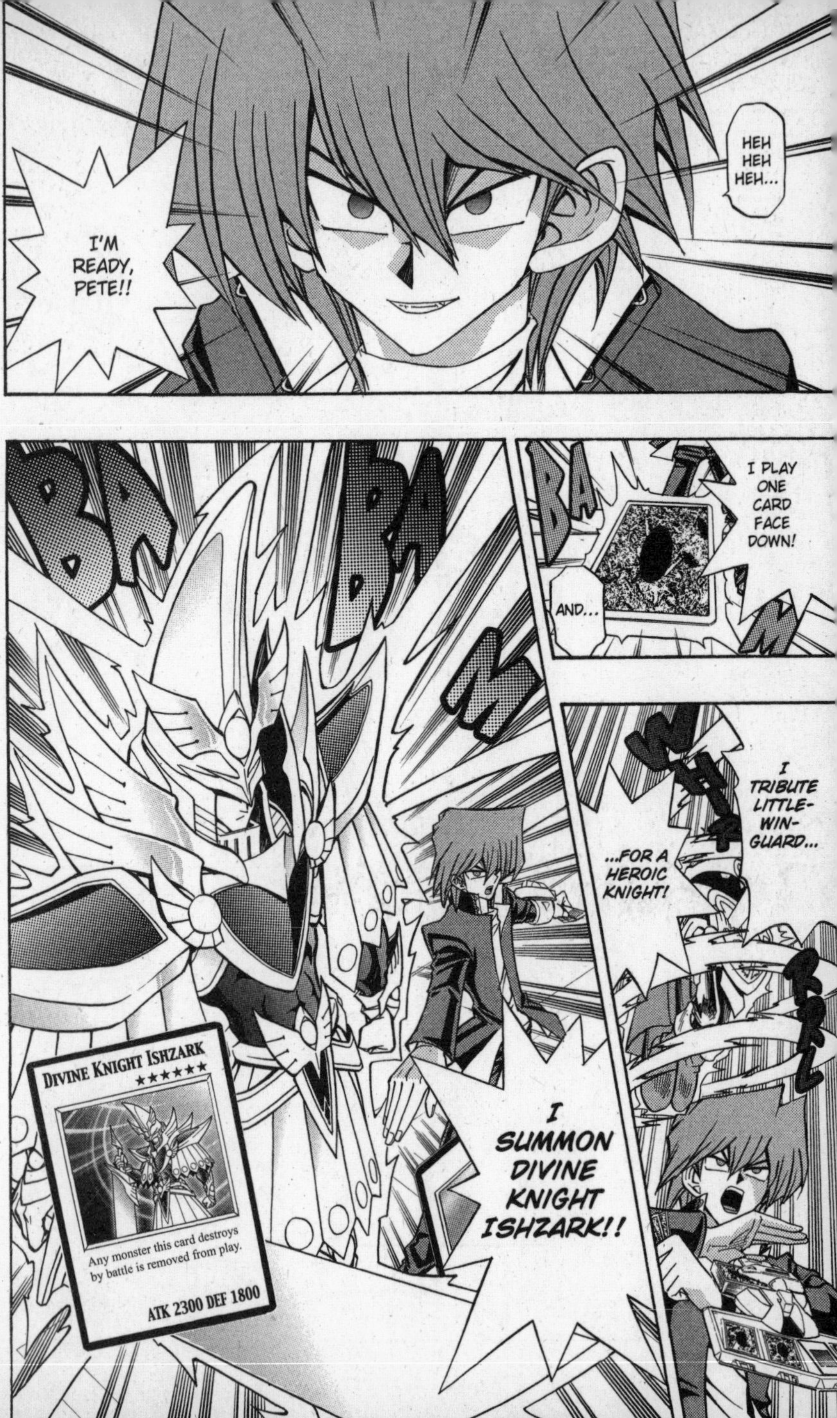
HEH HEH HEH...
I'M READY, PETE!!
BAM
I PLAY ONE CARD FACE DOWN!
AND...
I TRIBUTE LITTLE-WINGUARD...
...FOR A HEROIC KNIGHT!
I SUMMON DIVINE KNIGHT ISHZARK!!
DIVINE KNIGHT ISHZARK
★★★★★★
Any monster this card destroys by battle is removed from play.
ATK 2300 DEF 1800

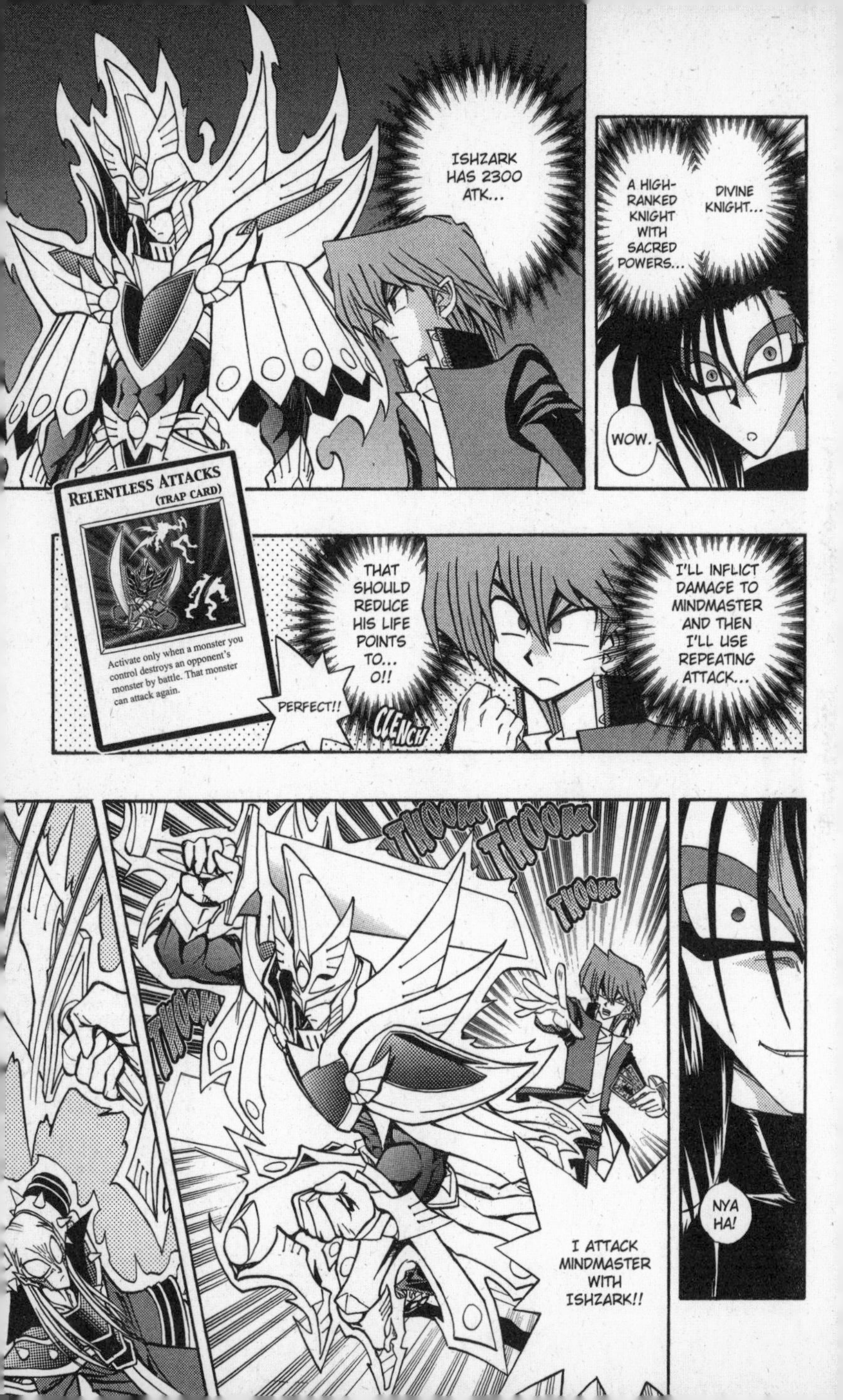
DIVINE KNIGHT...
A HIGH-RANKED KNIGHT WITH SACRED POWERS...
WOW.
ISHZARK HAS 2300 ATK...
I'LL INFLICT DAMAGE TO MINDMASTER AND THEN I'LL USE REPEATING ATTACK...
THAT SHOULD REDUCE HIS LIFE POINTS TO... 0!!
CLENCH
PERFECT!!
RELENTLESS ATTACKS
(TRAP CARD)
Activate only when a monster you control destroys an opponent's monster by battle. That monster can attack again.
NYA HA!
THOOM THOOM
THOOM
THOOM
I ATTACK MINDMASTER WITH ISHZARK!!

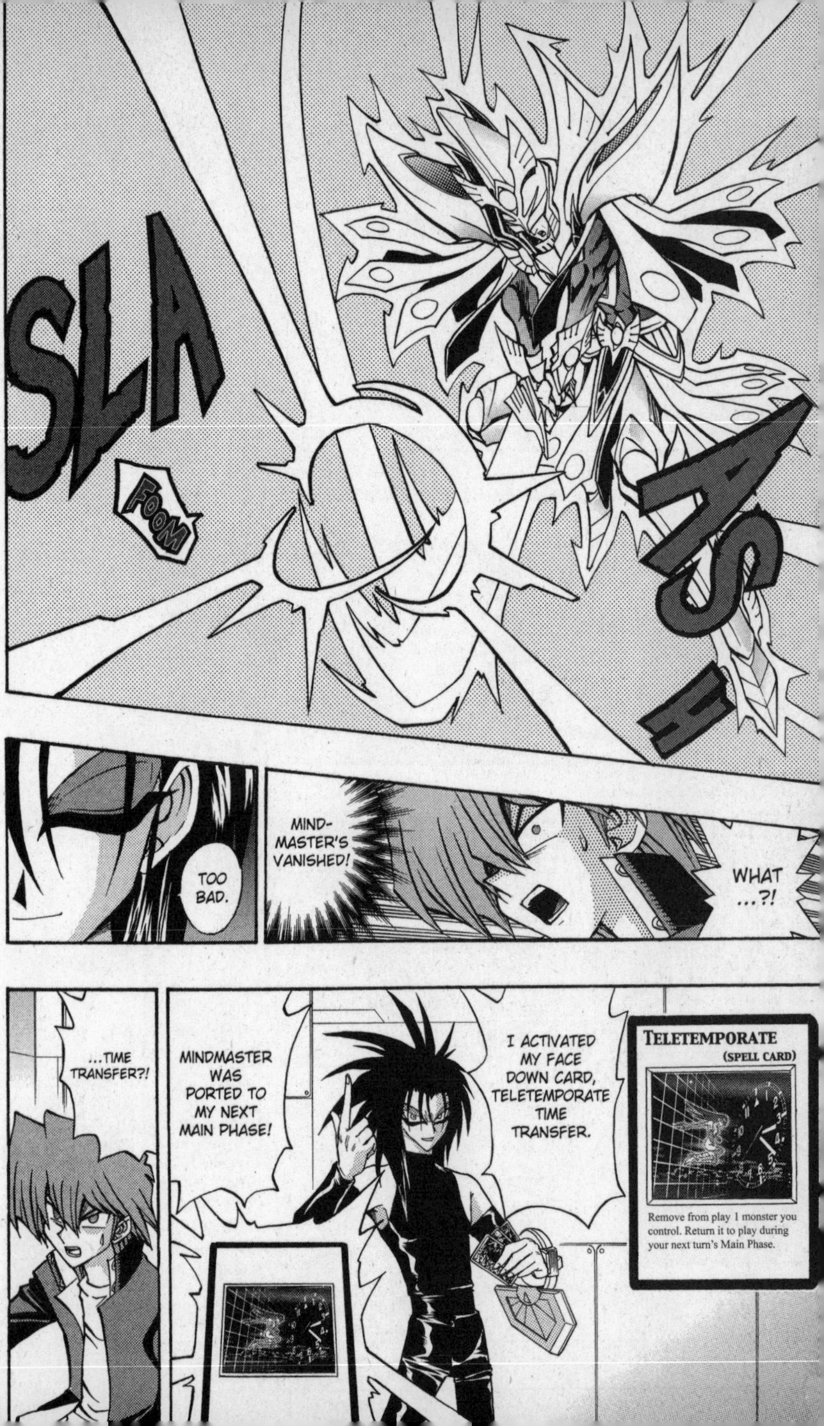
SLA
FOOM
ASH
WHAT ...?!
MIND-MASTER'S VANISHED!
TOO BAD.
TELETEMPORATE
(SPELL CARD)
Remove from play 1 monster you control. Return it to play during your next turn's Main Phase.
I ACTIVATED MY FACE DOWN CARD, TELETEMPORATE TIME TRANSFER.
MINDMASTER WAS PORTED TO MY NEXT MAIN PHASE!
...TIME TRANSFER?!

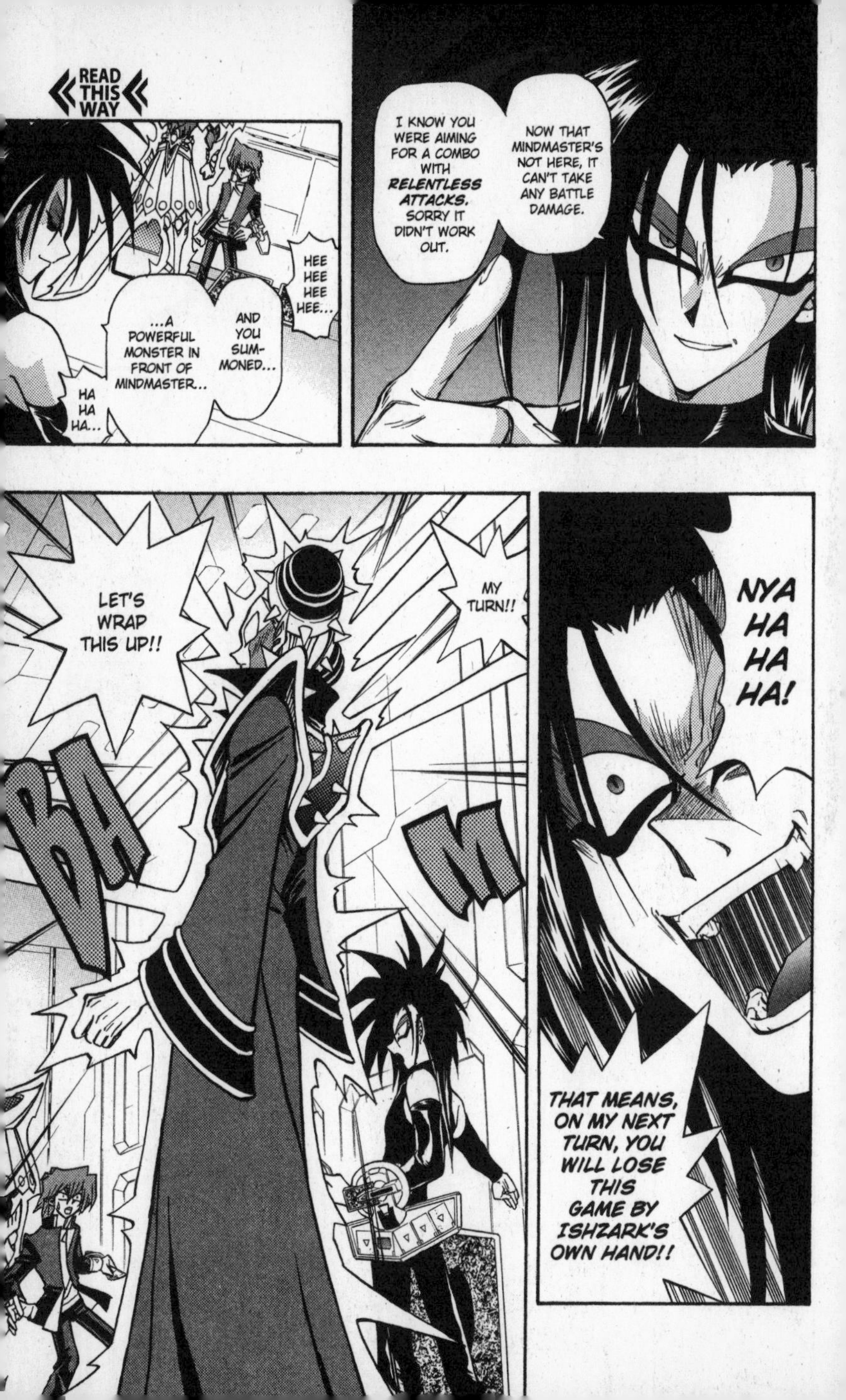
READ THIS WAY
NOW THAT MINDMASTER'S NOT HERE, IT CAN'T TAKE ANY BATTLE DAMAGE.
I KNOW YOU WERE AIMING FOR A COMBO WITH ***RELENTLESS ATTACKS.*** SORRY IT DIDN'T WORK OUT.
HEE HEE HEE HEE...
AND YOU SUMMONED...
...A POWERFUL MONSTER IN FRONT OF MINDMASTER...
HA HA HA...
NYA HA HA HA!
THAT MEANS, ON MY NEXT TURN, YOU WILL LOSE THIS GAME BY ISHZARK'S OWN HAND!!
MY TURN!!
LET'S WRAP THIS UP!!
BAM

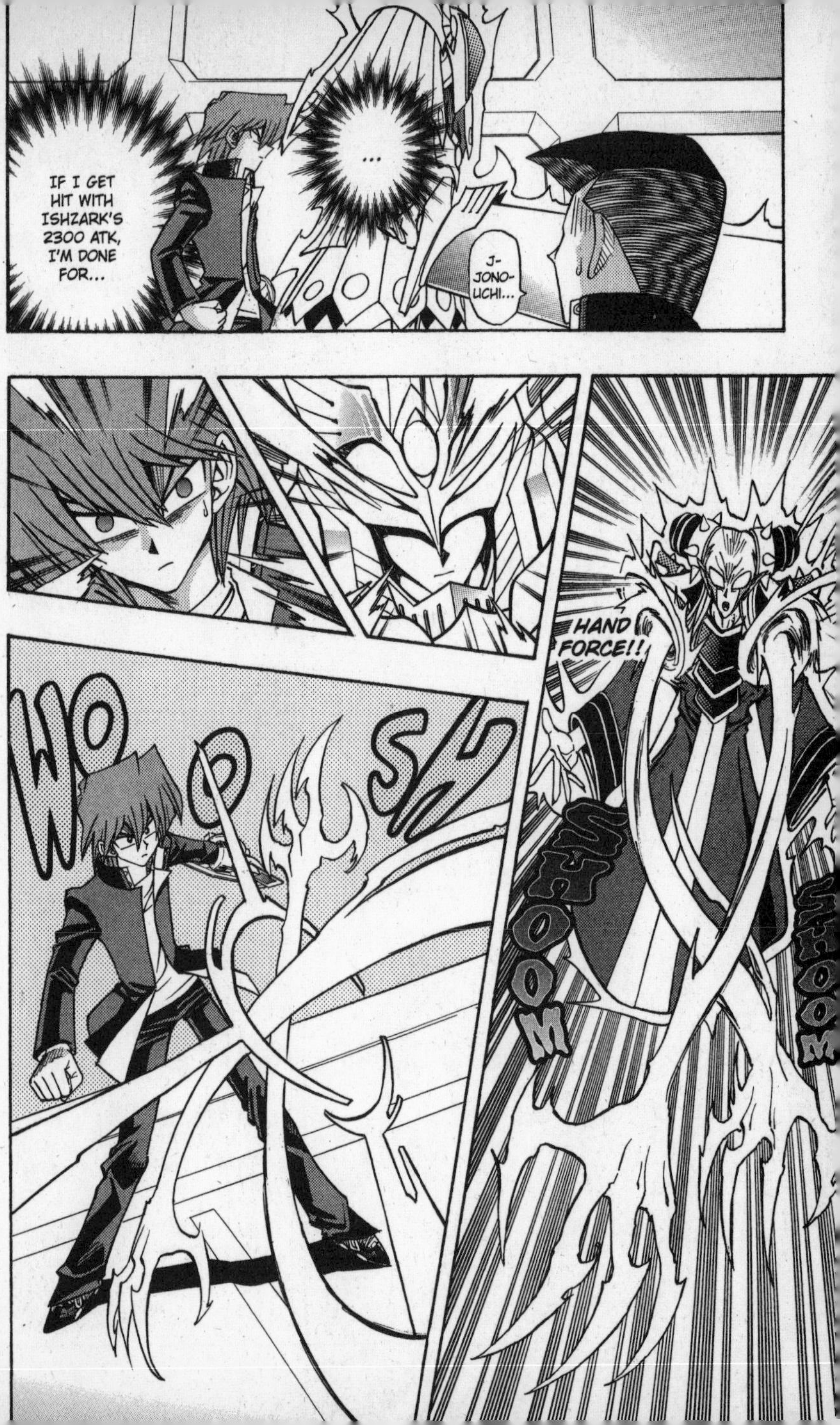
J-JONOUCHI...
...
IF I GET HIT WITH ISHZARK'S 2300 ATK, I'M DONE FOR...
HAND FORCE!!
SHOOM
SHOOM
WHOOSH

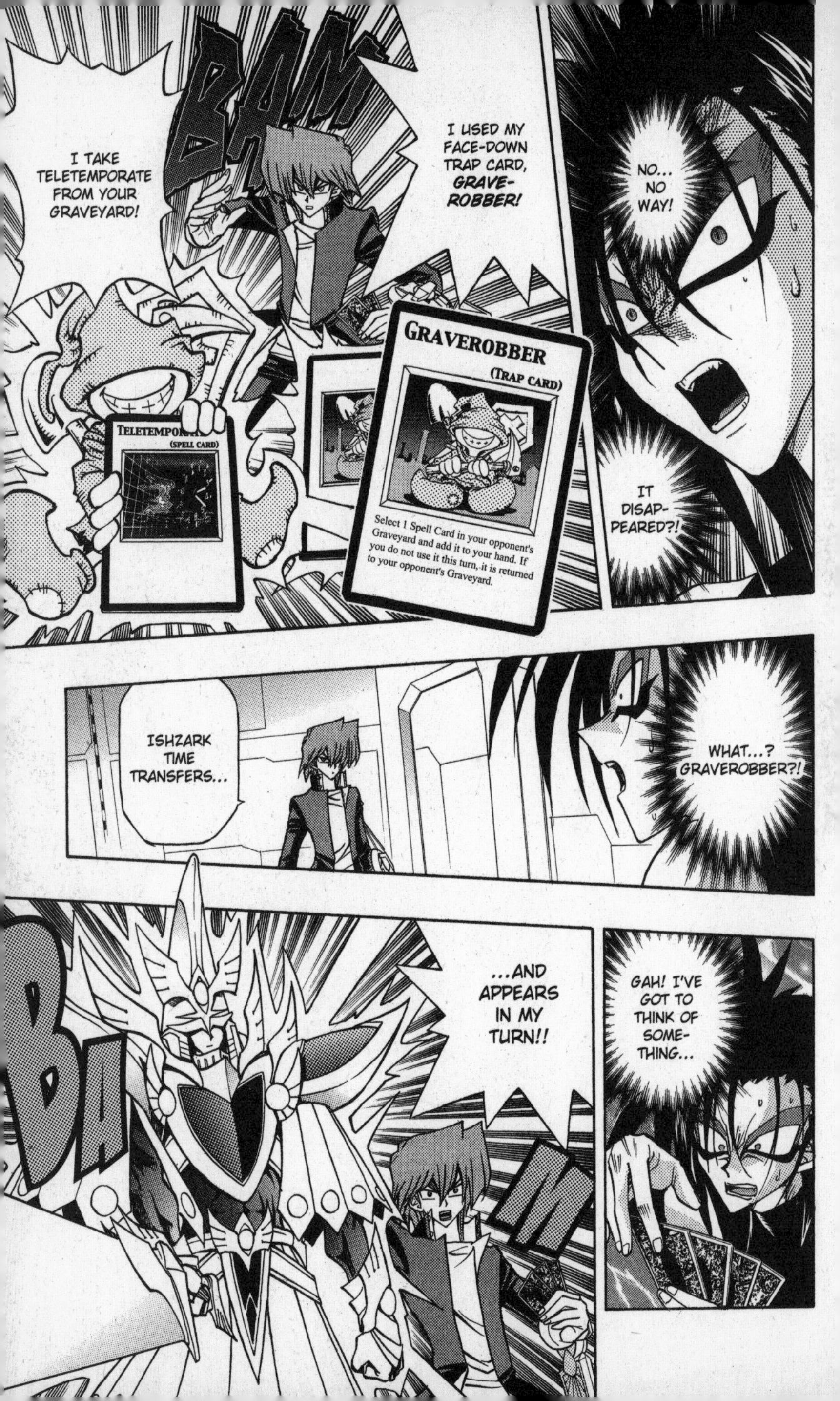

NO... NO WAY!
IT DISAPPEARED?!
BAM
I USED MY FACE-DOWN TRAP CARD, GRAVE-ROBBER!
I TAKE TELETEMPORATE FROM YOUR GRAVEYARD!
GRAVEROBBER
(TRAP CARD)
Select 1 Spell Card in your opponent's Graveyard and add it to your hand. If you do not use it this turn, it is returned to your opponent's Graveyard.
(SPELL CARD)
WHAT...? GRAVEROBBER?!
ISHZARK TIME TRANSFERS...
GAH! I'VE GOT TO THINK OF SOME-THING...
...AND APPEARS IN MY TURN!!

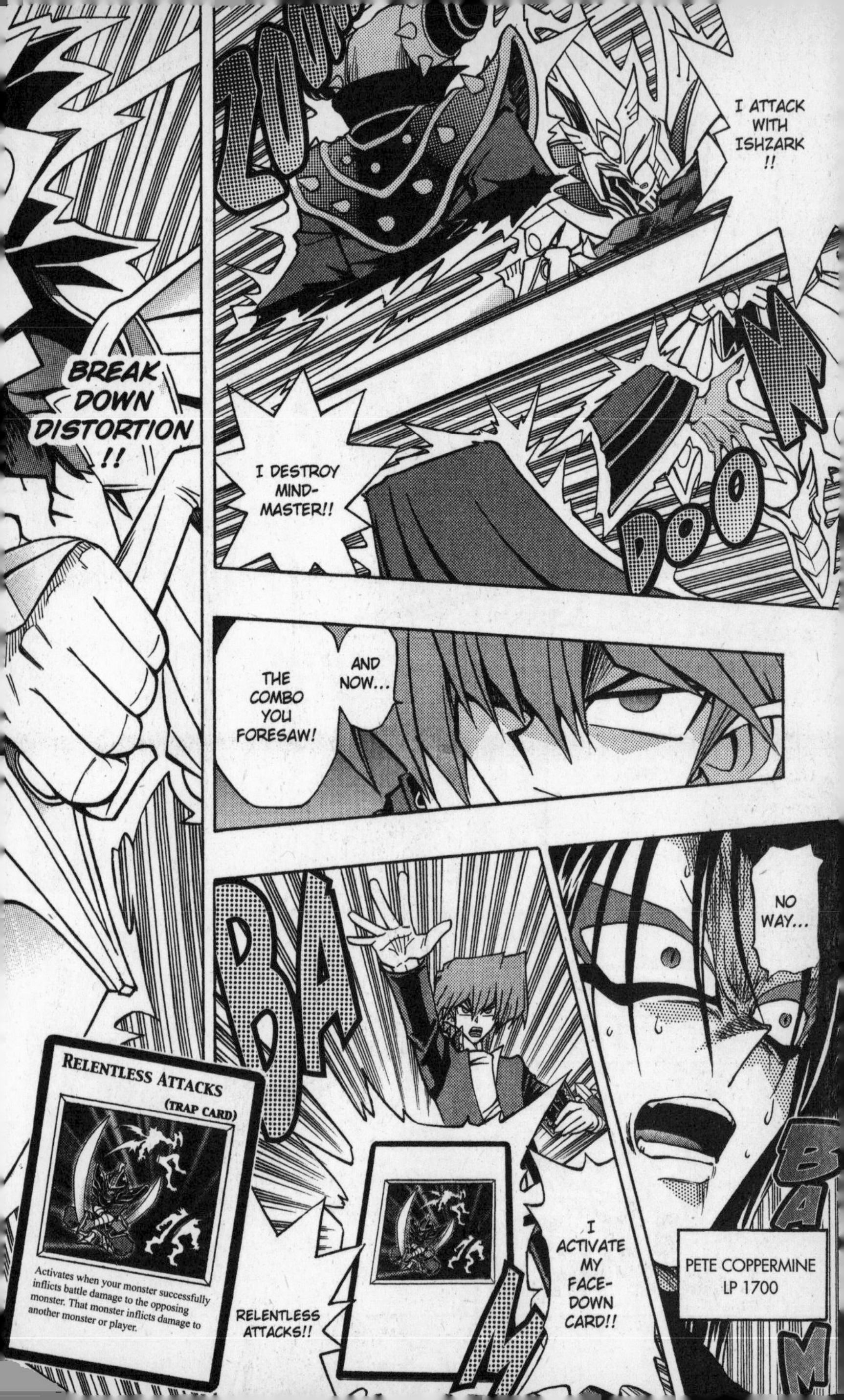
I ATTACK WITH ISHZARK!!
I DESTROY MIND-MASTER!!
AND NOW...
THE COMBO YOU FORESAW!
NO WAY...
PETE COPPERMINE
LP 1700
I ACTIVATE MY FACE-DOWN CARD!!
RELENTLESS ATTACKS!!
BREAK DOWN DISTORTION!!
RELENTLESS ATTACKS
(TRAP CARD)
Activates when your monster successfully inflicts battle damage to the opposing monster. That monster inflicts damage to another monster or player.

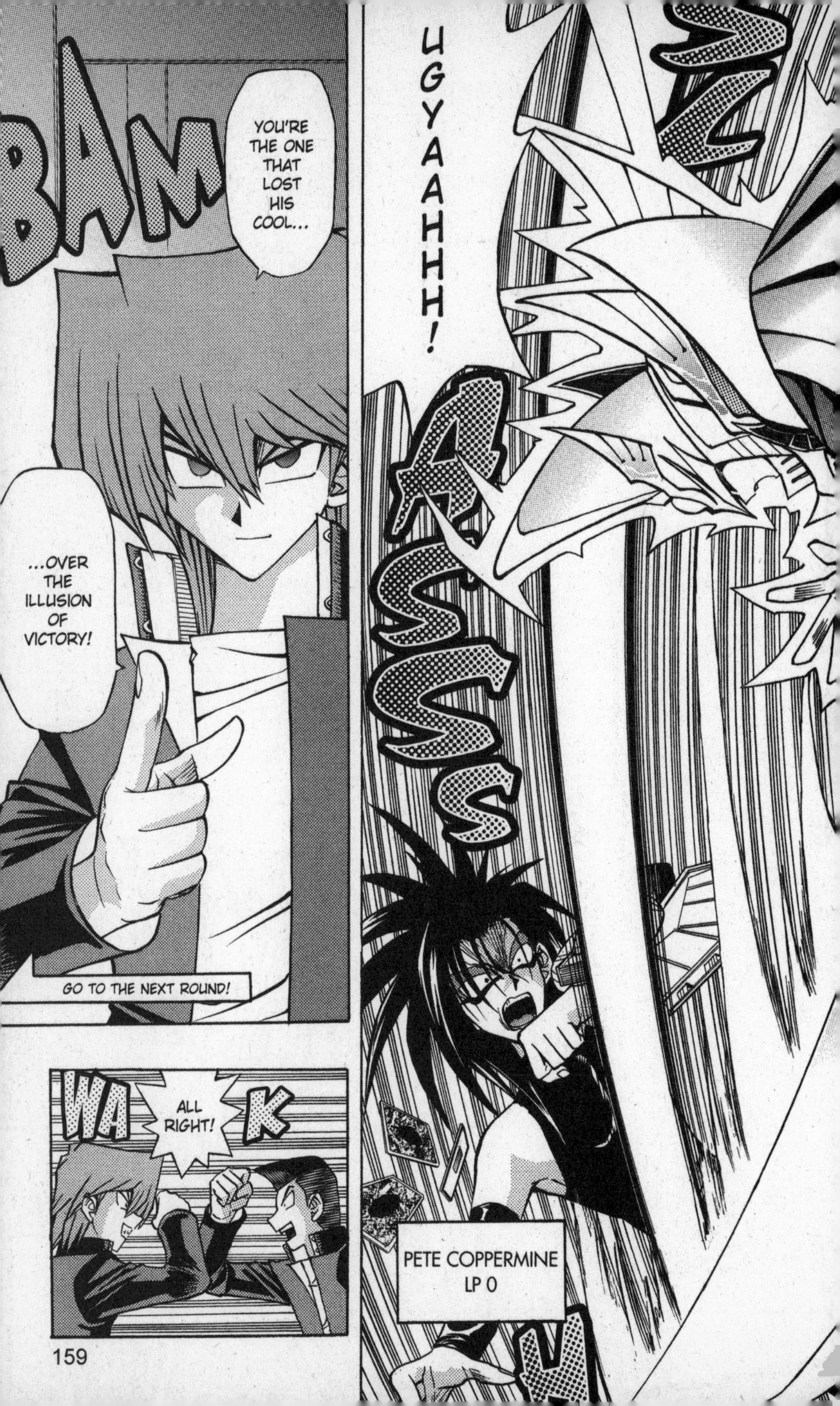
UGYAAHHH!
PETE COPPERMINE
LP 0
BAM
YOU'RE THE ONE THAT LOST HIS COOL...
...OVER THE ILLUSION OF VICTORY!
GO TO THE NEXT ROUND!
WAK
ALL RIGHT!

Duel Round 8: Dweller in the Dark!!

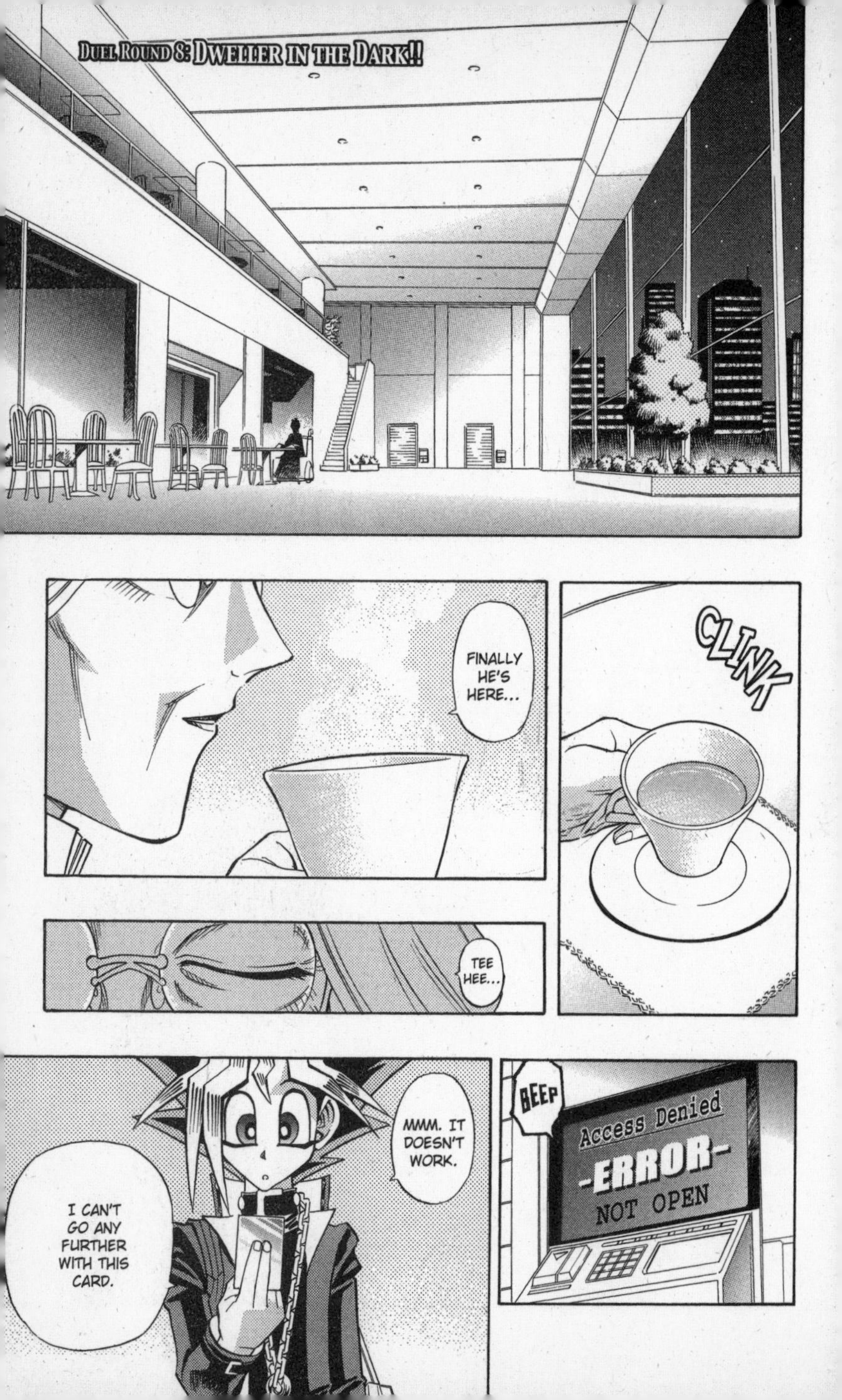

CLINK
FINALLY HE'S HERE...
TEE HEE...
BEEP
Access Denied
-ERROR-
NOT OPEN
MMM. IT DOESN'T WORK.
I CAN'T GO ANY FURTHER WITH THIS CARD.

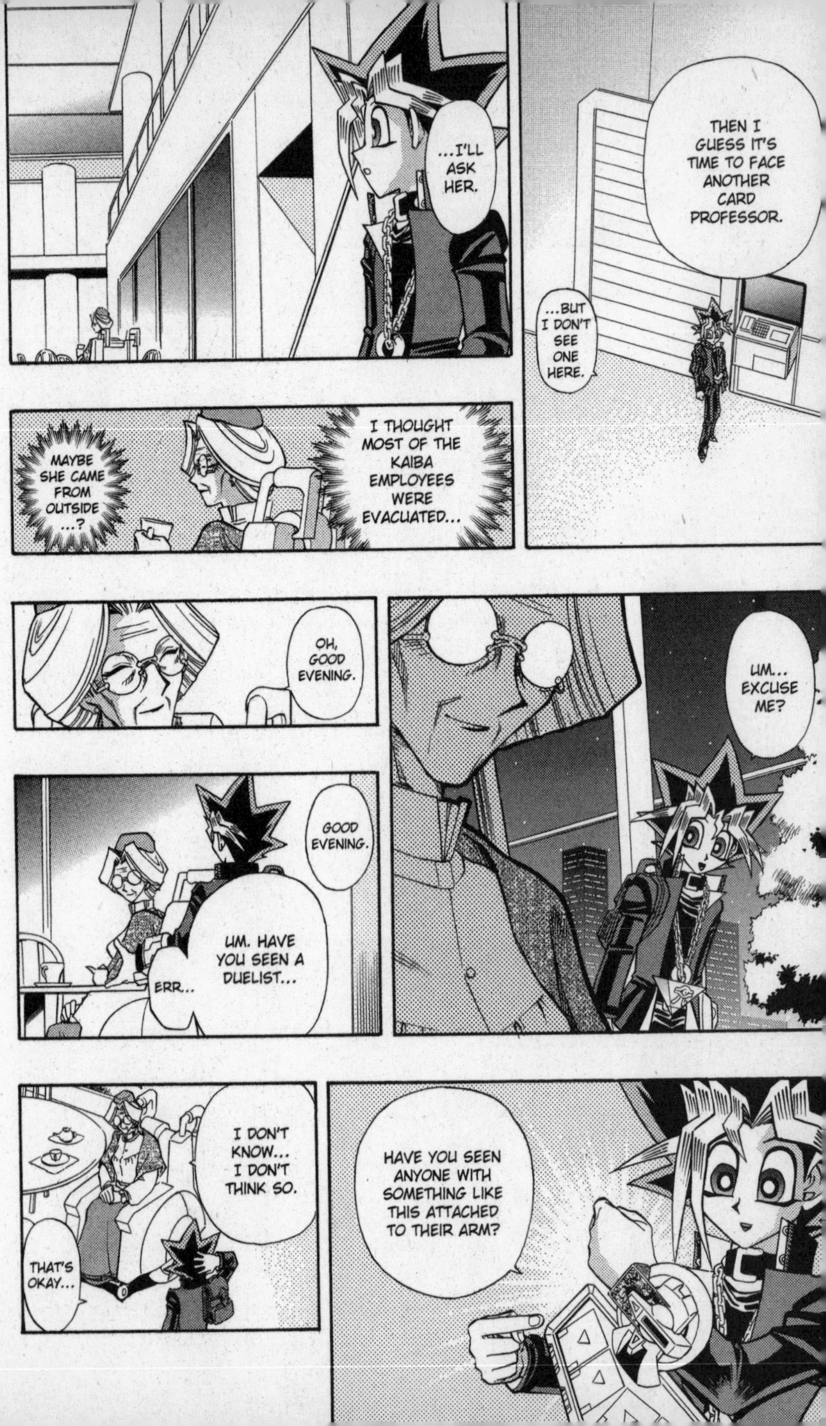
THEN I GUESS IT'S TIME TO FACE ANOTHER CARD PROFESSOR.
...BUT I DON'T SEE ONE HERE.
...I'LL ASK HER.
I THOUGHT MOST OF THE KAIBA EMPLOYEES WERE EVACUATED...
MAYBE SHE CAME FROM OUTSIDE ...?
UM... EXCUSE ME?
OH, GOOD EVENING.
GOOD EVENING.
UM. HAVE YOU SEEN A DUELIST...
ERR...
HAVE YOU SEEN ANYONE WITH SOMETHING LIKE THIS ATTACHED TO THEIR ARM?
I DON'T KNOW... I DON'T THINK SO.
THAT'S OKAY...

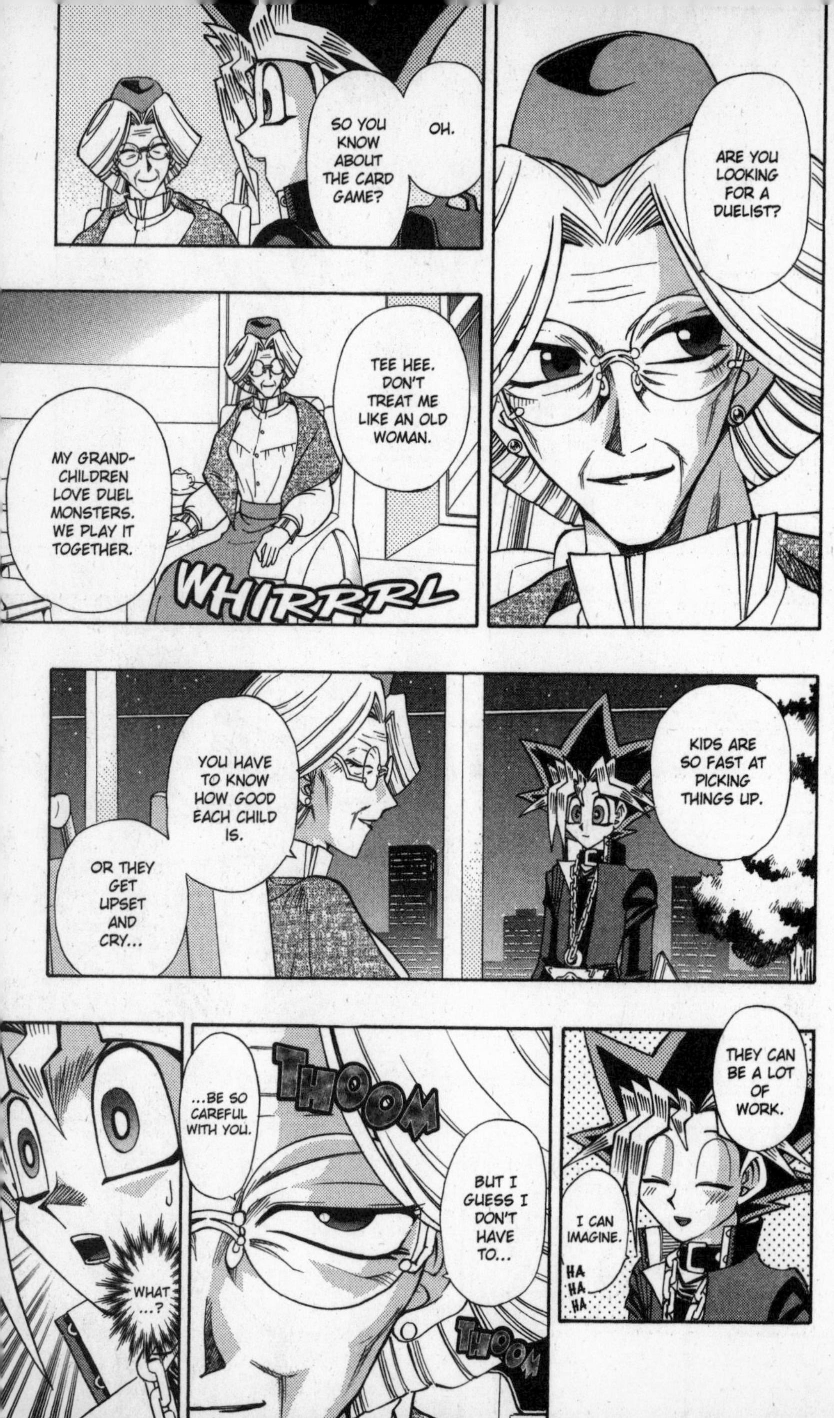
ARE YOU LOOKING FOR A DUELIST?
OH.
SO YOU KNOW ABOUT THE CARD GAME?
TEE HEE. DON'T TREAT ME LIKE AN OLD WOMAN.
MY GRAND-CHILDREN LOVE DUEL MONSTERS. WE PLAY IT TOGETHER.
WHIRRRL
KIDS ARE SO FAST AT PICKING THINGS UP.
YOU HAVE TO KNOW HOW GOOD EACH CHILD IS.
OR THEY GET UPSET AND CRY...
THEY CAN BE A LOT OF WORK.
I CAN IMAGINE.
HA HA HA
THOOM
BUT I GUESS I DON'T HAVE TO...
...BE SO CAREFUL WITH YOU.
THOOM
WHAT ...?

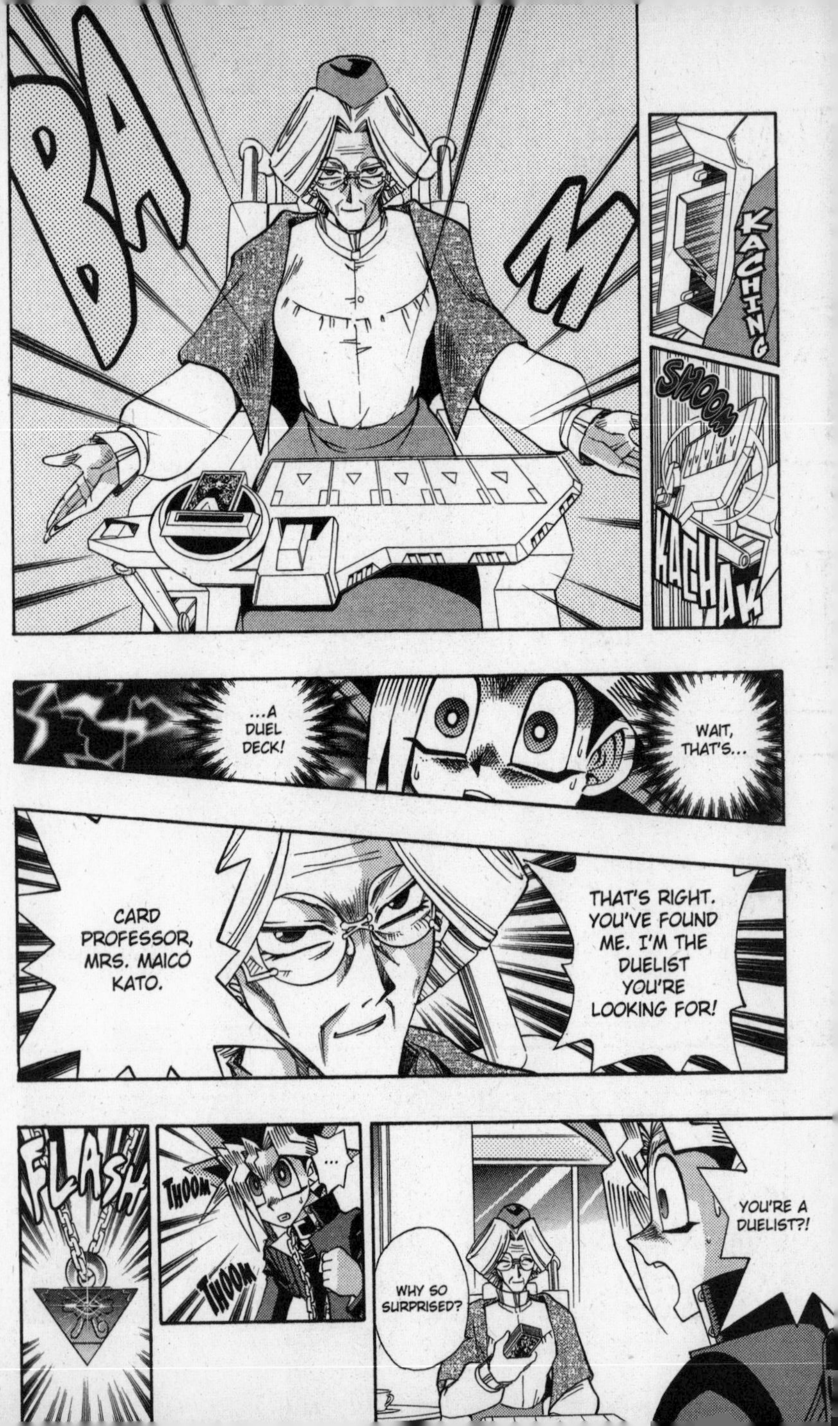
KACHING
SHOOM
KACHAK
BAM
WAIT, THAT'S...
...A DUEL DECK!
THAT'S RIGHT. YOU'VE FOUND ME. I'M THE DUELIST YOU'RE LOOKING FOR!
CARD PROFESSOR, MRS. MAICO KATO.
YOU'RE A DUELIST?!
WHY SO SURPRISED?
...
THOOM
THOOM
FLASH

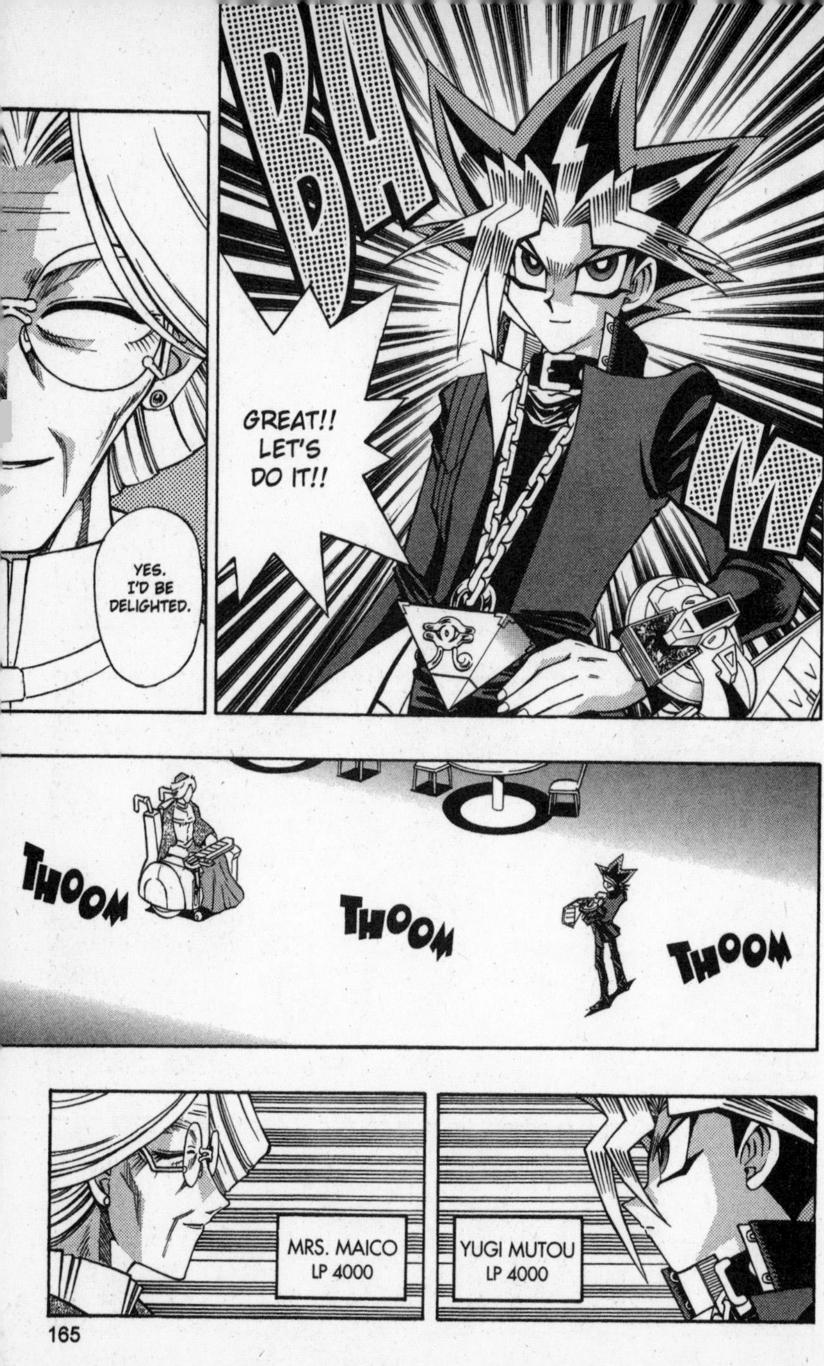
BAM
GREAT!! LET'S DO IT!!
YES. I'D BE DELIGHTED.
THOOM
THOOM
THOOM
YUGI MUTOU LP 4000
MRS. MAICO LP 4000

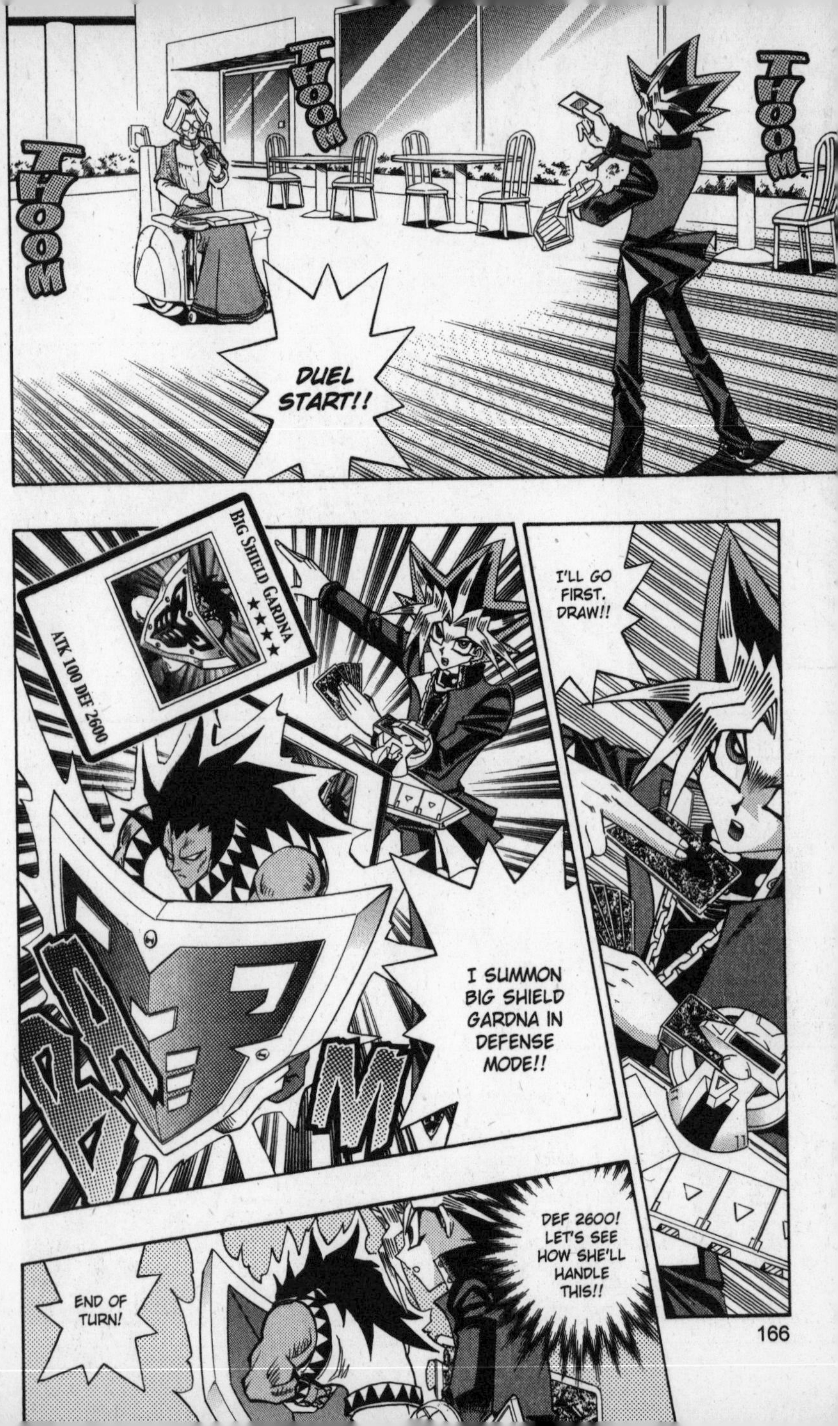
THOOM
THOOM
THOOM
DUEL START!!
I'LL GO FIRST. DRAW!!
BIG SHIELD GARDNA
ATK 100 DEF 2600
I SUMMON BIG SHIELD GARDNA IN DEFENSE MODE!!
DEF 2600! LET'S SEE HOW SHE'LL HANDLE THIS!!
END OF TURN!

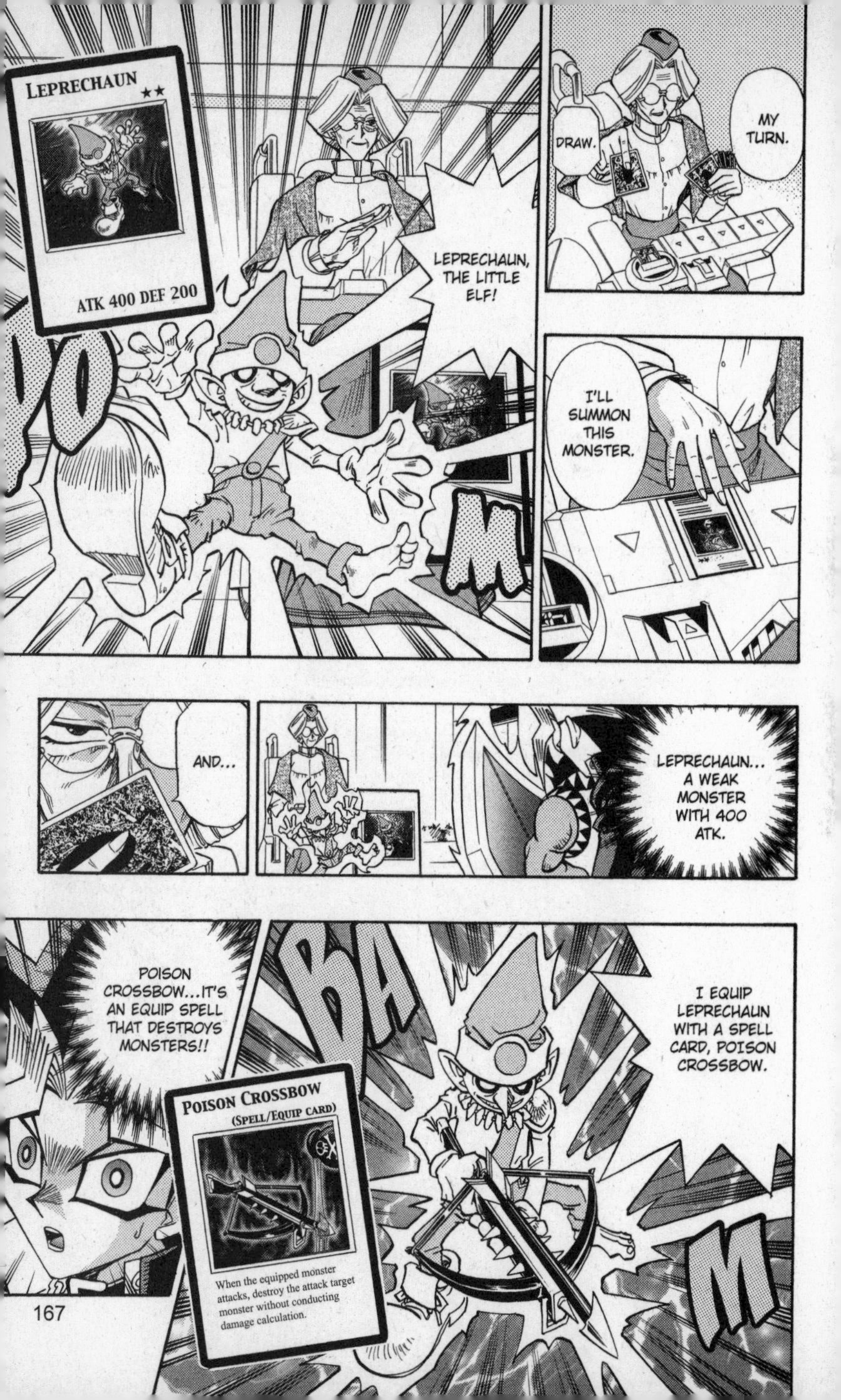
MY TURN.
DRAW.
I'LL SUMMON THIS MONSTER.
LEPRECHAUN, THE LITTLE ELF!
LEPRECHAUN ★★
ATK 400 DEF 200
PO
M
LEPRECHAUN... A WEAK MONSTER WITH 400 ATK.
AND...
I EQUIP LEPRECHAUN WITH A SPELL CARD, POISON CROSSBOW.
M
BA
POISON CROSSBOW...IT'S AN EQUIP SPELL THAT DESTROYS MONSTERS!!
POISON CROSSBOW
(SPELL/EQUIP CARD)
When the equipped monster attacks, destroy the attack target monster without conducting damage calculation.

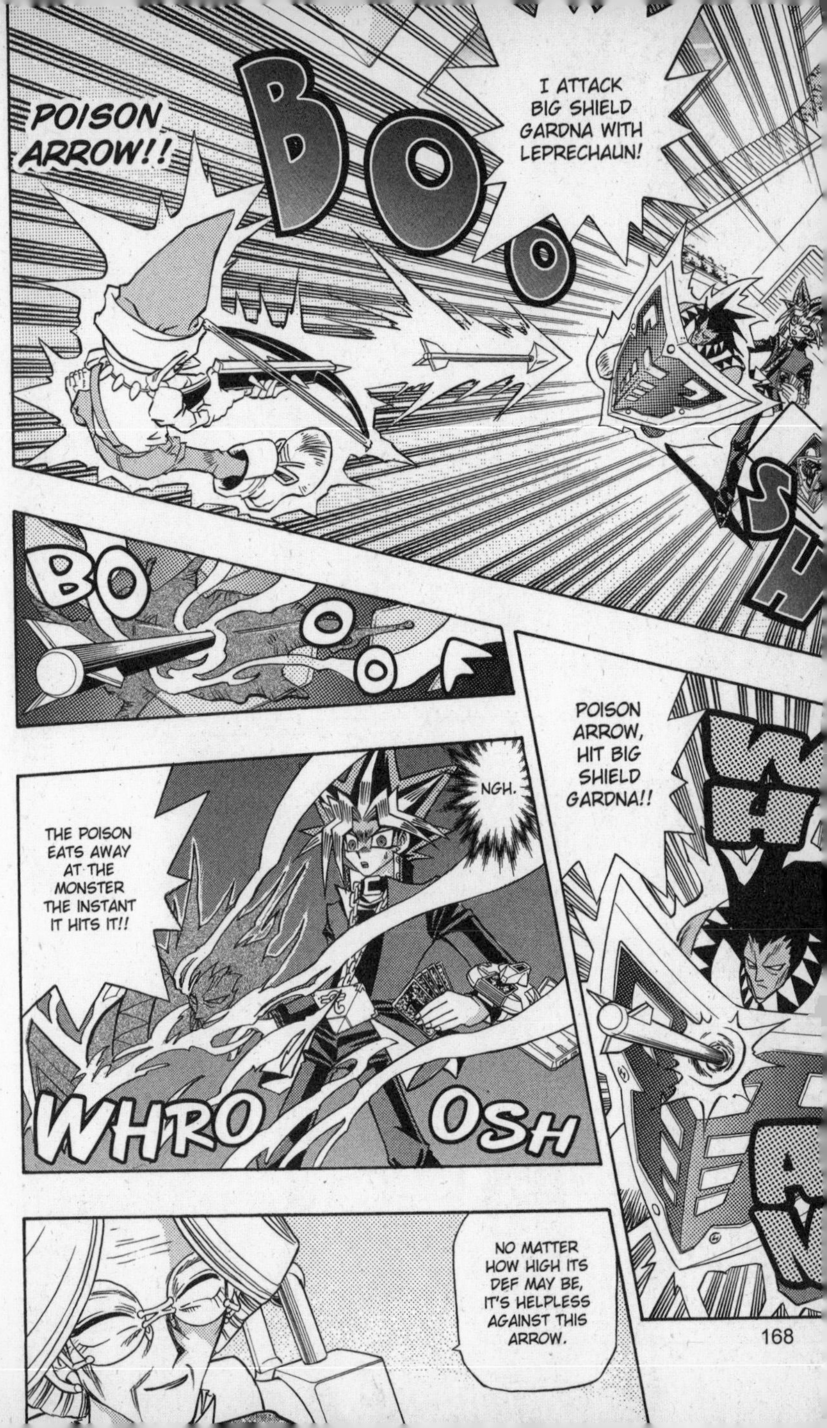
I ATTACK BIG SHIELD GARDNA WITH LEPRECHAUN!
BOOO
POISON ARROW!!
SH
POISON ARROW, HIT BIG SHIELD GARDNA!!
BOOOF
NGH.
THE POISON EATS AWAY AT THE MONSTER THE INSTANT IT HITS IT!!
WHROOSH
NO MATTER HOW HIGH ITS DEF MAY BE, IT'S HELPLESS AGAINST THIS ARROW.

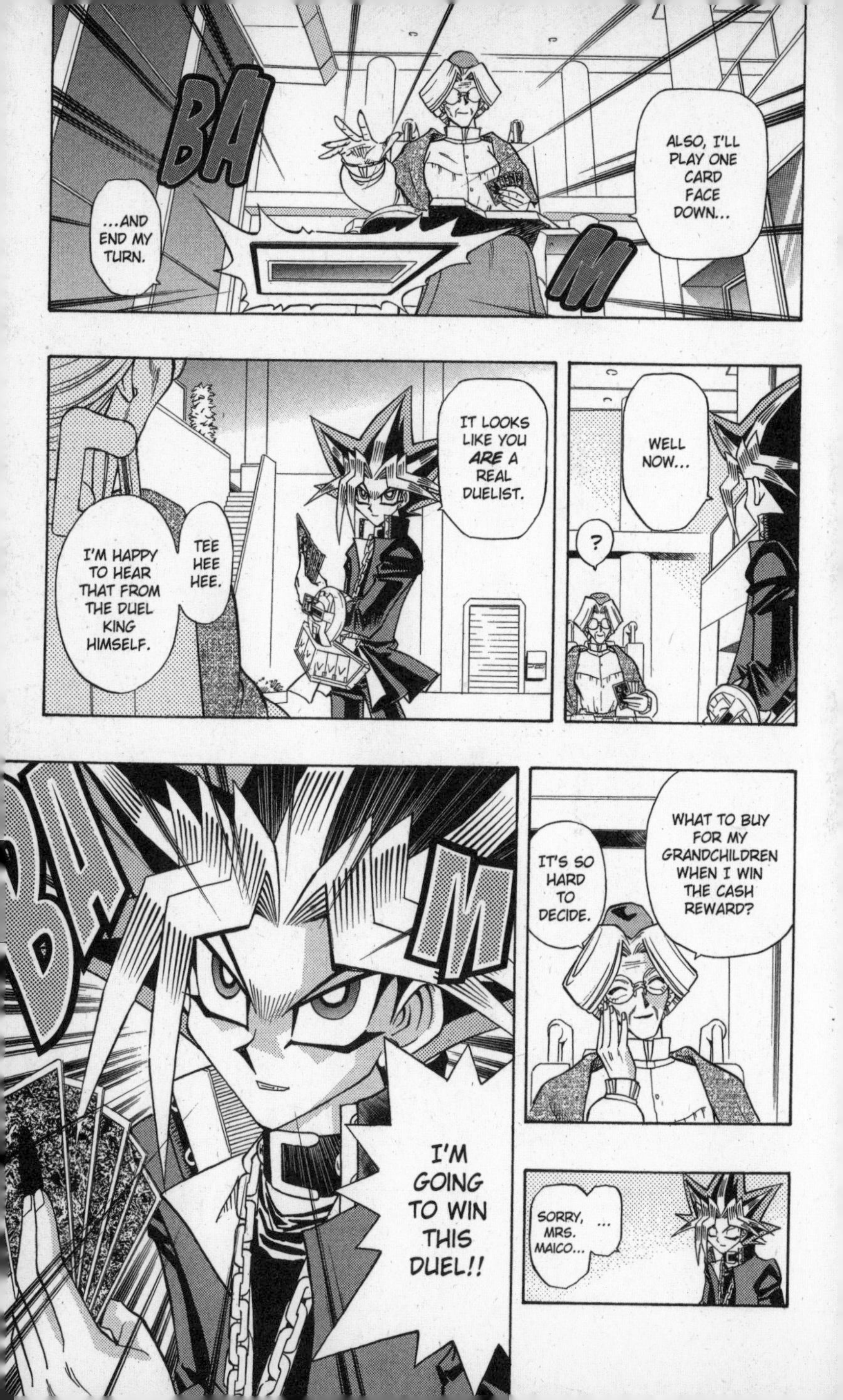
ALSO, I'LL PLAY ONE CARD FACE DOWN...
BAM
...AND END MY TURN.
WELL NOW...
?
IT LOOKS LIKE YOU *ARE* A REAL DUELIST.
TEE HEE HEE.
I'M HAPPY TO HEAR THAT FROM THE DUEL KING HIMSELF.
WHAT TO BUY FOR MY GRANDCHILDREN WHEN I WIN THE CASH REWARD?
IT'S SO HARD TO DECIDE.
...
SORRY, MRS. MAICO...
BAM
I'M GOING TO WIN THIS DUEL!!

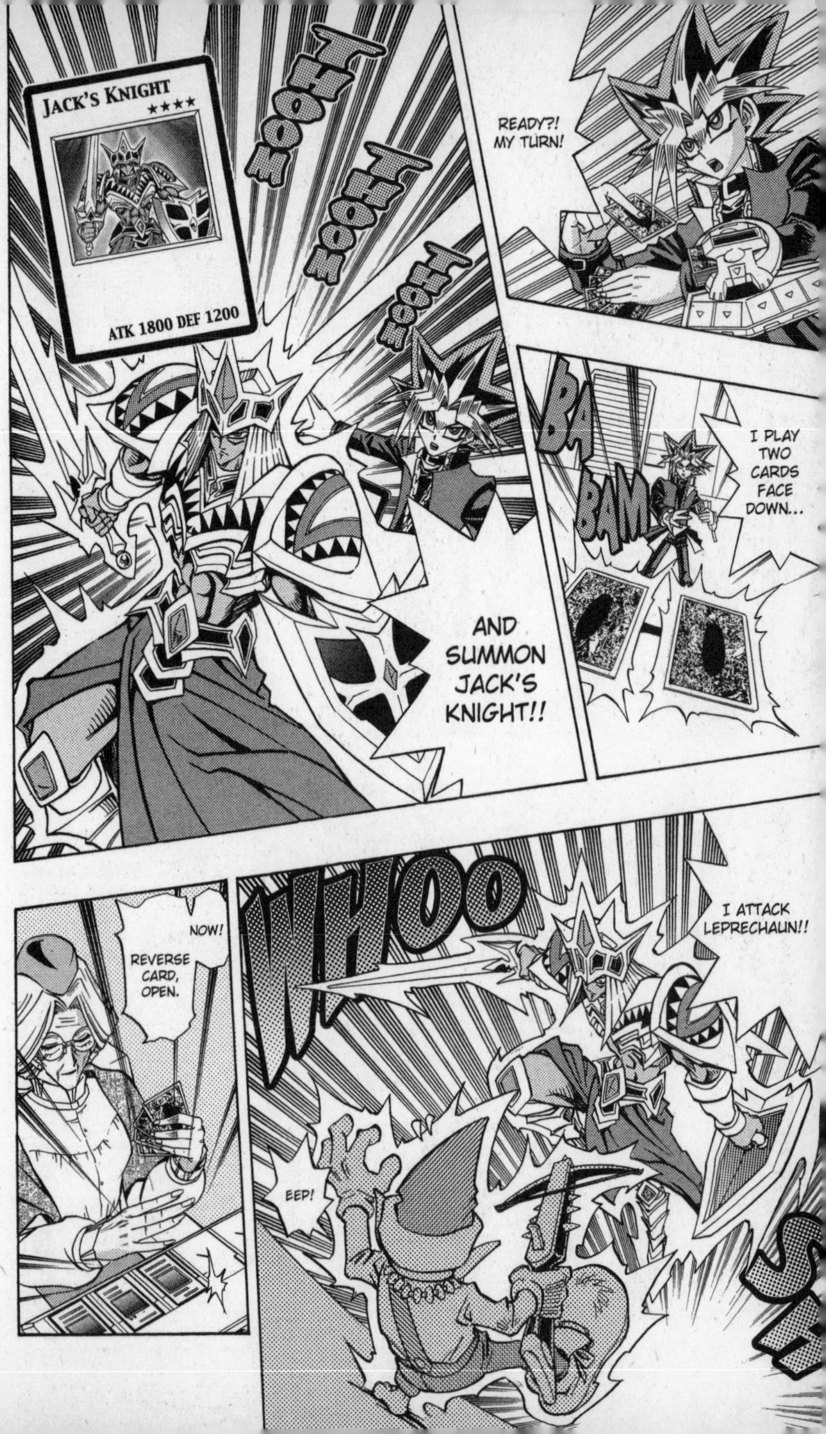
READY?! MY TURN!
BAM
BAM
I PLAY TWO CARDS FACE DOWN...
JACK'S KNIGHT
★★★★
ATK 1800 DEF 1200
THOOM
THOOM
THOOM
AND SUMMON JACK'S KNIGHT!!
WHOO
I ATTACK LEPRECHAUN!!
EEP!
NOW!
REVERSE CARD, OPEN.

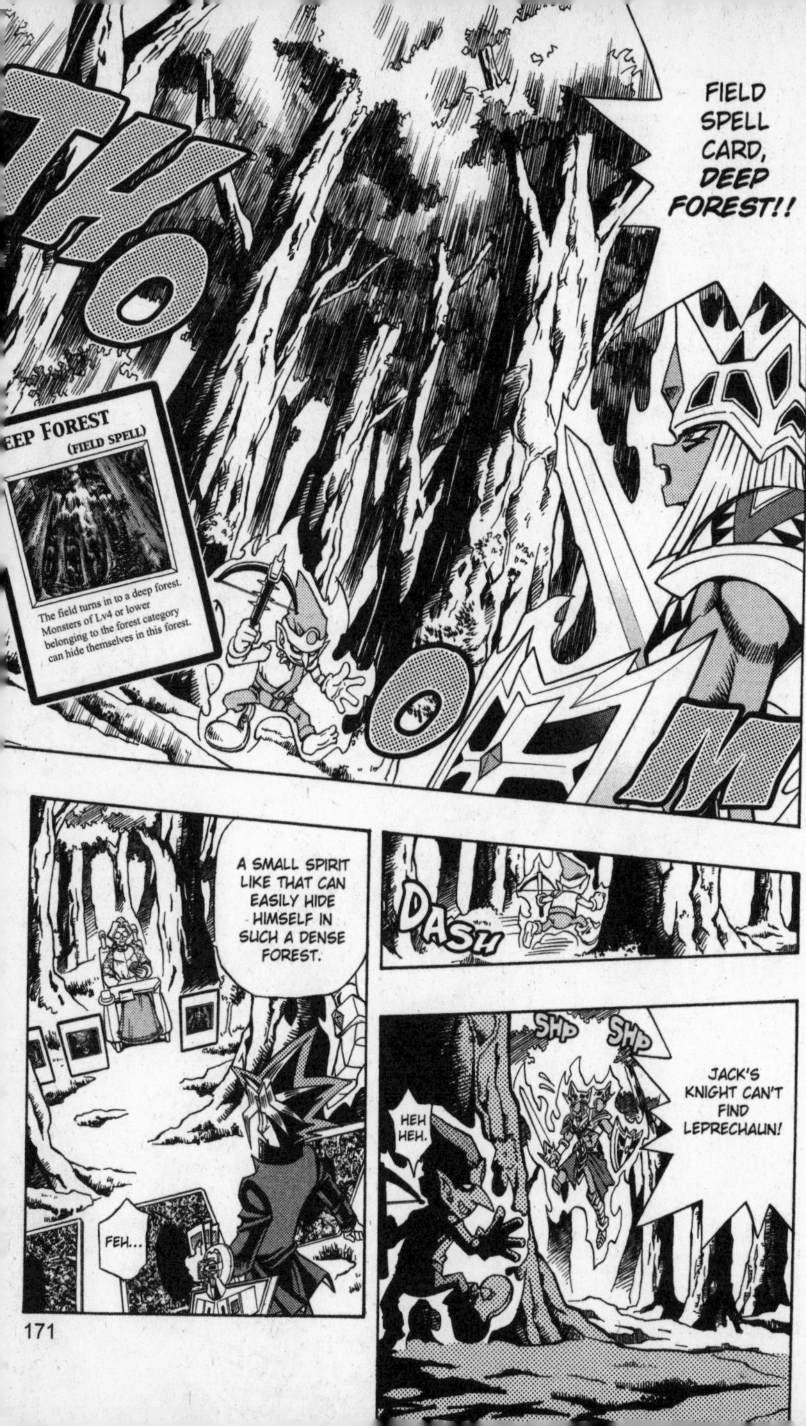
FIELD SPELL CARD, DEEP FOREST!!
EEP FOREST
(FIELD SPELL)
The field turns in to a deep forest. Monsters of Lv4 or lower belonging to the forest category can hide themselves in this forest.
DASH
SHP
SHP
JACK'S KNIGHT CAN'T FIND LEPRECHAUN!
HEH HEH.
A SMALL SPIRIT LIKE THAT CAN EASILY HIDE HIMSELF IN SUCH A DENSE FOREST.
FEH...

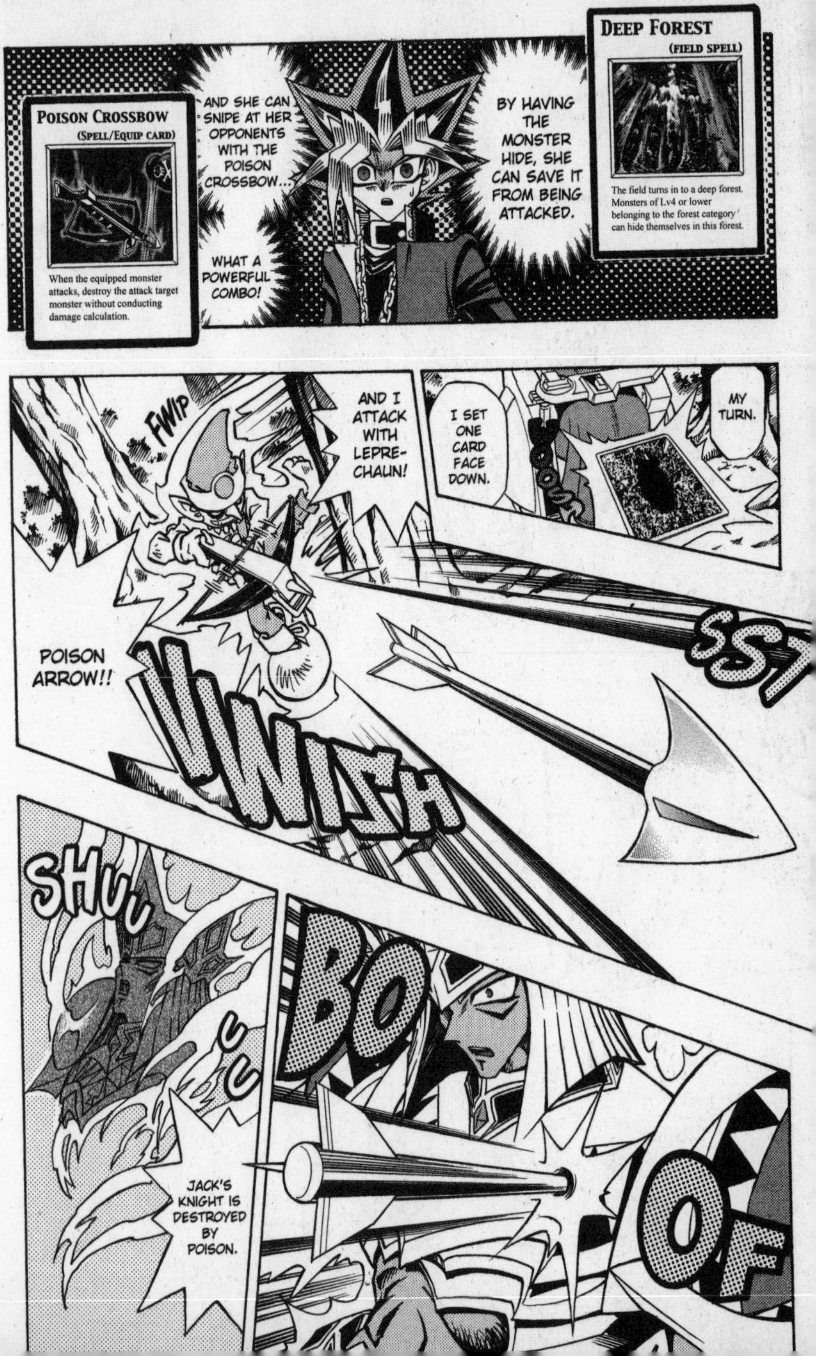
DEEP FOREST
(FIELD SPELL)
The field turns in to a deep forest. Monsters of Lv4 or lower belonging to the forest category can hide themselves in this forest.
BY HAVING THE MONSTER HIDE, SHE CAN SAVE IT FROM BEING ATTACKED.
AND SHE CAN SNIPE AT HER OPPONENTS WITH THE POISON CROSSBOW...
WHAT A POWERFUL COMBO!
POISON CROSSBOW
(SPELL/EQUIP CARD)
When the equipped monster attacks, destroy the attack target monster without conducting damage calculation.
MY TURN.
I SET ONE CARD FACE DOWN.
AND I ATTACK WITH LEPRE-CHAUN!
FWIP
SST
POISON ARROW!!
VWISH
BO
OF
SHUU
JACK'S KNIGHT IS DESTROYED BY POISON.

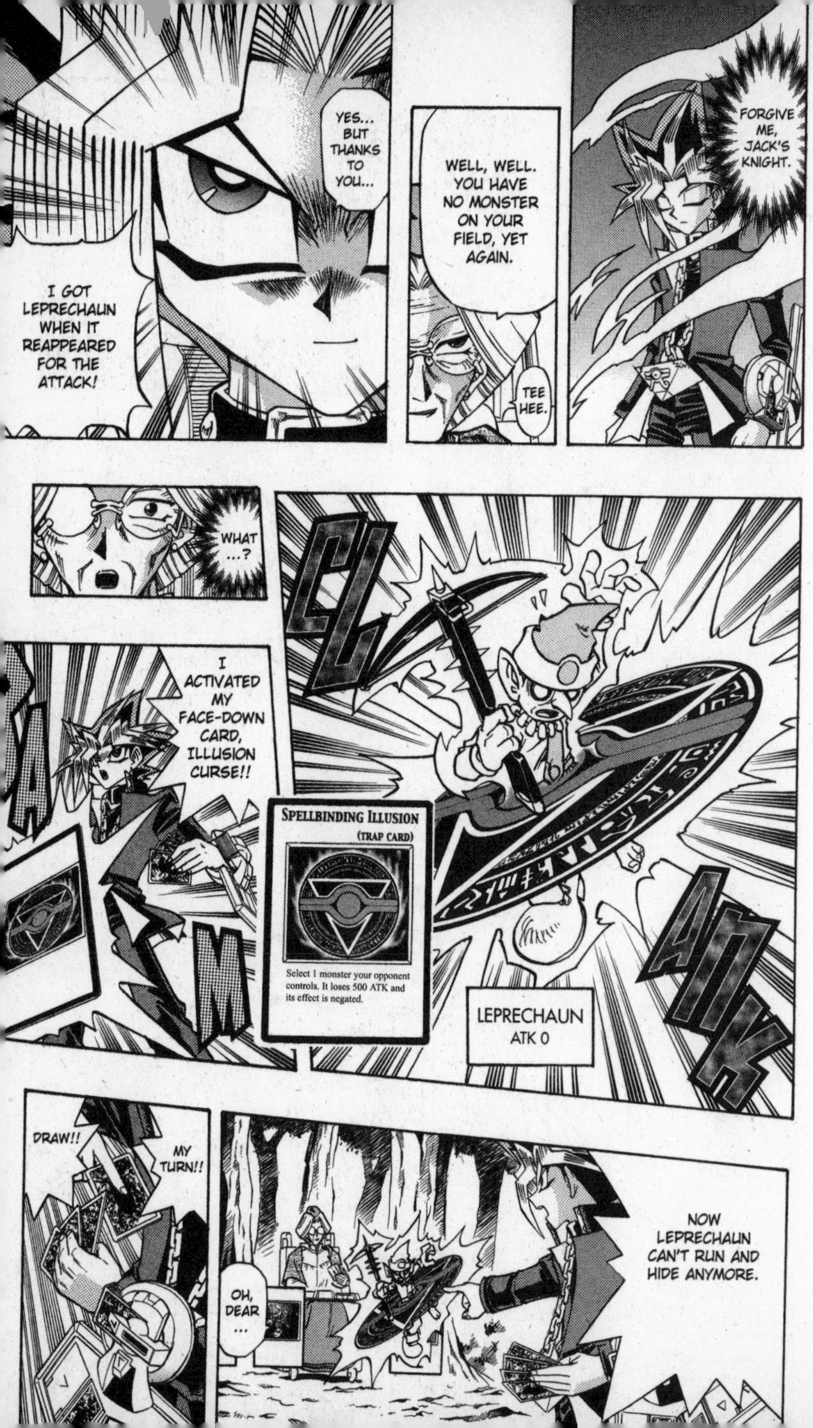
FORGIVE ME, JACK'S KNIGHT.
WELL, WELL. YOU HAVE NO MONSTER ON YOUR FIELD, YET AGAIN.
TEE HEE.
YES... BUT THANKS TO YOU...
I GOT LEPRECHAUN WHEN IT REAPPEARED FOR THE ATTACK!
LEPRECHAUN ATK 0
WHAT ...?
I ACTIVATED MY FACE-DOWN CARD, ILLUSION CURSE!!
SPELLBINDING ILLUSION
(TRAP CARD)
Select 1 monster your opponent controls. It loses 500 ATK and its effect is negated.
NOW LEPRECHAUN CAN'T RUN AND HIDE ANYMORE.
OH, DEAR ...
MY TURN!!
DRAW!!

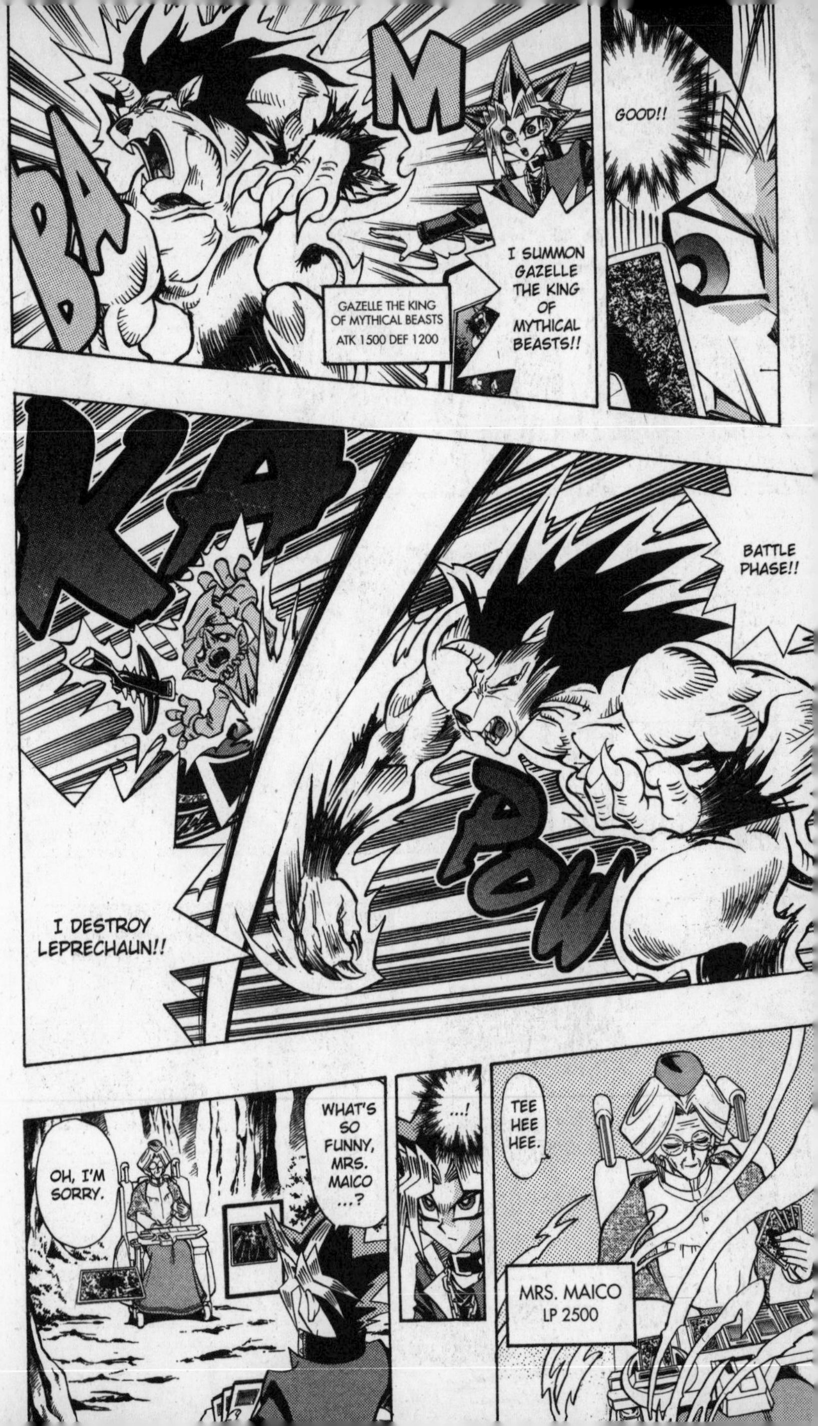
GOOD!!
I SUMMON GAZELLE THE KING OF MYTHICAL BEASTS!!
GAZELLE THE KING OF MYTHICAL BEASTS
ATK 1500 DEF 1200
M
BA
BATTLE PHASE!!
POW
I DESTROY LEPRECHAUN!!
TEE HEE HEE.
MRS. MAICO
LP 2500
...!
WHAT'S SO FUNNY, MRS. MAICO ...?
OH, I'M SORRY.

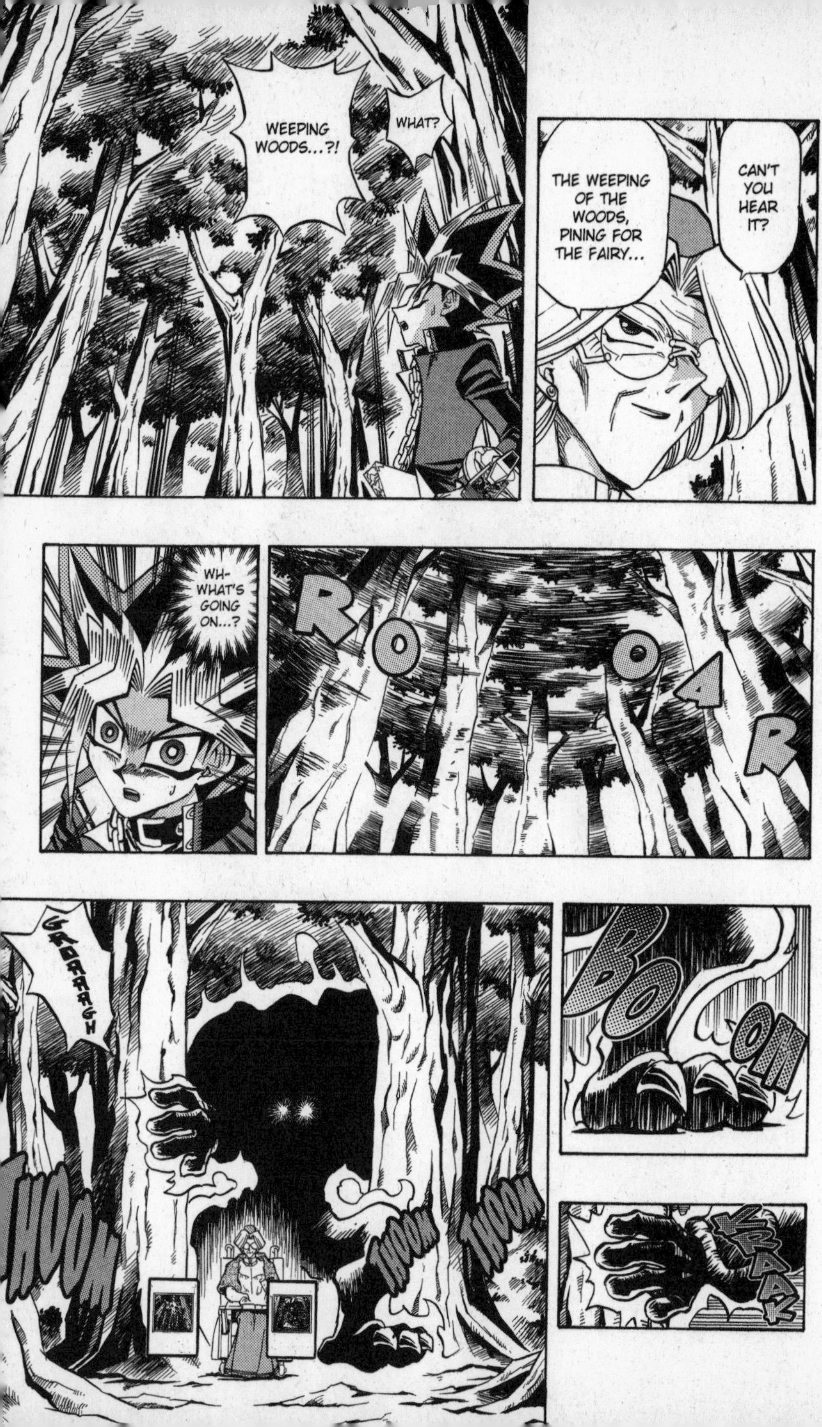
CAN'T YOU HEAR IT?
THE WEEPING OF THE WOODS, PINING FOR THE FAIRY...
WHAT?
WEEPING WOODS...?!
ROOAR
WH-WHAT'S GOING ON...?
BOOOM
KRAAK
GROAAAGH
THOOM
THOOM
THOOM

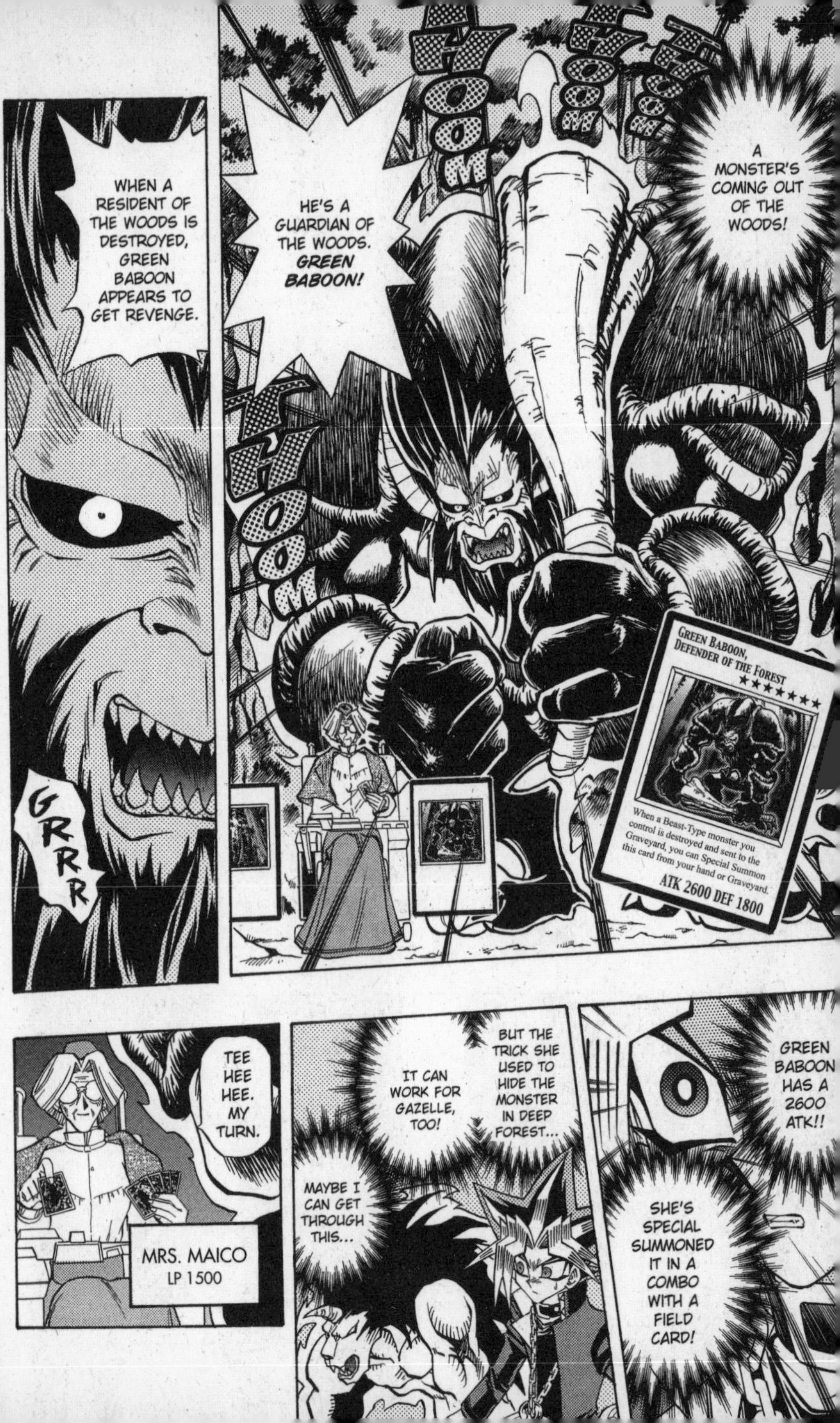

A MONSTER'S COMING OUT OF THE WOODS!
HE'S A GUARDIAN OF THE WOODS. GREEN BABOON!
VOOOM
GREEN BABOON, DEFENDER OF THE FOREST
When a Beast-Type monster you control is destroyed and sent to the Graveyard, you can Special Summon this card from your hand or Graveyard.
ATK 2600 DEF 1800
WHEN A RESIDENT OF THE WOODS IS DESTROYED, GREEN BABOON APPEARS TO GET REVENGE.
GRRR
GREEN BABOON HAS A 2600 ATK!!
SHE'S SPECIAL SUMMONED IT IN A COMBO WITH A FIELD CARD!
BUT THE TRICK SHE USED TO HIDE THE MONSTER IN DEEP FOREST...
IT CAN WORK FOR GAZELLE, TOO!
MAYBE I CAN GET THROUGH THIS...
TEE HEE HEE. MY TURN.
MRS. MAICO LP 1500

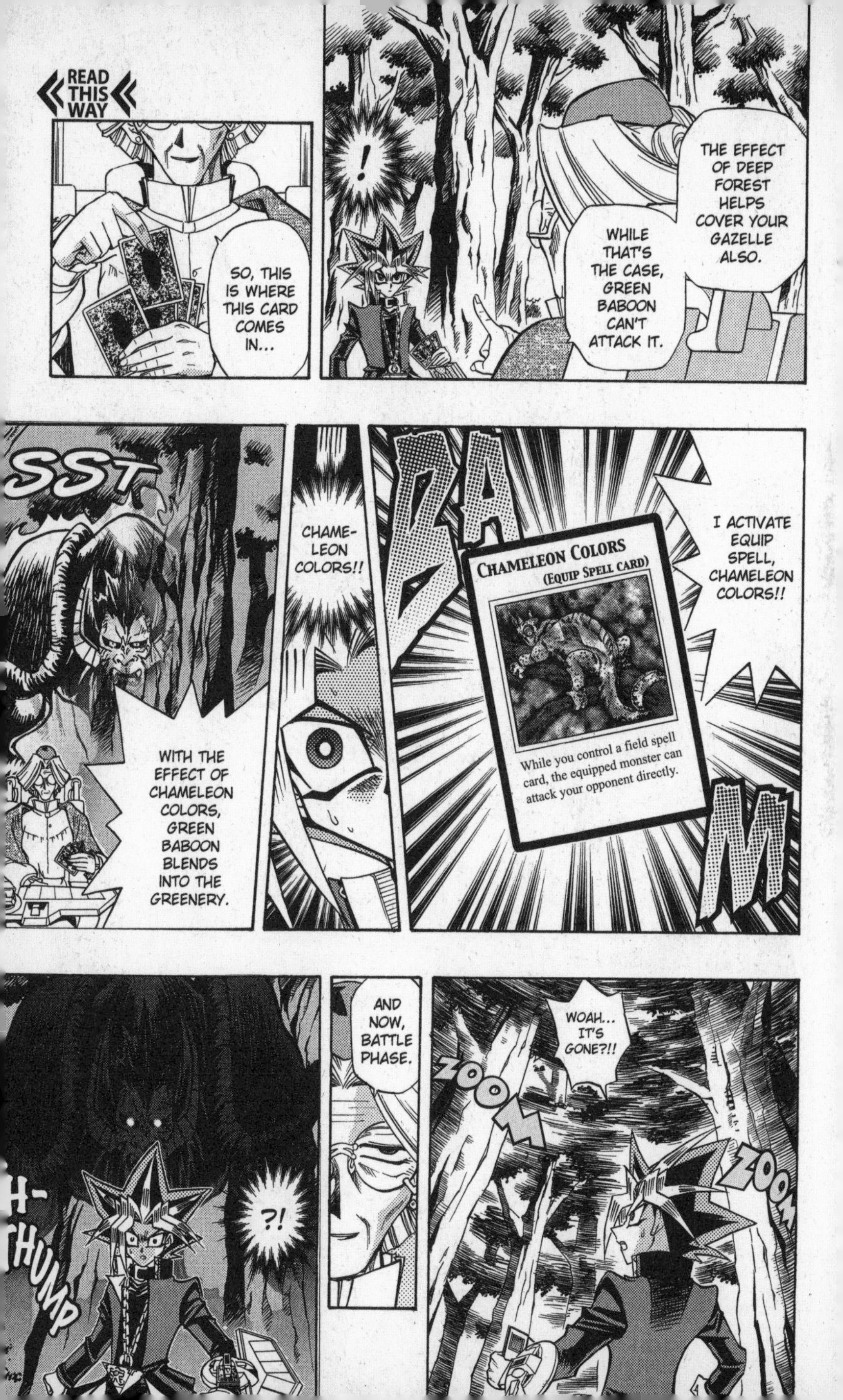
READ THIS WAY
THE EFFECT OF DEEP FOREST HELPS COVER YOUR GAZELLE ALSO.
WHILE THAT'S THE CASE, GREEN BABOON CAN'T ATTACK IT.
!
SO, THIS IS WHERE THIS CARD COMES IN...
I ACTIVATE EQUIP SPELL, CHAMELEON COLORS!!
ZAM
CHAMELEON COLORS
(EQUIP SPELL CARD)
While you control a field spell card, the equipped monster can attack your opponent directly.
CHAME-LEON COLORS!!
SST
WITH THE EFFECT OF CHAMELEON COLORS, GREEN BABOON BLENDS INTO THE GREENERY.
WOAH... IT'S GONE?!!
ZOOM
ZOOM
AND NOW, BATTLE PHASE.
?!
THUMP

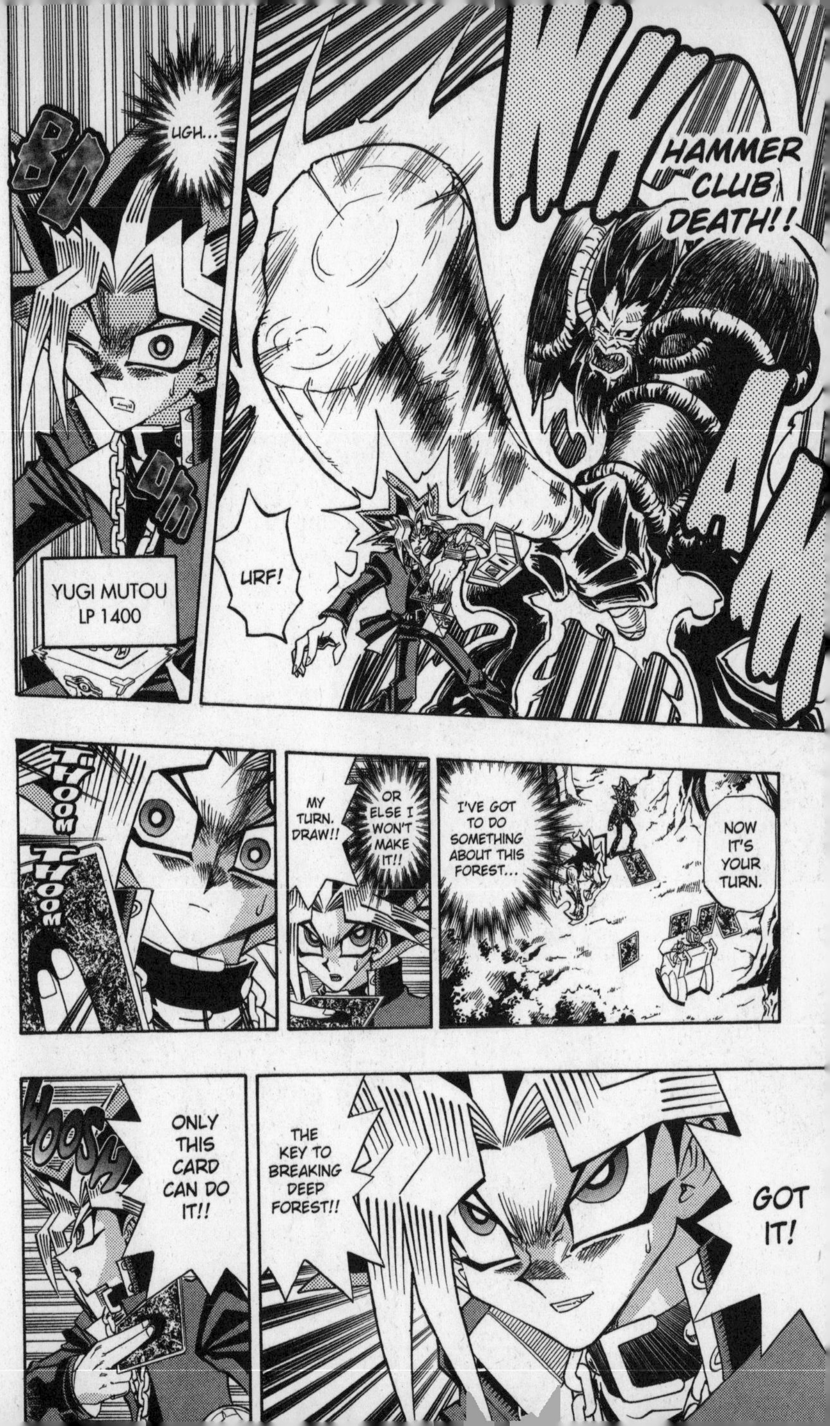
HAMMER CLUB DEATH!!
URF!
UGH...
YUGI MUTOU
LP 1400
NOW IT'S YOUR TURN.
I'VE GOT TO DO SOMETHING ABOUT THIS FOREST...
OR ELSE I WON'T MAKE IT!!
MY TURN. DRAW!!
THOOM
THOOM
GOT IT!
THE KEY TO BREAKING DEEP FOREST!!
ONLY THIS CARD CAN DO IT!!

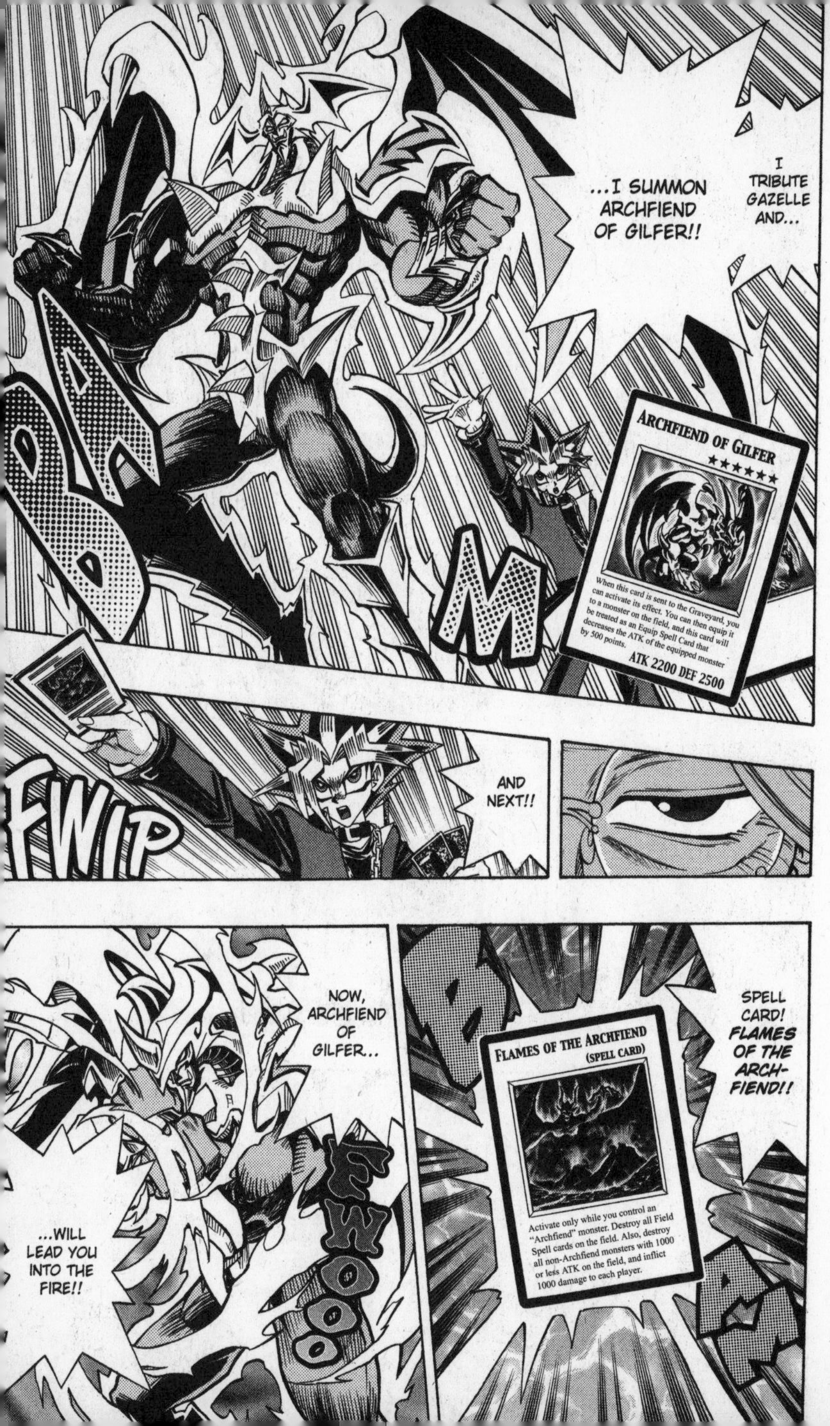
I TRIBUTE GAZELLE AND...
...I SUMMON ARCHFIEND OF GILFER!!
ARCHFIEND OF GILFER
When this card is sent to the Graveyard, you can activate its effect. You can then equip it to a monster on the field, and this card will be treated as an Equip Spell Card that decreases the ATK of the equipped monster by 500 points.
ATK 2200 DEF 2500
AND NEXT!!
FWIP
SPELL CARD! FLAMES OF THE ARCH-FIEND!!
FLAMES OF THE ARCHFIEND
(SPELL CARD)
Activate only while you control an "Archfiend" monster. Destroy all Field Spell cards on the field. Also, destroy all non-Archfiend monsters with 1000 or less ATK on the field, and inflict 1000 damage to each player.
NOW, ARCHFIEND OF GILFER...
...WILL LEAD YOU INTO THE FIRE!!

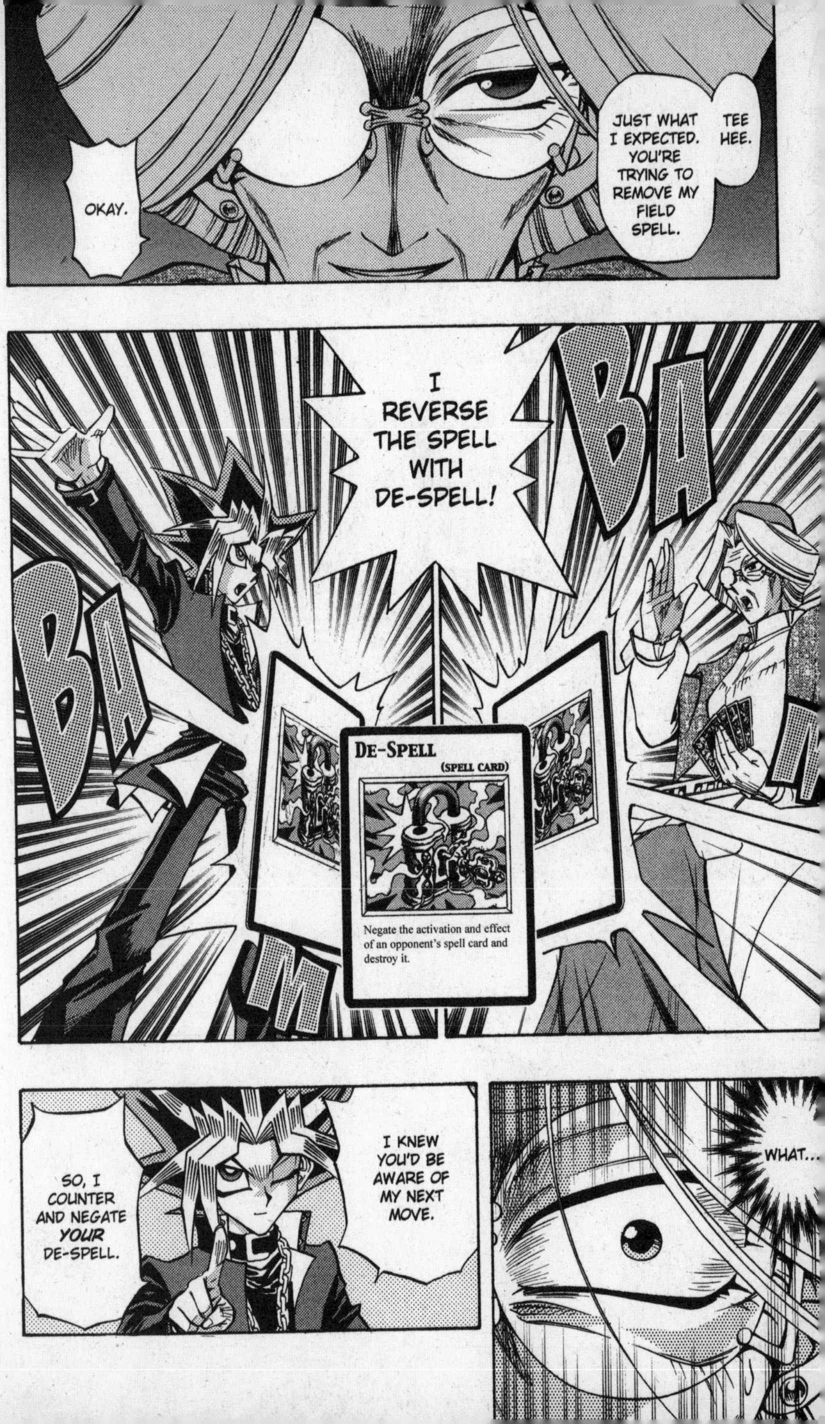
JUST WHAT I EXPECTED. YOU'RE TRYING TO REMOVE MY FIELD SPELL.
TEE HEE.
OKAY.
BA
I REVERSE THE SPELL WITH DE-SPELL!
BA
DE-SPELL
(SPELL CARD)
Negate the activation and effect of an opponent's spell card and destroy it.
M
WHAT...
I KNEW YOU'D BE AWARE OF MY NEXT MOVE.
SO, I COUNTER AND NEGATE *YOUR* DE-SPELL.

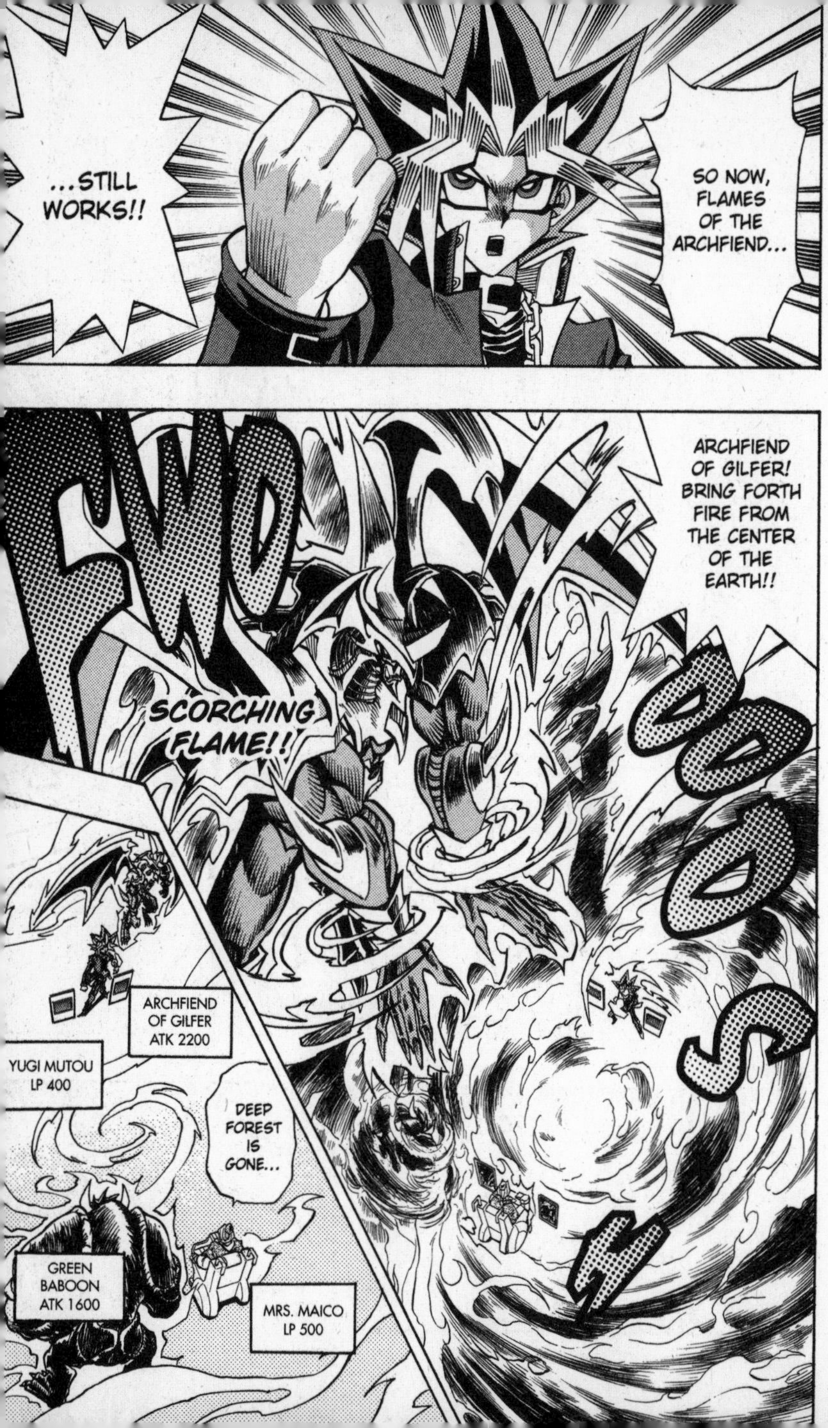
SO NOW, FLAMES OF THE ARCHFIEND...
...STILL WORKS!!
ARCHFIEND OF GILFER! BRING FORTH FIRE FROM THE CENTER OF THE EARTH!!
SWOOOSH
SCORCHING FLAME!!
ARCHFIEND OF GILFER ATK 2200
YUGI MUTOU LP 400
DEEP FOREST IS GONE...
GREEN BABOON ATK 1600
MRS. MAICO LP 500

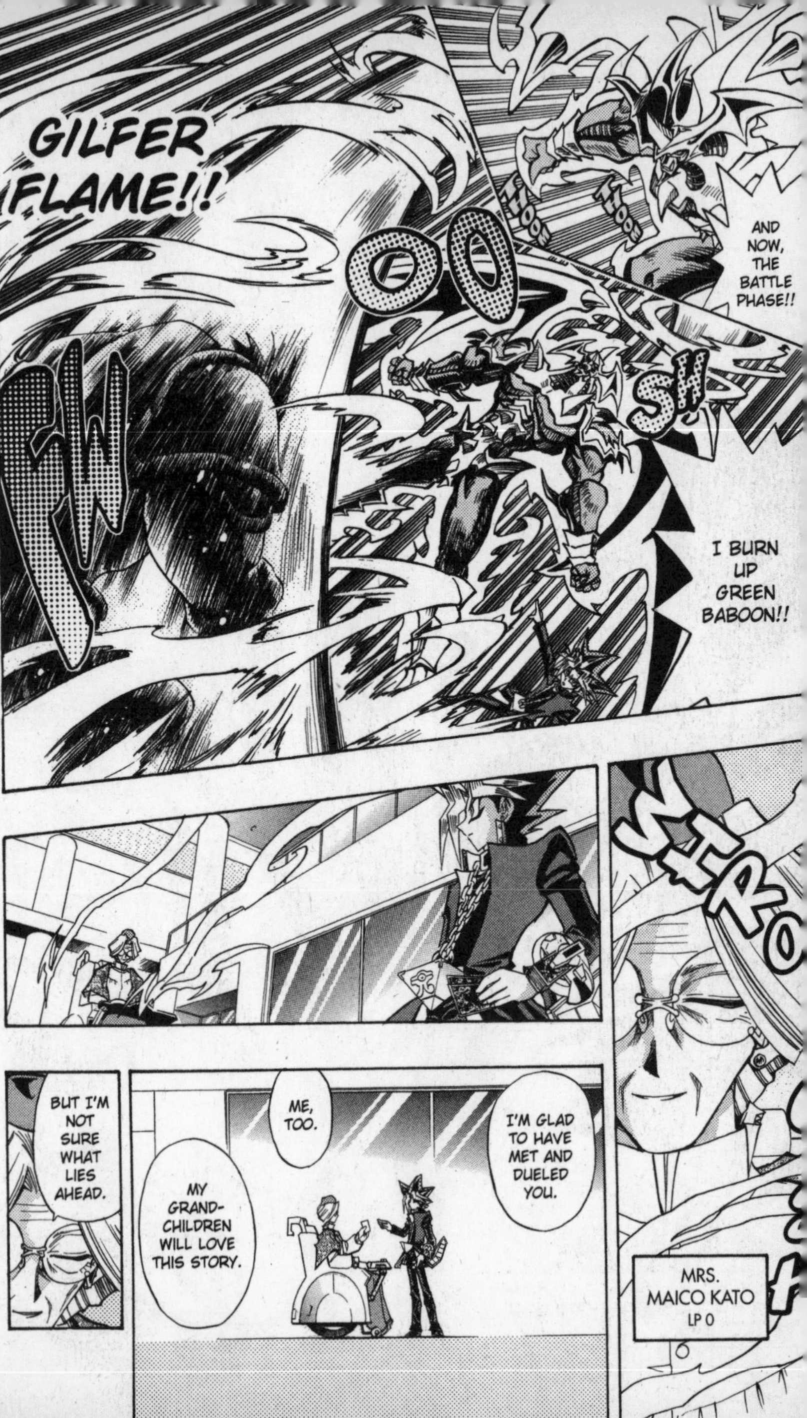
AND NOW, THE BATTLE PHASE!!
I BURN UP GREEN BABOON!!
GILFER FLAME!!
MRS. MAICO KATO
LP 0
I'M GLAD TO HAVE MET AND DUELED YOU.
ME, TOO.
MY GRAND-CHILDREN WILL LOVE THIS STORY.
BUT I'M NOT SURE WHAT LIES AHEAD.

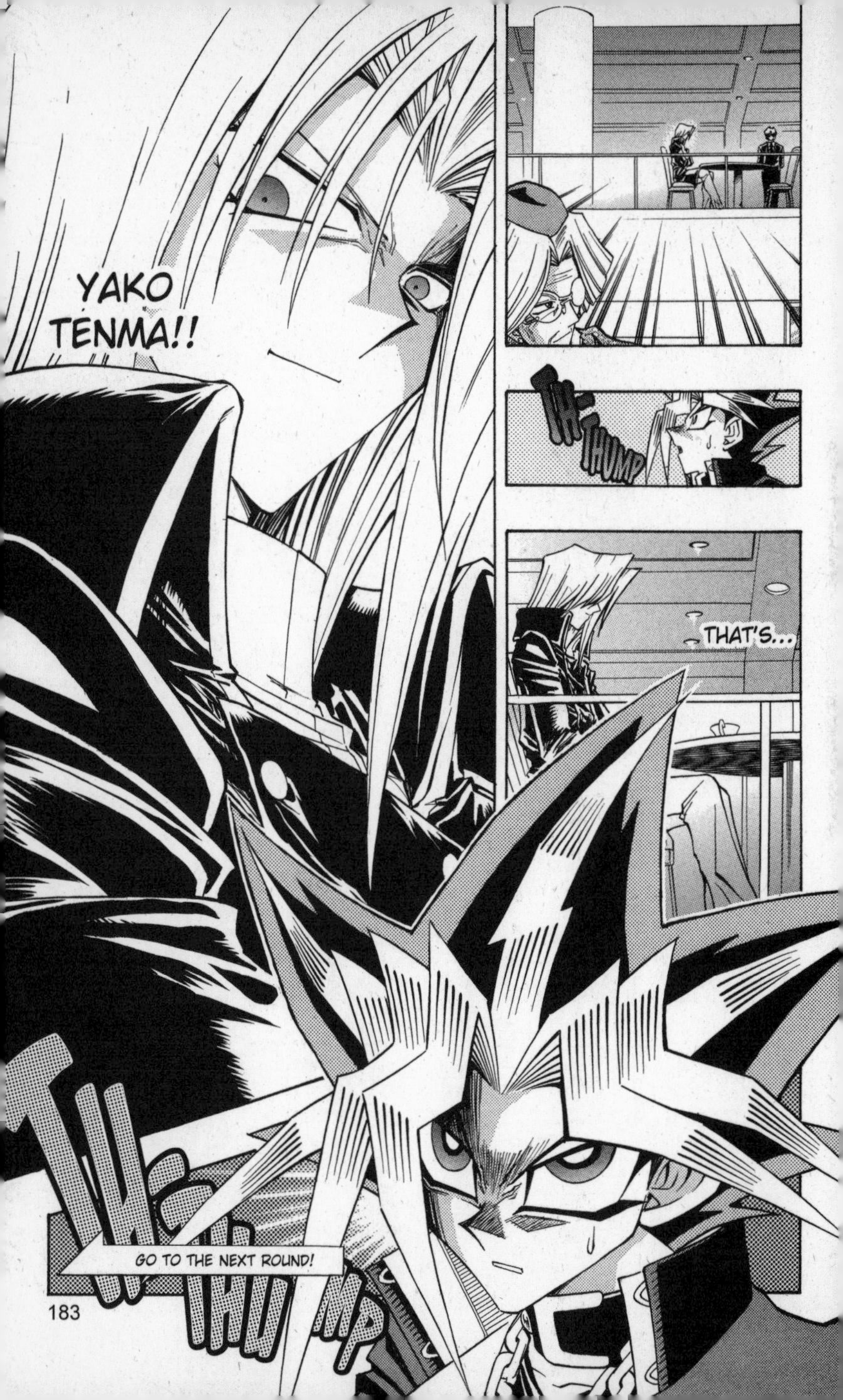
THA-THUMP
THAT'S...
YAKO TENMA!!
THA-THUMP
GO TO THE NEXT ROUND!

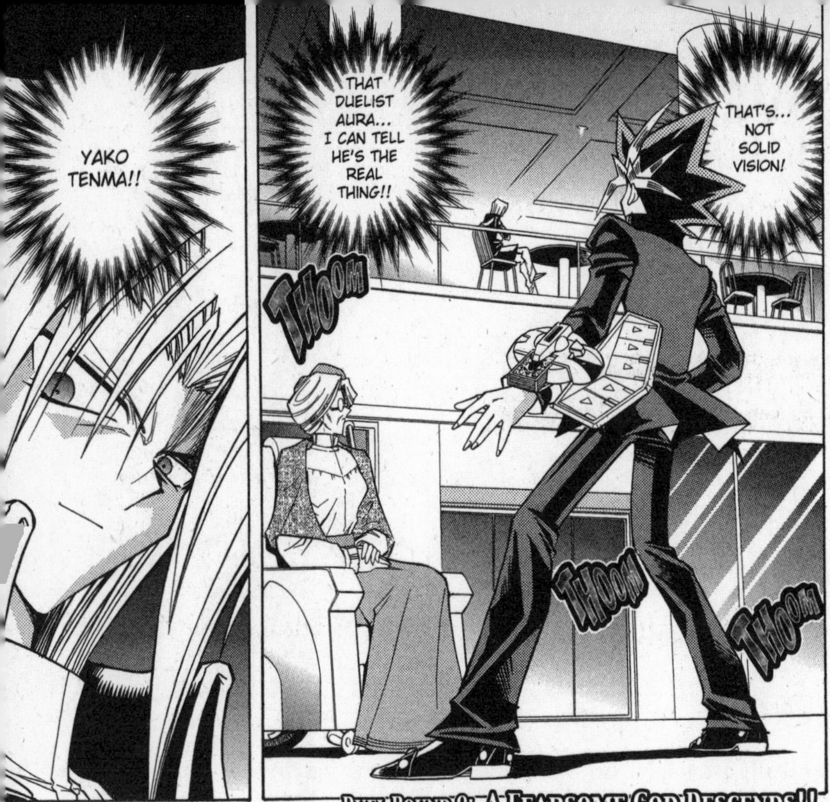
THAT'S... NOT SOLID VISION!
THAT DUELIST AURA... I CAN TELL HE'S THE REAL THING!!
THOOM
THOOM
THOOM
YAKO TENMA!!

Duel Round 9: A Fearsome God Descends!!

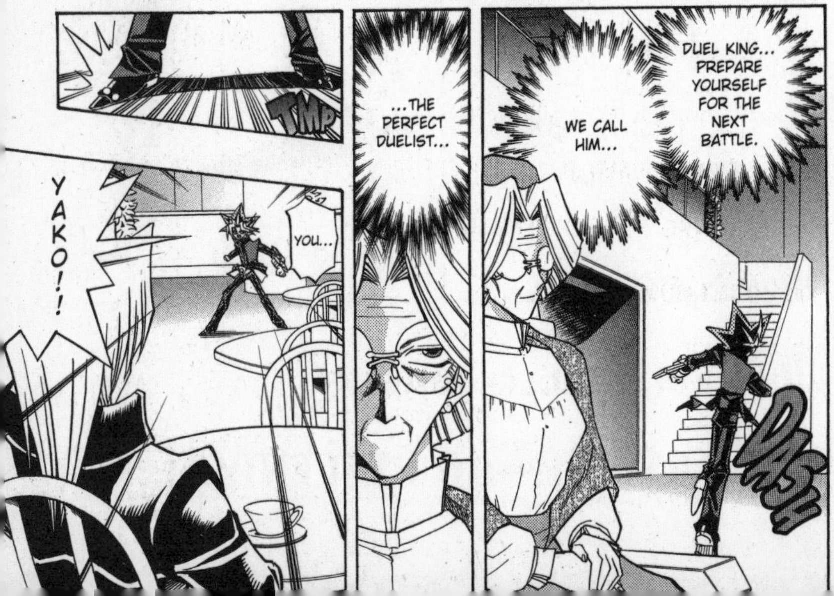
DUEL KING... PREPARE YOURSELF FOR THE NEXT BATTLE.
WE CALL HIM...
DASH
...THE PERFECT DUELIST...
TMP
YOU...
YAKO!!

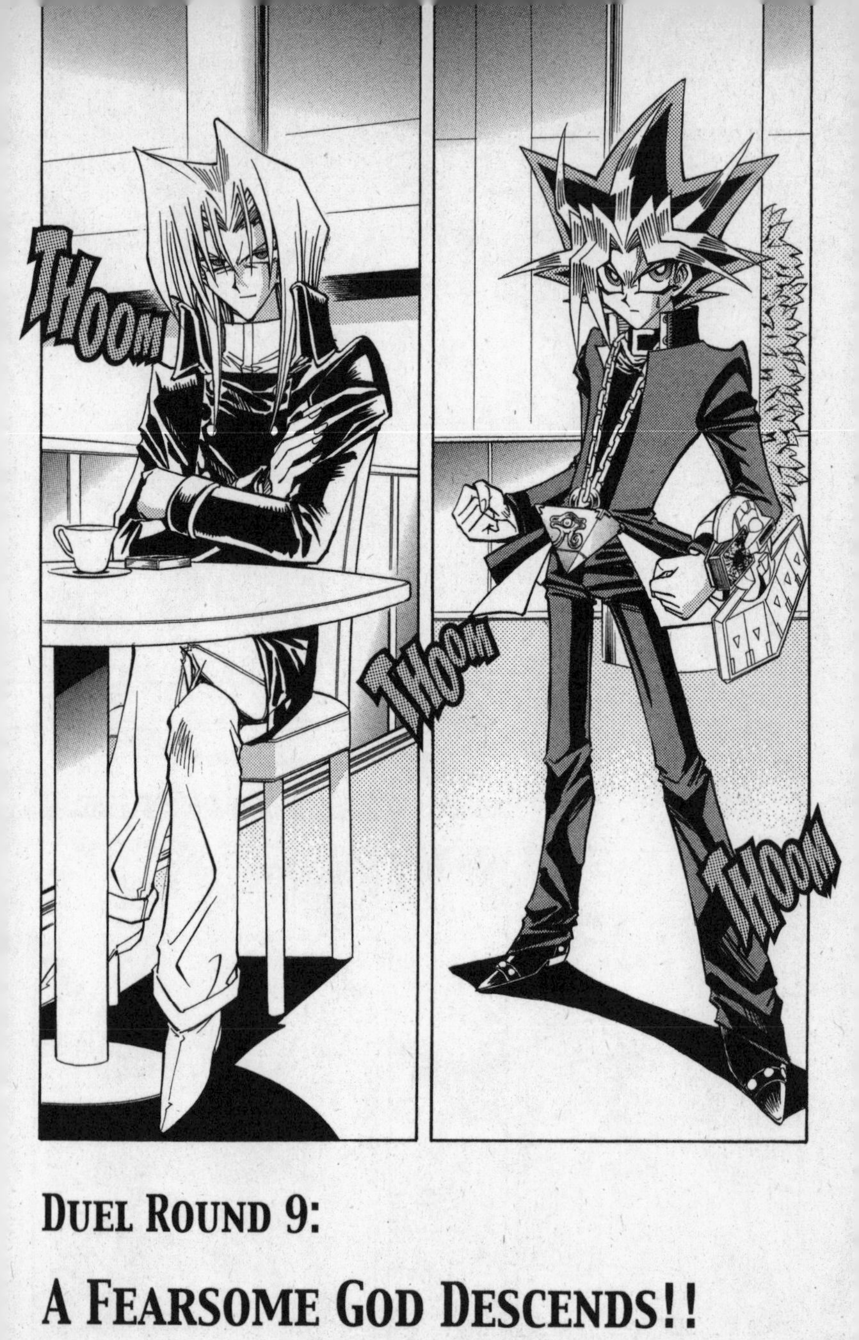
THOOM
THOOM
THOOM

DUEL ROUND 9:

A FEARSOME GOD DESCENDS!!

READ THIS WAY

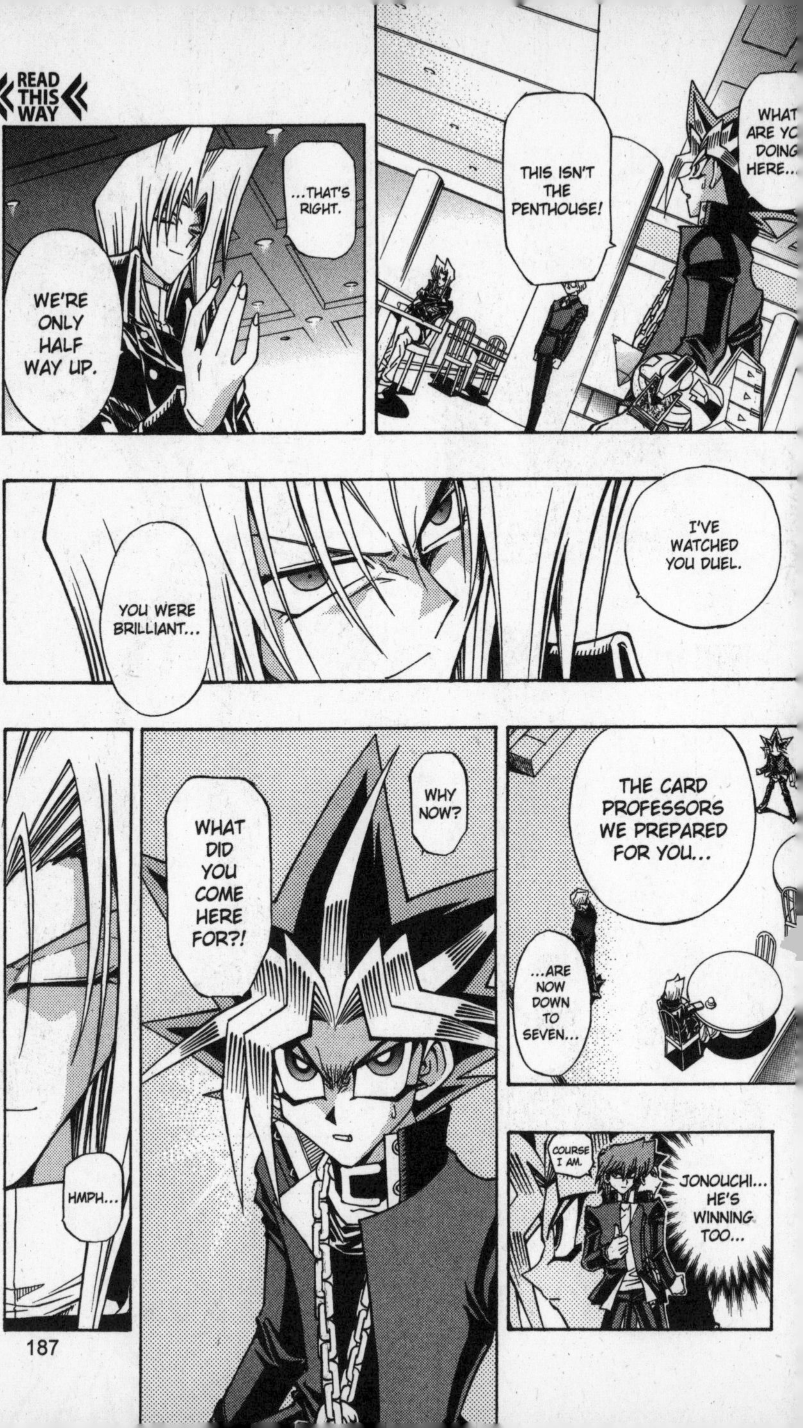
WHAT ARE YO DOING HERE...
THIS ISN'T THE PENTHOUSE!
...THAT'S RIGHT.
WE'RE ONLY HALF WAY UP.
I'VE WATCHED YOU DUEL.
YOU WERE BRILLIANT...
THE CARD PROFESSORS WE PREPARED FOR YOU...
...ARE NOW DOWN TO SEVEN...
JONOUCHI... HE'S WINNING TOO...
COURSE I AM.
WHY NOW?
WHAT DID YOU COME HERE FOR?!
HMPH...

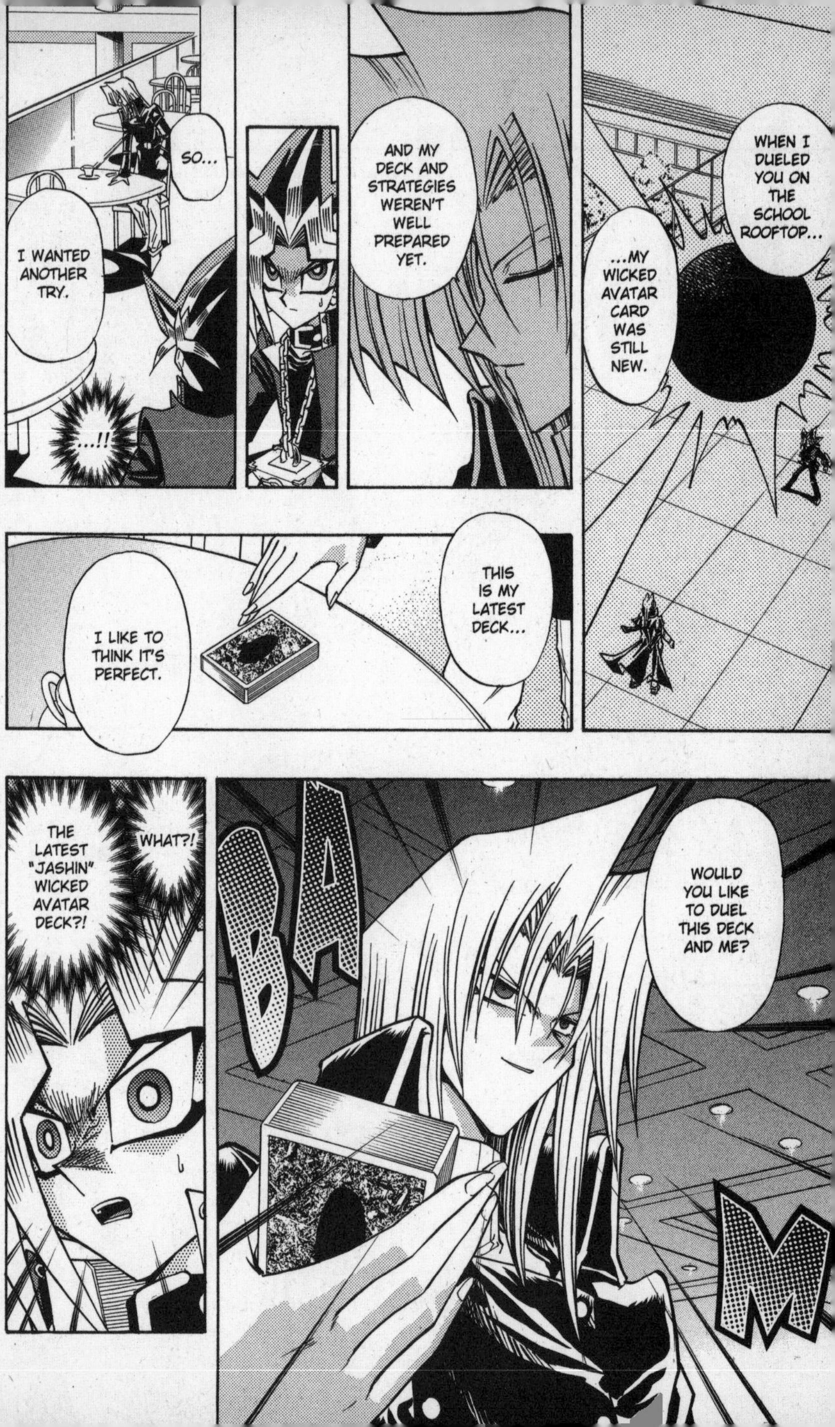
WHEN I DUELED YOU ON THE SCHOOL ROOFTOP...
...MY WICKED AVATAR CARD WAS STILL NEW.
AND MY DECK AND STRATEGIES WEREN'T WELL PREPARED YET.
SO...
I WANTED ANOTHER TRY.
...!!
THIS IS MY LATEST DECK...
I LIKE TO THINK IT'S PERFECT.
WOULD YOU LIKE TO DUEL THIS DECK AND ME?
BAM
WHAT?!
THE LATEST "JASHIN" WICKED AVATAR DECK?!

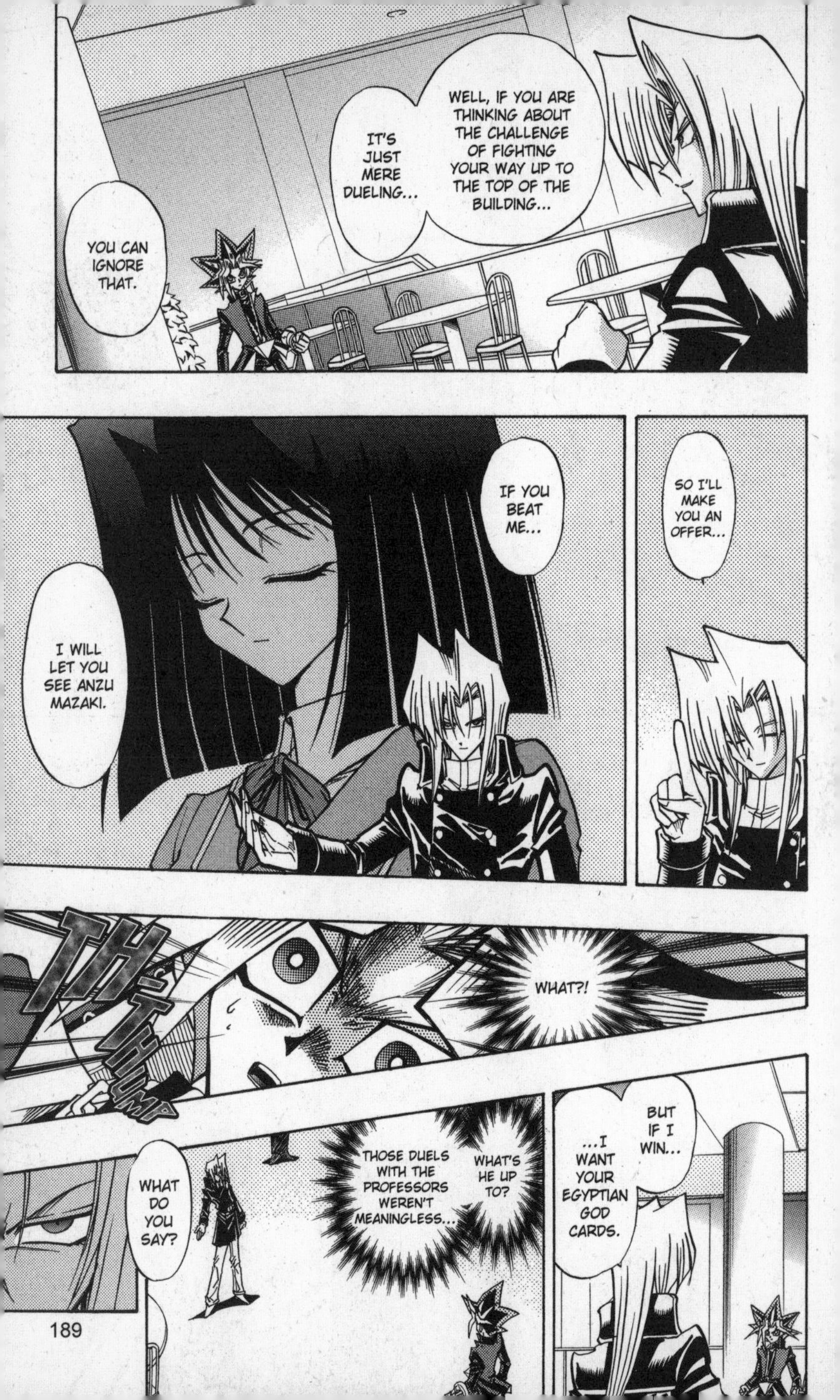
WELL, IF YOU ARE THINKING ABOUT THE CHALLENGE OF FIGHTING YOUR WAY UP TO THE TOP OF THE BUILDING...
IT'S JUST MERE DUELING...
YOU CAN IGNORE THAT.
SO I'LL MAKE YOU AN OFFER...
IF YOU BEAT ME...
I WILL LET YOU SEE ANZU MAZAKI.
WHAT?!
TH-THUMP
BUT IF I WIN...
...I WANT YOUR EGYPTIAN GOD CARDS.
WHAT'S HE UP TO?
THOSE DUELS WITH THE PROFESSORS WEREN'T MEANINGLESS...
WHAT DO YOU SAY?

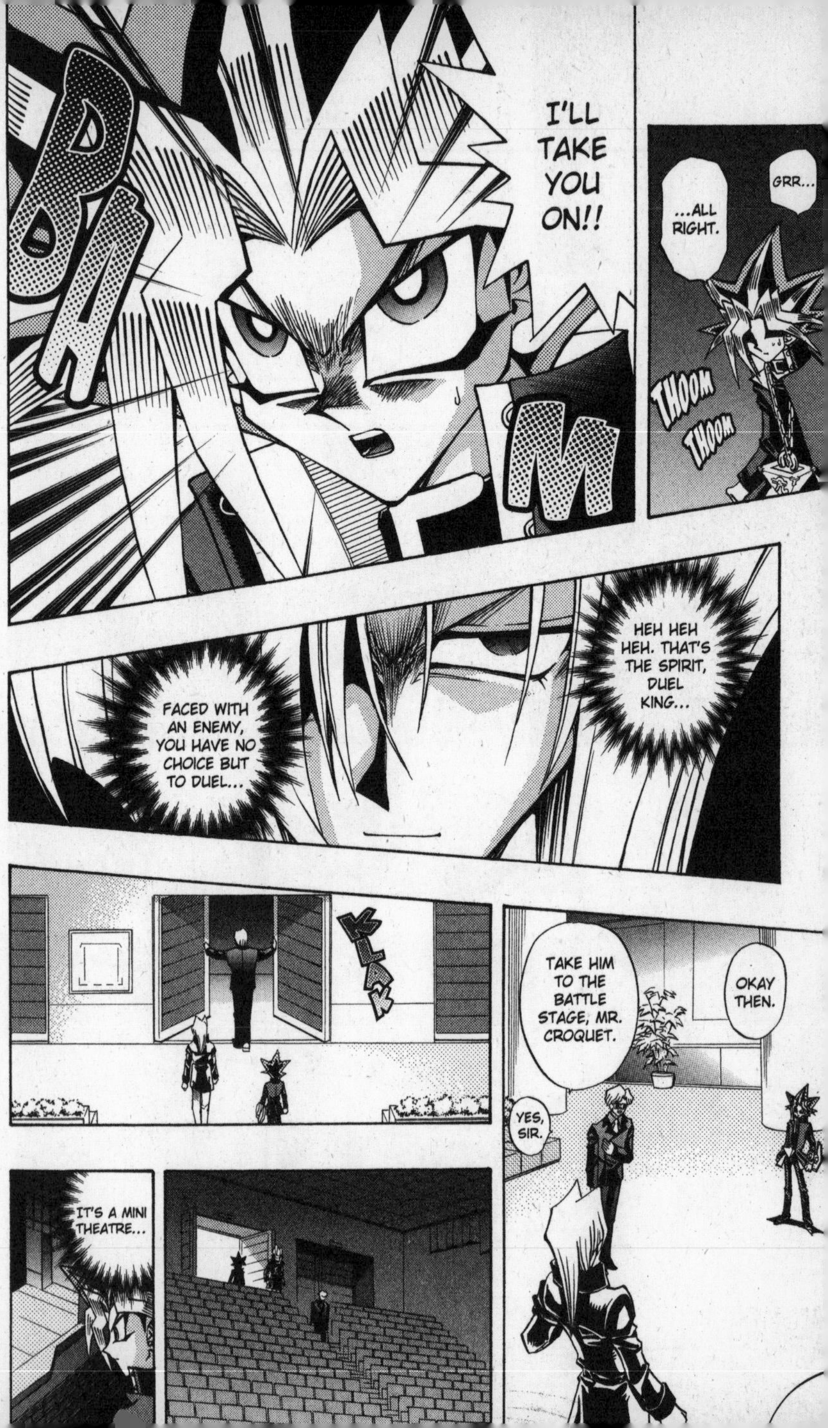
GRR...
...ALL RIGHT.
THOOM
THOOM
I'LL TAKE YOU ON!!
HEH HEH HEH. THAT'S THE SPIRIT, DUEL KING...
FACED WITH AN ENEMY, YOU HAVE NO CHOICE BUT TO DUEL...
TAKE HIM TO THE BATTLE STAGE, MR. CROQUET.
OKAY THEN.
YES, SIR.
KLAK
IT'S A MINI THEATRE...

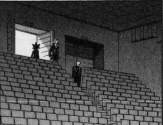

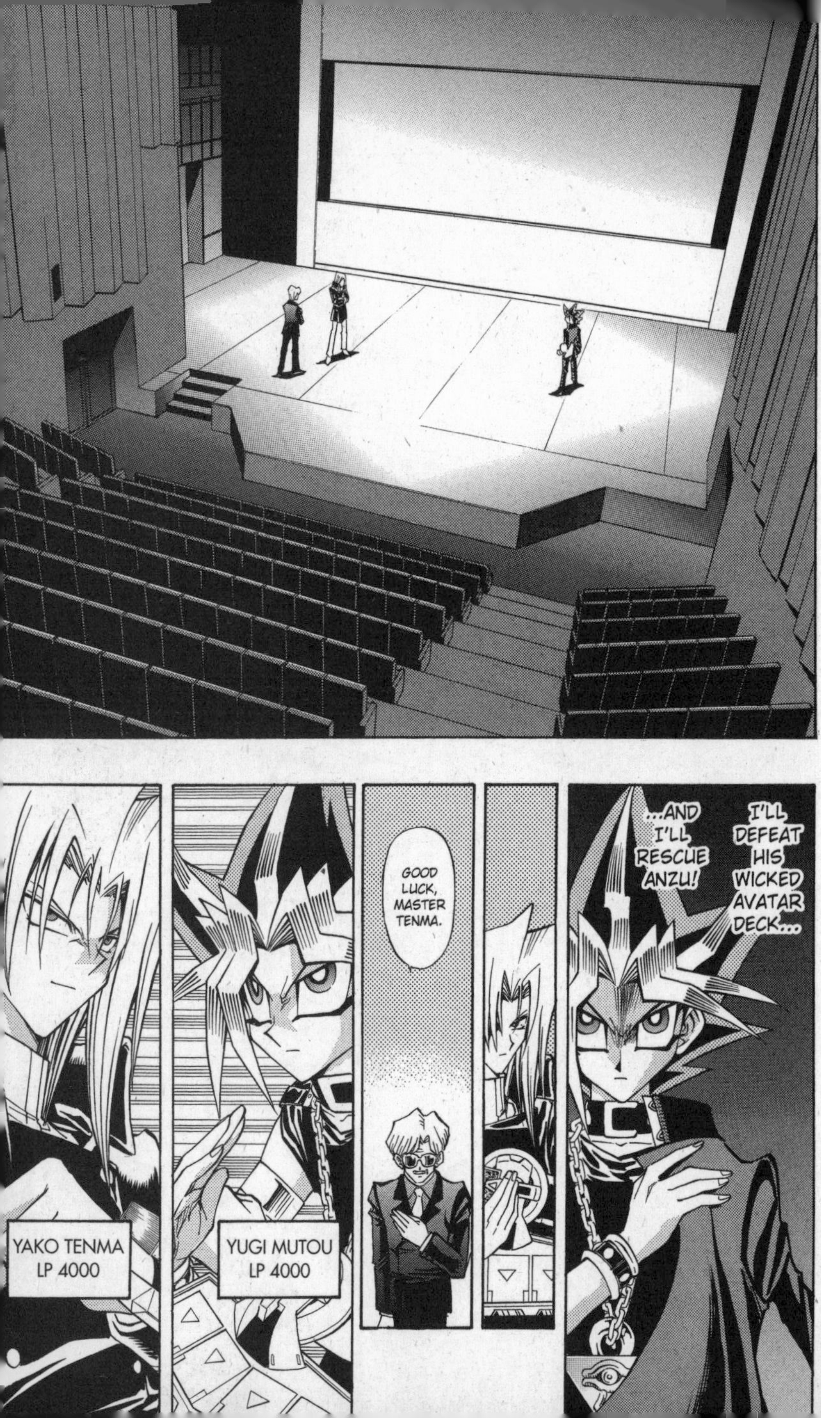
I'LL DEFEAT HIS WICKED AVATAR DECK...
...AND I'LL RESCUE ANZU!
GOOD LUCK, MASTER TENMA.
YUGI MUTOU
LP 4000
YAKO TENMA
LP 4000

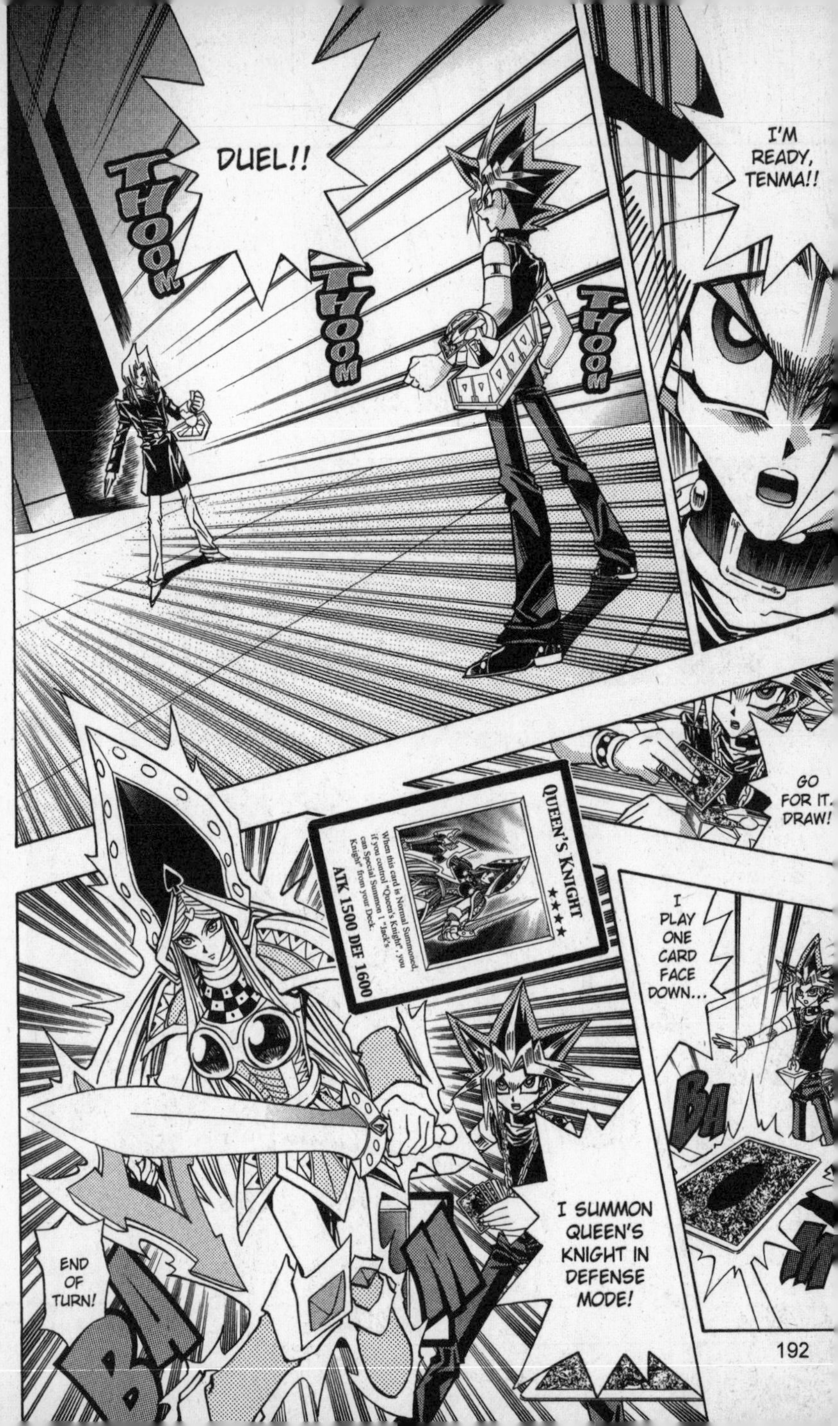
I'M READY, TENMA!!
THOOM
DUEL!!
THOOM
THOOM
GO FOR IT. DRAW!
QUEEN'S KNIGHT
When this card is Normal Summoned, if you control "Queen's Knight", you can Special Summon 1 "Jack's Knight" from your Deck.
ATK 1500 DEF 1600
I PLAY ONE CARD FACE DOWN...
I SUMMON QUEEN'S KNIGHT IN DEFENSE MODE!
END OF TURN!

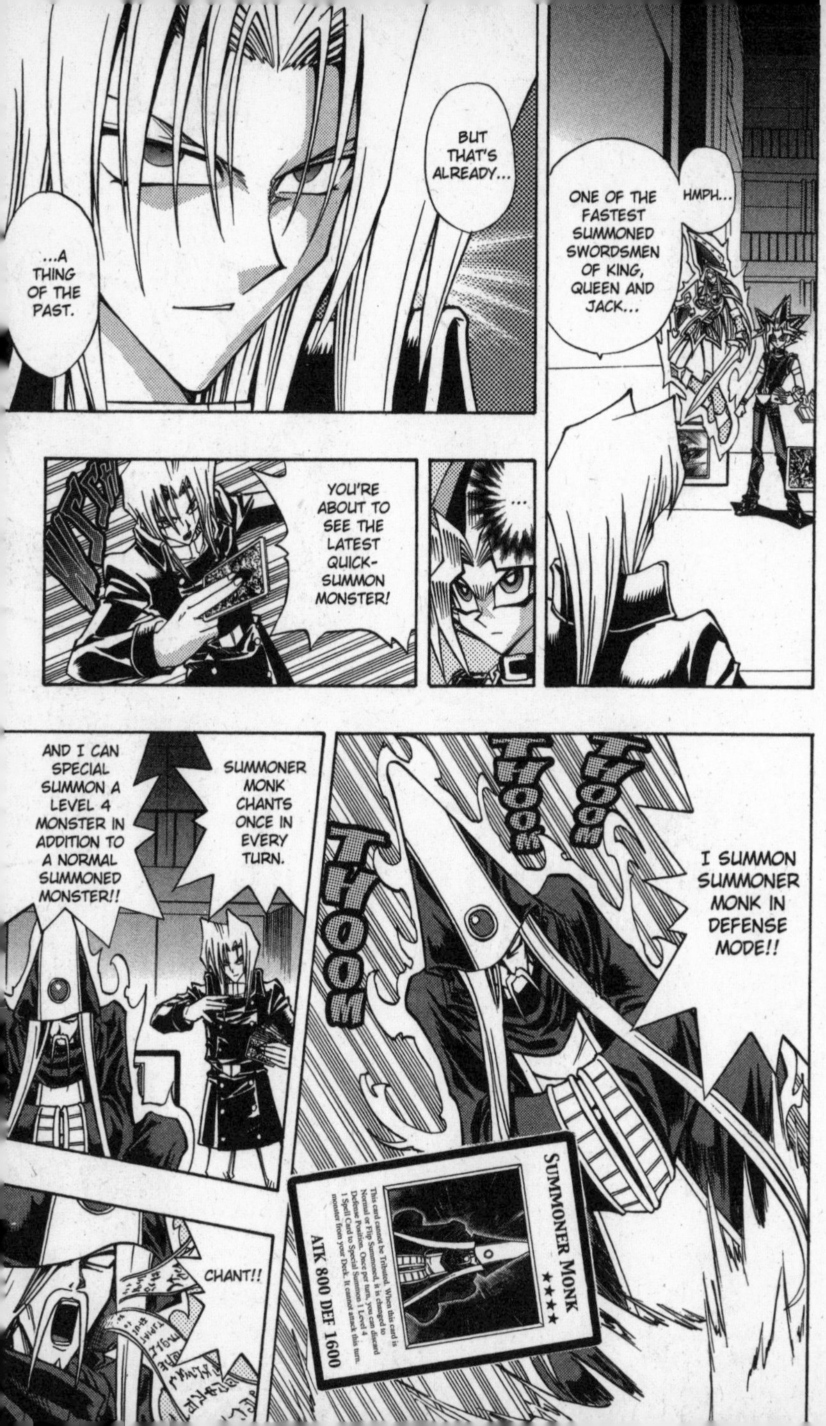
HMPH...
ONE OF THE FASTEST SUMMONED SWORDSMEN OF KING, QUEEN AND JACK...
BUT THAT'S ALREADY...
...A THING OF THE PAST.
...
YOU'RE ABOUT TO SEE THE LATEST QUICK-SUMMON MONSTER!
THOOM
THOOM
THOOM
I SUMMON SUMMONER MONK IN DEFENSE MODE!!
SUMMONER MONK
This card cannot be Tributed. When this card is Normal or Flip Summoned, it is changed to Defense Position. Once per turn, you can discard 1 Spell Card to Special Summon 1 Level 4 monster from your Deck. It cannot attack this turn.
ATK 800 DEF 1600
SUMMONER MONK CHANTS ONCE IN EVERY TURN.
AND I CAN SPECIAL SUMMON A LEVEL 4 MONSTER IN ADDITION TO A NORMAL SUMMONED MONSTER!!
CHANT!!

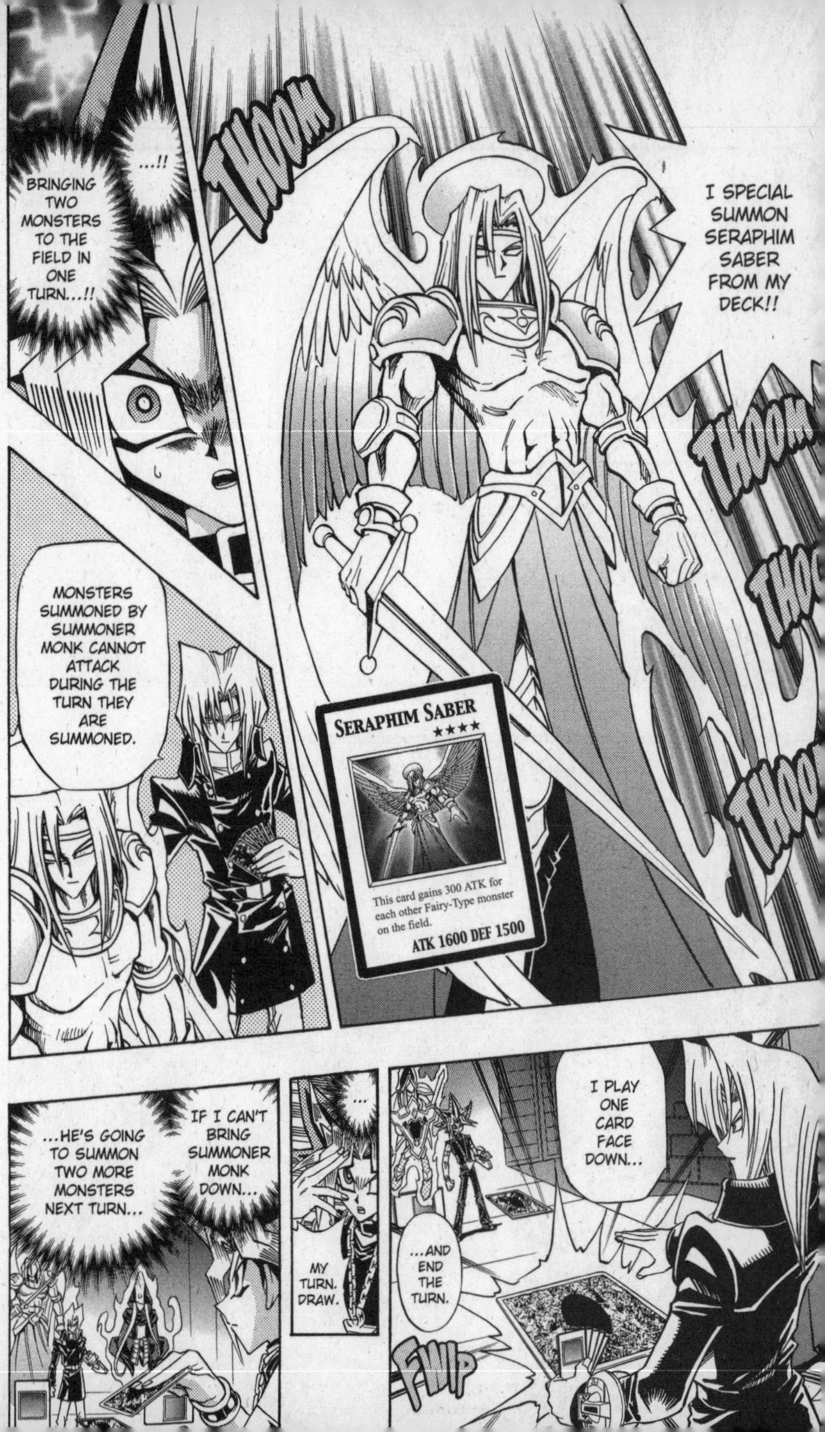
I SPECIAL SUMMON SERAPHIM SABER FROM MY DECK!!
THOOM
THOOM
THOOM
THOOM
SERAPHIM SABER
★★★★
This card gains 300 ATK for each other Fairy-Type monster on the field.
ATK 1600 DEF 1500
...!!
BRINGING TWO MONSTERS TO THE FIELD IN ONE TURN...!!
MONSTERS SUMMONED BY SUMMONER MONK CANNOT ATTACK DURING THE TURN THEY ARE SUMMONED.
I PLAY ONE CARD FACE DOWN...
...AND END THE TURN.
FWIP
...
MY TURN. DRAW.
IF I CAN'T BRING SUMMONER MONK DOWN...
...HE'S GOING TO SUMMON TWO MORE MONSTERS NEXT TURN...

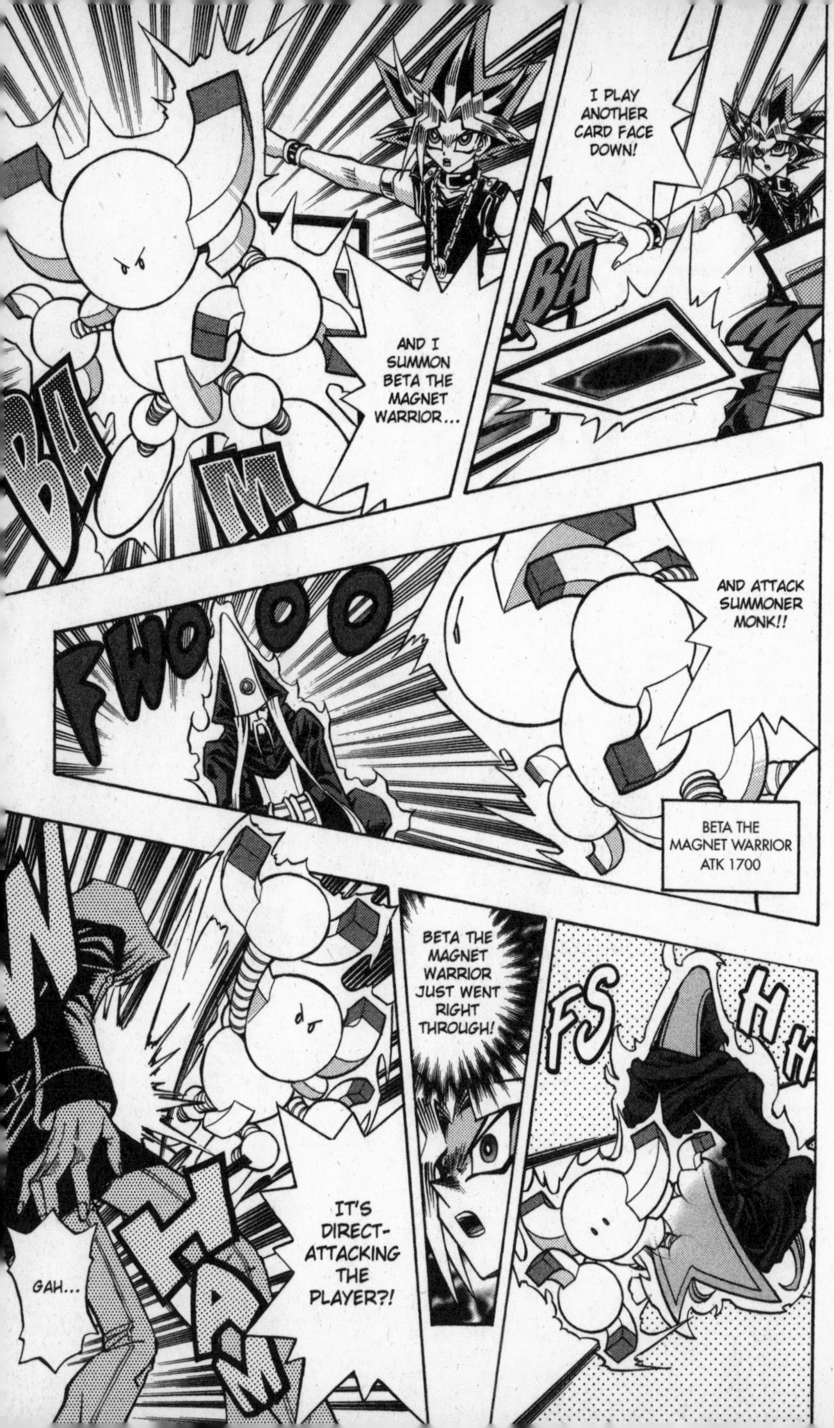
I PLAY ANOTHER CARD FACE DOWN!
AND I SUMMON BETA THE MAGNET WARRIOR...
AND ATTACK SUMMONER MONK!!
BETA THE MAGNET WARRIOR ATK 1700
BETA THE MAGNET WARRIOR JUST WENT RIGHT THROUGH!
IT'S DIRECT-ATTACKING THE PLAYER?!
GAH...

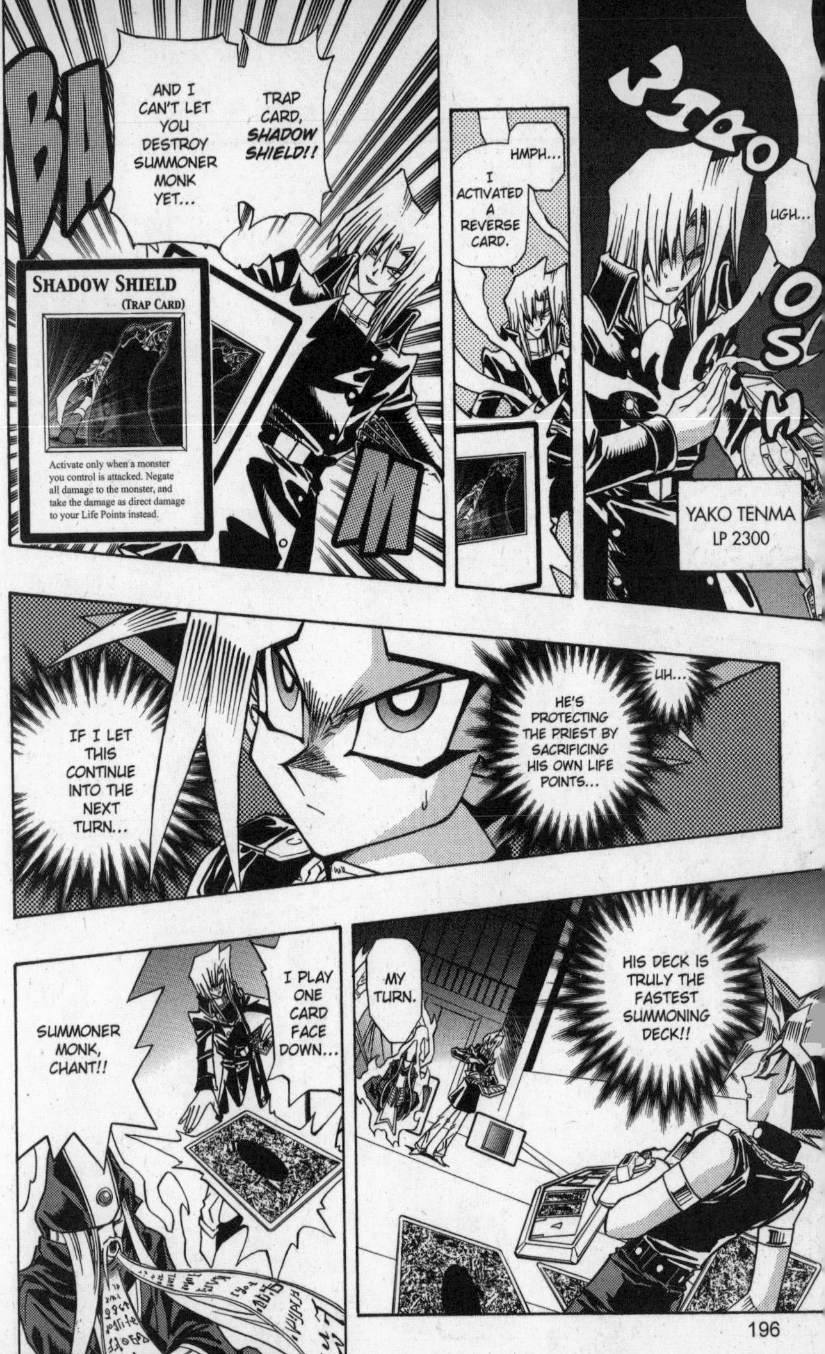
UGH...
YAKO TENMA
LP 2300
HMPH...
I ACTIVATED A REVERSE CARD.
TRAP CARD, SHADOW SHIELD!!
AND I CAN'T LET YOU DESTROY SUMMONER MONK YET...
SHADOW SHIELD
(TRAP CARD)
Activate only when a monster you control is attacked. Negate all damage to the monster, and take the damage as direct damage to your Life Points instead.
UH...
HE'S PROTECTING THE PRIEST BY SACRIFICING HIS OWN LIFE POINTS...
IF I LET THIS CONTINUE INTO THE NEXT TURN...
HIS DECK IS TRULY THE FASTEST SUMMONING DECK!!
MY TURN.
I PLAY ONE CARD FACE DOWN...
SUMMONER MONK, CHANT!!

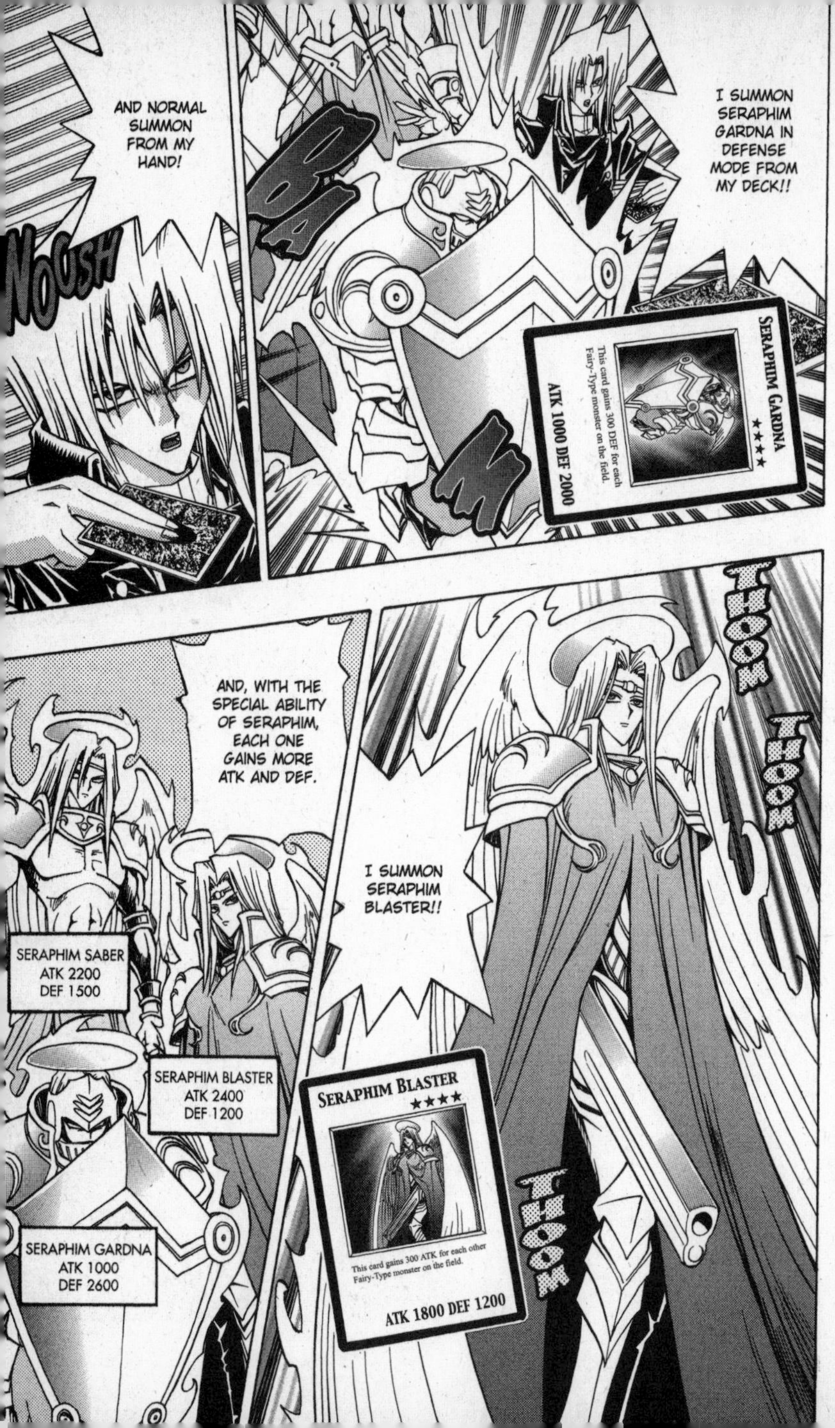
I SUMMON SERAPHIM GARDNA IN DEFENSE MODE FROM MY DECK!!
SERAPHIM GARDNA
★★★★
This card gains 300 DEF for each Fairy-Type monster on the field.
ATK 1000 DEF 2000
AND NORMAL SUMMON FROM MY HAND!
NOOSH
THOOM
THOOM
I SUMMON SERAPHIM BLASTER!!
THOOM
SERAPHIM BLASTER
★★★★
This card gains 300 ATK for each other Fairy-Type monster on the field.
ATK 1800 DEF 1200
AND, WITH THE SPECIAL ABILITY OF SERAPHIM, EACH ONE GAINS MORE ATK AND DEF.
SERAPHIM SABER ATK 2200 DEF 1500
SERAPHIM BLASTER ATK 2400 DEF 1200
SERAPHIM GARDNA ATK 1000 DEF 2600

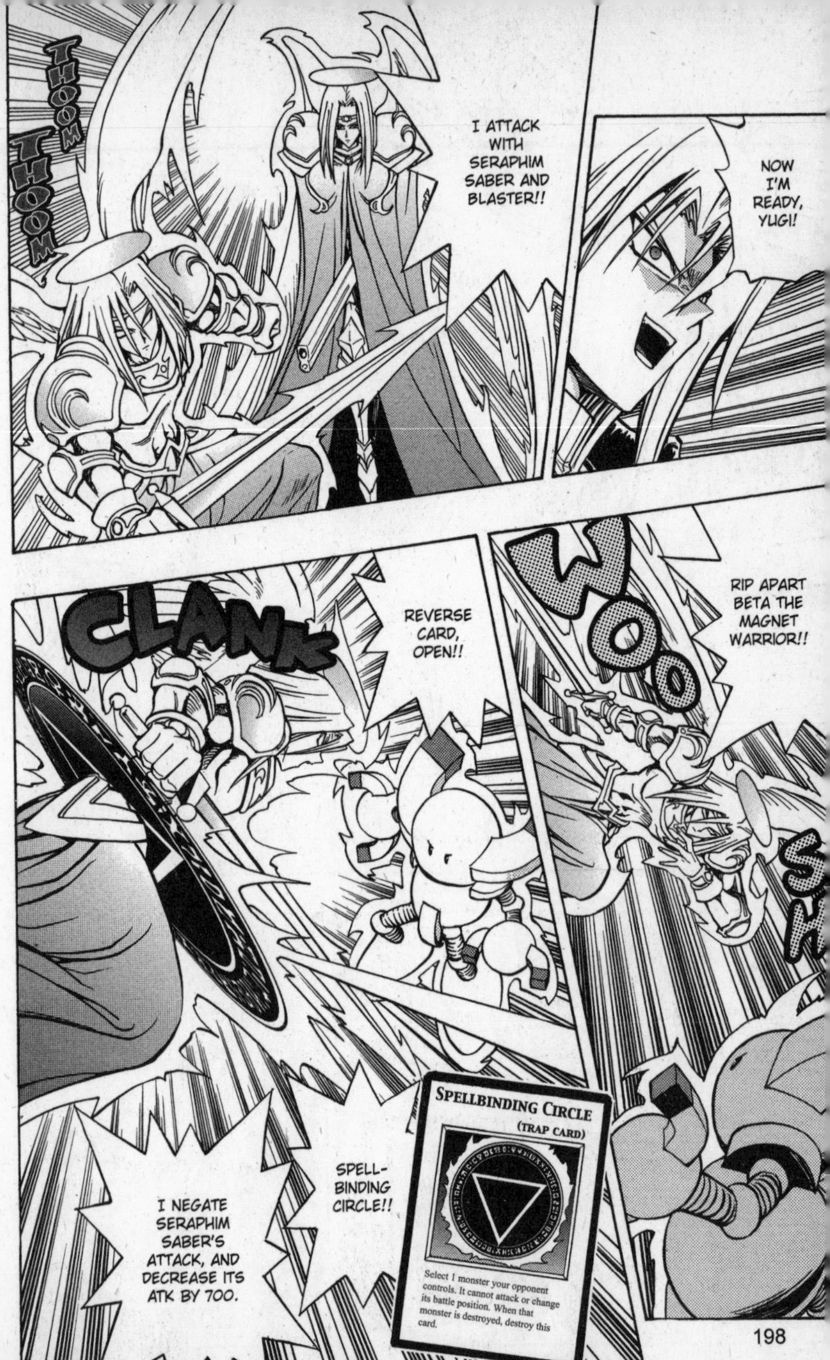
NOW I'M READY, YUGI!
I ATTACK WITH SERAPHIM SABER AND BLASTER!!
THOOM THOOM
WOO
RIP APART BETA THE MAGNET WARRIOR!!
REVERSE CARD, OPEN!!
CLANK
SPELLBINDING CIRCLE
(TRAP CARD)
Select 1 monster your opponent controls. It cannot attack or change its battle position. When that monster is destroyed, destroy this card.
SPELL-BINDING CIRCLE!!
I NEGATE SERAPHIM SABER'S ATTACK, AND DECREASE ITS ATK BY 700.

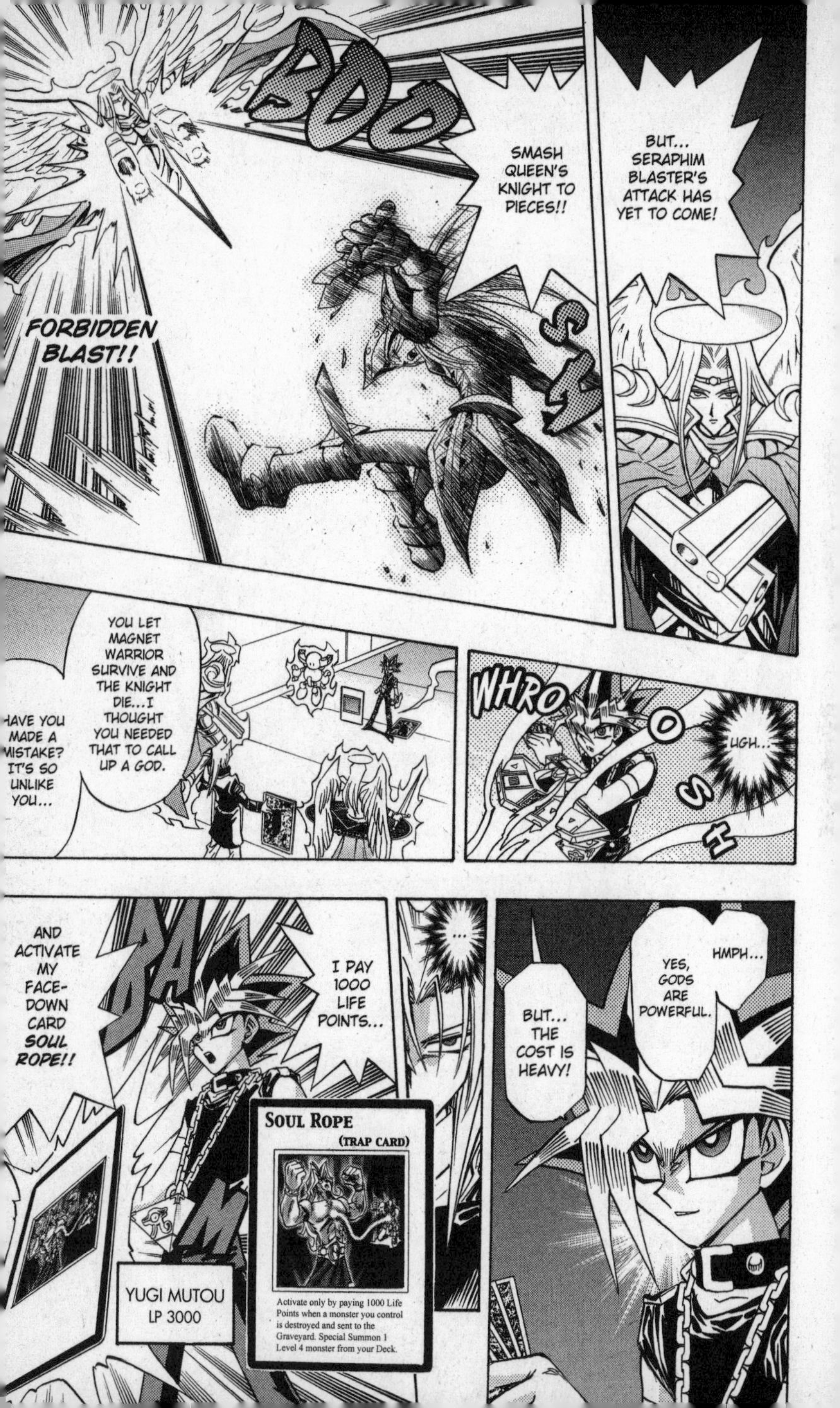
BUT... SERAPHIM BLASTER'S ATTACK HAS YET TO COME!
SMASH QUEEN'S KNIGHT TO PIECES!!
BOO
FORBIDDEN BLAST!!
WHROOSH
UGH...
YOU LET MAGNET WARRIOR SURVIVE AND THE KNIGHT DIE...I THOUGHT YOU NEEDED THAT TO CALL UP A GOD.
HAVE YOU MADE A MISTAKE? IT'S SO UNLIKE YOU...
HMPH...
YES, GODS ARE POWERFUL.
BUT... THE COST IS HEAVY!
...
I PAY 1000 LIFE POINTS...
AND ACTIVATE MY FACE-DOWN CARD SOUL ROPE!!
BAM
SOUL ROPE
(TRAP CARD)
Activate only by paying 1000 Life Points when a monster you control is destroyed and sent to the Graveyard. Special Summon 1 Level 4 monster from your Deck.
YUGI MUTOU
LP 3000

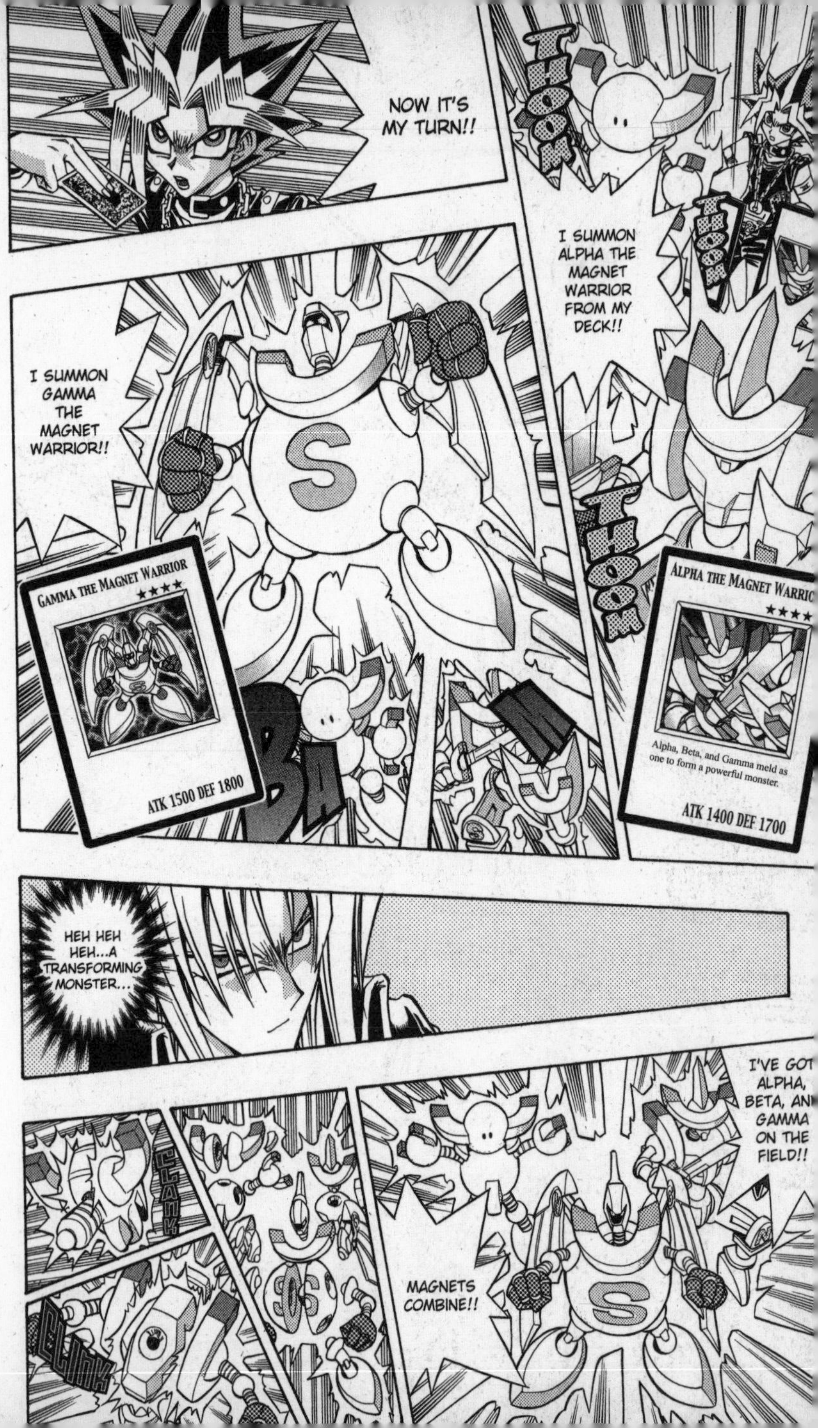

THOOM
THOOM
I SUMMON ALPHA THE MAGNET WARRIOR FROM MY DECK!!
THOOM
ALPHA THE MAGNET WARRIO
★★★★
Alpha, Beta, and Gamma meld as one to form a powerful monster.
ATK 1400 DEF 1700
NOW IT'S MY TURN!!
I SUMMON GAMMA THE MAGNET WARRIOR!!
GAMMA THE MAGNET WARRIOR
★★★★
ATK 1500 DEF 1800
BA
HEH HEH HEH...A TRANSFORMING MONSTER...
I'VE GOT ALPHA, BETA, AN GAMMA ON THE FIELD!!
MAGNETS COMBINE!!
CLANK
CLINK

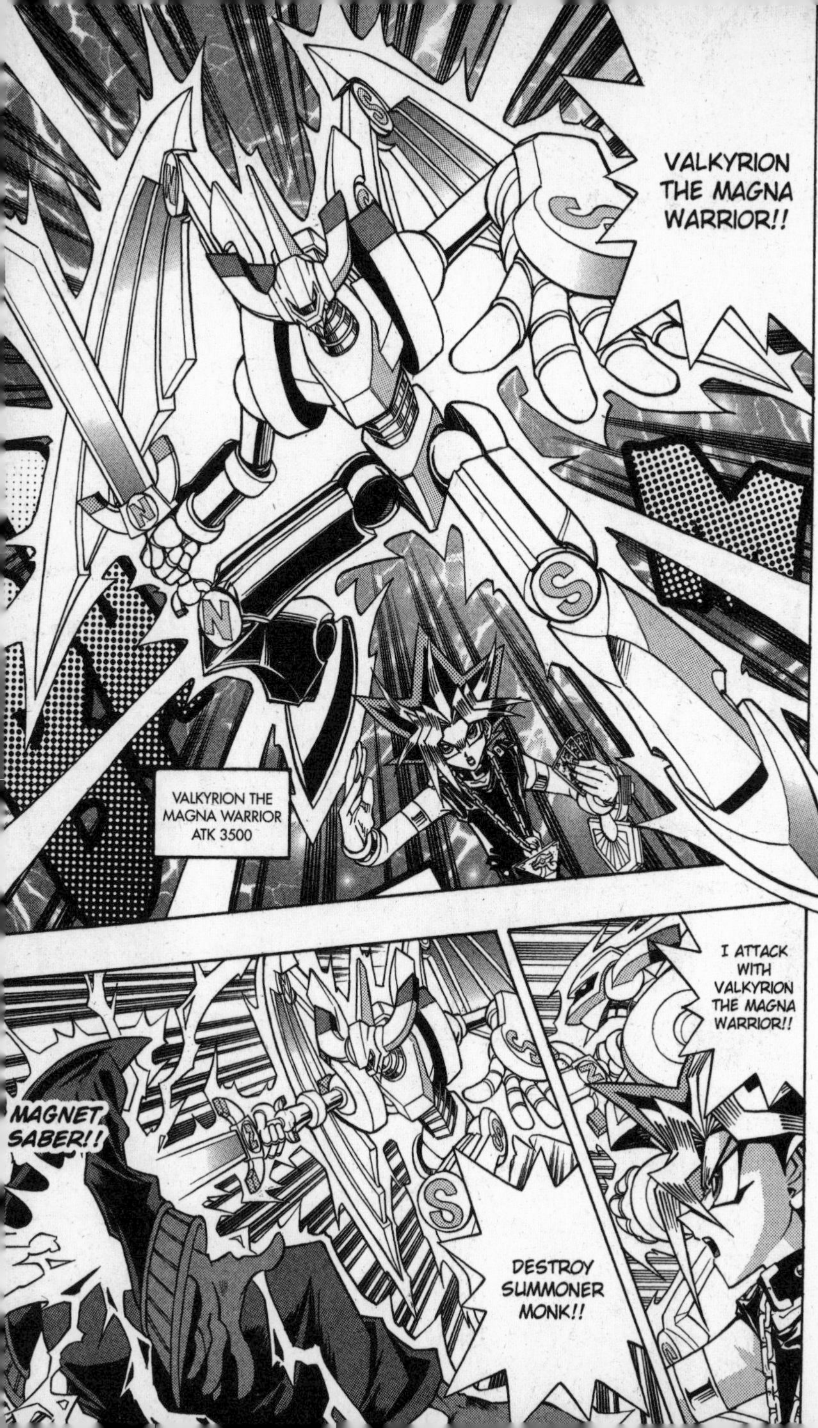
VALKYRION THE MAGNA WARRIOR!!
VALKYRION THE MAGNA WARRIOR ATK 3500
I ATTACK WITH VALKYRION THE MAGNA WARRIOR!!
DESTROY SUMMONER MONK!!
MAGNET SABER!!

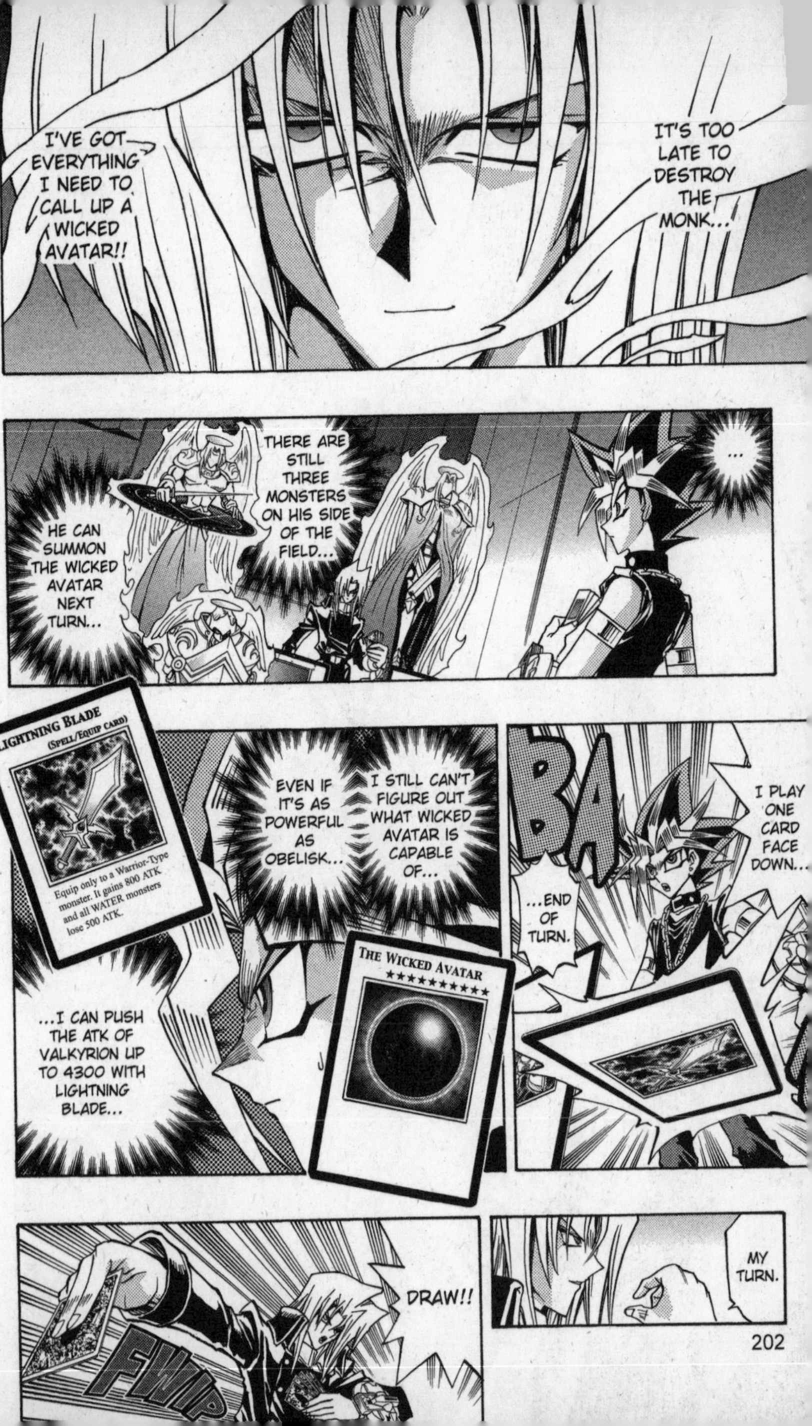
IT'S TOO LATE TO DESTROY THE MONK...
I'VE GOT EVERYTHING I NEED TO CALL UP A WICKED AVATAR!!
...
THERE ARE STILL THREE MONSTERS ON HIS SIDE OF THE FIELD...
HE CAN SUMMON THE WICKED AVATAR NEXT TURN...
I PLAY ONE CARD FACE DOWN...
BA
...END OF TURN.
I STILL CAN'T FIGURE OUT WHAT WICKED AVATAR IS CAPABLE OF...
EVEN IF IT'S AS POWERFUL AS OBELISK...
LIGHTNING BLADE
(SPELL/EQUIP CARD)
Equip only to a Warrior-Type monster. It gains 800 ATK and all WATER monsters lose 500 ATK.
...I CAN PUSH THE ATK OF VALKYRION UP TO 4300 WITH LIGHTNING BLADE...
THE WICKED AVATAR
MY TURN.
DRAW!!
FWIP

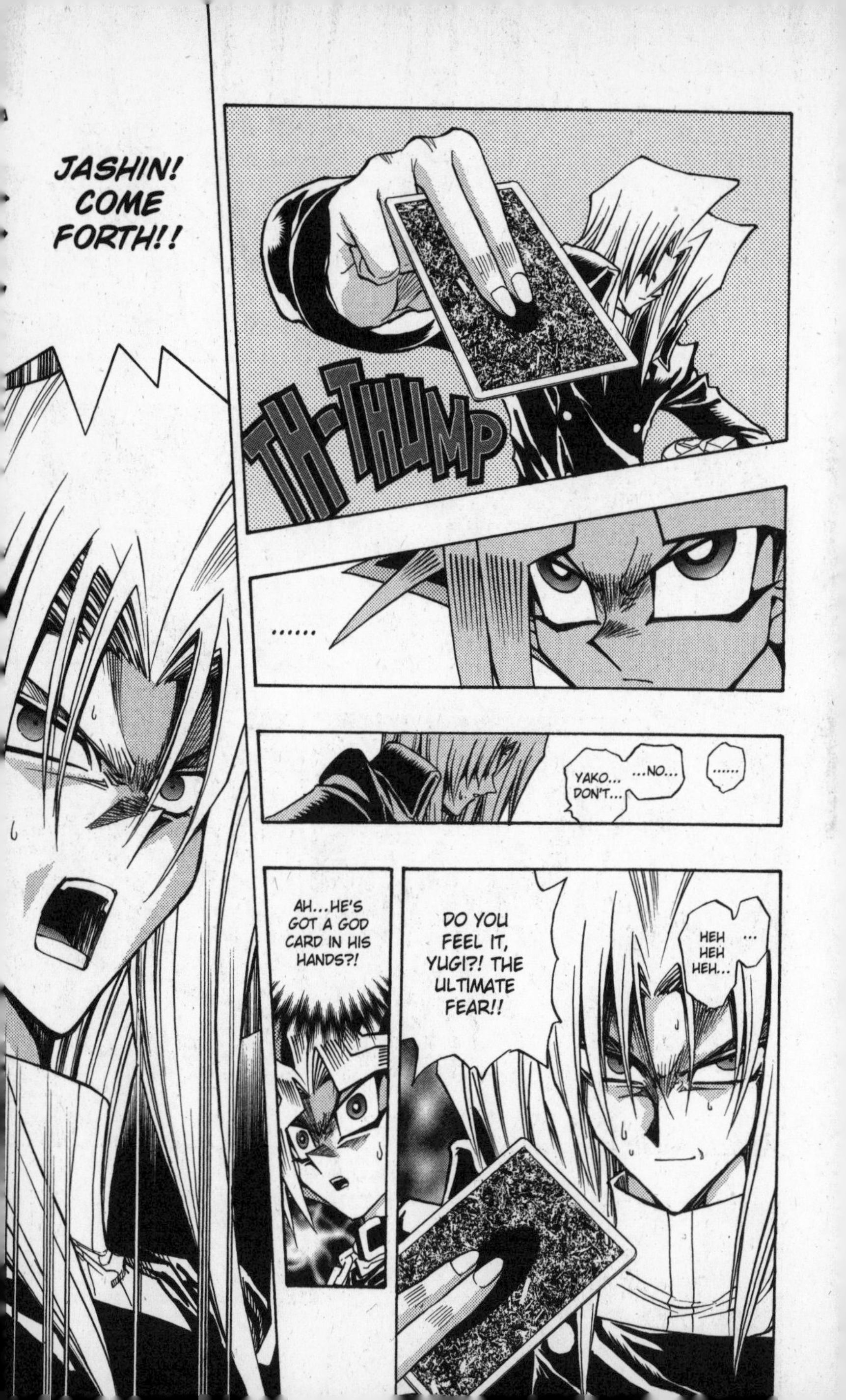
TH-THUMP
......
......
...NO...
YAKO... DON'T...
HEH HEH HEH...
DO YOU FEEL IT, YUGI?! THE ULTIMATE FEAR!!
AH...HE'S GOT A GOD CARD IN HIS HANDS?!
JASHIN! COME FORTH!!

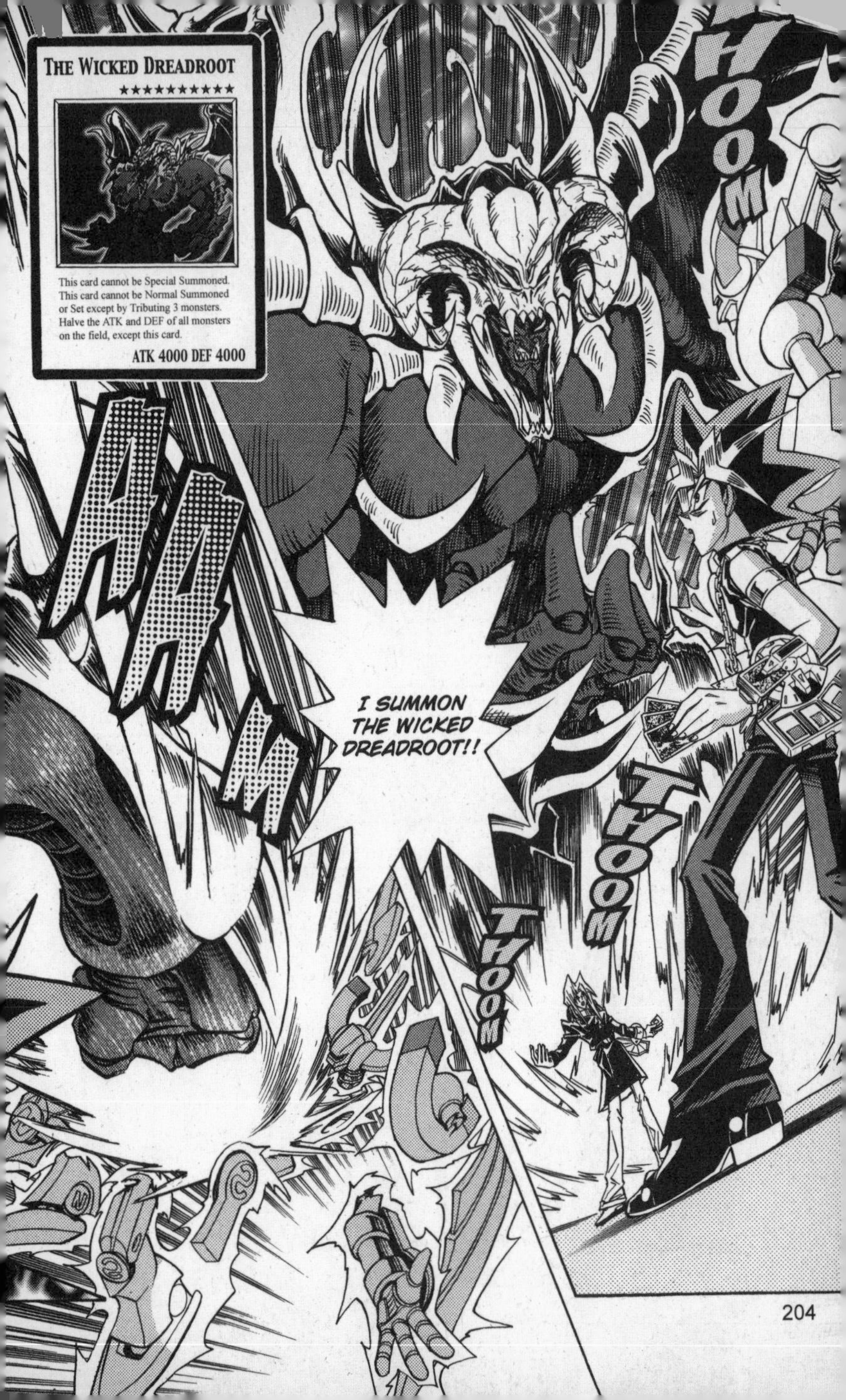
HOOM
THE WICKED DREADROOT
★★★★★★★★★★★★
This card cannot be Special Summoned. This card cannot be Normal Summoned or Set except by Tributing 3 monsters. Halve the ATK and DEF of all monsters on the field, except this card.
ATK 4000 DEF 4000
I SUMMON THE WICKED DREADROOT!!
THOOOM
THOOOM

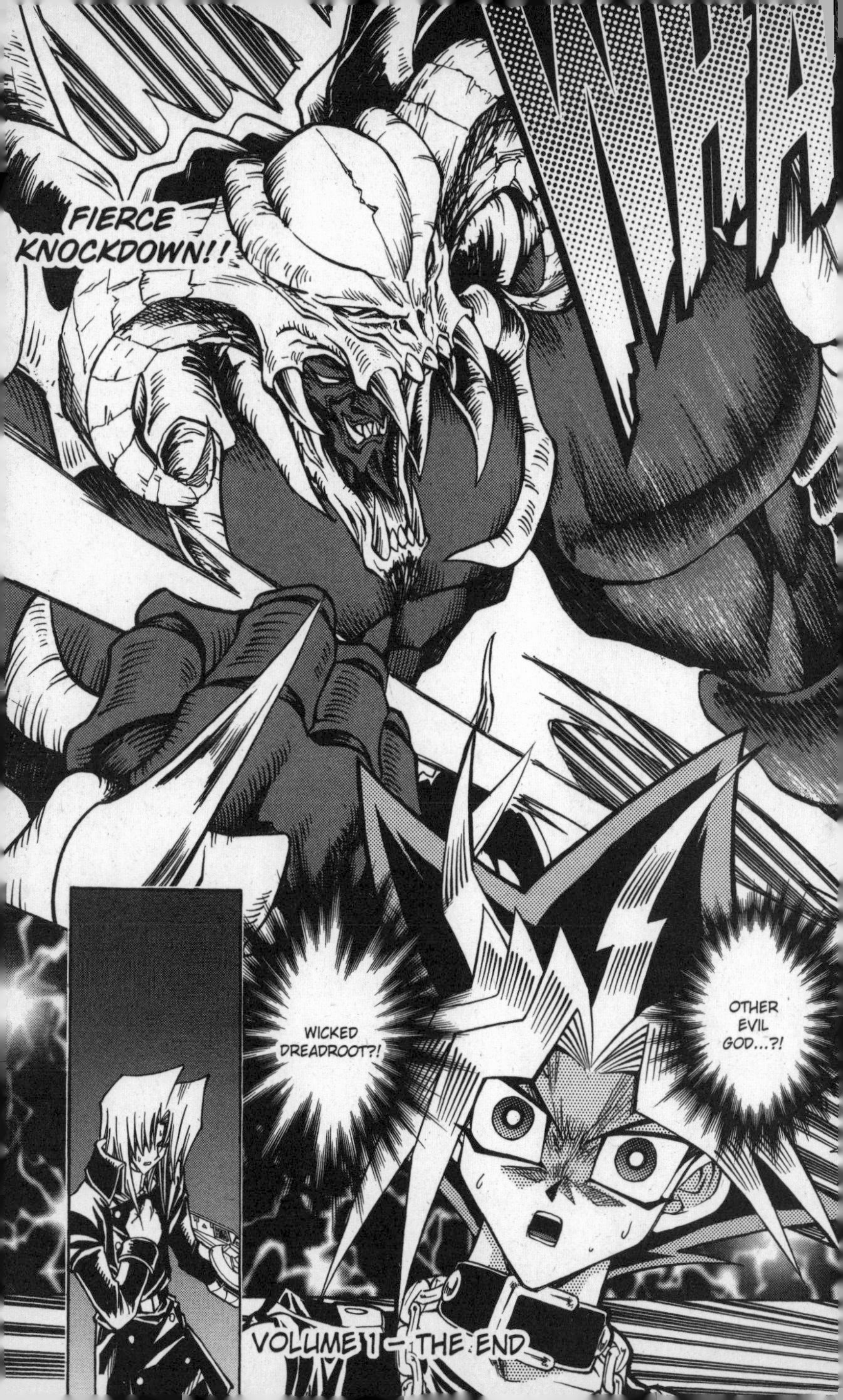
FIERCE KNOCKDOWN!!
OTHER EVIL GOD...?!
WICKED DREADROOT?!
VOLUME 1 – THE END

MASTER OF THE CARDS

Yu-Gi-Oh! R is an original story that takes place after *Yu-Gi-Oh!: Duelist* but before *Yu-Gi-Oh!: Millennium World*. It features many new cards never seen before in the manga or anime. As with all original *Yu-Gi-Oh!* cards, names can differ slightly between the Japanese and English versions, so we're showing you both for reference. Plus, we show you the card even if the card itself doesn't show up in the manga but the monster or trap does! And some cards you may have already seen in the original *Yu-Gi-Oh!*, but we still note them the first time they appear in this volume anyway!

First Appearance in This Volume	Japanese Card Name	English Card Name <<!>> = Not yet available in the TCG.
p.20	*Osiris no Tenkuryû (aka Saint Dragon—The God of Osiris)* オシリスの天空竜	Slifer the Sky Dragon
p.23	*Moku suru Shisha* 黙する死者	Silent Doom
p.25	*The Devils Avatar*	The Wicked Avatar
p.30	*The Sun of God Dragon*	The Winged Dragon of Ra (aka The Sun Dragon Ra)
p.30	*The God of Obelisk*	Obelisk the Tormentor (aka The God of the Obelisk)
p.50	*Tamashii no Rôgoku* 魂の牢獄	Soul Prison <<!>>
p.53	*Queens Knight* クイーンズ・ナイト	Queen's Knight
p.53	*Kidô Toride no Gear Golem* 機動砦のギアゴーレム	Gear Golem the Moving Fortress
p.54	*Kings Knight* キングス・ナイト	King's Knight
p.55	*Jacks Knight* ジャックス・ナイト	Jack's Knight
p.55	*Inazuma no Ken* 稲妻の剣	Lightning Blade
p.57	*Castle Gate* キャッスル・ゲート	Castle Gate
p.58	*Sennô –Brain Control–* 洗脳－ブレイン・コントロール－	Brain Control

p.61	*Black Magician* ブラック・マジシャン	Dark Magician
p.62	*Gôin na Torihiki* 強引な取引き	Forceful Deal
p.63	*Shoyûsha no Kokuin* 所有者の刻印	Owner's Seal
p.74	*Blood Sucker* ブラッド・サッカー	Blood Sucker
p.75	*Magnet Warrior Beta* マグネット・ウォリアーベータ	Beta the Magnet Warrior
p.76	*Chi no Kawaki* 血の渇き	Blood Curse <<!>>
p.78	*Curse of Vampire* カース・オブ・ヴァンパイア	Vampire's Curse
p.80	*Tamashii no Tsuna* 魂の綱	Soul Rope
p.80	*Magnet Warrior Gamma* マグネット・ウォリアーガンマ	Gamma the Magnet Warrior
p.80	*Genjûô Gazelle* 幻獣王ガゼル	Gazelle the King of Mythical Beasts
p.81	*Union Attack* ユニオン・アタック	Union Attack
p.84	*Iatsu suru Magan* 威圧する魔眼	Evil Eye of Coercion <<!>>
p.86	*Buster Blader* バスター・ブレイダー	Buster Blader
p.86	*Mahô Utsushi* 魔法移し	Bounce
p.94	*Booby Trap* ブービートラップ	Booby Trap <<!>>
p.99	*Ari Jigoku* アリジゴク	Antlion <<!>>
p.100	*Tetsu no Kishi Gear Fried* 鉄の騎士ギア・フリード	Gearfried the Iron Knight
p.103	*Kaki Tsuki Kikô Yoroi* 火器付機甲鎧	Laser Cannon <<!>>
p.103	*Worm Drake* ワーム・ドレイク	Worm Drake
p.105	*Rocket Senshi* ロケット戦士	Rocket Warrior
p.106	*Evolution 2* エボリューション2	Double Evolution <<!>>
p.107	*Magic Arm Shield*	Magic Arm Shield

p.108	*Roulette Spider* ルーレット・スパイダー	Roulette Spider <<!>>
p.110	*Kakuritsu Hendô* 確率変動	Probability Change <<!>>
p.118	*Magnet Warrior Alpha* マグネット・ウォリアーアルファ	Alpha the Magnet Warrior
p.119	*Machiners Soldier* マシンナーズ・ソルジャー	Machine Soldier <<!>>
p.120	*Dôhô no Kizuna* 同胞の絆	Ties of the Brethren <<!>>
p.120	*Machiners Sniper* マシンナーズ・スナイパー	Machine Sniper<<!>>
p.120	*Machiners Defenser* マシンナーズ・ディフェンサー	Machine Defender <<!>>
p.122	*Black Magician Girl* ブラック・マジシャン・ガール	Dark Magician Girl
p.123	*Tekishû Keihô—Yellow Alert* 敵襲警報ーイエローアラートー	Intruder Alarm—Yellow Alert <<!>>
p.124	*Powered Caterpillar* パワードキャタピラー	Caterpillar Tank <<!>>
p.125	*Sankakusei no Jûbaku* 三角星の呪縛	Spellbinding Circle
p.126	*Tokusenkan Covington* 督戦官コヴィントン	Commander Covington <<!>>
p.127	*Machiners Force* マシンナーズ・フォース	Machine Force <<!>>
p.129	*Gensô no Jûbaku* 幻想の呪縛	Spellbinding Illusion <<!>>
p.130	*Kakusan suru Hadô* 拡散する波動	Diffusion Wave-Motion
p.143	*Little Winguard* リトルウィンガード	Little Winguard
p.143	*Para Mutant* パラ・ミュータント	Para Mutant <<!>>
p.144	*Shikkoku no Hyôsenshi* *Panther Warrior* 漆黒の豹戦士パンサーウォリアー	Panther Warrior
p.145	*Jûka no Hôshu* 獣化の宝珠	Gem of Lycanthropy <<!>>
p.147	*Miraiyochi no Me* 未来予知の眼	All-Seeing Eye <<!>>
p.147	*Rengeki* 連撃	Relentless Attacks <<!>>
p.147	*Otoshi Ana* 落とし穴	Pit Trap <<!>>

p.148	*Mutant Highbrain* ミュータント・ハイブレイン	Mutant Mindmaster
p.152	*Saint Knight Ishzark* セイントナイトイシュザーク	Divine Knight Ishzark
p.154	*Teletemporate* テレテンポレート	Teletemporate <<!>>
p.157	*Haka Arashi* 墓荒し	Graverobber
p.166	*Big Shield Gardna* ビッグ・シールド・ガードナー	Big Shield Gardna
p.167	*Leprechaun* レプレカーン	Leprechaun <<!>>
p.167	*Poison Bowgun* ポイズンボーガン	Poison Crossbow <<!>>
p.171	*Fukaki Mori* 深き森	Deep Forest <<!>>
p.176	*Mori no Bannin Green Baboon* 森の番人グリーン・バブーン	Green Baboon, Defender of the Forest
p.177	*Chameleon Colored* カメレオン・カラード	Chameleon Colors <<!>>
p.179	*Ankoku Mazoku Gilfer Demon* 暗黒魔族ギルファーデーモン	Archfiend of Gilfer
p.179	*Jigoku no Retsukaen* 地獄の烈火炎	Flames of the Archfiend <<!>>
p.180	*Mahô Kaijô* 魔法解除	De-Spell
p.193	*Shôkansô Summon Priest* 召還僧サモンプリースト	Summoner Monk <<!>>
p.194	*Seraphim Saber* セラフィムセイバー	Seraphim Saber <<!>>
p.196	*Zanzô no Tate* 残像の盾	Shadow Shield
p.197	*Seraphim Gardna* セラフィムガードナー	Seraphim Gardna <<!>>
p.197	*Seraphim Gunner* セラフィムガンナー	Seraphim Blaster <<!>>
p.201	*Jishaku no Senshi Magnet Valkyrion* 磁石の戦士マグネット・ ウォリアー	Valkyrion the Magna Warrior
p204	*The Devils Dread-Root*	The Wicked Dreadroot

IN THE NEXT VOLUME...

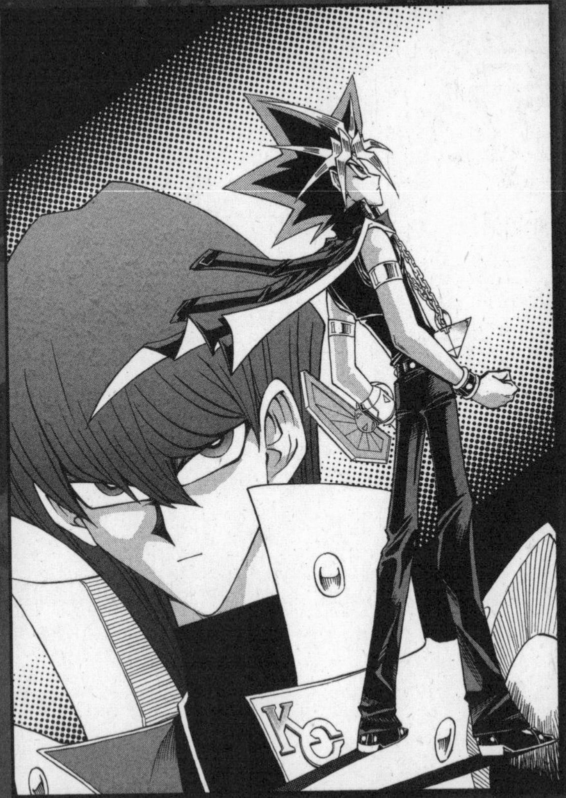

KC

What is the truth behind the mysterious "R.A. Project"? To find out, Yugi must face the terrifying power of the Three Evil Gods! But while Yugi fights for his friend's life, another duelist races across the Atlantic Ocean to join in the battle. Kaiba is back, but whose side will he be on?

COMING DECEMBER 2009!

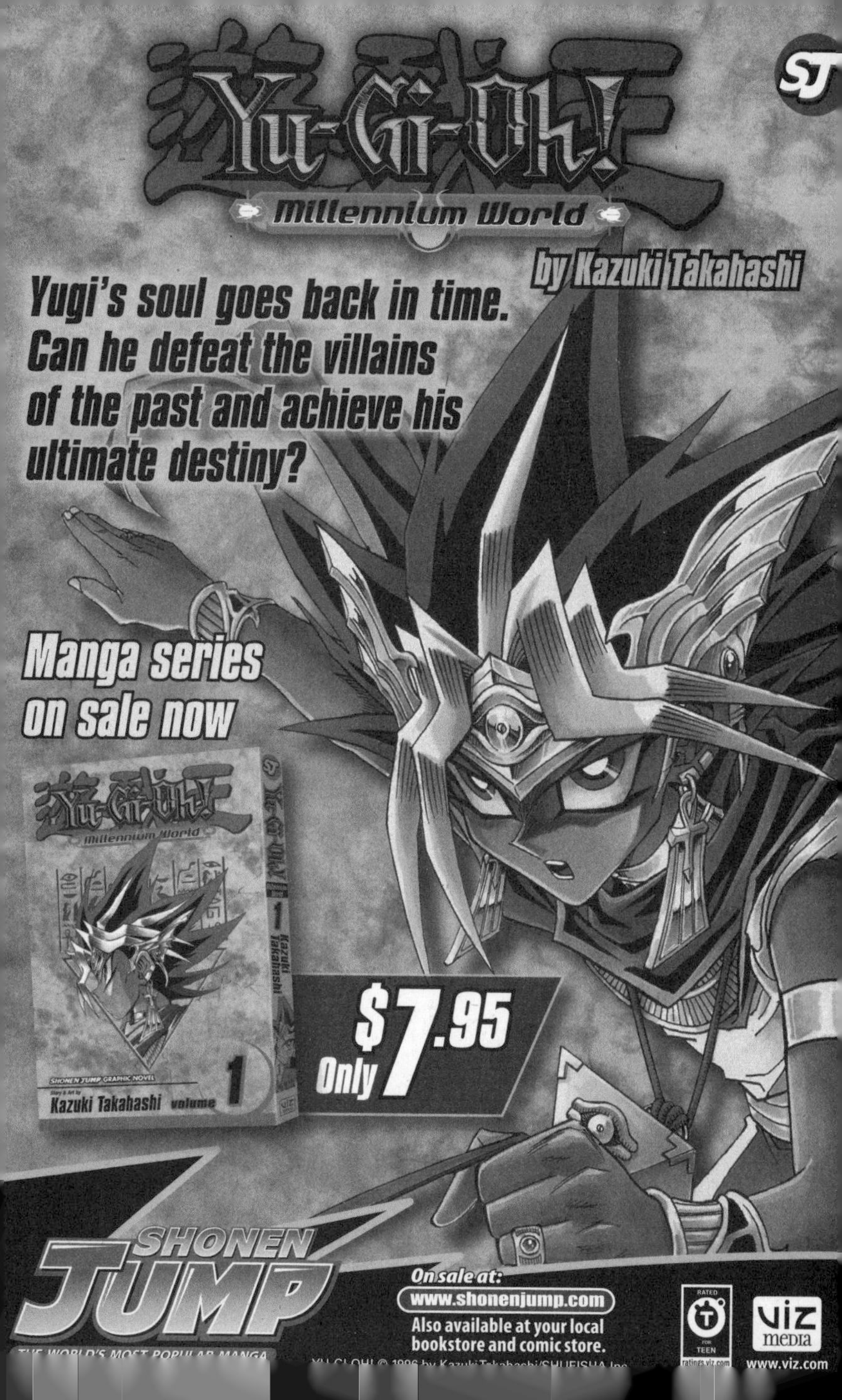

SJ
YU-GI-OH!
Millennium World
by Kazuki Takahashi
Yugi's soul goes back in time. Can he defeat the villains of the past and achieve his ultimate destiny?
Manga series on sale now
YU-GI-OH! Millennium World
SHONEN JUMP GRAPHIC NOVEL
Story & Art by Kazuki Takahashi volume 1
Only $7.95
SHONEN JUMP
On sale at:
www.shonenjump.com
Also available at your local bookstore and comic store.
RATED T FOR TEEN ratings.viz.com
VIZ media
www.viz.com

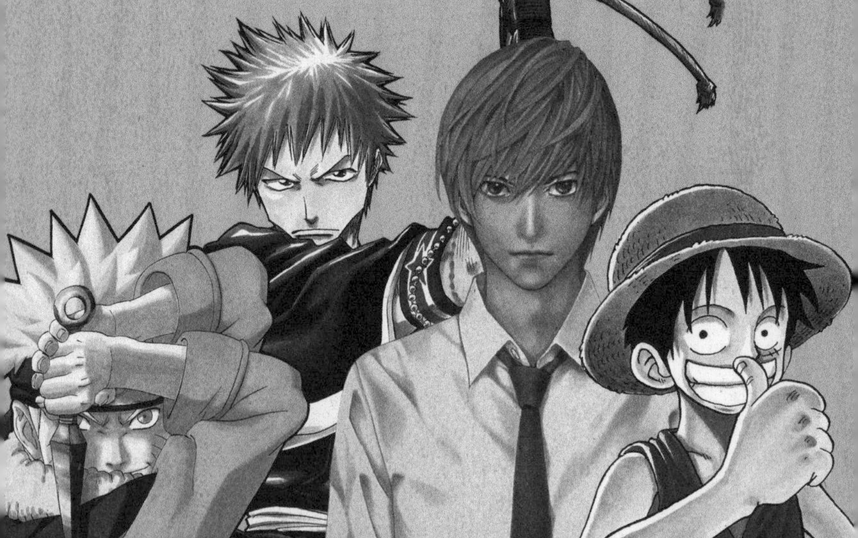